The Funniest Thing You Never Said 2

To Mum

The Funniest Thing You Never Said 2

THE ULTIMATE COLLECTION OF
HUMOROUS
QUOTATIONS

ROSEMARIE JARSKI

3 5 7 9 10 8 6 4 2

First published in 2010 by Ebury Press, an imprint of Ebury Publishing
A Random House Group company

The Random House Group Limited Reg. No. 954009

Addresses for companies within the Random House Group can be found at
www.randomhouse.co.uk

A CIP catalogue record for this book is available from the British Library

The Random House Group Limited supports the Forest Stewardship Council® (FSC®), the leading
international forest certification organisation. All our titles that are printed on Greenpeace approved
FSC® certified paper carry the FSC® logo. Our paper procurement policy can be found at
www.randomhouse.co.uk/environment

Designed and set by seagulls.net

Printed in the UK by CPI Mackays, Chatham, ME5 8TD

ISBN 9780091924515

To buy books by your favourite authors and register for offers visit
www.randomhouse.co.uk

Grant me a sense of humour, Lord,
The saving grace to see a joke,
To win some happiness from life,
And pass it on to other folk.

Old Irish toast

CONTENTS

FOOD & DRINK 1

Food & Drink – General 2
Cooking 7
Cannibal 12
Vegetarian 13
Alcohol 13
Restaurants & Cafés 22

SEX & DATING 29

Attraction 30
Dating 32
Machismo 34
My Dick is so Big... 35
Sex 36
Love 44
Hate 46
Pornography 47
Prostitute 48

MONEY MATTERS 49

Money 50
Taxation 53

Debt 57
Bankruptcy 59
Capitalism & Communism 60
Economics 61
Recession 64
Banks & Borrowing 65
Investment Banks 66
Investing & the Stock Market 69
Saving & Thrift 72
Meanness 73
Rich 74
Poor 77
Charity 78

APPEARANCE & FASHION 81

Appearance – General 82
Make-Up 86
Breasts 87
Hair 88
Fashion & Dress 90
Beauty 96
Ugly 97
Cosmetic Surgery 98
Nose Job 99
Beauty Treatments 101
Personal Hygiene 102

ANIMALS & NATURE 105

Animals – General 106
Pets 109
Cat 110
Dog 112
Birds 114

Insects 115
Nature & Country Life......................................116
Weather 118
Garden & Flowers...120
Environment & Green Issues 123
Agriculture..125

PEOPLE...**127**

Names..128
Good Name...Bad Name 129
People 130
There Are Two Kinds of People in the World.........131
Men 132
Women..133
Battle of the Sexes..135
Gender 138
Race & Ethnicity 140
Racism & Prejudice 141
Friends & Enemies..142

BOOKS & LANGUAGE.......................................**145**

Languages 146
Words 149
Grammar & Punctuation...................................150
Books..152
Writer 155
Diary...160
Autobiography & Biography 161
Publishing 163
Poetry 164
Critic...166

MARRIAGE & FAMILY LIFE 171

Marriage 172
Married Life.................................174
Single Life 177
Family Life..................................178
Grandparents 179
Mother-in-Law.............................181
Children.....................................182
Sex Education 191
House & Home 192
Housework 193
DIY...195
Cheating 196
Separation & Divorce 198
Remarriage 199

COMMUNICATION 201

Conversational Ice-Breakers..............202
Conversation................................202
Conversation-Stoppers 204
Gossip..205
Secrets..206
Letter 207
Telephone....................................209
Public Speaking.............................211
News – General 213
Newspapers & Journalism.................214
Television News 216

CHARACTER & HUMAN NATURE...................219

Character – General........................220
Ego 221
Bores & Boredom...........................222

Anger & Argument...223
Right & Wrong...225
Good & Bad 226
Beliefs 227
Astrology 228
Truth & Lies..229
Smells...231
Voice..232
Optimism & Pessimism 234
Luck...236
Happiness & Sadness..237

MANNERS & BEHAVIOUR **241**

Manners & Etiquette – General..............................242
Gentleman 245
Lady...246
Polite Euphemisms for Relieving a Wedgie 246
Punctuality..247
Compliments & Flattery 248
Swearing 249
Modern Curses 251
Insults 252

SPORTS...**255**

Sports – General 256
Horse Racing 258
Cricket 260
Football 261
Golf 265
Golf Terms..269
Boxing 270
Tennis 271
Baseball...273
Basketball 275

WORK & BUSINESS 277

Work...278
Idleness 280
Problems 281
Mistakes 282
Success & Failure............................283
Awards...286
Business 288
Advertising......................................291
Insurance 292

HOBBIES & LEISURE 293

Hobbies & Recreations......................294
'Who's Who' Recreations....................296
Fishing 297
Gambling 298
Amusement Parks 299
Consumerism 300
Shopping...301
Unseemly Greetings Cards for Unlikely Occasions..302
Gift 304
Holiday...305
Hotel..307
Dinner Party 308
Christmas..312

POLITICS 315

Power..316
Government 317
Election...318
Politics – General 320
Politicians 330
House of Lords 335

Political Speeches 336
Foreign Affairs & Diplomacy 338
Bureaucracy 339
US Politics..341
Leaving Political Office............................344

ARTS & ENTERTAINMENT 347

Music..348
Musical Instrument..................................356
Opera..359
Dance..361
Art 363
Sculpture...367
Photography 368
Film & Hollywood 369
Agent 373
Musical 374
Theatre 375
Playwright...377
Shakespeare 378
Actors & Acting 381
Fame & Celebrity 384
Publicity..388
Television 389
Radio 390
Comedy 391
Heckle...393

TRANSPORT.......................................395

Transport – General.................................396
Car...397
Bicycle...400
Train 401
Air Travel...402
Sea Travel 404

TRAVEL & COUNTRIES 407

Travel & Tourism 408
Countries – General 412
America 414
American Places 417
Australia 419
Canada 420
Great Britain – General...........................421
Mottos for Modern Britain 422
England..423
Ireland 425
Scotland...426
Wales 428

SCIENCE & TECHNOLOGY 429

Computer..430
Internet 432
Science & Scientists 434
Evolution & Creationism..........................437
Time...438
Mathematics 439
Statistics..441
Inventions 442
Astronomy 443
Extraterrestrial Life...................................445

SOCIETY & LAW 447

Class 448
Royalty 449
Aristocracy..451
Class Consciousness.................................453
Law & Lawyers...454
Crime...456

In Court 460
Prison..462
History..463
War & Peace..465
Terrorism 470
Violence & Weapons 471

HEALTH, MEDICINE & DRUGS.........473

Weight 474
Diet..475
Healthy Eating...................................478
Exercise...480
Health & Medicine.............................481
Dentist 485
Disability 486
Drugs & Addiction 488
Smoking...490
Depression 491
Psychiatry & Therapy........................492

EDUCATION & THINKING...............499

Education & Schools 500
Teacher 502
Exams & Tests.....................................504
College...505
Knowledge 506
Intelligence...507
Stupidity 508
Thinking 510
Philosophy 511

LIFE, AGEING & DEATH.....................................513

Life 514
Living..515
Age & Ageing 516
Memory 521
Retirement 521
Death & Dying 523
Last Words...525
Suicide 526
Funeral..527

RELIGION 529

Religion – General 530
God...532
Jew...534
Christian 535
Catholic 537
Muslim 538
Immortality...539
Heaven & Hell 540

INDEX 542

FOOD
& DRINK

FOOD & DRINK
– GENERAL

'Life,' said Emerson, 'consists in what a man is thinking all day.' If that be so, then my life is nothing but a big intestine.

Henry Miller

Show me another pleasure like dinner, which comes every day and lasts an hour.

Charles-Maurice de Talleyrand

Oh, boy, dinner time! The perfect break between work and drunk.

Homer Simpson

I'm so hungry I could eat a bowl of lard with a hair in it.

Corsican Brother, *Cheech & Chong's The Corsican Brothers*

I'm so hungry I could eat the dates off a calendar.

Helen Rudge, quoting her uncle

I'm so hungry I could eat a vegetable.

Al Bundy, *Married With Children*

—You seem to have a good appetite.
—Not at all, madam, but, thank God, I am very greedy.

Fellow Diner and Anthony Trollope

He's had more hot dinners than you've had hot dinners.

Anon, on Cyril Smith, MP

He's 20 stones. For his salad, you just pour vinegar and oil on your lawn and let him graze.

Jim Bakken

—What would you like for breakfast?
—Just something light and easy to fix. How about a dear little whiskey sour?

Joe Bryan and Dorothy Parker

To open champagne at breakfast is premature, like uncovering the font at a wedding.

Pierce Synnott

I always have a boiled egg. A three-minute egg. Do you know how I time it? I bring it to the boil and then conduct the overture to *The Marriage of Figaro*. Three minutes exactly.

Sir John Barbirolli

I marmaladed a slice of toast with something of a flourish.

P.G. Wodehouse, *Stiff Upper Lip, Jeeves*

A Texas breakfast is a two-pound hunk of steak, a quart of whiskey and a hound dog. If you're wondering why you need the dog – well, somebody has to eat the steak.

Texas Bix Bender

Sex: Breakfast of Champions

Badge on the racing suit of James Hunt, champion racing driver

Yogurt is one of only three foods that taste exactly the same as they sound. The other two are goulash and squid.

Henry Beard

Peach flavour yogurt tastes best on the way back up.

Brüno Gehard, aka Sacha Baron Cohen

Ah, Wensleydale! The Mozart of cheeses.

T.S. Eliot

I hate clams. To me, they're like God's little bed-pans.

Sylvester Stallone

I am known to cross a street whenever I see an anchovy coming.

Jeffrey Steingarten

A winkle is just a bogey with a crash helmet on.

Mick Miller

Canapé: a sandwich cut into 24 pieces.

Billy Rose

Buffet: a French word that means, 'Get up and get it yourself.'

Ron Dentinger

The better a pie tastes, the worse it is for you.

Ed Howe

I never drink tap water in London, because the water here is hard, limey and tastes like it's been used to rinse false teeth.

A.A. Gill

I never drink water. I'm afraid it will become habit-forming.

W.C. Fields

I drank some boiling water because I wanted to whistle.

Mitch Hedberg

It's half past four, I think we'll have tea. Put the kettle on, Harnsworth. Oh, you've put the kettle on. It suits you.

Tony Hancock

'Spit and polish' – surely one of the worst crisp flavours ever devised.

Humphrey Lyttelton, *I'm Sorry I Haven't a Clue*

With this sauce a man might eat his father.

Leigh Hunt, quoting the verdict of a jury of taste-testers on a new sauce

Garlic is the ketchup of intellectuals.

Anon

Hotter than hell in a heatwave.

Gary O'Shea, eating the naga-bih jolokia, the world's hottest chilli

American Danish can be doughy, heavy, sticky, tasting of prunes and is usually wrapped in cellophane. Danish Danish is light, crisp, buttery and often tastes of marzipan or raisins; it is seldom wrapped in anything but loving care.

R.W. Apple, Jr.

—What is Osama Bin Laden's favourite dessert?
—Terrormisu.

Popbitch.com

As a boy, I was seduced by the honeycomb centre of a Crunchie. I'm sure I wasn't alone in trying to make a deep hole in the honeycomb with my tongue, before the chocolate collapsed around it.

Simon Hopkinson, *Roast Chicken and Other Stories*

Liquorice is the liver of candy.

Michael O'Donoghue

Fry's Turkish Delight...a refrigerated human organ dipped in chocolate.

Charlie Brooker

Tinned soups, unless you happen to like the taste of tin, are universally displeasing.

Elizabeth David

Rightly thought of there is poetry in peaches, even when they are canned.

Harvey Granville Barker

Raspberries are best not washed. After all, one must have faith in something.

Ann Batchelder

—What's red and sits in a corner?
—A naughty strawberry.

Alan Davies, *QI*

Kiwi: a Draylon-covered tasteless fruit.

Mike Barfield, *Dictionary for our Time*

Jerusalem artichokes...are none the worse for not being artichokes and having nothing at all to do with Jerusalem.

Jane Grigson

The French'll eat anything. Over here, My Little Pony is a toy; over there, it's a starter.

Paul Merton, *Room 101*

Whilst in Normandy last summer, I found Bisto gravy powder in a hardware shop on the same shelf as colouring for tile grout.

M.J.J. Tanner

I visited a supermarket in southern Italy, where I found Bird's Custard on shelves reserved for pet foods.

I.S. Harrison

Somewhere lives a bad Cajun cook, just as somewhere must live one last ivory-billed woodpecker. For me, I don't expect ever to encounter either one.

William Least Heat-Moon

—Why is parsley like pubic hair?
—You push it aside and keep eating.

Anon

—Is it true that the Chinese will eat anything with four legs, unless it's a table?

—Yes. And anything with wings, unless it's a plane.

Andrew Purvis and Xu Ying Jie

The story about the Indian and the Cantonese confronted by a creature from outer space: the Indian falls to his knees and begins to worship it, while the Chinese searches his memory for a suitable recipe.

Paul Lévy, Out to Lunch

Some of the food looks good enough to eat.

Paul Merton, in India

Photographs fade, bric-a-brac gets lost, busts of Wagner get broken, but once you absorb a Bayreuth-restaurant meal, it is your possession and your property until the time comes to embalm the rest of you.

Mark Twain, dining in Germany

I feel like a bus on a wet day: full up inside.

Monica Nash, quoting an acquaintance

Always get up from the table feeling as if you could still eat a penny bun.

Joyce Grenfell and Hugh Casson, quoting 'Nanny'

COOKING

I miss my wife's cooking – as often as I can.

Henny Youngman

It took her the first 3 months of married life to discover you can't open an egg with a can opener.

Joey Adams

She has the only dining room with a garbage disposal for a centrepiece.

Bob Hope

My wife can't cook at all. She made chocolate mousse. An antler got stuck in my throat.

Rodney Dangerfield

She loves to make soup – especially 'cream of yesterday'.

Milton Berle

Hey, I stuck that in the microwave, pressed 'power', pressed 'time', pressed 'start', and this is the thanks I get?

Roseanne Conner, *Roseanne*

—This hot chocolate you made…tastes like some warm water that has had a brown crayon dipped in it.
—[*sips it*] You're right. I'll go put in another crayon.

Lucy and Linus van Pelt, *Peanuts*

The husband that uncomplainingly eats what's set before him may live more peacefully, but not as long.

Kin Hubbard

I tried boiling pig's feet once, but I couldn't get the pig to stand still.

Groucho Marx

I'm an all right cook. It depends on how much I want to sleep with you, really.

Benjamin Zephaniah

Here, taste my tuna casserole and tell me if I put in too much hot fudge.

Larry Lipton, *Manhattan Murder Mystery*

I have enough fruitcakes in my freezer to enlarge my patio.

Erma Bombeck

Mammy's cakes are so heavy the post office won't take them.

Ernest Matthew Mickler

All you used to give me was TV dinners or convenience food... If you'd been in charge of the Last Supper, it would have been a takeaway.

Rodney Trotter, to Del Boy, *Only Fools and Horses*

Who bothers to cook TV dinners? I suck them frozen.

Woody Allen

I don't even butter my bread; I consider that cooking.

Katherine Cebrian

Cook book: a collection of recipes arranged in such a fashion that the cook must turn the page just after the point where a thick paste of flour, water and lard is mixed by hand.

Henry Beard

Skid Road Stroganoff... Add the flour, salt, paprika and mushrooms, stir, and let it cook five minutes while you light a cigarette and stare sullenly at the sink.

Peg Bracken

My favourite recipe: Warm up car. Let stand for an hour next to restaurant.

Margery Eliscu

Chef: any cook who swears in French.

Henry Beard

A lot of chefs stick a banana up a duck and call themselves geniuses.

Sanche de Gramont

—What's the difference between Gordon Ramsay and a cross country run?
—One is a pant in the country...

Popbitch.com

I'm not a smarmy arse. I don't think you should walk into the dining room and grace tables, standing there like some starched stiff erection, gawping at customers and asking how the food was.

Gordon Ramsay

If you give Heston Blumenthal a human brain he might poach it lightly in a reduction of 1978 Cornas and top it with a mortarboard made of liquorice.

Julian Barnes

Heston Blumenthal could probably make you a cloud sandwich if you asked.

Charlie Brooker

I'm sure Nigella's cooking is fantastic, but a bit wasted on me. I like toast with Dairylea, followed by Weetabix for supper.

Charles Saatchi, on his wife, Nigella Lawson
My Name is Charles Saatchi and I am an Artoholic

Was there ever anything more absurd than the cult of the stellar egg-flipper?

Will Self

I met a famous chef a few years ago: he said that while cooking was undoubtedly an art, it was the only one the products of which ended up in the sewer.

Alice Thomas Ellis

The only good vegetable is Tabasco sauce.

P.J. O'Rourke

Give peas a chance.

Tom Brokaw

—These peas are a bit big.
—They're sprouts.

Morecambe and Wise

New potatoes in their jackets or, as the Italian expression has it, in their nightshirts.

John Lanchester, *The Debt to Pleasure*

You say potato, I say vodka.

Karen Walker, *Will and Grace*

Veal is a very young beef and, like a very young girlfriend, it's cute but boring and expensive.

P.J. O'Rourke

Roast Beef, Medium, is not only a food. It is a philosophy.

Edna Ferber

Tongue – well, that's a very good thing when it ain't a woman's.

Charles Dickens, *The Pickwick Papers*

Roadkill: a roast with a lingering hint of tarmac.

Sandi Toksvig

Pâté: nothing more than a French meat loaf that's had a couple of cocktails.

Carol Cutler

There is no light so perfect as that which shines from an open fridge door at 2am.

Nigel Slater

The cold pork in the fridge was wilting at the edges; it and I exchanged looks of mutual contempt, like two women wearing the same hat in the Royal Enclosure at Ascot.

Kyril Bonfiglioli, After You With the Pistol

CANNIBAL

—What's the definition of trust?
—Two cannibals giving each other a blow job.

Anon

A cannibal is one who goes into a café and orders the waiter.

Anon

A cannibal is a man who loves his neighbour. With sauce.

Jean Riguax

A cannibal goes to the missionary who is in the pot, 'Would you mind telling me how you spell your name. We are making out the menu.'

Larry Adler

Did you hear about the vegetarian cannibal? He would only eat Swedes.

Anon

VEGETARIAN

I can smell burning flesh – and I hope to God it's human!

Morrissey, vegetarian, walking offstage in protest about a backstage barbecue

The gorilla is a strict vegetarian like the elephant and buffalo – three of the four most dangerous animals of Africa. It behooves one to walk softly with vegetarians!

Mary Hastings Bradley

If meat is murder, does that mean eggs are rape?

P.J. O'Rourke

What I always say about your salads, Annie, is that I may not enjoy eating them but I learn an awful lot about insect biology.

Reg, *Table Manners*

—I'm a vegan. Do you know what a vegan is?
—Absolutely, I never missed an episode of *Star Trek*.

Graham Perry and Vince Pinner, *Just Good Friends*

ALCOHOL

A skeleton walks into a bar and says, 'Give me a beer and a mop.'

Anon

Drunk for 1d, dead drunk for 2d, clean straw for nothing.

Sign outside a gin shop in Southwark in the 18th century

Let's get something to eat. I'm thirsty.

Nick Charles, *After the Thin Man*

I don't mind eating if it's possible to make a Martini sandwich.

Captain Benjamin 'Hawkeye' Pierce, *M*A*S*H*

—Hey, Mr Peterson, there's a cold one waiting for you.
—I know, and if she calls, I'm not here.

Woody Boyd and Norm Peterson, *Cheers*

A woman is only a woman but a frothing pint is a drink.

P.G. Wodehouse, *Pigs Have Wings*

Say when? When it's running over my knuckles.

Sir Les Patterson

Alcohol is a very necessary article... It enables Parliament to do things at eleven at night that no sane person would do at eleven in the morning.

George Bernard Shaw

Whiskey is carried into committee rooms in demijohns and carried out in demagogues.

Mark Twain

Bourbon does for me what the piece of cake did for Proust.

Walker Percy

The only time I ever said no to a drink was when I misunderstood the question.

Tom Sykes

I never worry about being driven to drink. I just worry about being driven home.

W.C. Fields

Somebody's gotta be the designated drinker.

Karen Walker, *Will and Grace*

The chief reason for drinking is the desire to behave in a certain way, and to be able to blame it on alcohol.

Mignon McLaughlin

—A friend of mine used alcohol as a substitute for women.
—Yeah, what happened?
—He got his penis stuck in the neck of the bottle.

Anon

I drink to forget I drink.

Joe E. Lewis

—What are you having?
—Not much fun.

Bartender and Dorothy Parker

I like a drink as much as the next man – unless the next man is Mel Gibson.

Ricky Gervais, Golden Globe Awards

Most of my Irish friends liked to drink to excess, on the principle that otherwise they might as well not drink at all.

Hugh Leonard

I'm an occasional drinker, the kind of guy who goes out for a beer and wakes up in Singapore with a full beard.

Raymond Chandler, *The Simple Art of Murder*

If you go to Germany and get drunk, at some point you're going to look up Hitler in the phone book.

Dave Attell

—What's the difference between London beer and making love in a punt?
—They're both fucking close to water.

Victor Lewis-Smith

Beer is not a good cocktail-party drink, especially in a home where you don't know where the bathroom is.

Billy Carter

A good Martini should be strong enough to make your eyeballs bubble, so cold your teeth will ache, and you'll think you're hearing sleigh bells.

L.G. Shreve

You can no more keep a Martini in the refrigerator than you can keep a kiss there.

Bernard De Voto

A cocktail is to a glass of wine as rape is to love.

Paul Claudel

—My father fell down the stairs with three quarts of liquor.
—Did he spill it?
—No, silly. He kept his mouth closed.

Gracie Allen and George Burns

It's like pouring diamonds into a tulip.

Advertising slogan for Dom Ruinart champagne

'He was drinking champagne out of my wife's shoe.' 'Yeah, and he wasted a good bottle of champagne. Your wife was wearing open-toed shoes.'

Larry Hagman, *Hello Darlin'*

I'll stick with gin. Champagne is just ginger ale that knows somebody.

Captain Benjamin 'Hawkeye' Pierce, *M*A*S*H*

Champagne and orange juice is a great drink. The orange improves the champagne. The champagne definitely improves the orange.

Prince Philip, Duke of Edinburgh

Gimme a bottle of Bourbon! I got a new liver and I'm breakin' it in!
Wealthy Texan, *The Simpsons*

A wonderful drink wine. Did you ever hear of a bare-footed Italian grape-crusher with athlete's foot?

W.C. Fields

By making this wine vine known to the public, I have rendered my country as great a service as if I had enabled it to pay back the national debt.

Thomas Jefferson, US president and wine importer

It's lucid, yes, but almost Episcopalian in its predictability.

Dave Barry, at a wine tasting

Being a Scotsman, I am naturally opposed to water in its undiluted state.

Alistair MacKenzie

I know bourbon gets better with age, because the older I get, the more I like it.

Booker Noe

I make it a point never to consume anything that's been aged in a radiator.

Major Charles Winchester, *M*A*S*H*

A sudden violent jolt of it has been known to stop the victim's watch, snap his suspenders and crack his glass eye right across.

Irvin S. Cobb, on moonshine corn whiskey

A toast! To my uncle, who taught me that you should always stop drinking when you can't spell your name backwards... here's to Uncle Bob!

Dan Chopin

That Scotch egg you had… I think there was more 'scotch' in it than 'egg'.

James Lipton, to Ricky Gervais

Pour him out of here!
Mae West, when W.C. Fields showed up drunk on the set of *My Little Chickadee*

Who's sober enough to drive? No one? Okay, who's drunk, but that special kind of drunk where you're a better driver because you know you're drunk?

Peter Griffin, *Family Guy*

Man, I was an embarrassing drunk. I'd get pulled over by the cops, I'd be so drunk I'd be out dancing in their lights thinking I'd made it to the next club.

Bill Hicks

I had to stop drinking because I got tired of waking up in my car driving ninety.

Richard Pryor

I've been drunk only once in my life. But that lasted for 23 years.

W.C. Fields

Anyone who stayed drunk 25 years, as I did, would have to be in trouble. Hell, I used to take two-week lunch hours.

Spencer Tracy

When doctors operated on Richard Burton three years before he died they found that his spine was coated with crystallized alcohol.

Graham Lord

Doctors don't ask the right questions to find out whether you have a drink problem. They should ask things like, 'Have you ever woken up on a plane to Turkey?'

Jenny Lecoat

An alcoholic has been...defined as a man who drinks more than his own doctor.

Alvan L. Barach

Excessive drinking of beer is likely to make the consumer fall forward; anyone overestimating his powers in regard to cider invariably falls backward.

William Pett Ridge

Mankind's Ten Stages of Drunkenness... Witty and Charming; Rich and Powerful; Benevolent; Clairvoyant; Fuck Dinner; Patriotic; Crank up the Enola Gay; Witty and Charming, Part II; Invisible; Bulletproof.

Dan Jenkins, *Baja Oklahoma*

It takes that *je ne sais quoi* which we call sophistication for a woman to be magnificent in a drawing-room when her faculties have departed but she herself has not yet gone home.

James Thurber

I am sparkling; *you* are unusually talkative; *he* is drunk.

R.E. Kitching

In response to the question, 'What were you doing in Central Park, in Bethesda Fountain, at one in the morning, naked?' he replied, 'The backstroke.'

Leo Silver, *My Favorite Year*

Never get drunk when you're wearing a hooded sweatshirt, cos you will eventually think there's someone right behind you.

Dave Attell

Staggering home from the pub one night, Murphy passed through the cemetery, tripped into a freshly-dug grave and fell fast asleep. Next morning he awoke, looked around and said, 'Good heavens! The Day of Judgement and I'm the first up!'

Anon

Uncle Seamus, the notorious and poetic drunk... would sit down at the breakfast table the morning after a bender, drain a bottle of stout and say, 'Ah, the chill of consciousness returns.'

Molly O'Neill

The noise of the cat stamping about in the passage outside caused him exquisite discomfort.

P.G. Wodehouse, *Mr Mulliner Speaking*

I feel like the floor of a taxi cab.

Egon Spengler, *Ghostbusters*

—What hit me?
—The last Martini.

Nora and Nick Charles, *The Thin Man*

While I was asleep someone had come in and carpeted my throat.

Alan Coren

I feel like a midget with muddy feet has been walking over my tongue all night.

W.C. Fields

Be wary of strong drink. It can make you shoot at tax collectors – and miss.

Robert A. Heinlein

By the time a bartender knows what drink a man will have before he orders, there is little else about him worth knowing.

Don Marquis

—What's up, Mr Peterson?
—The warranty on my liver.

Woody Boyd and Norm Peterson, *Cheers*

He sees a psychiatrist once a week to make him stop drinking – and it works. Every Wednesday, between 5 and 6, he doesn't drink.

Joe E. Lewis

When anyone announces to you how little they drink you can be sure it's a regime they just started.

F. Scott Fitzgerald

One of life's puzzling oddities is that every centenarian has either used alcohol most of his life or has let it strictly alone.

Arnold H. Glasow

One knows where one is with a drunk, but teetotalism in an Irishman is unnatural; if it is not checked, he becomes unpredictable and repays watching.

Hugh Leonard

Don Marquis came downstairs after a month on the wagon, ambled over to the bar, and announced: 'I've conquered that goddamn willpower of mine. Gimme a double scotch.'

E.B. White

I haven't touched a drop of alcohol since the invention of the funnel.

Malachy McCourt

RESTAURANTS & CAFÉS

I had the most expensive meal of my life today: breakfast at the airport.

Elayne Boosler

There was no place to eat last night, so I went to a kebab shop and had a doner. Which my body rejected.

Emo Philips

Don't eat anything that's served to you out of a window unless you're a seagull.

Bill Maher

I went to an authentic Mexican restaurant. The waiter poured the water and warned me not to drink it.

Brad Garrett

Never eat at a restaurant where you see a cockroach bench-pressing a burrito.

Pat McCormick

For the first time in history McDonald's had a loss. How? Everybody gets the urge for chewy meat under incredibly bright fluorescent lights.

David Letterman

It gets so your blood turns to ketchup.

Jerry Pelletier, assistant dean, McDonald's Hamburger University, on his dedication to hamburgers

COURTEOUS AND EFFICIENT SELF-SERVICE

Sign in a New York restaurant

—How do you want your steak?
—Just knock the breath out of it.

Waiter and Dan Manoukian

My steak was a little gristly, but what do you expect from a place decorated with a mural depicting the Heimlich Manoeuvre.

Cliff Clavin, dining at 'The Hungry Heifer', *Cheers*

To get a better piece of chicken, you'd have to be a rooster.

Advertising slogan, Mickey Mantle's Country Cooking Restaurant Chain

God, I hate gastropubs. What with all the twice-baked goats' cheese soufflés and geranium-scented panna cotta there's nowhere to put your pint down anymore.

Nigel Slater

For me, fancy food in a traditional old pub is about as inviting as the phrases 'hot male-on-male action', or 'tonight Billy Joel live!' or 'free prostate exam with every drink.'

Anthony Bourdain

At a Chinese restaurant in Barmouth, I asked what they had for pudding. The waiter said, 'Peaches or fruit salad,' while presenting me with both tins.

Listener, *The Radcliffe and Maconie Show*

I've never been to a hotel with a rotating restaurant on top, but one time I took my girlfriend to a merry-go-round, and I gave her a burrito.

Mitch Hedberg

Sushi must have been created by two Jews thinking, 'How can we open a restaurant without a kitchen?'

Jackie Mason

A tablecloth restaurant is still one of the great rewards of civilization.

Harry Golden

COME IN, OR WE'LL BOTH STARVE

Sign in a restaurant window

Give me a table near a waiter!

Henny Youngman

The head-waiter began to drift up like a bank of fog.

P.G. Wodehouse, *The Indiscretions of Archie*

Just as a horse knows immediately and instinctively when its rider is an idiot, so a head waiter greets my entrance to a restaurant with a knowing aside to his assistants, 'Nous avons a right one here.'

Harry Secombe

When a waiter asks you to taste the wine and you're clueless, sip it and then say, 'Yeah, that should get me hammered.'

Carol Leifer

What wine goes with mood stabilizers?

Will Truman, *Will and Grace*

We began with a *truite au bleu* – a live trout simply done to death in hot water, like a Roman emperor in his bath. It was served up with enough melted butter to thrombose a regiment.

A.J. Liebling

An aubergine had simply been put in an oven until it was slightly deflated, and then served. It was depressed rather than cooked, and tasted like an aubergine that had just lost its job.

Giles Coren

The potatoes looked as if they had committed suicide in their own steam.

George Meredith

The *haricots vert* resembled decomposed whiskers from a theatrical-costume beard.

A.J. Liebling

I don't like *al dente* vegetables. What upsets me most is a green bean that squeaks when you eat it.

Simon Hopkinson

Surrounded with cold, white fat, the rabbit legs looked like maps of Greenland, and tasted like a dryad's inner thigh.

Clive James, *Unreliable Memoirs*

As any fool knows, seaweed looks and tastes like the pubic hair of a Rhinemaiden.

Will Self

It was like eating freshly extracted breast implants.

Hermione Eyre, on pigs' cheeks

Nowhere else in the world has anyone thought of burying a shark for a year and then putting it in their mouths... You know the burning sensation of an Extra Strong Mint or a Victory V? Well, imagine that, but with the flavour of a Turkish long-drop lav – in August.

A.A. Gill, on an Icelandic speciality

The baklava tasted like balaclava.

Victor Lewis-Smith

I've tasted nicer ointments.

Jay Rayner, on the dill sauce at Blue Kangaroo, London

Someone at the table, whose order had not yet arrived, said, 'I think "waiter" is such a funny word. It is we who wait.'

Muriel Spark, *The Finishing School*

The service is like herpes: absent for long stretches, and then suddenly impossible to get rid of.

Jay Rayner, at Cecconi's, London

Waiters must never 'who gets the soup?' interrupt.

Alan Richman

Could we have some more virgin olive oil? This one's kinda trampy.

Ellen DeGeneres

An inferno of blood-curdled oil, Bruegelishly bobbing with tripe and lurking flesh, scabbed with chilli...looked like nothing so much as the bucket under a field-hospital operating table.

A.A. Gill, on the offal stew at Bar Shu, London

A customer...called the waitress after sniffing the food she had served him. 'Do you know what the cook did to this fish?' he asked. 'Sure,' said the waitress, 'she grilled it.' 'So now you should take it back to her,' said the customer. 'It's ready to talk.'

Milton Shulman

Quite often the worst place to eat fish is beside the sea. People who catch it are not necessarily the best at cooking it, just as gynaecologists are not necessarily the best lovers.

A.A. Gill

I was polishing off the last mouthful of a dish in a restaurant when I heard one waiter whisper to another: 'He's actually eating it...'

Gilbert Harding

I have eaten the still-beating heart of a fucking cobra!

Anthony Bourdain, in Saigon

[*Jerry has been served with a large, live snake*] —Jerry, you all right? You haven't even touched your food.
—My food is still eating.

Steve Tobias and Jerry Peyser, *The In-Laws*

I ate a kangaroo's anus – and do you know, they hadn't even waxed it.

Kim 'Queen of Clean' Woodburn, on a bush-tucker trial
for *I'm a Celebrity Get me Out of Here!*

Jim Grimson had never planned to eat his father's balls.

Philip José Farmer, *Red Orc's Rage*

If you have enough butter, anything is good.

Julia Child

There are several ways of calculating the tip after a meal. I find the best is to divide the bill by the height of the waiter. Thus, a bill of 12 dollars brought by a six-foot waiter calls for a 2-dollar tip.

Miss Piggy

For that kind of money a lot of chefs I know will come round to your house, cook your dinner and shampoo your carpets into the bargain.

Will Self, on Le Manoir Aux Quat' Saisons, Oxfordshire

Eat, drink and be merry for tomorrow they may recall your credit cards!

Anon

SEX & DATING

ATTRACTION

—What's the difference between Roseanne Barr and a bowling ball?
—If I really had to, I'd eat the bowling ball.

Chevy Chase

There she was – dejected, desperate and stoned. Everything I could have hoped for in a woman.

Louie De Palma, *Taxi*

I don't know what we should do first, have lunch or have sex.
Michael Hutchence, on a first date with Kylie Minogue

I have to find a girl attractive or it's like trying to start a car without an ignition key.

Jonathan Aitken

I like my women like I like my wine: red and full of alcohol.
Fez, *That 70s Show*

The best way to attract a man immediately is to have a magnificent bosom and a half-size brain and let both of them show.

Zsa Zsa Gabor

He looked at my face – a rare thing for me.

Dolly Parton, on first meeting her husband-to-be

Looking at cleavage is like looking at the sun. You don't stare at it. It's too risky. You get a sense of it, then you look away.

Jerry Seinfeld, *Seinfeld*

Her eyes were like two teaspoonfuls of the Mediterranean.

Michael Arlen

She has eyes that folks adore so, and a torso even more so.

Groucho Marx

I love it when I get whistled at by builders. If they don't, I'll walk past again until they do.

Su Pollard

This girl is ugly. She hands out whistles to construction workers.

Jean Sorensen

The thing that attracted me to my husband was his pride. I'll never forget the first time I saw him, standing up on a hill, his hair blowing in the breeze – and he too proud to run and get it.

Jean Carroll

I don't know what she sees in him – I wouldn't fancy him baked.

W.S. Hardy, quoting her mother

Throw away this absurd Vera Wang shopping list which says of a man that he has to earn £100,000 a year, that he has to be able to cut down a tree, play the Spanish guitar, make love all night and cook me a cheese soufflé.

Joanna Trollope

I require only three things of a man. He must be handsome, ruthless and stupid.

Dorothy Parker

Lord, any mammal with a day job.

Carol Leifer

My ideal man is kind, sensitive, intelligent, 6ft 2", 180lbs, and made of solid milk chocolate.

Patrick Hardin, cartoon caption

DATING

Dating is a social engagement with the threat of sex at its conclusion.

P.J. O'Rourke

—Would you sleep with someone on the first date?
—I wouldn't even need the date.

Andrea McLean and Carol McGiffin, *Loose Women*

She was as easy as the TV Guide crossword.

Tom Witte

I went out with a promiscuous impressionist. She did everyone.

Jay London

—Are you seeing anyone right now?
—Well, there was this one girl in my apartment complex I was seeing on a regular basis – but then she bought curtains.

Annie Spadaro and Charlie, *Caroline in the City*

Employees make the best dates. You don't have to pick them up and they're always tax-deductible.

Andy Warhol

—You know what I do when I have a problem with a woman?
—Deflate her?

Roy Biggins and Antonio Scarpaggi, *Wings*

S.W.M. haemophiliac seeks S.W.F. knife thrower.

Allen Jones

I like to date schoolteachers. If you do something wrong, they make you do it over again.

Rodney Dangerfield

He had one of those trophy girlfriends – well, I say, trophy girlfriend, she was more like third prize.

Jonathan Ross

I like my whiskey old and my women young.

Errol Flynn

I won't say his girlfriend is young, but when he said, 'I love you,' she said, 'Then buy me a pony.'

Jeffrey Ross

You know your girlfriend is young when you haven't seen her in a couple of weeks and she's actually gotten taller.

Dom Irrera

Steer well clear of the knight in shining armour. He'll only want you to polish it.

Anon

—Can you give me one good reason why you shouldn't come back to my hotel room?
—I could give you several.

Peter Firth and Jenny Agutter

Why does a man take it for granted that a girl who flirts with him wants him to kiss her – when, nine times out of ten, she only *wants* him to want to kiss her?

Helen Rowland

I've kissed so many women I could do it with my eyes closed.

Henny Youngman

In order to avoid being called a flirt, she always yielded easily.

Charles-Maurice de Talleyrand

If men knew all that women think, they'd be twenty times more daring.

Alphonse Karr

—Roz, you've broken up with a lot of people. How do you do it?
What do you say to them?
—I love you and I want to have your baby.

Frasier Crane and Roz Doyle, *Frasier*

—Admit it, you're still not over me.
—Not over you? I've taken more time getting over speed bumps.

Joe Hackett and Helen Chapel, *Wings*

If you come home, and he's using your diaphragm for an ashtray,
it's over.

Carol Siskind

Will always follow you. On Twitter.

Mircea Lungu

My girlfriend broke up with me because she says we have no future
together. Oh well, at least I still have my wife.

Brian, *Mystic Seven*

MACHISMO

Nothing brings out the woman in the woman more than the man in
the man!

Gomez Addams, *The Addams Family*

When two men fight over a woman, it's the fight they want not the woman.

Brendan Francis

The tragedy of machismo is that a man is never quite man enough.

Germaine Greer

The American male is the world's fattest and softest; this might explain why he also loves guns – you can always get your revolver up.

Gore Vidal

This guy says, 'I'm perfect for you because I'm a cross between a macho man and a sensitive man.' I said, 'Oh, a gay trucker?'

Judy Tenuta

MY DICK IS SO BIG...

...there's still snow on it in the summertime.

John Caponera

...it has castors.

Les Firestein

...I have to check it as luggage when I fly.

Anon

...I can braid it.

Anon

...Stephen Hawking has a theory about it.

Eddie Gorodetsky

...movie theaters now serve popcorn in small, medium, large, and My Dick.

Eddie Gorodetsky

...it won't return Spielberg's calls.

Terry Mulroy

...a homeless family lives underneath it.

Les Firestein

...when it's Eastern Standard Time at the tip, it's Central Mountain Time at my balls.

Eddie Gorodetsky

...they use a bullet train to test my condoms.

Marcy Woolard

...I was once in Ohio and got a blow job in Tennessee.

Monty Hoffman

SEX

A little boy says, 'Dad, can I have $50 for a blow job?' He says, 'I don't know, are you any good?'

Gilbert Gottfried

—I want it to be the right time, the right place...
—It's not a space shuttle launch, it's sex.

Vicky and Jessica, *American Pie*

—Where did you lose your virginity?
—In a vagina.

Audience Member and Jimmy Carr

My first sexual experience took about a minute and a half – and that includes my buying the dress.

Joan Rivers

How long should sexual intercourse last? As a rule, women would like to devote as much time to foreplay and the sex act as men would like to devote to foreplay, the sex act and building a garage.

Dave Barry

Trust me, there is only one man who can satisfy a woman in two minutes: Colonel Sanders.

Sylvia Fine, *The Nanny*

If you have an obsession about a man, sometimes you have to go to bed with him to get over it.

Jackie Bisset

If I were asked for a one-line answer to, 'What makes a woman good in bed?' I would say, 'A man who is good in bed.'

Bob Guccione

Errol Flynn is priapic! The man never stops! They should tell the birds and the bees about *him*.

Anita Louise

The last woman I had sex with just hated me. I could tell by the way she asked for the money.

Drew Carey

I was dating this girl for a while, and the first time she saw me naked, she said: 'Is everything a joke with you?'

Jeffrey Ross

—I can't have sex with you. It's disgusting.
—How can it be? I don't have my clothes off yet.

Adrian and Andrew, *A Midsummer Night's Sex Comedy*

My biggest sex fantasy is we're making love and I realize I'm out of debt.

Beth Lapides

In sex as in banking there is a penalty for early withdrawal.

Cynthia Nelms

I sometimes wonder if necrophiliacs are really into dead people or if they just enjoy the quiet.

Doug Stanhope

Latin men are incredibly noisy in bed – I had no idea that there even were that many saints.

Caroline Rhea

I was so good, I screamed out my own name!

Roy Biggins, *Wings*

Post coitum omne animal triste – praeter asinum et sacerdotem.
Every animal is sad after copulation – except the ass and the priest.

Ernest Renan

Remember, what happens in Vegas stays in Vegas. Except for herpes.

Sid Garner, *The Hangover*

My girlfriend has crabs. I bought her fishnet stockings.

Jay London

I had an unusual case of crabs. Most people get that from someone else who has it already. I got it directly from a crabmeat cocktail.

Ed Bluestone

What I like about masturbation is that you don't have to talk afterwards.

Milos Forman

—What's the ultimate rejection?
—When you're masturbating and your hand falls asleep.

Anon

He's the only man who fakes an orgasm during masturbation.

Rob Reiner

—Was I the first, darling?
—Why does everyone always ask me that?

Bridegroom and Bride

I've had more women than most people have noses.

Steve Martin

A woman who has known but one man is like a person who has heard only one composer.

Isadora Duncan

She was 21 before she knew an automobile had a front seat.

Lewis Grizzard

—I'm not a whore.
—I wouldn't pay.

Alice and Larry, *Closer*

I'm a virgin. I'm just not very good at it.

Ramada Thompson, *Hot Shots!*

Today's Tuesday. You were Monday.

Unidentified Woman, turning down Jeffrey Bernard after a one-night stand

Sex is a beautiful thing between two people. Between five, it's fantastic.

Woody Allen

My sister was with two men in one night. She could hardly walk after that. Can you imagine? Two dinners!

Sarah Silverman

The difference between sex and love is that sex relieves tension and loves causes it.

Woody Allen

If you're going to have sex with an animal, always make it a horse. That way, if things don't work out, at least you know you've got a ride home.

Willie Nelson

The last girl I made love to, it was not going well. Anytime you make love and have to give her the Heimlich manoeuvre at the same time, it's not a good thing.

Garry Shandling

Never do anything to a clitoris with your teeth that you wouldn't do to an expensive waterproof wristwatch.

P.J. O'Rourke

A guy gets into bed with his wife and he's really horny. She says, 'Not tonight. I'm going to the gynaecologist tomorrow and I want to be fresh.' He says, 'Well, you're not going to the dentist are you?'

Jackie Martling

Oral sex is like being attacked by a giant snail.

Germaine Greer

If they didn't show it on the screen, most people would never know about oral sex.

Mary Whitehouse

From the movies we learn precisely how to hold a champagne flute, kiss a mistress, pull a trigger, turn a phrase...[but] the movies spoil us for life; nothing ever lives up to them.

Edmund White

Anal sex has one serious advantage: there are few cinematic precedents that instruct either party how they should *look*.

Don Paterson, *The Book of Shadows*

I was in bed one night when my boyfriend Ernie said, 'How come you never tell me when you're having an orgasm?' I said to him, 'Ernie, you're never around.'

Bette Midler

The purpose of sexual intercourse is to get it over with as long as possible.

Steven Max Singer

Guys want us to go from 0 to 60 in 5.5 seconds. We're not built like that. We stall.

Anita Wise

He, labouring away, pauses to ask, 'Are you nearly there?' 'It's hard to say,' she says. He plunges on. 'If you imagine it as a journey from here to China, where would you be?' She considers. 'The kitchen.'

Jenny Lecoat

Guys always wonder, why do we fake it? To get you the hell *off* us!

Wanda Sykes

Germaine Greer once gave a lecture at Oxford, arguing that the female orgasm was not only a facet of gender tyranny but was also vastly overrated. A male student raised his hand. 'About that overrated orgasm,' he drawled. 'Won't you give a Southern boy another chance?' The speaker was a young Rhodes scholar called Bill Clinton.

Caitlin Moran

—What do you do with 365 used rubbers?
—Melt them down, make a tyre and call it a good year.

Anon

You have to keep taking the pill every day, regardless of what's going on in your love life... Can you imagine if men had to wear a condom for 30 days just in case they might need it? 'It's Day 28, but somebody might call.'

Caroline Rhea

Scientists have announced the invention of a women's condom. The condom works by fitting snugly over a woman's wine glass.

Kevin Nealon

Margaret Sanger said the best birth control is to make your husband sleep on the roof.

Adela Rogers St Johns

I bought my wife a sex manual but half the pages were missing. We went straight from foreplay to post-natal depression.

Bob Monkhouse

Sex in marriage is like medicine. Three times a day for the first week. Then once a day for another week. Then once every three or four days until the condition clears up.

Peter De Vries

—Why can't our sex life be like it was 12 years ago?
—Why? Because the maid quit, that's why.

Jack Carter

My wife was so frigid that when she opened her mouth, a light would come on.

Rip Taylor

I took my wife to a wife-swapping party. I had to throw in some cash.

Henny Youngman

Getting older is tough. I remember the last time I felt an erection. It was at the movies. The only trouble is, it belonged to the guy sitting next to me.

Rodney Dangerfield

I used to have four supple members and one stiff one. Now I have four stiff ones and one supple one.

Duc de Morny

—I'm only 80, but I can only have sex about once a month. Groucho Marx is 85 and he says he has sex twice a week.
—Okay, you say the same thing.

George Burns and Doctor

My gynaecologist surprised me the other day. I was climbing back into my clothing after an examination, and she said: 'Well, Esther, it's all in excellent working order; don't waste it.'

Esther Rantzen, aged 67

I don't like young guys. I'm always scared I'll wake up and think, is this my date, or did I give birth last night?

Joan Rivers

I just took two Viagra. Now I'm as hard as Chinese algebra.

Robin Williams

I accidentally mixed my Viagra with my iron pills and now I can't stop pointing north.

Anon

I feel so uncomfortable...he's been undressing me with his cataracts.

Judy Gold

Viagra is now available in powder form for your tea. It may not enhance your sexual performance but it will stop your biscuit going soft.

Anon

The only way Hugh Hefner can get stiff now is through *rigor mortis*.

Gilbert Gottfried

LOVE

Love and marriage go together like angel cake and anthrax.

Julie Burchill

In how many lives does Love really play a dominant part? The average taxpayer is no more capable of a 'grand passion' than of a grand opera.

Israel Zangwill

I thought I was in love once, and then later I thought maybe it was just an inner-ear imbalance.

Benton Fraser, *Due South*

—Have you told her you love her?
—Are you kidding? That's like firing first in a duel. If you miss you're fucked.

Jeremy Osborne and Mark Corrigan, *Peep Show*

American men say 'I love you' as part of the conversation.

Liv Ullmann

Valentine's Day: Make her believe you love her – even if you don't.

Sign seen in a shop in Windsor

When you are in love with someone, you want to be near him all the time, except when you are out buying things and charging them to him.

Miss Piggy

It is an extra dividend when you like the girl you've fallen in love with.

Clark Gable

We like someone because. We love someone although.

Henri de Montherlant

Of all the paths that lead to a woman's love, pity's the straightest.

Beaumont & Fletcher

You holding my hair, me puking.

Diana Greiner

Never judge someone by who he's in love with; judge him by his friends. People fall in love with the most appalling people.

Cynthia Heimel

Oh, Marge. If there was a reality show named *Fat Guys Who Really Love Their Wives*, not only would it be an enormous ratings success, but I'd be the first one on it.

Homer Simpson

Love one another and you will be happy. It's as simple and as difficult as that.

Michael Leunig

HATE

Hate is such a luxurious emotion, it can only be spent on one we love.

Bob Udkoff

Dad, I hate you. I hate you more than I hate Barry Manilow!

Chris Lahr

If you want to make someone hate you, explain to them, logically and politely, why they are wrong.

Phil Simborg

There is nothing in the whole world so painful as feeling that one is not liked. It always seems to me that people who hate me must be suffering from some strange form of lunacy.

Sei Shōnagon

I don't want everyone to like me; I should think less of myself if some people did.

Henry James

—I don't know how you keep going.
—I just get up in the morning to confound my enemies.

Pat and Richard Nixon, during the Watergate scandal, noted by their daughter, Julie

There is no fate that cannot be surmounted by scorn.

Albert Camus

Someone asked me the other day, 'What's your pet hate?' I said, 'It doesn't really like things shoved up its arse.'

Popbitch.com

PORNOGRAPHY

A mother finds her teenage son's bedroom closet full of gay-bondage porno. 'What are we going to do?' she asks her husband. 'Well,' he says, 'I can't spank him.'

Bruce Vilanch

Women do not believe that men believe what pornography says about women. But they do. From the worst to the best of them, they do.

Andrea Dworkin

I turned down 'Playboy'. I had a lot of requests to do a centrefold. But my husband was opposed to it. He said if he can't see it, why should other people.

Dame Edna Everage

Laughter serves to neutralise pornography, and is therefore anathema to most pornographers.

Malcolm Muggeridge

It'll be a sad day for sexual liberation when the pornography addict has to settle for the real thing.

Brendan Francis

I don't need pornography – I've got Wagner.

Bernard Levin

PROSTITUTE

A man goes to a house of ill-repute. He's got both legs in a cast, both arms in a cast. The Madam opens the door, takes one look at him and says: 'What d'you want?' The man says, 'I rang the bell, didn't I?'

Redd Foxx

I only like high-class escorts. I don't like sleeping with people I really love.

Karl Lagerfeld

Whores are the most honest girls. They present the bill right away.
The others hang on and never let you go.

Alberto Giacometti

Sex is the great amateur art. The professional, male or female, is frowned on; he or she misses the whole point and spoils the show.

David Cort

MONEY
MATTERS

MONEY

Money is something you got to make in case you don't die.

Max Asnas

Money was invented so we could know exactly how much we owe.

Cullen Hightower

Money is what you'd get on beautifully without if only other people weren't so crazy about it.

Margaret Case Harriman

Money differs from an automobile, a mistress or cancer in being equally important to those who have it and those who do not.

J.K. Galbraith

Money is, in its effects and laws, as beautiful as roses.

Ralph Waldo Emerson

If you see a £20 note on the pavement, pick it up. Something valuable may be under it.

Anon

I don't feel like I get germs when I hold money. Money has a certain kind of amnesty... When I pass my hand over money, it becomes perfectly clean to me.

Andy Warhol

It isn't enough for you to love money – it's also necessary that money should love you.

Baron Rothschild

I can remember when you used to kiss your money goodbye. Now you don't even get a chance to blow in its ear.

Robert Orben

Right now I'd do anything for money. I'd kill somebody for money. I'd kill *you* for money. Ha ha, no, you're my friend. I'd kill you for nothing!

Chico Marx, *The Cocoanuts*

It is easy to make money. You put up the sign 'Bank' and someone walks in and hands you his money. The facade is everything.

Christina Stead

I believe that one's basic financial attitudes are – like a tendency toward fat knees – probably formed *in utero*.

Peg Bracken

When I was brought up we never talked about money because there was never enough to furnish a topic of conversation.

Mark Twain

It is physically impossible for a well-educated, intellectual, or brave man to make money the chief object of his thoughts.

John Ruskin

One should look down on money, but never lose sight of it.

André Prévot

I don't like money, but it quiets my nerves.

Joe Louis

Money is a good thing to have. It frees you from doing things you dislike. Since I dislike doing nearly everything, money is handy.

Groucho Marx

I have never been in a situation where having money made it worse.

Clinton Jones

Not having to worry about money is almost like not having to worry about dying.

Mario Puzo

If women didn't exist, all the money in the world would have no meaning.

Aristotle Onassis

—You said that money was no object!
—Oh, honey, that's just a saying, like, 'Ooh, that sounds like fun' or 'I love you'.

Grace Adler and Karen Walker, *Will and Grace*

'Extra' money is defined as that which you have in your possession just before the car breaks down.

Dick Armey

—Well, Marge, he's got all the money in the world, but there's one thing he can't buy.
—What's that, Homer?
—A dinosaur.

Homer and Marge Simpson

—Money doesn't buy happiness.
—But it upgrades despair so beautifully.

Oliver and Laurie, *Hurrah at Last*

If money doesn't make you happy, give it back!

Jules Renard

TAXATION

Taxes are a form of capital punishment.

Eddie George, governor of the Bank of England

There is no art which one government sooner learns of another than that of draining money from the pockets of the people.

Adam Smith

If you make any money, the government shoves you in the creek once a year with it in your pockets, and all that don't get wet you can keep.

Will Rogers

The taxpayer – that's someone who works for the federal government but doesn't have to take a civil service examination.

Ronald Reagan

One third of a pint of beer is tax. Not until about halfway through your pint do you stop drinking for the Government and start drinking for yourself.

Al Murray, The Pub Landlord

We've got so much taxation. I don't know of a single foreign product that enters this country untaxed except the answer to prayer.

Mark Twain

To tax and to please, no more than to love and be wise, is not given to men.

Edmund Burke

Everyone should pay tax – however rich they are.

Sir Lawrence Airey, Chairman of the Board of Inland Revenue

For several days before you put it in the mail, carry your tax return under your armpit. No Inland Revenue Service agent is going to want to spend hours poring over a sweat-stained document.

Dave Barry

I always put a dab of perfume on my tax return. Considering what they're doing to me, I might as well get them in the mood.

Bob Monkhouse

Simplified Tax Form: How much money did you make last year? Mail it in.

Stanton Delaplane

I said to my Tax Inspector, 'Have a heart!' He took it.

Bob Monkhouse

Every year, the night before he paid his taxes, my father had a ritual of watching the news. We figured it made him feel better to know that others were suffering.

Kevin Arnold, *The Wonder Years*

Do you know what Margaret Thatcher did in her first budget? Introduced VAT on yachts! It somewhat ruined my retirement.

Edward Heath

There's nothing wrong with waiting for your ship to come in, but you can be sure that if it ever does, the Receiver of Revenue will be right there to help you unload it.

David Biggs

We all hate paying taxes, but the truth of the matter is that without our tax money, many politicians would not be able to afford prostitutes.

Jimmy Kimmel

Last year I had difficulty with my income tax. I tried to take my analyst off as a business deduction. The government said it was entertainment. We compromised finally and made it a religious contribution.

Woody Allen

Last year, I deducted 10,697 cartons of cigarettes as a business expense. The tax man said: 'Don't ever let us catch you without a cigarette in your hand.'

Dick Gregory

If you sell your soul to the Devil, do you need a receipt for tax purposes?

Mark Russell

It's true that nothing is certain but death and taxes. Sometimes I wish they came in that order.

Sam Levenson

The only difference between death and taxes is that death doesn't get worse every time Congress meets.

Will Rogers

People love the words 'tax-free'. It is like saying 'I love you'.

Diane Saunders

Next to being shot at and missed, nothing is really quite as satisfying as an income tax refund.

F.J. Raymond

Don't get excited about a tax cut. It's like a mugger giving you back your bus fare.

Arnold H. Glasow

The avoidance of taxes is the only intellectual pursuit that carries any reward.

John Maynard Keynes

The difference between tax avoidance and tax evasion is the thickness of a prison wall.

Denis Healey

Creative Accounting is a victimless crime – like tax evasion or public indecency.

Karen Walker, *Will and Grace*

You must pay taxes. But there's no law that says you gotta leave a tip.

Advertising slogan, Morgan Stanley Financial Services

Tax loopholes are like parking spaces – they all seem to disappear by the time you get there.

Joey Adams

I contact Alun Owen in Eire and ask him what the tax advantages would be if I became domiciled in Dublin. 'None,' he says. 'What you save on tax you spend on drink.'

Spike Milligan

Philosophy teaches a man that he can't take it with him; taxes teach him he can't leave it behind either.

Mignon McLaughlin

No taxation without respiration.

Steve Forbes, on the US 'death tax', a compulsory fee to pay for social care payable after death

I can't pay death duties – I do self-assessment.

Jeremy Hardy, *The News Quiz*

There's no tax on brains – the revenue would be too small.

Evan Esar

DEBT

A reminder to anyone spending like there is no tomorrow: there *is* a tomorrow.

Advertisement, Chase Manhattan Bank

I feel these days like a very large flamingo. No matter what way I turn, there is always a very large bill.

Joseph O'Connor, *The Secret World of the Irish Male*

I know at last what distinguishes man from animals: financial worries.

Jules Renard

Annual income twenty pounds, annual expenditure nineteen nineteen six, result happiness. Annual income twenty pounds, annual expenditure twenty pounds ought and six, result misery.

Charles Dickens, *David Copperfield*

Strange things happen when you're in debt. Two weeks ago, my car broke down and my phone got disconnected. I was one electric bill away from being Amish.

Tom Ryan

—We wouldn't be in this mess if you just paid the heating bill.
— I thought global warming would take care of it. Can't Al Gore do anything right?

Marge and Homer Simpson

A man properly must pay the fiddler. In my case…a whole symphony orchestra had to be subsidized.

John Barrymore

You can't put your VISA bill on your American Express card.

P.J. O'Rourke

All right, so I like spending money. But name one other extravagance!

Max Kauffmann

Thousands upon thousands are yearly brought into a state of real poverty by their great *anxiety not to be thought poor*.

William Cobbett, on keeping up appearances

When I was born, I owed twelve dollars.

George S. Kaufman

A terrible thing happened to me last week. I tried to live within my means and was picked up for vagrancy.

Robert Orben

I'm going to live within my income this year even if I have to borrow money to do it.

Mark Twain, New Year's resolution

BANKRUPTCY

Bankruptcy is a proceeding in which you put your money in your pants pocket and give your coat to your creditors.

Joey Adams

How can they say I'm bankrupt? I owe a billion dollars!

William Zeckendorf, US property developer

'How did you go bankrupt?' Bill asked. 'Two ways,' Mike said. 'Gradually and then suddenly.'

Ernest Hemingway, *The Sun Also Rises*

I've often known people more shocked because you are not bankrupt than because you are.

Margaret Baillie Saunders

I know a man who had to file for bankruptcy. He couldn't afford his kids' allowance.

Phyllis Diller

Bankruptcy stared me in the face, but one thought kept me calm; soon I'd be too poor to need an anti-theft alarm.

Gina Rothfels

Capitalism without bankruptcy is like Christianity without hell.

Frank Borman

CAPITALISM & COMMUNISM

Capitalism is the astounding belief that the most wickedest of men will do the most wickedest of things for the greatest good of everyone.

William Maynard Keynes

Capitalism is the legitimate racket of the ruling classes.

Al Capone

The trouble with the profit system has always been that it was highly unprofitable to most people.

E.B. White

The capitalist system does not guarantee that everybody will become rich, but it guarantees that anybody can become rich.

Raul R. de Sales

I am not a Capitalist, by the way; you will not find many Socialists who are not.

George Bernard Shaw

All I know is I'm not a Marxist.

Karl Marx

I ain't a communist necessarily, but I been in the red all my life.

Woody Guthrie

The capitalist system is not going to be destroyed by an outside challenger like communism – it will be destroyed by its own internal greed.

Molly Ivins

When it comes time to hang the capitalists they will compete with each other to sell us the rope at a lower price.

Vladimir Ilich Lenin

In the Soviet Union, capitalism triumphed over communism. In the United States, capitalism triumphed over democracy.

Fran Lebowitz, 1997

ECONOMICS

Two economists are walking down the street. One sees a £10 note lying on the pavement and asks, 'Isn't that a £10 note?' 'Obviously not,' says the other. 'If it were, someone would have already picked it up.'

Anon

Economic theory is a systematic application and critical evaluation of the basic analytic concepts of economic theory, with an emphasis on money and why it's good.

Woody Allen

Economics is the science of greed.

F.V. Meyer

The Dismal Science.

Thomas Carlyle

Economics is what economists do.

Jacob Viner

Economics is extremely useful as a form of employment for economists.

J.K. Galbraith

An economist is a man who knows 100 ways of making love but doesn't know any women.

Art Buchwald, *attrib*.

An economist is someone who, if you have forgotten your telephone number, will estimate it for you.

Eddie Kent, quoting his maths tutor

An economist is someone who, by looking out of the rear window of a car, can tell the driver where he is going.

Clive Wismayer

An economist is someone who knows more about money than people who have got it.

Arthur S. Hoffman

Once economists were asked: 'If you're so smart, why ain't you rich?' Today they're asked: 'Now you've proved you ain't so smart, how come you got so rich?'

Edgar R. Fiedler

All races have produced notable economists, with the exception of the Irish who doubtless can protest their devotion to higher arts.

J.K. Galbraith

Economists are like Bangkok taxi-drivers; put two of them together and you will have four opinions, any of which will take you careering off in the wrong direction at great expense.

Mike Carlton

If all economists were laid end to end, they would not reach a conclusion.

George Bernard Shaw, *attrib*.

I was in search of a one-armed economist so that the guy could never make a statement and then say, 'on the other hand'.

Harry S. Truman

An economist is a man that can tell you anything. His guess is liable to be as good as anybody else's, too.

Will Rogers

There are only two kinds of economic forecasters – those who don't know, and those who don't know they don't know.

J.K. Galbraith

Every statement in regard to economic affairs which is short is a misleading fragment, a fallacy or a truism.

Alfred Marshall

—I don't think Sir Humphrey understands economics, Prime Minister; he did read Classics, you know.
—What about Sir Frank? He's head of the Treasury!
—Well, I'm afraid he's at an even greater disadvantage in understanding economics: he's an economist.

Bernard Woolley and Jim Hacker, *Yes, Prime Minister*

When I have to read economic documents I have to have a box of matches and start moving them into position to illustrate and simplify the points to myself.

Sir Alex Douglas-Home

'How do you treat a cold?' One nanny said, 'Feed a cold' – she was a neo-Keynesian. Another nanny said, 'Starve a cold' – she was a monetarist.

Harold Macmillan

A man explained inflation to his wife thus: 'When we married you measured 36-24-36. Now you're 42-42-42. There's more of you, but you're worth less.

Joel Barnett, attrib.

I'm 300 per cent against inflation!

Anon

There are three things not worth running for – a bus, a woman, or a new economic panacea; if you wait a bit another one will come along.

Derick Heathcoat-Amory, Chancellor of the Exchequer

No real English gentleman, in his secret soul, was ever sorry for the death of a political economist: he is much more likely to be sorry for his life.

Walter Bagehot

RECESSION

A recession is when my neighbour loses his job. A depression is when I lose my job. A panic is when my wife loses her job.

Edgar R. Fiedler

The Great Depression, 1931, that was the year when our family ate the piano.

James C. Wright, Jr.

The stock market has predicted nine out of the last five recessions.

Paul Samuelson

Let Wall Street have a nightmare and the whole country has to help get them back in bed again.

Will Rogers, after the Wall Street Crash, 1929

Wall Street owns America. It is no longer a government of the people, by the people and for the people, but a government of Wall Street, by Wall Street and for Wall Street... Money rules.

Mary E. Lease, 1890

[*urging patience after measures had been taken to promote recovery after the Wall Street Crash of 1929*] —You can't expect to see calves running in the field the day after you put the bull to the cows.
—No, but I would expect to see contented cows.

Calvin Coolidge and President Herbert Hoover, 1932

The complex mechanisms of the modern world depend as certainly on the faith in money as the structures of the medieval world depended on faith in God.

Lewis H. Lapham

There's a phrase we live by in America: 'In God We Trust'. It's right there where Jesus would want it: on our money.

Stephen Colbert

BANKS & BORROWING

A bank is a place that will lend you money if you can prove that you don't need it.

Bob Hope

Students: Left school? No job? No money? No prospects? Then fuck off!

Advert for Gnat West (The Frank Bank), *Viz magazine*

To borrow money, big money, you have to wear your clothes in a certain way, and have about you an air of solemnity and majesty – something like the atmosphere of a Gothic cathedral.

Stephen Leacock

It is no accident that banks resemble temples, preferably Greek, and that the supplicants who come to perform the rites of deposit and withdrawal instinctively lower their voices into the registers of awe.

Lewis H. Lapham

I hesitate to deposit money in a bank. I am afraid I shall never dare to take it out again. When you go to confession and entrust your sins to the safe-keeping of the priest, do you ever come back for them?

Jean Baudrillard

There are two kinds of people in the world: those who, when taking money from a bank, carefully count it before putting it away, and those who put it away immediately, as if they can't quite believe they've actually been given it and there is a risk of their being asked for it back if they leave it in their hands for a moment longer.

Miles Kington

I think our bank is in trouble. I was about to complete a withdrawal at the cashpoint and the machine asked if I wanted to go double or quits.

The Rotarian

INVESTMENT BANKS

—A banker, stock broker and a politician jump off the Empire State Building at the same time. Which one hits the ground first?
—Who cares?

Anon

Jump, you bastards, jump!
 Protestor's call to bankers on Wall Street after the collapse of investment banks, 2008

Bankers collectively occupy a place in public opinion significantly lower than cannibalistic paedophile global-warming deniers.

Boris Johnson

If you talk to 100 people, 102 will tell you they hate bankers.

Craig Warner, *The Last Days of Lehman Brothers*

What does being an investment banker mean? It means always having to say, 'I'm sorry, it seemed like a good idea at the time' all the time.

Bird and Fortune

When I was young, people called me a gambler. As the scale of my operations increased I became known as a speculator. Now I am called a banker. But I have been doing the same thing all the time.

Sir Ernest Cassel, private banker to King Edward VII

Bankers are just like anybody else, except richer.

Ogden Nash

The only two places a 28-year-old can make a half million dollars – Wall Street and dealing dope.

Ross Perot

We need three things to trade successfully... bucks, brains and balls.

Toni Turner

There are only two emotions in Wall Street: fear and greed.

William M. Lefevre, Jr.

Goldman Sachs...the world's most powerful investment bank is a great vampire squid wrapped around the face of humanity, relentlessly jamming its blood funnel into anything that smells like money.

Matt Taibbi

Banking establishments are more dangerous than standing armies.

Thomas Jefferson

Just as war is waged with the blood of others, so fortunes are made with other people's money.

André Suarès

The City is like an orgy where no one stops to have a bath.

Charlie Richardson

For decades mortgage dealers insisted that home buyers be able to produce a down payment of 10 percent or more, show a steady income and good credit rating, and possess a real first and last name. Then, at the dawn of the new millennium, they suddenly threw all that shit out the window and started writing mortgages on the backs of napkins to cocktail waitresses and ex-cons carrying five bucks and a Snickers bar.

Matt Taibbi, on the origins of the subprime lending crisis of 2007

If you were alive, they would give you a loan. Actually, I think if you were dead, they would still give you a loan.

Steven M. Knoebel, on the lax lending policy of Washington Mutual Bank, which went into receivership in 2008

Chicken Licken on Wall Street: 'Thy sky is making a technical correction!'

Current Comedy

The banks fell over like fat Labradors running over a wet kitchen floor.

Hedge Fund Manager, 2008

[*shop assistant to customer paying with a credit card*] Your card is fine. I'm just checking that your bank hasn't expired.

Matthew 'Matt' Pritchett, cartoon caption

There was a time when a fool and his money were soon parted, but now it happens to everybody.

Adlai Stevenson

Now I'm in real trouble. First my laundry called and said they lost my shirt, and then my broker said the same thing.

Leopold Fechtner

All I lost was $240,000. I would have lost more but that was all the money I had.

Groucho Marx, during the Wall Street Crash, 1929

Someone said that if it had been Lehman Sisters, instead of Lehman Brothers, there might not have been so much difficulty.

Harriet Harman, MP, after the collapse of the investment bank in 2008

It's only when the tide goes out that you learn who's been swimming naked.

Warren Buffett

Where large sums of money are concerned, it is advisable to trust nobody.

Agatha Christie

—How did you survive the 1974 banking crash?
—Quite simple, really. I only lent money to people who had been to Eton.

**Lord Cowdray and Lord Poole,
Chairman of Lazard Investment Bank and Old Etonian**

INVESTING &
THE STOCK MARKET

Jesus saves! But wouldn't it be better if he invested?

Anon

With a million bucks and a hot tip you can go broke in a year.

Warren Buffet, *attrib*.

This year I invested in pumpkins. They've been going up the whole month of October and I got a feeling they're going to peak right around January. Then bang! That's when I'll cash in.

Homer Simpson

I can calculate the motion of heavenly bodies but not the madness of people.

Isaac Newton, who lost a fortune in the South Sea Bubble of 1720

No warning can save a people determined to grow suddenly rich.

Lord Overstone

It's not the bulls and bears you need to avoid – it's the bum steers.

Chuck Hillis

Never invest in a going concern until you know which way it's going.

Lord Dewar

We own a lot of Gillette and you can sleep pretty well at night if you think of a couple of billion men with their hair growing on their faces. It is growing all night while you sleep. Women have two legs, it is even better. So it beats counting sheep.

Warren Buffett

There's nothing so disastrous as a rational investment policy in an irrational world.

John Maynard Keynes

I like buying companies that can be run by monkeys – because one day they will be.

Peter Lynch

Never invest in any idea you can't illustrate with a crayon.

Peter Lynch

I have...been speculating...in English stocks, which are springing up like mushrooms this year...forced up to a quite unreasonable level and then, for the most part, collapse. In this way, I have made over £400... It's a type of operation that makes small demands on one's time, and it's worth while running some risk in order to relieve the enemy of his money.

Karl Marx, in a letter to his uncle, Lion Philips, 1864

Don't gamble; take all your savings and buy some good stock and hold it till it goes up, then sell it. If it don't go up, don't buy it.

Will Rogers

I'm putting all my money in taxes – it's the only thing sure to go up.

Anon

Buying a stock is exactly the same thing as going to a casino, only with no cocktail service.

Ted Allen

Playing the stock market is analogous to entering a newspaper beauty-judging contest in which one must select the six prettiest faces out of a hundred photographs, with the prize going to the person whose selections most nearly conform to those of the group as a whole.

John Maynard Keynes

One of the funny things about the stock market is that every time one man buys, another sells, and both think they are astute.

William Feather

—Do you play the market?
—No, the ukulele.

Joe (Tony Curtis) and Sugar Kane Kowalczyk (Marilyn Monroe), *Some Like it Hot*

Stock prices plunged sharply today as investors reacted to the discovery that Saturn actually has six moons rather than five, as we believed previously.

Dave Barry

I made a fortune getting out too soon.

J.P. Morgan

Trying to catch the bottom on a falling stock is like trying to catch a falling knife. It's normally a good idea to wait until the knife hits the ground.

Peter Lynch

I made a killing on Wall Street a few years ago... I shot my broker.

Groucho Marx

SAVING & THRIFT

If you gave up your morning coffee for a year, you could make an extra mortgage payment. But, man, you'd be grumpy.

Advertisement, Citibank

I had a nest egg, but I lost it gambling. I was betting I'd be dead by now.

Drew Carey

My grandfather always said, 'Don't watch your money; watch your health.' So one day while I was watching my health, someone stole my money. It was my grandfather.

Jackie Mason

Remember, if you save nothing, you can't take it with you.

Stan Laurel

Never economize on luxuries.

Angela Thirkell

A penny saved is a penny.

Philip J. Frankenfield

If you had a penny and you were on top of the Empire State Building, and you took that penny and threw it off the Empire State Building and it hit somebody on the head, it would kill him. Talk about getting your money's worth.

Heywood Banks

I know how we can save money, mum. By not buying broccoli.

Karen Brockman, aged 5 years, *Outnumbered*

Living on a budget is the same as living beyond your means, except that you have a record of it.

Anon

—Did you put something away for a rainy day?
—Yes, my wellingtons.

Anon

MEANNESS

'Stand behind your lover,' said the Scotsman to his unfaithful wife. 'I'm going to shoot you both.'

Joey Adams

He's that mean that when a fly lands in his sugar he shakes its feet before he kills it.

Bill Wannan

He quit playing golf, then took it up again 14 years later. He found his ball.

Bob Kaliban

He throws nickels around like they were manhole covers.

Mike Ditka

He'd live in one of your ears and rent out the other as flats.

Patrick O'Keefe

'Goodbye,' said McIntosh, 'and don't forget to take little Donald's glasses off when he isn't looking at anything.'

Joey Adams

RICH

'Take a pencil and paper,' the teacher said, 'and write an essay with the title: "If I Were a Millionaire".' Everyone but Philip began to write furiously. 'What's the matter?' the teacher asked. 'Why don't you begin?' 'I'm waiting for my secretary.'

Bernadette Nagy

Every man nourishes within himself a secret plan for getting rich that will not work.

Grierson's Law of Minimal Self-Delusion

If I had a dollar for every time I heard, 'My God! He's covered in some sort of goo,' I'd be a rich man.

Homer Simpson

It's not the mustard that people eat that made Coleman rich, but that left on the plate!

Anon

What's the quickest way to become a millionaire? Borrow fivers off everyone you meet.

Richard Branson

Making the first million is hard, making the next hundred million is easy.

Theo Paphitis

To turn $100 into $110 dollars is work. But to turn $100 million into $110 million is inevitable.

Edgar Bronfman

The only thing I like about rich people is their money.

Nancy Astor

Sure a lot of people have money to burn. Why not? It's cheaper than gas!

Joey Adams

Those people were so rich they had a Persian rug made out of real Persians.

Henny Youngman

Once I dated a girl whose father was so rich, he had Swiss money in American banks.

Joey Adams

There are two classes of people: the have-nots and the have-yachts.

Evan Esar

If you can count your money you don't have a billion dollars.

John Paul Getty

We may see the small value God has for riches, by the people he gives
them to.

Alexander Pope

Donald Trump – a man so obscenely rich he could afford to buy all the
oxygen in the world, then rent it back to us at a profit if he so chose.

Charlie Brooker

He has an edifice complex. Buying buildings is his sex life.

Caroline Llewellyn, *Life Blood*

Greta Garbo earned a lot of money, and it was well invested for her.
When she went shopping on Rodeo Drive, it wasn't for dresses or for
jewellery; it was for Rodeo Drive.

George Cukor

You know what rich is? If Oprah ever calls you for a loan, you know you've made it.

Joan Rivers

My father somehow managed to live all his life with the gusto and
philanthropy of an extremely wealthy man – without being burdened
with the many complications of actually possessing any money.

Peter Ustinov

H.L. Mencken always said that every man ought to feel rich whether he
had a cent or not to his name, and to that end had a habit of distributing
10-dollar bills in out-of-the-way corners of his jackets and pants pockets.
'When I accidentally come upon one of the bills,' he assured me, 'I always
feel a satisfactory glow come over me and the surprise does me no end of
good.' Whereupon he would lead me into the nearest drink house and set
them up.

George Jean Nathan

Associate with people of cultivated tastes, and some of the culture may rub off on you. Hang around musical folk and you may, with luck, get to know Brahms from Beethoven. But keep company with the very rich and you'll end up picking up the bill.

Stanley Walker

POOR

The other day I told my wife, 'I lost my wallet, I'm very depressed.' She said, 'That makes two of you – you and the guy who found it.'

Rodney Dangerfield

I am never in during the afternoon, except when I am confined to the house by a sharp attack of penury.

Oscar Wilde

I know a fellow who's as broke as the Ten Commandments.

John Marquand

There were times my pants were so thin I could sit on a dime and tell if it was heads or tails.

Spencer Tracy

When I was a kid, my family was so poor, I had to wear my brother's hand-me-downs at the same time he was wearing them.

Redd Foxx

We were so skint when I was young that for Christmas dinner we used to have to go down to Kentucky Fried Chicken and lick other people's fingers.

Victor Lewis-Smith

Have you seen, lemons are 28 pence each? I'm having to squirt lemon washing up liquid into my gin and tonics.

Sandi Toksvig

You're not really poor until you put water on your cornflakes.

Elaine Marskon

Cuando merda tiver valor, pobre nasce sem cu.
When shit becomes valuable, the poor will be born without assholes.

Portuguese proverb

CHARITY

—I'm sick of this Tarzan movie.
—Dad, it's a documentary about the homeless.

Homer and Lisa Simpson

Times have sure changed. Yesterday, a bum asked me for $2.75 for a double cappuccino with no foam.

Bill Jones

Tramps: watch Ray Mears' *World of Survival* in Dixon's window to open your eyes to a whole host of natural foodstuffs.

Top Tip, *Viz* magazine

I've been doing lots of charity gigs lately – it's just in case I catch anything.

Noel Gallagher

Helping people is never more rewarding than when it's in your own self-interest.

Richard Fish, *Ally McBeal*

The rich man never really gives anything, he only distributes part of the surplus. It is the person of moderate means who really gives.

George Eastman

When they asked Jack Benny to do something for the Actors' Orphanage, he shot both his parents and moved in.

Bob Hope

He read in the papers that it takes 10 dollars a year to support a kid in India. So he sent his kid there.

Red Buttons

Charity is taking an ugly girl to lunch.

Warren Beatty

I'd like to help you out. Which way did you come in?

Henny Youngman

APPEARANCE & FASHION

APPEARANCE
– GENERAL

[*into the mirror*] Good morning, Starshine!

Karen Walker, *Will and Grace*

I got pulled over this morning for having all the mirrors in the Mercedes turned so I could see myself.

Suzanne Sugarbaker, *Designing Women*

I'm so gorgeous, there's a six-month waiting list for birds to suddenly appear every time I am near.

The Cat, *Red Dwarf*

Many times on the beach a good looking lady will say to me, 'I want to touch you.' I always smile and say, 'I don't blame you lady.'

Arnold Schwarzenegger, as Mr Universe

I'm afraid his body went to his head.
Dorothy Parker

—Oh, father, I am guilty of the sin of vanity. Every morning when I look in the mirror I think how beautiful I am.
—Never fear, my girl. That isn't a sin, it's only a mistake.

Young Girl and Father Healey of Dublin

I'm about 8 feet tall with a face like a reflection in a spoon.

Joyce Grenfell

Her face, even with its powder, looked more than ever as if it should have been resting over the top rail of a paddock fence.

Dorothy Parker

A nose like a piece of cuttlefish bone stuck between the wires of a budgerigar's cage.

Anthony Burgess, *The Worm and the Ring*

Her mouth was like a garment whose elastic had perished.

Clare Boylan, *Black Baby*

She's well-built without being in the slightest bit sexy – like a junior minister's wife.

Denis Norden

As for Gussie Fink-Nottle, many an experienced undertaker would have been deceived by his appearance and started embalming him on sight.

P.G. Wodehouse, *Right Ho, Jeeves*

In the short distance between the two houses, he had somehow managed to acquire the ragged, spent look of a man who had crossed a continent on horseback.

Lucille Kallen, *The Tanglewood Murder*

The great drapery of chin and neck was reminiscent of drought-resistant cattle from India.

Peter Carey, *The Chance*

My uncle had long fingers. He could put his finger in one ear and beckon to you through the other one.

Fred Allen

—Must you wear glasses?
—Oh, no, sir. Only when I want to see.

Football Coach and 'Junior' Jackson, *That's My Boy*

His genitals looked like a foetal mouse on a bed of radicchio.

Jonathan Ross

Jewish guys don't have big cocks. I have no cock. When I take a piss, it's like a turtle. I have to put a piece of lettuce there for the head to come out.

Stewie Stone

His dick looks just like him only it has more hair.

David Hyde Pierce

—Hey, dad, I got the biggest cock in the fourth grade. Is that cos I'm black?
—No, son, it's because you're 19.

Chevy Chase

British people are very reserved physically. I know I am. I keep the strip in my bikini bottoms after I've bought them.

Victoria Wood

Never work with any actor smaller than his Oscar.

Larry Gelbart, on Dustin Hoffman

He reminded one of a bottle with the cork driven in too far. One longed to get hold of his head and pull it out sharply so as to give him a bit more neck.

Christianna Brand, *Green for Danger*

You are one tiny, loudmouth fairy! You're the only guy who takes a stepladder into a glory hole.

Greg Giraldo

He's so short – once he was masturbating he almost poked his eye out.

Joy Behar

Get out of my face, you half-a-motherfucker!

Lester Young, to 'Pee Wee' Marquette, the pint-sized master of ceremonies at Birdland jazz club in New York

He shrugs and grins his slow grin, the big face breaking up reluctantly, like a cliff being dynamited.

William Hall, on Robert Mitchum

His smile was as faint as a fat lady at a fireman's ball.

Raymond Chandler, *The High Window*

The mute orgasm of the smile.

Jean Baudrillard

I can hear people smile.

David Blunkett

You know, every time Dick Cheney smiles like that, an angel gets waterboarded.

Jon Stewart

It's that laugh, the one that sounds like a pubescent hyena with its knackers caught in a mangle.

Woof73, on Ricky Gervais

He was born with a gift of laughter and a sense that the world was mad.

Rafael Sabatini, *Scaramouche*

She has a laugh so hearty it knocks the whipped cream off an order of strawberry shortcake on a table fifty feet away.

Damon Runyon

I will always pass up a diamond for a laugh.

Anita Loos

She had a beautiful laugh which was like rain water pouring over daffodils made from silver.

Richard Brautigan, *Sombrero Fallout*

Whether laughter is healthful or not depends on the size of the fellow you're laughing at.

Anon

MAKE-UP

The most beautiful make-up of a woman is a passion. But cosmetics are easier to buy.

Yves Saint Laurent

Make-up is such a weird concept. I'll wake up in the morning and look in the mirror. 'Gee, I really don't look so good. Maybe if my eyelids were blue, I'd be more attractive.'

Cathy Ladman

I was working in a cosmetics shop. A woman came in looking for something to bring out her bright blue eyes. I gave her meat skewers.

Hattie Hayridge

Never wear yellow lipstick; never braid your eyelashes; never powder your tongue.

Miss Piggy, make-up rules

Ladies, leave your eyebrows alone. Here's how much men care about your eyebrows: do you have two of them? Okay, we're done.

Bill Maher

I did not use paint. I made myself up morally.

Eleanora Duse, actress

—I couldn't get Mimi to take off her make-up.
—I heard they tried once, and there was a whole other painting underneath it.

Lisa Robinns and Drew Carey, *The Drew Carey Show*

I have no time to put on make-up. I need that time to clean my rifle.

Henriette Mantel

—Do you have any beauty secrets?
—For attractive lips, speak words of kindness.

Interviewer and Audrey Hepburn

BREASTS

Here they are......Jayne Mansfield!

Dick Cavett

People always ask me if they're mine. Yes, they are...all bought and paid for.

Dolly Parton

Don't try to run a *salon*. You have too luscious a bosom to keep the conversation general.

Madame Aubernon

I have little feet because nothing grows in the shade.

Dolly Parton

A lot of people say: 'Oh, Pamela Anderson wouldn't be anyone without her tits.' That's not true. She'd be Paris Hilton.

Sarah Silverman

My breasts have a career of their own. Theirs is going better.

Jennifer Love Hewitt

Released from their support, her breasts dropped like hanged men.

Gowan McGland, *Reuben, Reuben*

My breasts are so versatile now – I can wear them down, up, or side by side.

Cybill Shepherd

—Guess what? I'm going to have a boob job.
—Well, I'm having my asshole bleached.
—Really? I can't picture your husband as a blonde.

Anon

HAIR

When you're not blonde and thin, you come up with a personality real quick.

Kathy Najimy

A woman with her hair up always looks as if she were going some place – either to the opera or the shower.

Orson Welles

—Snow White – was she blonde or brunette?
—Only Walt Disney knows for sure.

Peter Marshall and Paul Lynde

It is great to be a blonde. With low expectations it's very easy to surprise people.

Pamela Anderson

My husband decided that blondes have more fun so he bleached his hair and asked me for a divorce.

Phyllis Diller

A man is usually bald four or five years before he knows it.

Ed Howe

Balderdash — a rapidly receding hairline.

Paul Kocak

The most expensive haircut I ever had cost a tenner. And £9 went on the search fee.

William Hague

Iain Duncan Smith and William Hague looked like two boiled eggs in blue eggcups. Their pates gleamed in unison. I gazed from the balcony in awe. If you'd stuck a few sequins on their heads they'd have looked like Dolly Parton's cleavage.

Simon Hoggart, at the Tory Party Conference

His toupee makes him look 20 years sillier.

Bill Dana

I have the insane desire to take off your toupee and butter the inside of it.

Buster Crabbe

Once a year they should have No Hairpiece Day. So everyone could see what all these baldy-headed, fake-hair jerkoffs look like.

George Carlin

Guys are lucky because they get to grow moustaches. I wish I could. It's like having a little pet for your face.

Anita Wise

When you spend weeks growing a moustache you almost fall in love with it. I had a big, thick moustache once. Everything you drink with it, you drink twice.

Bill Cosby

—Why do gay men have moustaches?
—To hide the stretch marks.

Anon

Of the Seven Dwarfs, the only one who shaved was Dopey. That should tell us something about the wisdom of shaving.

Tom Robbins, *Skinny Legs and All*

It isn't a beard until you have to decide whether to sleep with it inside or outside the duvet.

Phil Ridgway

Duvet? Who needs one if you're a real beardie? Mine's a tog factor 12.5.

Julian Heddy

FASHION & DRESS

—Why do Hell's Angels wear leather?
—Because chiffon wrinkles too easily.

Peter Marshall and Paul Lynde

Does fashion matter? Always – though not quite as much after death.

Joan Rivers

Just around the corner, in every woman's mind – is a lovely dress, a wonderful suit, or entire costume, which will make an enchanting new creature of her.

Wilhela Cushman

You could come a real cropper facing the real world after being immersed in *Vogue*.

Audrey Withers, former editor of *Vogue*

You look like a victim of designer drive-by.

Carol Muske Dukes, *Saving St Germ*

You couldn't tell if she was dressed for an opera or an operation.

Irvin S. Cobb

The prettiest dresses are worn to be taken off.

Jean Cocteau

You got to shave before you leave the house in a dress like that... and I don't mean your legs.

Don Cleveland, *The Adventures of Ford Fairlane*

I can't take you seriously if your skirt is so short I can see your tampon string.

Rachel Goodwin

Never wear anything that panics the cat.

P.J. O'Rourke

I just bought a new nightgown that would turn a monk into Jack the Ripper.

Robert J. Serling, *Wings*

—That's a beautiful nightgown.
—Yes, I spent all summer looking for a night to go with that nightgown.

Friend and Djuna Barnes

There were nine buttons on her nightgown, but she could only fascinate.

Homer Haynes

People's innermost thoughts are never as revealing as their jackets.

Fran Lebowitz

I'm trying to think of a word that describes what you're wearing...
affordable!

Dame Edna Everage

—You got that entire outfit for free?
—Absolutely *au gratin*.

Landlord and Mr Glum, *The Glums*

June 14: Suit of clothes for $18 – cheaper than stealing.

Mark Twain, notebook entry

—How would you describe your style?
—I'm an intergalactic bejewelled pirate, a spindly sex stick, a he-witch
scarecrow dressed by Dior.

Dan Rookwood and Russell Brand

Even on Central Avenue, not the quietest dressed street in the world, he
looked about as inconspicuous as a tarantula on a slice of angel food.

Raymond Chandler, *Farewell, My Lovely*

I had a pair of jeans with studs all over them, and my friend and art
critic, John Richardson, said to me: 'Ooh, you look just like a Queen
Anne chair, dear.'

Nicky Haslam

I hold that gentleman to be the best
dressed whose dress no one observes.

Anthony Trollope

Practical, simple, cheap and does not go out of fashion.

Fidel Castro, on battledress

Don't itch when wearing armour.

Stanislaw J. Lec

A guy goes to a fancy dress party wearing nothing but a pair of boxers. The host says, 'What the hell are you supposed to be?' The guy says, 'A premature ejaculation – I just came in my pants.'

Anon

A man wearing only bathing-shorts looks fully dressed, but a man wearing only underpants looks naked.

Miles Kington

Judge not a man by his clothes, but by his wife's clothes.

Thomas R. Dewar

If I am at home… I mostly wear leggings and an old zip-up fleece. I am really more sheep than woman.

Emma Thompson, actress

If you have a pear-shaped body, you should not wear pear-coloured clothes, or act juicy.

Demetri Martin

My clothes are addressed to women who can afford to travel with 40 suitcases.

Yves Saint Laurent

What's in a name? A 35 per cent mark-up!

Vince Thurston, retailer, on designer names

—You paid $500 for shoes?!
—*Boots*, Todd. I'm not an idiot.

Todd Garrett and Toni Childs, *Girlfriends*

High heels were invented by a woman who had been kissed on the forehead.

Christopher Morley

—Why are so many gay men drawn to designing women's clothes?
—Because we're too scared to be plumbers.

Alex Bilmes and Alexander McQueen, fashion designer

Naomi – she's amazing – 20 years in the business and all the pressure and fame hasn't changed her a bit – she's remained a total bitch.

Brüno Gehard, aka Sacha Baron Cohen

I hate turtlenecks. Wearing a turtleneck is like being strangled by a really weak guy – all day.

Mitch Hedberg

Do you know that if you hold a shell suit up to your ear you can hear Romford?

Linda Smith, *I Think the Nurses are Stealing my Clothes*

My sister has a social conscience now. She still wears her fur coat, but across the back she's embroidered a sampler that says: 'Rest in Peace.'

Julia Willis

—You know, Gracie, it takes 30 minks to make one fur coat.
—Really? How long does it take them?

George Burns and Gracie Allen

Kind-hearted Cynthia. You refused to wear fur coats taken from animals. Yes, you grew your own.

Milton Berle

I'm jealous of a woman and her purse. We men have to shove our whole lives in a little square of leather. Then we have to sit on it.

Hal Wilkerson, *Malcolm in the Middle*

When I was six I made my mother a little hat – out of her new blouse.

Lilly Daché

Top hats look like very sensible containers, suitable for holding almost everything with the exception of the human head.

George Mikes

If I ever get burned beyond recognition, and you can't decide if it's me or not, just put my funny fisherman's hat on my 'head'. See, it's me!

Jack Handey

Never try to wear a hat that has more character than you do.

Lance Morrow

All I want to know is, when are people going to stop wearing their baseball caps backwards?

Spalding Gray

When I wear a tuxedo I look like a truck driver out on a date.

Gene Kelly

I'm going to a State Dinner tonight. What do you wear to a recession?

Buffalo Bill Cody, noted by Sheldon Keller

—Do you ever wear pink?
—Only in the privacy of my own home.

Reporter and David Cameron

There will be little change in men's pockets this year.

Wall Street Journal

BEAUTY

[*in a taxi*] You look so beautiful, I can hardly keep my eyes on the meter.

Woody Allen

If you were a Broadway musical, people would be humming your face.

Elliot Garfield, *The Goodbye Girl*

She's got legs going up to her armpits – not literally; that would be hideous.

Alan Partridge

Sometimes I think this leg is the most beautiful one in the world, and sometimes the other; I suppose the truth lies somewhere in between.

Peter De Vries

The legs aren't so beautiful. I just know what to do with them.

Marlene Dietrich

All I ever seemed to get was the kind of woman who had a special dispensation from Rome to wear the thickest part of her legs below the knees.

Hugh Leonard

—Do you think a woman should be beautiful before breakfast?
—It would never occur to me to look at a woman before breakfast.

Reporter and George Sanders

But these women! If put into rough wrappers in a turnip-field, where would their beauty be?

Thomas Hardy, at a society party

No matter how hot a girl is, there's always someone who's tired of fucking her.

Clint Eastwood, *attrib*.

Flaubert...proclaimed...that beauty was not erotic, that beautiful women were not meant to be bedded, that the only useful purpose they served was inspiring statuary.

Edmond and Jules de Goncourt

Let us leave pretty women to men without imagination.

Marcel Proust

Of course, every cat is really the most beautiful woman in the room.

E.V. Lucas

UGLY

—Models... take away all their make-up, all their expensive haircuts and those bodies, and what have you got?
—You!

Diane Chambers and Carla Tortelli, *Cheers*

I was in a beauty contest once. I not only came last, I was hit in the mouth by Miss Congeniality.

Phyllis Diller

A peeping Tom threw up on her window sill.

Jack Carter

I once took her to a masquerade party. At the stroke of midnight, I ripped off her mask and discovered I had beheaded her.

Oscar Levant, on Elsa Maxwell

By god, you'd have to go to night school to be as ugly as that.

Les Brandon, *I Didn't Know You Cared*

I know I'm ugly. My dog closes his eyes before he humps my leg.

Rodney Dangerfield

Nothing is more moving than beauty which is unaware of itself, except for ugliness which is.

Robert Mallet

COSMETIC SURGERY

Time marches on. And eventually you realize it's marching across your face.

Robert Harling

If I see something sagging, dragging or bagging, I get it sucked, tucked or plucked.

Dolly Parton

Joan Rivers passed away four years ago, but nobody told her face.

Jeffrey Ross

—How old does she look after her facelift?
—A very old twelve.

Friend and Noël Coward

You used to look your age. Now you don't even look like your species.

Greg Giraldo, to Joan Rivers

Your face has been lifted more than Bristol Palin's prom dress.

Brad Garrett, to Joan Rivers

Joan Rivers came to see me backstage on Broadway and she'd had so much work done, I couldn't tell if she liked the show.

Dame Eileen Atkins

Did you see her facelift? You may be looking at a brand new face, but you'll still be hearing the same old mouth.

Florida Evans, *Maude*

When I went for a hysterectomy I asked for a tummy tuck at the same time. I was the only woman in the hospital who wasn't sobbing when I woke up. I couldn't wait to get to the beach.

Joan Rivers

Anne Robinson's face now appears so tight and Botoxed she seems to be pushing it through the taut skin of a tambourine.

Charlie Brooker

[*doctor to female patient*] I'm not sure we should get rid of your cellulite – it may be all that's holding you together.

Good Housekeeping magazine, cartoon caption

I've had a little bit of work done. I've had a penis reduction. Just got the one now.

Ricky Gervais, *Golden Globe Awards*

NOSE JOB

A plastic surgeon's office is the only place where no one gets offended when you pick your nose.

MAD magazine

One's nose is rather like one's club or religion: there is not much really wrong with any of them, but there is something quite vulgar in wanting to change them.

Julian Fellowes

It's hard having a big nose. I can't go in the ocean. I'll be doing backstroke and someone'll shout, 'Shark!'

Rick Corso

He's the only man who can take a shower and smoke a cigar at the same time.

Wilson Mizner, on a long-nosed movie magnate

Are you eating a tomato or is that your nose?

Charlie McCarthy, to W.C. Fields

We get nose jobs all the time in the National Hockey League, and we don't even have to go to the hospital.

Brad Park, ice hockey player

Fanny Brice cut off her nose to spite her race.

Dorothy Parker, on the Jewish 'Funny Girl' who had rhinoplasty

I've always been proud of the Jews, but never so proud as tonight, because tonight I wish I had my old nose back.

Jean Carroll, actress, at a benefit for the United Jewish Appeal in May 1948 when Israel was declared a state

I spent a thousand dollars to have my nose fixed, and now my brain won't work.

Woody Allen

BEAUTY TREATMENTS

My wife went to the beauty parlour. She got a mud pack. She looked nice for a couple of days. Then the mud fell off.

Henny Youngman

I wouldn't have a coffee enema. Aren't they horrible? I suppose you go into Starbucks and ask for the screens to be put around. Anyway, who wants part of their anatomy awake all night?

Dame Edna Everage

Cleopatra always used to bathe in milk. When she was in a hurry, I suppose she used to get under the cow and take a shower.

Beryl Reid

Go into the royal gardens at dawn and gather dew-drenched peach blossoms, which should then be crushed with oil of almonds by the light of the moon.

16th-century Physician, advice to Catherine de Medici on how to keep her youthful appearance

My secret for staying young is good food, plenty of rest, and a make-up man with a spray gun.

Bob Hope

The dimmer switch – the greatest sex and beauty aid known to womankind.

Kathy Lette

—How do you keep your youthful appearance?
—Gin and drugs, madam, gin and drugs!

Unidentified Lady and T.S. Eliot

The only way to look younger is not to be born so soon.

Barbara Johnson

PERSONAL HYGIENE

I spied the following sign in a car park on the Isle of Wight: 'Toilets Pay & Display'. I declined.

Ray Perkins

The toilet, like the harp, is essentially a solo instrument.

Anon

I have to read when I'm on the throne. Have to read. Harpic bottle, tube of toothpaste, doesn't matter what it is. Even a book sometimes.

Stephen Fry, *A Bit of Fry and Laurie*

Who invented the brush they put next to the toilet? That things hurts!

Andy Andrews

—Why don't you wash your face? I can see what you had for breakfast this morning!
—Oh, yeah! What did I have?
—Bacon and eggs and tomato sauce.
—Wrong! That was *yesterday* morning!

Morecambe and Wise

If only he'd wash his neck, I'd wring it.

John Sparrow

I'm sweatin' like a hooker at a Viagra convention.

Pat Mulligan

I'm sweating like George Bush on Judgement Day.

Dan Dunne, *Half Nelson*

Sorry 'bout the sweat, honey. That's just holy water.

Little Richard

If you don't eat garlic, they'll never smell it on your breath.

Sholom Aleichem

Don't bathe. I'm coming home.

Napoleon, preferring his wife, Josephine, to smell *au naturel*,
in a letter to her after the Battle of Marengo, 1800

ANIMALS
& NATURE

ANIMALS – GENERAL

Once upon a time there were three bears – Papa Bear, Mama Bear, and Camembert.

George S. Kaufman

The bull grizzly bear is 7 feet tall, weighs more than a Mazda Miata, and can tear through a tree like a Jewish mother through self-esteem.

Grant Connor, *The Simpsons*

Playing dead not only comes in handy when face to face with a bear, but also at important business meetings.

Jack Handey

Two dumb guys go bear hunting. They see a sign saying, 'Bear left,' so they went home.

Henny Youngman

An American visiting the Moscow zoo was amazed to see a lion and a lamb in the same cage. 'Do they get along well?' he asked the Russian guide. 'They get along fine,' the Russian replied, adding, 'Of course, we have to put in a new lamb every day.'

Leo Aikman

On your report of the escaped snow leopard, I see a spokesman said: 'So far the animal has not been spotted.' I beg to differ. Leopards are always spotted.

Spike Milligan, letter to the *Daily Telegraph*

The Giant Panda – what a beautiful creature! A word of warning, though, its fur is not machine washable.

Brüno Gehard, aka Sacha Baron Cohen

As an experiment, Hugh Fearnley-Whittingstall set up his own intensive chicken farm, one half intensive, the other free-range. Before he knew it, he had 3,000 chickens... Looking around at the cramped conditions, Hugh sobbed, 'What animal of any kind would want to live in a place like this?' Er... a fox?

Harry Hill, *Harry Hill's TV Burp*

—Animals have rights too, you know. A battery chicken's life isn't worth living. Would you want to spend your life packed in with 600 other desperate, squawking, smelly creatures, unable to breathe fresh air, unable to move, unable to stretch, unable to think?
—Certainly not: that is why I never stood for Parliament.

Agnes Moorhouse and Sir Humphrey Appleby, *Yes, Minister*

Man is the only animal that blushes. Or needs to.

Mark Twain

I'm not over-fond of animals. I am merely astounded by them.

David Attenborough

Sponges live in the ocean – that kills me. I wonder how much deeper the ocean would be if that didn't happen.

Steven Wright

People laugh when I say that I think a jellyfish is one of the most beautiful things in the world. What they don't understand is, I mean a jellyfish with long, blonde hair.

Jack Handey

A dolphin will jump out of the water for a piece of fish. Imagine what he'd do for some chips.

Harry Hill

The shark must be the stupidest animal in the world. Can't he figure out to swim a foot lower on approach? When is he going to realize that that fin is tipping everybody off?

Russ Meneve

—What do you get when you cross an onion with a donkey?
—Most of the time you just get an onion with long ears, but every once in a while you get a piece of ass that brings tears to your eyes.

Anon

Whenever you observe an animal closely, you feel as if a human being sitting inside were making fun of you.

Elias Canetti

Which do you think we will achieve first, communication with the dead or with animals? Which of these will be the greater benefit to mankind?

Joseph Bryan

You would be surprised to hear a cow speak English. But believe me, after the tenth time you would resent the fact that it did not have an Oxford accent. Of course, if you could tell the difference.

Stanislaw J. Lec

A baby mouse and his mother were walking through a cave. A bat flew by, and the baby looked up and said, 'Look, Mama, an angel!'

Joey Adams

—Love is what separates us from animals.
—No. What separates us from animals is that we don't use our tongues to clean our own genitals.

Dave Lister and Arnold Rimmer, *Red Dwarf*

PETS

—Marge, can I get a duck?
—You already have a monkey.
—Can *he* get a duck?

Homer and Marge Simpson

I don't mind you having goldfish provided you don't let 'em out of the bowl.

Mrs Partington, *I Didn't Know You Cared*

Deter goldfish from having sex by throwing a small bucket of air over any you catch in the act.

Top Tip, *Viz* magazine

I got a horse for my wife. I thought it was a fair swap.

Bob Monkhouse

There are two things you should avoid approaching from the rear: restaurants and horses.

Evelyn Waugh

You can lead a horse to water but you can't make it throw Zara Phillips.

Arthur Smith, *The Smith Lectures*

—What do you call an Amish guy with his hand up a horse's ass?
—A mechanic.

Anon

He flung himself from the room, flung himself upon his horse and rode madly off in all directions.

Stephen Leacock

My parakeet died. We were playing badminton.

Danny Curtis

A child began eagerly stroking the shell of the turtle. 'Why are doing that?' said my father. 'Oh, to please the turtle.' 'Why, child, you might as well stroke the dome of St Paul's to please the Dean and Chapter.'

Rev. Sydney Smith

My brother had a hamster. He took it to the vet. It's like bringing a disposable lighter in for repairs.

Wayne Cotter

People often say to me, 'Vets must know just as much as doctors,' but when it comes to the crunch they are never very keen to let me treat them.

James Herriot

A little old lady…buys a couple of monkeys and she becomes very attached to them. As happens, both monkeys die one day. Not wanting to part with them, she takes the dead monkeys to a taxidermist. The taxidermist asks her, 'Would you like them mounted?' The old woman replies, 'No, just holding hands.'

Gregory Peck

CAT

—What does a cat on the beach have in common with Christmas?
—Sandy Claws.

Anon

I have often put to myself the question: what is a cat for? This is as futile an exercise as asking what laughter is for.

Hugh Leonard

He marvelled at the fact that cats had two holes cut in their fur at precisely the spot where their eyes were.

Georg Christoph Lichtenberg

I wish I could write as mysterious as a cat.

Edgar Allan Poe

I have found my love of cats most helpful in understanding women.

John Simon

A cat isn't fussy – just so long as you remember he likes his milk in the shallow, rose-patterned saucer and his fish on the blue plate. From which he will take it, and eat it off the floor.

Arthur Bridges

Cats understand plain English as well as anybody. How else would it be possible for them to so uncannily do just the opposite?

Stephen Baker

Cats remember everything. This is why we always lock them out of the room when we call in sick.

H. Thomas (Collins) Yu

Everything I know I learned from my cat: when you're hungry, eat. When you're tired, nap in a sunbeam. When you go to the vet's, pee on your owner.

Gary Smith

I rarely meddled in the cat's personal affairs and she rarely meddled in mine. Neither of us was foolish enough to attribute human emotions to our pets.

Kinky Friedman

Cat's motto: no matter what you've done wrong, always try to make it look like the dog did it.

Anon

DOG

And now a word for dog lovers. Kinky.

I'm Sorry I'll Read That Again

I love a dog. He does nothing for political reasons.

Will Rogers

How can people love something so much that they're willing to walk behind it and retrieve its faeces with their own hands every day? I have yet to meet a woman for whom I'd do that.

Joel Stein

I named my Boston terrier Woodrow Wilson because he was full of shit.

Dorothy Parker

My dog is blind. His name is Blind Spot.

Craig Sharf

When I woke up this morning, I could feel Tension mounting. Tension is my dog.

Tom Cotter

He saved himself from a pit bull that was humping his leg by faking an orgasm.

Dick Capri

I always call dogs 'he'. It don't do to notice everything.

Mrs Gordon, *The Ladies of the Corridor*

She said, 'Rex is just like one of the family.' And without thinking I said, 'Really? Which one?'

Bob Monkhouse

It is dogs, not wives, that men choose because they are like their mothers.

Roy Hattersley

The shar-pei looks like a miniature hippopotamus with badly fitting pantyhose all over.

Roger Caras

The dachshund is one of those dogs that is a dog-and-a-half long and only half-a-dog high.

Anon

Dachshunds are ideal dogs for small children, as they are already stretched and pulled to such a length that the child cannot do much harm one way or the other.

Robert Benchley

I've got a Chihuahua. They're good. If you lose one, just empty out your purse.

Jean Carroll

Corgis, of course, are bred to approve gas fitters.

Harry Hill, *Harry Hill's TV Burp*

They say dog is man's best friend. Well, that was until man discovered drugs.

Bob Reinhard

A dog really is a man's best friend. If you don't believe it, try this experiment. Put your dog and your wife in the boot of the car for an hour. When you open the boot, who is really happy to see you?

Anon

Your dog won't bring you chicken noodle soup when you're sick, but neither would your last wife.

Lewis Grizzard

In my entire life, my dog is the only person I've slept in the same bed with that didn't sue me for alimony.

Alan Harper, *Two and a Half Men*

If dogs could talk, perhaps we'd find it just as hard to get along with them as we do people.

Karel Čapek

The advantage of whiskey over a dog as a companion are legion. To begin with, whiskey does not need to be periodically wormed.

W.C. Fields

My terrier's got mange. He *said* he got it from a lamp post.

Dorothy Parker

I took my dog for a cat scan. They found three in his stomach.

Myq Kaplan

And now, here are the results of the Sheepdog Trials: all the sheepdogs were found not guilty.

Keith Waterhouse

BIRDS

I bought a bird-table labelled 'self-assembly'. I put it in the garden but when I looked a few days later it was still in the box. Those little blighters still hadn't put it up.

Barry Pullen

I note that a clever thrush, and a stupid nightingale, sing very much alike.

Thomas Hardy

To a man, ornithologists are tall, slender, and bearded so that they can stand motionless for hours, imitating kindly trees, as they watch for birds.

Gore Vidal

I wonder what kind of bird Humpty-Dumpty would have hatched out to, had he lived?

Harry Hill

Every day the hummingbird eats its own weight in food. You may wonder how it weighs the food. It doesn't. It just eats another hummingbird.

Steven Wright

INSECTS

Two fleas are leaving a restaurant. One says to the other: 'Shall we walk or take a dog?'

Anon

I was reading how a female spider will eat the male spider after mating. I guess female spiders know that life insurance is easier to collect than child support.

Janine DiTullio

Ants can carry 20 times their own body weight, which is useful information if you're moving out and you need help getting a potato chip across town.

Ron Darian

I sort of felt sorry for the damn flies... Even though they were supposed to carry disease, I never heard anybody say he caught anything from a fly. My cousin gave two guys the clap, and nobody ever whacked her with a newspaper.

Lenny Bruce

Flies spread disease. Keep yours zipped.

Anon

NATURE &
COUNTRY LIFE

—Oh, I just love nature!
—That's loyalty – after what nature did to her.

Dowager and Groucho Marx

When I am on the Sussex Downs in the morning I feel that I am having a cocktail with God.

Lydia Lopokova

I like a lot of things about the city, but prefer the country because here I don't have to wear a tie.

Alexander Calder, American artist, inventor of the mobile (sculpture not phone!)

The modern city is a place for banking and prostitution and very little else.

Frank Lloyd Wright

It is only in the country that we can get to know a person or a book.

Cyril Connolly

The best part of living in the country is the people you don't meet.

Evan Esar

Beauty-spot: a wood with a car park attached.

Mike Barfield, *Dictionary for our Time*

Turn the eyes upside down, by looking at the landscape through your legs, and how agreeable is the picture, though you have seen it any time in these 20 years!

Ralph Waldo Emerson

A beech wood, which – like all beech woods – was pretending to be a cathedral.

Beverley Nichols

There is nothing like walking to get the feel of a country. A fine landscape is like a piece of music; it must be taken at the right tempo. Even a bicycle goes too fast.

Paul Scott Mowrer

The best place for a picnic is always just a little further on.

Evan Esar

In Africa you can't walk in the countryside and think. You might be eaten by a lion.

A.C. Grayling

I hate the outdoors. To me, the outdoors is where the car is.

Will Durst

One thing that's certain about going outdoors: when you come back inside, you'll be scratching.

P.J. O'Rourke

I love Nature. I just don't want to get any on me!

Roxanne Martin

WEATHER

On cable TV they have a weather channel – 24 hours of weather. We had something like that where I grew up. We called it a window.

Dan Spencer

Yesterday evening Mrs Arundel insisted on my going to the window, and looking at the glorious sky, as she called it... And what was it? It was simply a very second-rate Turner.

Oscar Wilde

Generally Pre-Raphaelist in feeling, sunsets sometimes descend to the level of Corot, and bad Corot at that. At their worst they are sheer calendar art.

Peter De Vries

The sunset displayed rich, spectacular hues like a .jpg file at 10 per cent cyan, 10 per cent magenta, 60 per cent yellow and 10 per cent black.

Jennifer Hart

There's an old song to the effect that the sun never sets on the British Empire. Well, while we were there, it never even rose.

Ring Lardner

New York just had the first white Christmas in 30 years. A note, though, to you guys in Greenwich Village: when you build a snowman, the carrot goes on the *nose*.

Conan O'Brien

You know in *Rocky* he prepares for the fight by punching sides of raw beef? Well, yesterday it was as cold as that meat locker he was in.

Alan S. Jarvis

It was so cold in New York today the guy who gives me the finger was wearing mittens and said I'd have to take his word for it.

David Letterman

As a child growing up in Malaysia I longed to be cold. Putting on a cardigan was a huge treat.

Joanna Lumley

Louisiana in September was like an obscene phone call from nature. The air – moist, sultry, secretive, and far from fresh – felt as if it were being exhaled into one's face. Sometimes it even sounded like heavy breathing.

Tom Robbins, *Jitterbug Perfume*

It's humid. The air tastes like it's been strained through a hot leotard.

Charlie Brooker

I said to the First Officer, 'Gad, that sun's hot,' to which he replied, 'Well, you shouldn't touch it.'

Spike Milligan

It's so hot that even the statues have armpit stains.

Dave Barry

The Welsh are not meant to go out in the sun. They photosynthesize.

Rhys Ifans

There's a hurricane on the way. They said today that we should stock up on canned goods. So I went out and bought a case of beer.

John Gretchen

There was a 4.5 earthquake in Alabama – a tragedy. It'll spawn at least ten thousand country and western songs.

Craig Kilborn

Has the tsunami created any tsilly tsubconscious tside effects in tsome tsections of tsociety?

Michael Leunig, cartoon caption

We're going on honeymoon to India next month and I wanted to know what the weather was going to be like, so I phoned my bank.

Shappi Khorsandi

GARDEN & FLOWERS

Welcome to the Garden of Weedin'.

Anon

A weed is a flower growing in the wrong place.

George Washington Carver

Perennial: any plant which, had it lived, would have bloomed year after year.

Henry Beard

No man ought to be compelled to live where a rose cannot grow.

George Cadbury, who built the model village of Bournville to house the workers in his chocolate factory

As we all know, the only way to plant daffodils it to pile them on a tray, and then to run into the orchard and hurl the tray into the air, planting them exactly where they fall.

Beverley Nichols

Last year, at the beginning of August, we planted our first bulb and at Christmas we had the most charming little bedside lamp.

Eric Morecambe

The fuchsia is the world's most carefully spelled flower.

Jimmy Barnes

If one tried to hybridize a fuchsia and a yew, would you have a fuchyew?

Professor Robert C. Art

The life expectancy of a houseplant varies inversely with its price and directly with its ugliness.

Britt's Green Thumb Postulate

Pay a visit to the nurseries... To buy a tree, even a baby, from a catalogue is as foolish as to adopt a child by parcel post.

Beverley Nichols

Trees are your best antiques.

Alexander Smith

Grass simply invites you to walk on it, run on it or even throw yourself on it. I have decided to grow English grass in the front of my house at home.

Marijan Mrmić, Croatian goalkeeper

You might be a redneck if you've ever cut your grass and found a car.

Jeff Foxworthy

'I want to be a lawn.' Greta Garbo.

W.C. Sellar & R.J. Yeatman

If our band moved next door to you, your lawn would die.

Lemmy Kilmister, of heavy metal band, Motörhead

The back garden was small. There was a patch of deeply worried lawn.

Peter Tinniswood, *Uncle Mort's North Country*

If the grass is greener on the other side of the fence, you can be sure the water bill is higher.

Anon

A garden is never so good as it will be next year.

Thomas Cooper

Taking a cutting is miraculous. It is exactly as though you were to cut off your wife's leg, stick it in the lawn, and be greeted on the following day by an entirely new woman, sprung from the leg, advancing across the lawn to meet you.

Beverley Nichols

—What can I do about carrot-fly attacking my carrots?
—Go to Sainsbury's.

Questioner and Gardening Expert, *The Richard Bacon Show*, Radio 5 Live

To turn ordinary clothes into gardening clothes, simply mix with compost.

Guy Browning

I knew a man who grew the most wonderful dahlias. When I asked him the secret he told me that he fed them on Mackeson Stout. It was some time later that he added that he did this each evening on his return from the village inn, after enjoying the stout.

Neville Denson

I'm not a dirt gardener. I sit with my walking stick and point things out that need to be done. After many years, the garden is now totally obedient.

Hardy Amies

Make no mistake: the weeds will win; nature bats last.

Robert M. Pyle

ENVIRONMENT & GREEN ISSUES

Environmentalists tell us that every day an area of rainforest the size of Wales is destroyed. Why is it never Wales?

Jimmy Carr, *The Naked Jape*

Destroying a rain forest for economic gain is like burning a Renaissance painting to cook a meal.

Edward O. Wilson

We're not allowed to do anything to nature anymore, except look at it. It's like porn with leaves.

Dennis Miller

All in favor of conserving gasoline please raise your right foot.

Sign on a California freeway

Kilometres are shorter than miles. Save gas, take your next trip in kilometres.

George Carlin

Has anyone noticed the similarity between carbon offsetting and the medieval practice of selling indulgences – where a sinner would 'offset' his wickedness with a paid-for prayer at a handy monastery.

Paul Dornan

Green is the first socio-political movement in which every single leader and spokesperson is filthy rich. They make the Conservative Party look like the Jarrow marchers.

Julie Burchill

Remember when atmospheric contaminants were romantically called stardust?

Lane Olinghouse

This planet is getting hot. And the only way to solve Global Warming is to elect Hillary Clinton... because that is one cold bitch.

Dana Cavey

Global warming? When my globes get warm, I just take off my sweater.

Dolly Parton

I have never met anyone who wanted to save the world without my financial support.

Robert Brault

Let me tell you something that we Israelis have against Moses. He took us 40 years through the desert in order to bring us to the one spot in the Middle East that has no oil.

Golda Meir

The era of low-cost energy is almost dead. Popeye has run out of cheap spinach.

Peter Peterson

I can download 3 million vaginas on to my iPhone. Don't tell me we can't come up with alternative energy.

Lewis Black

If sunbeams were weapons of war, we would have had solar energy centuries ago.

George Porter

—Which of our natural resources do you think will become exhausted first?
—The taxpayer.

Winston K. Pendleton

I'll really laugh if the world ends just before they manage to destroy it.

Stanislaw J. Lec

Save the earth! It's the only planet with chocolate.

Anon

AGRICULTURE

Man – despite his artistic pretensions, his sophistication, and his many accomplishments – owes his existence to a six-inch layer of topsoil and the fact that it rains.

Anon

There are three ways a man can be ruined: women, gambling, and farming. My father chose the most boring.

Pope John XXIII

A guy told me, 'To a farmer manure smells like money.' I said, 'Maybe he should start keeping his wallet in his front pocket.'

Tammy Patorelli

A farm is a hunk of land on which, if you get up early enough mornings and work late enough nights, you'll make a fortune – if you strike oil on it.

Jim Jordan

A gentleman farmer raises nothing but his hat.

Anon

Earth is here so kind, that just tickle her with a hoe and she laughs with a harvest.

Douglas Jerrold, on Australia

My interest in agriculture is limited to breakfast cereals.

S.J. Perelman

PEOPLE

NAMES

[*man introducing himself to a stranger at a party*] Hi. I'm, I'm, I'm...
You'll have to forgive me. I'm terrible with names.

Robert Mankoff, cartoon caption

What I should have said: I loved last night, Jane.
What I did say: I loved last night, Joan.

Anon

How many men mind if, while making love, the woman calls out
someone else's name? What if the name is Fido?

Johnny Carson

Tarquin Olivier? Now there's a name that smacks of overkill.

Texan Businessman, on being introduced to the son of Laurence Olivier

People give their children all sorts of rummy names... I have a pal in
England who was christened Cuthbert de la Hay Horace. Fortunately
everyone calls him Stinker.

P.G. Wodehouse, *The Indiscretions of Archie*

Nigel Lawson named his daughter Nigella. It's a good thing Salman
Rushdie didn't follow suit.

Roy Harris

I wish my name was Todd, because then I could say, 'Yes, my name's
Todd. Todd Blankenship.' Oh, also I wish my last name was Blankenship.

Jack Handey

Barack Obama has named Nobel Prize-winning physicist, Steve Chu, as
his energy secretary, unless he was just sneezing.

Amy Poehler

The one thing I do not want to be called is First Lady. It sounds like a saddle horse.

Jacqueline Kennedy

Have you ever exchanged three words with an American without being told his name?

Kyril Bonfiglioli, *Don't Point That Thing at Me*

Rimsky Korsakov – what a name! It suggests fierce whiskers stained with vodka.

Music Correspondent, *Musical Courier*

If the Lords Cardigan and Sandwich had each borne the other's name we might today have been wearing sandwiches and eating cardigans.

Lewis Barton

GOOD NAME... BAD NAME

Cheerios is a good name for a cereal but a bad name for a funeral home.

Anon

Domino's is a good name for a pizza place but a bad name for a construction company.

Tiffany Getz

Just Do It is a good slogan for Nike but a bad slogan for a suicide relief centre.

Jeff Keenan

First Impressions is a good name for a dating service but not a bungee jumping centre.

Russell Beland

Air France is a good name for an airline but a bad name for a deodorant.

Danny Bravman

Kleenex may be a good name for a tissue, but it's an excellent name for a divorce law firm.

Paul Kondis

BP is a good name for a gas company but a bad name for a honey company.

Elden Carnahan

Virgin Airways is okay as a name for an airline but not for a cigarette.

Russell Beland

Excalibur is a good name for a security company but a bad name for a tampon.

Jeff Brechlin

Nordic Track is a good name for exercise equipment but a bad name for an affirmative action program.

Larry Phillips

PEOPLE

There is a great deal of human nature in people.

Mark Twain

I am learning about people the hard way, by being one.

Ashleigh Brilliant

Three people to avoid: a man who has recently lost his luggage at an airport, a woman who has recently joined a reading group, and a child who has recently been given a how-to-be-a-magician kit.

Miles Kington

People like Coldplay and voted for the Nazis. You can't trust people.

Super Hans, *Peep Show*

I gave up trying to understand people long ago. Now I just let them try to understand me.

Snoopy, *Peanuts*

In the end we're all Jerry Springer Show guests; we just haven't been on the show.

Marilyn Manson

THERE ARE TWO KINDS OF PEOPLE IN THE WORLD...

...those who turn off a light when they leave a room, and those who don't.

Kathryn Leibovich

...those who use coasters and those who don't.

Jura Koncius

...those who brake for amber lights, and those who accelerate.

Diane White

...those who, when buying petrol, always know what the number of their pump is when asked by the cashier, and those to whom it has never occurred to look, even though this is the thousandth time they have been asked.

Miles Kington

...those who want to get to the airport two hours before flight time, and those who think they're wasting their lives if they don't leap on board as the door is closing.

Richard Reeves

...those who borrow and those who lend.

Charles Lamb

...those who laugh at their own jokes and those who don't.

Thomas Hurka

...those who hate clowns... and clowns.

D.J. MacHale, *The Quillan Games*

...cannibals and lunch.

Eric Overmyer

MEN

There's only two kinds of guys, *a prick* and *not a prick*.

Margaret Atwood

The more I study men, the more I realize that they are nothing in the world but boys grown too big to be spankable.

Jean Webster

Batteries are cheap. Who needs men?

Rebecca McLenna

Men have wonderful minds. So much is stored inside – all those sports scores and so on.

Jane Seymour

No one knows 'men' as such, any more than anyone knows 'women'… You don't know a vast crowd of identical men who roam around the place like some amorphous blob of pure, distilled masculinity. They just don't exist. Unless you count Il Divo, of course.

Julie Burchill

Men have two emotions: hungry and horny. If I don't have an erection, make me a sandwich.

Anon

The true man wants two things: danger and play. For that reason, he wants woman, as the most dangerous plaything.

Friedrich Nietzsche

Women give us solace, but if it were not for women we should never need solace.

Don Herold

WOMEN

Woman: a diet waiting to happen.

Serena Gray

Being a woman is a terribly difficult task, since it consists principally in dealing with men.

Joseph Conrad

I hate women because they always know where things are.

James Thurber

What passes for woman's intuition is often nothing more than man's transparency.

George Jean Nathan

Give a woman an inch and she'll park a car on it.

E.P.B. White

Marge, you can't keep blaming yourself. Just blame yourself once, then move on.

Homer Simpson

There are only two kinds of women – goddesses and doormats.

Pablo Picasso

Don't take for granted the English weather or the English women.

Sir Frank Worrell

They all start out as Juliets and wind up as Lady Macbeths.

Bernie Dodd, *The Country Girl*

To be a woman is something so strange, so confusing, and so complicated that only a woman could put up with it.

Søren Kierkegaard

Trust not a woman, even when dead.

Latin proverb

BATTLE OF THE SEXES

So it's *our* car, *our* flat and *our* money, but I notice it's always *her* tits.
There's feminism for you.

Neil, *Viz* magazine

I'm a feminist. Not the fun kind.
Andrea Dworkin

I could never be a feminist/lesbian as there is nothing more pleasurable to me than the sight of the bottom of the washing basket on a wash day.
Mrs Merton, aka Caroline Aherne

I can't be a rose in any man's lapel.

Margaret Trudeau

Until Eve arrived, this was a man's world.

Richard Armour

Sigmund Freud asked the question: 'What is it that women want?'…But
it's obvious, isn't it? They want the central heating turned up, don't they?
Al Murray, *The Pub Landlord's Book of Common Sense*

Women have very little idea of how much men hate them.
Germaine Greer, *The Female Eunuch*

How do I feel about men? With my fingers.

Cher

The only time I use women, they're either naked or dead.

Joel Silver, film producer of movies including *Lethal Weapon* and *Die Hard*

I asked a Burmese why women, after centuries of following their men, now walk ahead. He said there were many unexploded landmines since the war.

Robert Mueller

I treat women as my equal. Of course, most women don't like to be treated like a paranoid balding Jew with contact lenses.

David Feldman

On the one hand, we'll never experience childbirth; on the other hand, we can open all our own jars.

Bruce Willis

What would happen if suddenly, magically, men could menstruate and women could not?...Men would brag about how long and how much... Sanitary supplies would be federally funded and free... Street guys would invent slang: 'He's a three-pad man'.

Gloria Steinem

Did you ever put those maxipads on adhesive side up? Makes you cranky, don't it?

Roseanne

My sister claimed sexual harassment on the job, which was a little surprising since she's a hooker.

George Miller

—Lemon, I'm impressed. You're beginning to think like a businessman.
—A business*woman*.
—I don't think that's a word.

Jack Donaghy and Liz Lemon, *30 Rock*

I love the word 'girl'. 'Gal' is pretty great, too. I don't just want to be called a 'woman'. It sounds like someone with a moustache.

Bette Midler

If the men in the room would only think how they would feel graduating with a 'spinster of arts' degree they would see how important language reform is.

Gloria Steinem, at Yale University, 1981

—Do you prefer the title 'chairperson'?
—I'd rather be a 'chairman'. They make more.

Lawyer and Dr Estelle Ramey

What is asserted by a man is an opinion; what is asserted by a woman is opinionated.

Marya Mannes

Very few men care to have the obvious pointed out to them by a woman.

Margaret Baillie Saunders

There will always be a battle between the sexes because men and women want different things. Men want women, and women want men.

George Burns

Women can do everything; men can do the rest.

Russian proverb

GENDER

[*surveying a packed room*] —Well, there's one thing you can say for Frankie Howerd. He certainly puts bums on seats.
—Yes, safest place for them.

Unidentified Friend and Tommy Cooper, at a showbiz dinner, 1966

There's more mince in that walk than there is in the freezer!

Derek Laud, *Big Brother 6*

I was the pink sheep of the family.

Alexander McQueen, fashion designer

At the Catholic high school I attended, they spent so much time telling us how sinful heterosexual relations before marriage are, that I had a hundred homosexual experiences before I knew it was sinful.

Dick Leitsch

Noël Coward put his sexuality in a little silver box and sniffed it.

Derek Jarman

If he was any further back in the closet, he'd be in Narnia.

Daniel Bryan, *Big Brother 5*

My cousin is an agoraphobic homosexual, which makes it kind of hard for him to come out of the closet.

Bill Kelly

When asked, 'Shall I tell my mother I'm gay?' I reply, 'Never tell your mother *anything*.'

Quentin Crisp

In America, of course, they're all homosexual.

Barbara Cartland

We were talking about gay marriages and my brother, Greg, said: 'Bob you're gay, what do you think?' And my mother said, 'Greg, that's not nice. Don't remind him.' Oh, yeah, Mom. That had slipped my mind.

Bob Smith

Sometimes I think if there was a third sex men wouldn't get so much as a glance from me.

Amanda Vail

If all lesbians suddenly turned purple today, society would be surprised at the number of purple people in high places.

Sidney Abbott & Barbara Love

Lesbians make ideal house-guests. No mess, short grunts instead of conversation, and they spend most of their time outside chopping wood and smoking pipes.

Julian Clary

Let's encourage lesbians so we can breed out feminists.

David Bailey, photographer

Oh, wouldn't it be great being a lesbian? All the advantages of being a man, but with less embarrassing genitals.

Jeff Murdock, *Coupling*

—Why in the world would you want to have a sex-change operation?
—I hear women live longer.

Nurse and Patient, *Soap*

If you're sure you want a sex-change, all I can really say is: don't try to perm your own hair, and don't wear high heels on a soggy lawn.

Shirlee Kenyon, *Straight Talk*

I could never be a woman because I'd just stay home and play with my breasts all day.

Harris T. Telemacher, *L.A. Story*

To be truthful, I missed my penis.

Charles Kane, who had a sex-change, then had it reversed

If I had a cock for a day I would get myself pregnant.

Germaine Greer

Nobody is 100 per cent anything. Someone once asked Tallulah Bankhead if Montgomery Clift was queer. She replied: 'I don't know, darling, but he never sucked *my* cock!'

Jonathan Williams

RACE & ETHNICITY

—True or false: Bill Cosby was the world's first black man.
—It's false, of course. The first black man was Sidney Poitier.

Vic Reeves and Bob Mortimer, *Shooting Stars*

—Do you think some of the vitriolic reaction to your health care plan is driven partly by racism?
—I think it's important to realise that I was actually black before the election.
—Really? How long have you been a black man?

David Letterman and President Barack Obama

Barack Obama is a Hawaiian Kenyan, which makes for a great president but a lousy pizza.

John Sergeant

My mom was Hungarian; dad, Italian. Mom always said to me that they were 'paprika and garlic' – boy oh boy, what a mix!

Suzi Quatro

Caucasian? It was on my army draft card. I thought it meant 'circumcised'.

Elvis Presley

Someone asked me where my roots were and I said, I hope in civilised behaviour.

Peter Ustinov

There are only two races on this planet – the intelligent and the stupid.

John Fowles

RACISM & PREJUDICE

Monday was Martin Luther King Day in America. Or as it's known in the South, Monday.

Jane Borden

I am really enjoying the new Martin Luther King Jr. stamp – just think about all those white bigots, licking the backside of a black man.

Dick Gregory

Bigotry started a long time ago – nobody knows where. Personally I think the French started it.

Johnny Caravella, *WKRP in Cincinnati*

Racism is just the golden hand-grenade that you lob at anyone – you know it's going to stick.

Martin Amis

Racial prejudice is stupid…because if you spend time with someone from another race and really get to know them, you can find other reasons to hate them.

Bernadette Luckett

It seems Suggs is marching against racism and homophobia. I mean, it's just Madness gone politically correct.

Popbitch.com

There's no colour prejudice in Hollywood. It's not black or white – it's green. All they're chasing is the buck.

Alan Parker, director

I lay awake amid sleeping Muslim brothers and I learned that pilgrims from every land – every colour, and class, and rank; high officials and the beggar alike – all snored in the same language.

Malcolm X

FRIENDS & ENEMIES

Friends are God's apology for relations.

Hugh Kingsmill

An Italian is criticizing his best friend: 'You come in da house, you eata alla da spaghetti, you drinka alla da chianti, you fucka da wife, you knocka da Jesus Christ offa da mantlepiece and breaka da legs. One day, ma friend, YOU GO TOO FAR!'

George Melly, *Slowing Down*

The holy passion of Friendship is of so sweet and steady and loyal and enduring a nature that it will last through a whole lifetime if not asked to lend money.

Mark Twain

Anybody can sympathize with the sufferings of a friend, but it requires a very fine nature to sympathize with a friend's success.

Oscar Wilde

I do with my friends, as I do with my books. I would have them where I can find them, but I seldom use them.

Ralph Waldo Emerson

I have 2 million friends on MySpace. That's a lot of time spent sitting in your underwear, eating Fruit Loops, clicking 'accept' over and over again.

Dane Cook

—Do you have many enemies?
—Yes, like a lot of people who can't stand idiots.

Interviewer and Bernard Blier

The French and the British are such good enemies that they can't resist being friends.

Peter Ustinov

One should forgive one's enemies, but not before they are hanged.

Heinrich Heine

BOOKS & LANGUAGE

LANGUAGES

Two sheep in a field. One turns to the other and says: 'Moo'. The other sheep says: 'What are you on about?' The first sheep says: 'I'm learning a foreign language.'

Anon

'Meow' means 'woof' in 'cat'.

George Carlin

A man who speaks three languages is trilingual. A man who speaks two languages is bilingual. A man who speaks only one language is English.

Claude Gagnière

Next to money, English is the leading international language.

Evan Esar

There is no such thing as 'The Queen's English'. The property has gone into the hands of a joint stock company, and we [Americans] own the bulk of the stock!

Mark Twain

French by sympathy, I am Irish by race, and the English have condemned me to speak the language of Shakespeare.

Oscar Wilde

English is a funny language. A fat chance and a slim chance are the same thing.

Jack Herbert

Saying, 'I apologise,' is the same as saying, 'I'm sorry.' Except at a funeral.

Demetri Martin

Very little thinking was ever done in English; it is not a language suited to logical thought. Instead, it's an emotive lingo beautifully adapted to concealing fallacies.

Robert A. Heinlein

Welsh is the only language you learn to be able to talk to fewer people.

A.A. Gill

The Romans would never have found time to conquer the world if they had been obliged first to learn Latin.

Heinrich Heine

Quidquid latine dictum sit, altum viditur.
Whatever is said in Latin sounds profound.

Anon

German is a language that has the unfortunate effect on the English ear and eye of seeming to contain nothing but orders.

Sandi Toksvig

When you start a sentence in German, you have to know in the beginning what the end will be.

Otto Friedrich

Whenever the literary German dives into a sentence, that is the last you are going to see of him till he emerges on the other side of the Atlantic with his verb in his mouth.

Mark Twain

I once heard a Californian student in Heidelberg say, in one of his calmest moods, that he would rather decline two drinks than one German adjective.

Mark Twain

I did German to A-Level…and the only use I've ever found for it is reading the sides of lorries when I'm stuck on the M20.

Marian Nyman

A French politician once wrote that it was a peculiarity of the French language that in it words occur in the order in which one thinks them.

Ludwig Wittgenstein

A peculiar virtue of French is that it enables you to say nothing more formidably than any other language I know.

H.J. Laski

If the English language made any sense, lackadaisical would have something to do with a shortage of flowers.

Doug Larson

—What word is always pronounced wrong?
—'Wrong'.

Anon

You can't be happy with a woman who pronounces both *d*s in Wednesday.

Peter De Vries

Life is a foreign language; all men mispronounce it.

Christopher Hampton

WORDS

Words fascinate me. They always have. For me, browsing in a dictionary is like being turned loose in a bank.

Eddie Cantor

Did you ever open the dictionary right to the page you want? Doesn't that feel good?

George Carlin

Words so affect me that a pornographic story, for example, excites me sexually more than a living person can do.

W.H. Auden

What's the sexiest four-word sentence in the English language? It's when a Southern woman says: 'Hey, y'all, I'm drunk.'

Jeff Foxworthy

Never use a long word when a diminutive one will do.

William Safire

Why are haemorrhoids called haemorrhoids and asteroids called asteroids? Wouldn't it make more sense if it was the other way around?

Robert Schimmel

For years, I thought *in loco parentis* meant 'My dad's an engine driver'.

Anon

'Vuja de' is that strange feeling that none of this has happened before.

George Carlin

I'd like to see a forklift lift a crate of forks. It would be so literal.

Mitch Hedberg

There is no linguistic impropriety more likely to upset people than a misspelling of their name.

Dvaid Crystal

Abso-bloody-exactly!

Alan Partridge

GRAMMAR & PUNCTUATION

All the grammar that any human being ever needs...can be learned in a few weeks from a little book as thin as a Ritz-Carlton sandwich.

Stephen Leacock

Never correct a man's grammar in bed.

Dodie Meeks

If you can't hear me, it's because I'm in parentheses.

Steven Wright

She felt in italics and thought in capitals.

Henry James

A tired exclamation mark is a question mark.

Stanislaw J. Lec

Do not be afraid of the semicolon; it can be most useful.

Ernest Gowers

A colon opens its mouth wide: woe to the writer who does not fill it with something nourishing.

Karl Krasus, noted by Theodor Adorno

—You told me about this yesterday.
—I know but I left out a comma.

Lady and Groucho Marx

The older I grow, the less important the comma becomes. Let the reader catch his own breath.

Elizabeth Zwart

No steel can pierce the human heart so chillingly as a full stop at the right moment.

Isaac Babel

Etc. – a sign used to make people believe you know more than you are telling them.

Herbert V. Prochnow

All of us recognise clichés. They fall like casual dandruff on the fabric of our prose. They are weary, stale, flat and unprofitable.

James J. Kilpatrick

Adjective salad is delicious, with each element contributing its individual and unique flavour; but a purée of adjective soup tastes yecchy.

William Safire

A line of dialogue is not clear enough if you need to explain how it's said.

Elmore Leonard

'Yes,' he said succinctly.

Danielle Steel, *Toxic Bachelors*

BOOKS

A man goes into a library and asks for a book on suicide. The librarian says: 'Fuck off, you won't bring it back.'

Anon

Libraries are brothels for the mind. Which means that librarians are the madams, greeting punters, understanding their strange tastes and needs, and pimping their books. That's rubbish, of course, but it does wonders for the image of librarians.

Guy Browning

On another small table stood Zuleika's library. Both books were in covers of dull gold.

Max Beerbohm, *Zuleika Dobson*

I divide all readers into two classes: those who read to remember and those who read to forget.

William Lyon Phelps

Whether it is fun to go to bed with a good book depends a great deal on who's reading it.

Kenneth Patchen

—For goodness sake, all day long you've had your nose stuck in that book – why?
—I lost my bookmark.

Dick Bentley and Jimmy Edwards, *Take it From Here*

He always held that the book with the best smell was the Harrap's French and English dictionary, a book he had bought...simply for the sake of its smell.

V.S. Naipaul, *The Mystic Masseur*

Books are useless! I only ever read one book, *To Kill a Mockingbird* and it gave me absolutely no insight on how to kill mockingbirds! Sure it taught me not to judge a man by the colour of his skin...but what good does that do me?

Homer Simpson

His favourite author is the guy who wrote, 'Pull tab to open.'

Gloria, *The Jewel of the Nile*

What happened to great literature? I mean, there's nothing like getting to the end of a good book and thinking to yourself, 'Ah, *there's* Wally!'

Milton Jones

In literature as in love, we are astonished at what is chosen by others.

André Maurois

There are two motives for reading a book: one, that you enjoy it; the other, that you can boast about it.

Bertrand Russell

I bored through *Middlemarch* the past week... and nearly died from the overwork.

Mark Twain

I know of no sentence that can induce such immediate and brazen lying as the one that begins: 'Have you read...'

Wilson Mizner

—Have you ever read a book that's changed your life?
—My vibrator instruction manual.

Interviewer and Kathy Lette

Grace Metalious...is one of my all time favourites. Primarily because she has the best author's picture of all author's pictures.

John Waters, on the author of *Peyton Place*

Naomi Klein's *No Logo* stares balefully at me from the shelf... How can I take seriously a woman who criticizes the media's obsession with beauty, and yet has such artful publicity shots?

S. Atkinson

Income tax returns are the most imaginative fiction being written today.

Herman Wouk

The ideal travel book should be perhaps a little like a crime story in which you're in search of something.

Christopher Isherwood

The smaller the ball used in the sport, the better the book. There are superb books about golf, very good books about baseball, not very many good books about basketball, and no good books on beach balls.

George Plimpton

The ideal mystery was one you would read if the end was missing.

Raymond Chandler

Mein Kampf is the fashion bible written by Austria's black sheep, Adolf. It literally translates as: 'My Flamboyance'.

Brüno Gehard, aka Sacha Baron Cohen

I speed-read my daughter's Harry Potter book in 45 minutes. It's about wizards.

Glenn Baron

One trouble with developing speed-reading skills is that by the time you realise a book is boring you've already finished it.

Franklin P. Jones

WRITER

—What do you call a carpenter from Salt Lake City?
—A Morman Nailer.

Anon

The true function of a writer is to produce a masterpiece and…no other task is of any consequence.

Cyril Connolly

In order to write a book, it is necessary to sit down (or stand up) and write. Therein lies the difficulty.

Edward Abbey

—How do you go about writing?
—With a pencil.

Interviewer and John Steinbeck

Have you got a pencil? I left my typewriter in my other pants.

Groucho Marx

Writing today is like being stood stark naked in Trafalgar Square and being told to get an erection.

Louis de Bernières, on writing the follow-up to the bestselling *Captain Corelli's Mandolin*

I get up and sit down at my computer with a cup of strong coffee…
I then begin to type, inspired by the thought of how the hell I'm going to pay the mortgage.

Iain Pattinson

Writing a novel is like making love, but it's also like having a tooth pulled. Pleasure and pain. Sometimes it's like making love while having a tooth pulled.

Dean Koontz

I get an urge, like a pregnant elephant, to go away and give birth to a book.

Stephen Fry

[*a man in agony is consulting his doctor*] —Help me doctor. I've got a book inside me!
—Most people have a book in them. Perhaps I can refer you to a publisher.

Michael Leunig, cartoon caption

At the end of every writing day I feel like I've been wrestling in radioactive quicksand with Xena the Warrior Princess and her five fat uncles.

Tom Robbins

The only people who like to write are the people who write terribly.

Franklin Pierce Adams

If I had told my father, a strict engineer, that I wanted to write, he would have said: 'To whom?'

Maurice Donnay

When...I told my father I wanted to be a writer, he had asked me to consider my unfortunate wife, who would have me about the house all day 'wearing a dressing gown, brewing tea and stumped for words'.

John Mortimer

What no wife of a writer can ever understand is that a writer is working when he's staring out of the window.

Burton Rascoe

Gazing at the typewriter in moments of desperation, I console myself with three thoughts: alcohol at six, dinner at eight, and to be immortal you've got to be dead.

Gyles Brandreth

—Did your wife help you in your career as a writer?
—She dusted my typewriter in 1922. Late one night in 1924 we got home from somewhere and I said I was hungry, and she gave me a verbal picture of the location of the pantry.

Interviewer and Ring Lardner

Never let a domestic quarrel ruin a day's writing. If you can't start the next day fresh, get rid of your wife.

Mario Puzo

I sometimes doubt that a writer should refine or improve his workroom by so much as a dictionary: one thing leads to another and the first thing you know he has a stuffed chair and is fast asleep in it.

E.B. White

This book was written in those long hours I spent waiting for my wife to get dressed to go out. And if she had never gotten dressed at all, this book would never have been written.

Groucho Marx, on his book, *Memoirs of a Mangy Lover*

The poet Walter de la Mare said that if there is a leak of attention when you are trying to concentrate, the leak can be stifled by smoking a cigarette, or in Schiller's case, by inhaling the rotten apples which he kept in a drawer.

Stephen Spender

When writer's block sets in, Dan Brown hangs upside-down, bat-like, until the ideas start flowing again.

Vanessa Allen

Only ambitious nonentities and hearty mediocrities exhibit their rough drafts. It is like passing around samples of one's sputum.

Vladimir Nabokov

The author should die once he has finished writing. So as not to trouble the path of the text.

Umberto Eco

I have heard of…a post-war writer who, after having finished his first book, committed suicide to attract attention to his work. Attention was in fact attracted, but the book was judged no good.

Albert Camus

The only advice I have to give a young novelist is to fuck a really good agent.

John Cheever

Write out of love, write out of instinct, write out of reason. But always for money.

Louis Untermeyer

I always start a book for money. If you're married five times you have to.

Norman Mailer

Girls Aloud popstrel Cheryl Cole has signed a five-million-pound deal to write romantic novels. 'She hadn't previously thought of writing, but she's come around to the idea,' said a source at HarperCollins.

Katy Guest

With the proceeds of *my* last novel [*The Wings of the Dove*], I purchased a small hand-barrow, on which my guests' luggage is wheeled from the station to my house. It needs a coat of paint. With the proceeds of my next novel, I shall have it painted.

Henry James, to Edith Wharton when she mentioned that she had bought a Panhard-Levassor motor car with part of her royalties

Royalties are nice and all that, but shaking the beads brings in money quicker.

Gypsy Rose Lee, striptease artiste

In America, you can make a fortune as a writer, but not a living.

James Michener

In Dublin you are worse off if you have written books than if you are illiterate.

Patrick Kavanagh

My earnings were just about sufficient to keep a goat alive.

Henry Miller

Das Kapital will not even pay for the cigars I smoked writing it.

Karl Marx

All the yachts you could build with your Canadian royalties you could sail in your bathtub.

Ernest Buckler, Canadian novelist

—Naomi Campbell has written a book. What do you think of that?
—I think I would like to go into modelling. Of course, I don't know how to do it, and wouldn't be any good at it if I did, so I'm going to employ someone to walk the catwalks on my behalf. It would still be *me*, of course...

Questioner and Terry Pratchett

I wrote a book under a pen name: Bic.

Buzz Nutley

If I'm a lousy writer, then a hell of a lot of people have got lousy taste.
Grace Metalious, author of *Peyton Place*

The literary equivalent of a Big Mac and a large fries from McDonald's.
Stephen King, on most of his novels

These big-shot writers…can never dig the fact that there are more salted peanuts consumed than caviar.
Mickey Spillane

I leave out the parts that people skip.
Elmore Leonard, on the popularity of his books

I have often thought what a good thing it would be if somebody would write a book that we could skip the whole of. I think a good many people would like to have such a book as that. I know I should.
William Henry Frost

DIARY

It's not a bad idea to get in the habit of writing down one's thoughts. It saves one having to bother anyone else with them.
Isabel Colegate, on keeping a diary, *The Shooting Party*

Diary-writing isn't wholly good for one… It leads to living for one's diary instead of living for the fun of living as ordinary people do.
James Agate

—If you don't keep a diary, how can you remember everything?
—The good shit sticks.
Cal Fussman and Harry Crews

The life of every man is a diary in which he means to write one story, and writes another.

J.M. Barrie

I sat down once with Alan Clark...and...we worked out that the four rules for a good political diarist were the four *i's*: immediate... indiscreet... intimate... and indecipherable.

Gyles Brandreth

AUTOBIOGRAPHY & BIOGRAPHY

Next to the writer of real estate advertisements, the autobiographer is the most suspect of prose artists.

Donal Henahan

Things I Did And Things I Think I Did

Jean Negulesco, title of his autobiography

—Your ex-husband, Tony Visconti, recently had his memoirs out... Did you read them with trepidation?
—No, I didn't read them at all. I like non-fiction.

Mark Lawson and Mary Hopkin, *Front Row*

I have been told that when the late Sir Edward Marsh, composing his memoir of Rupert Brooke, wrote 'Rupert left Rugby in a blaze of glory', the poet's mother, a lady of firm character, changed 'a blaze of glory' to 'July'.

F.L. Lucas

You want to hear the new title of my autobiography: *It Was No Fucking Picnic: The Jack Lucas Story.*

Jack Lucas, *The Fisher King*

We like to know the weakness of eminent men; it consoles us for our inferiority.

Madame de Lambert

I would rather read my own death certificate.

Rod Liddle, on most sports stars' autobiographies

The books aren't being incinerated, they've being pulped. My book could very well end up being reconstituted as a trestle table in a home for battered women. I'm putting something back!

Alan Partridge, on the failure of his autobiography, *Bouncing Back*

A well-written Life is almost as rare as a well-spent one.

Thomas Carlyle

Just how difficult it is to write biography can be reckoned by anybody who sits down and considers just how many people know the real truth about his or her love affairs.

Rebecca West

It's a wonder the prospect of having a biographer never discouraged anyone from having a life.

E.M. Cioran

Great geniuses have the shortest biographies. Their cousins can tell you nothing about them. They lived in their writings.

Ralph Waldo Emerson

I heard one of the people I'd written for interviewed on *Woman's Hour*, recounting a specific detail I'd invented to make her story come alive. I felt strangely flattered.

Mark McCrum, ghost writer of celebrity autobiographies

In heaven, we will all be ghost writers, if we write at all.

Robert Frost

PUBLISHING

Any fool can write a novel but it takes real genius to sell it.

J.G. Ballard

'You told them you were expecting to sell a hundred thousand copies?'
'We always tell them we're expecting to sell a hundred thousand copies,'
said Russell Clutterbuck, letting him in on one of the secrets of the
publishing trade.

P.G. Wodehouse, *French Leave*

My first idea was to print only three copies: one for myself, one for the
British Museum, and one for Heaven. I had some doubt about the
British Museum.

Oscar Wilde, anticipating the appeal of his poem 'The Sphinx'

I well remember the late Poet Laureate and publisher, Cecil Day Lewis,
telling me his two favourite literary forms, challenging in their brevity,
were the sonnet and the blurb.

H.R.F. Keating

It's just called *The Bible* now. We
dropped the word 'Holy' to give it a
more mass-market appeal.

Judith Young, *attrib.*

Novel: a short story padded.

Ambrose Bierce

Alan Coren wrote *Golfing For Cats*. He'd worked out that cats, golf and the Third Reich were the most popular subjects of that time, so they put a golfing cat and a swastika on the front. Today's equivalent might be 'The Incest Diet'.

Simon Hoggart

You know how it is in children's book publishing: it's bunny-eat-bunny.

Anon

Every book is a children's book if the kid can read.

Mitch Hedberg

Editors used to be known by their authors; now some of them are known by their restaurants.

Robert Giroux, *The Education of an Editor*

It is with publishers as with wives: one always wants somebody else's. And when you have them, where's the difference?

Norman Douglas, author

POETRY

Among America's 240 million people there aren't a thousand who want a book of poetry badly enough to pay the price of a small pizza for it.

Beverly Jarrett

I don't like to boast, but I have probably skipped more poetry than any other person of my age and weight in this country.

Will Cuppy

Most poets were little boys who couldn't play baseball or ride bicycles. So, the big boys got them down in the vacant lot, rubbed sand on their thing, and they eventually took to art.

Kenneth Rexroth

Never leave me alone with poets.

Harold Ross, editor, memo to his secretary

I have nothing against poetry. If it were not for poetry, Postman Pat would have a black-and-white dog.

Alan Coren, Chocolate and Cuckoo Clocks

Herman has taken to writing poetry. You need not tell anyone, for you know how such things get around.

Elizabeth Melville, his wife

Sometimes people say to me at poetry readings, 'What's the purpose of poetry?' And I say, 'To give novelists and playwrights titles.'

Peter Porter, poet

One, two, three,
Buckle my shoe.

Robert Benchley

—How are you?
—Not very well, I can only write prose today.

O'Connor and W.B. Yeats, attrib.

A true poet does not bother to be poetical. Nor does a nursery gardener scent his roses.

Jean Cocteau

The word 'poet' is a gift word: someone else has to call you a poet; you can't call yourself one.

Robert Frost

Wordsworth once told Matthew Arnold that for many years 'his poetry had never brought him in enough to buy his shoe-strings'.

Charles Dickens

For most of history, Anonymous was a woman.

Virginia Woolf

It is being said of a certain poet that though he tortures the English language, he had never yet succeeded in forcing it to reveal his meaning.

J.B. Morton

—How can you tell good poetry from bad?
—In the same way as you can tell fish. If it's fresh it's good, if it's stale it's bad, and if you're not certain, try it on the cat.

Questioner and Osbert Sitwell

I gave up on new poetry myself 30 years ago, when most of it began to read like coded messages passing between lonely aliens in a hostile world.

Russell Baker

I rather think poetry has given me up, which is a great sorrow to me. But not an enormous crushing sorrow. It's a bit like going bald.

Philip Larkin

CRITIC

Critics are eunuchs at a gang-bang.

George Burns

Critics are people who hated Mickey Mouse when they were children – if they ever were children.

Moss Hart

A critic is a man who expects miracles.

James Huneker

I'm so terribly clever you see... I have this extraordinary ability to see, after the event, why something didn't work, and communicate it so wittily.

Critic, played by Stephen Fry, *A Bit of Fry and Laurie*

Literature is strewn with the wreckage of men who have minded beyond reason the opinions of others.

Virginia Woolf

A fly, sir, may sting a stately horse and make him wince; but one is but an insect, and the other is a horse still.

Dr Samuel Johnson

A writer, like a woman, never knows why people like him, or why people dislike him. We never know.

Isaac Bashevis Singer

I take no more notice of the wind that comes out of the mouths of critics than of the wind expelled from their backsides.

Leonardo da Vinci

A good writer is not, *per se*, a good book critic. No more so than a good drunk is automatically a good bartender.

Jim Bishop

I was so long writing my review that I never got around to reading the book.

Groucho Marx

The music critic, Huneker, could never quite make up his mind about a new symphony until he had seen the composer's mistress.

H.L. Mencken

Mr Clarkson, the wig-maker, on being asked his opinion of a great Shakespearean production, declared it to be superb. 'You couldn't see a join,' said he.

Edward H. Sothern

One of the first and most important things for a drama critic to learn is how to sleep undetected at the theatre.

William Archer

You don't so much review a play as draw up a crushing brief against it.

Edmund Wilson

One of us is obviously mistaken. Knowing the paltry little I know, I cannot believe it is me.

William Saroyan, to 15 critics who panned his play

—What's the play about?
—It's about two hours long.

Critic and Edward Albee, his customary response when questioned by a critic

There are two kinds of dramatic critics; destructive and constructive. I am a destructive. There are two kinds of guns: Krupp and pop.

George Jean Nathan

I like only destructive critics, because they force me to be on my guard and readjust my ideas. To my mind, constructive critics are just impertinent.

Peter Ustinov

A negative judgement gives you more satisfaction than praise, provided it smacks of jealousy.

Jean Baudrillard

Genuine polemics approach a book as lovingly as a cannibal spices a baby.

Walter Benjamin

Listen carefully to first criticisms made of your work. Note just what it is about your work that the critics don't like – then cultivate it. That's the only part of your work that's individual and worth keeping.

Jean Cocteau

I divide all works into two categories: those I like and those I don't. I have no other criterion.

Anton Chekhov

Time is the only critic without ambition.

John Steinbeck

MARRIAGE & FAMILY LIFE

MARRIAGE

—Marge, will you marry me?
—Why? Am I pregnant?

Homer and Marge Simpson

It's a funny thing when a man hasn't anything on earth to worry about, he goes off and gets married.

Robert Frost

Let's get this straight: I can't sleep with anyone else for the rest of my life, and if things don't work out, you get to keep half my stuff?

Bobby Slayton

To marry, just as to become a monk, means to take an absolute risk.

Paul Evdokimov

I have a raging fear of commitment. I mean, I don't even like to write in pen.

Michael Somerville

There are men who would even be afraid to commit themselves on the doctrine that castor oil is a laxative.

Camille Flammarion

If I ever marry, it will be on a sudden impulse, as a man shoots himself.

H.L. Mencken

Prostitutes believe in marriage. It provides them with most of their trade.

Suzine, *Knave* magazine

Mother told me...'Sweetheart, settle down and marry a rich man.' I said, 'Mom, I *am* a rich man.'

Cher

Whenever you want to marry someone, go have lunch with his ex-wife.

Shelley Winters

Never marry a man you wouldn't want to be divorced from.

Nora Ephron

Dreadful flowers bought at a garage were a perfect metaphor for my wedding to Chris Evans: last-minute, cheap and dead within hours.

Carol McGiffin

Women your age are more likely to get mauled at the zoo than get married.

Jack Donaghy, *30 Rock*

They say I married my wife because her uncle left her a whole lot of money. That's not true. I would've married her no matter who left her the money.

Steve McFarlin

The way taxes are, you might as well marry for love.

Joe E. Lewis

I'm getting married on April 12th. My fiancé and I still haven't decided on the year.

Wendy Liebman

I'm so glad I didn't go for the wedding dress with the beaded top; I would've looked like an undefrosted freezer.

Vicky Hodges, *The Archers*

The bride wore her grandmother's dress. The grandmother was freezing.

Pam Ayres, *Ayres on the Air*

—What would you like to see on your honeymoon?
—Lots of lovely ceilings.

Jonas Cord and Monica Winthrop, The Carpetbaggers

He promised his fiancée the world, the moon and the stars. On their honeymoon, he took her to the planetarium.

Joey Adams

MARRIED LIFE

There's one consolation about matrimony. When you look around you can always see somebody who did worse.

Warren H. Goldsmith

I was always deeply devoted to Rex *before* we were married and *after* we were divorced. It was that little bit in between which proved so difficult.

Elizabeth Harrison

Marriage is like a bank account. You put it in, you take it out, you lose interest.

Irwin Corey

When a woman gets married, it's like jumping into a hole in the ice in the middle of winter; you do it once and you remember it the rest of your days.

Maxim Gorky

I had a patient once who dreamed she kept her husband in the deep freeze except for mating. Lots of men feel that way.

Robert A. Johnson, psychologist

The problem with marriage is that it ends every night after making love, and it must be rebuilt every morning before breakfast.

Gabriel García Márquez

I always take my wife morning tea in my pyjamas. But is she grateful? No, she says she'd rather have it in a cup.

Eric Morecambe

Jane says...she's found it helps to start each new day by arriving down at breakfast, throwing her arms in the air and announcing, apologetically, 'It's all my fault.'

Anne Robinson

I used to annoy my first wife so much. I used to do things deliberately to annoy her, I admit that. In the mornings, I'd wake up. God, she hated that.

Bob Monkhouse

We used to think it would be nice to sleep in one another's arms, but we never could go to sleep because our weight stopped our circulations just above the elbows.

George Bernard Shaw

What is it with men and scratching? You weren't so itchy before we were married. Why are you so itchy now we are?

Andrea McLean

I realized on our first wedding anniversary that our marriage was in trouble. My husband gave me luggage. It was packed. My mother damn near suffocated.

Phyllis Diller

I honestly thought my marriage would work because me and my wife did share a sense of humour. We had to, really, because she didn't have one.

Frank Skinner

Often the difference between a successful marriage and a mediocre one consists of leaving about three or four things a day unsaid.

Harlan Miller

I've been married 38 years myself, and I don't regret a day of it. The one day of it I don't regret was August 2nd 1936. She was off visiting her ailing mother at the time.

Eddie Mayehoff, *How to Murder Your Wife*

I sometimes feel like the beleaguered owner of a British bulldog with learning disabilities.

Caroline Bondy, on being the wife of Toby Young

My husband asked me if we have any cheese puffs. Like he can't go and lift that couch cushion up himself.

Roseanne

I got a teenage daughter and a menopausal wife. One's getting breasts, one's getting whiskers. My life is over.

Bobby Slayton

There are two kinds of marriages: where the husband quotes the wife and where the wife quotes the husband.

Clifford Odets

I never mind my wife having the last word. In fact, I'm delighted when she gets to it.

Walter Matthau

Despite all the advice about how to achieve connubial bliss, a happy marriage is usually an unearned miracle.

Sloan Wilson

SINGLE LIFE

It is always incomprehensible to a man that a woman should ever refuse an offer of marriage.

Jane Austen, *Emma*

Why get married and make one man miserable when I can stay single and make thousands miserable?

Carrie P. Snow

I'm single because I was born that way.
Mae West

Being an old maid is like death by drowning, a really delightful sensation after you cease to struggle.

Edna Ferber

One of the advantages of living alone is that you don't have to wake up in the arms of a loved one.

Marion Smith

Even if I should by some awful chance find a hair upon my bread and honey – at any rate it is my own hair.

Katherine Mansfield

—Who famously said 'I want to be alone'?
—Is it Terry Waite?
—Terry Waite was that poor sod held captive for five years tied to a radiator!
—Well, at least he was warm.

Jim and Barbara Royle, *The Royle Family*

There's one thing worse than being alone: wishing you were.

Bob Steele

FAMILY LIFE

Dignity, breeding and piles of money. That's all anyone has ever wanted from a family. But all anyone gets from most families is love.

P.J. O'Rourke

I came from a big family. Four of us slept in the same bed. When we got cold, Mother threw in another brother.

Bob Hope

I have one brother, five sisters. I had to wear a tampon just to fit in.

Dane Cook

The man with six kids will always be happier than the man with six million dollars, because the man with six million dollars always wants more.

William Feather

—I had a pretty tough childhood. At the age of 5 I was left an orphan.
—That's ridiculous. What could a 5-year-old do with an orphan?

Ernie Wise and Eric Morecambe

I come from a broken home. I broke it.

Lemmy Kilmister, of heavy metal band, Motörhead

Once you've driven your drunk father to your mom's parole hearing, what else is there?

Christopher Titus, *Titus*

What irritates me most about my family is that they don't drink alcohol and I do. The good thing is that I view them all as potential liver-donors.

Audience Member, *The Now Show*

My ol' man was tough. He allowed no drinking in the house. I had two brothers who died of thirst.

Rodney Dangerfield

Family love is messy, clinging, and of an annoying and repetitive pattern, like bad wallpaper.

P.J. O'Rourke

Maynards? So much incest in that family even the bulldog's got a club foot.

Viv Stanshall

Relations never lend one any money, and won't give one credit, even for genius. They are a sort of aggravated form of the public.

Oscar Wilde

A lot of people have been tracing their family histories on the Internet. I'm no exception, and what I've discovered is that I come from a very long line of dead people.

Pat Condell, *The Store*

Do you want to trace your family tree? Run for public office.

Patricia H. Vance

GRANDPARENTS

A Jewish grandmother is watching her grandchild playing on the beach when a huge wave comes and takes him out to sea. She pleads: 'Please God, save my only grandson. I beg of you, bring him back.' And a big wave comes and washes the boy back on to the beach, good as new. She looks up to heaven and says: 'He had a hat!'

Myra Cohen

A grandparent will put a sweater on you when she is cold, feed you when she is hungry, and put you to bed when she is tired.

Erma Bombeck

My parents used to send me to spend summers with my grandparents. I hate cemeteries!

Chris Fonseca

You should have met my granny. A marvellous woman. She lived on tinned salmon, snuff and porter and never got out of bed except for funerals.

Brendan Behan

Grandchildren can be annoying. How many times can you go, 'And the cow goes moo and the pig goes oink?' It's like talking to a supermodel.

Joan Rivers

'You're more trouble than the children are' is the greatest compliment a grandparent can receive.

Gene Perret

—Grandad, why are you sitting in the garden with no trousers on?
—Well, last week I sat out here with no shirt on and I got a stiff neck. This is your Grandma's idea.

Anon

Do you ever get your arthritic grandparents and take 'em out on the lawn and drag 'em around to rake the leaves?

Harland Williams

Today I picked up Grandma at the airport. She's now at that age where she doesn't remember. So I said: 'Thanks for coming... goodbye!'

Craig Kilborn

MOTHER-IN-LAW

—Have you ever in your life been totally and completely intimidated by another person?
—Yes. My husband's mother.

> Denis Ferrara and Madonna, on Guy Ritchie's mother

—What's Steve's mom like?
—Imagine Steve. In a wig. Drunk.

> Carrie Bradshaw and Miranda Hobbes, *Sex and the City*

When I got married, my mother-in-law said the bride and I made a perfect couple – except for me.

> George Burns

Two cannibals are having dinner. One says, 'I can't stand my mother-in-law.' The other says, 'Then just eat the rice.'

> Jerry Lewis

I should, many a good day, have blown my brains out, but for the recollection that it would have given pleasure to my mother-in-law.

> Lord Byron

I know a mother-in-law who sleeps with her glasses on, the better to see her son-in-law suffer in her dreams.

> Ernest Coquelin

What a wonderful place to drop one's mother-in-law!

> Marshal Ferdinand Foch, on seeing the Grand Canyon

—About your mother-in-law – should we embalm her, cremate her, or bury her?
—Do all three. Don't take chances.

Myron Cohen

Of all men, Adam was the happiest; he had no mother-in-law.

Paul Parfait

CHILDREN

I don't have any children – that I know of.

Carol Leifer

A man's desire for a son is usually nothing but the wish to duplicate himself in order that such a remarkable pattern not be lost to the world.

Helen Rowland

I worry about having a baby in case it grows up and can't find a parking space.

Victoria Wood

My wife and I have decided we don't want children. If anyone does, we can drop them off tomorrow.

Stewart Francis, *Loose Ends*

The greatest advantage of not having children must be that you can go on believing that you are a nice person: once you have children, you realise how wars start.

Fay Weldon

I guess the real reason that my wife and I had children is the same reason that Napoleon had for invading Russia: it seemed like a good idea at the time.

Bill Cosby

I'm pregnant. No need to applaud; I was asleep at the time.

Jeannie McBride

—Dorothy, are you all right?
—Well, let's see, everything's twice as big as it was nine months ago, and I'm growing another head inside me, let's start there.

Tony and Dorothy, *Men Behaving Badly*

I wanna open up a maternity shop and call it 'We're fucked'.

Zach Galifianakis

My wife's already baby-proofing the house. I've got to be out of the house by next week.

Chris Fonseca

You want to bring up a child? You couldn't bring up phlegm!

Sonia Fowler, *EastEnders*

Death and taxes and childbirth! There's never any convenient time for any of them.

Margaret Mitchell, *Gone With the Wind*

I told my mother I was going to have natural childbirth. She said to me: 'Linda, you've been taking drugs all your life. Why stop now?'

Linda Maldonado

People are giving birth underwater now. They say it's less traumatic for the baby because it's in water... But it's certainly more traumatic for the other people in the pool.

Elayne Boosler

I remember Melanie C saying when Melanie B was giving birth, 'It's not like the cat getting stuck behind the oven, when you know it's got in there, so it's got to get out.'

Victoria Beckham, *Learning to Fly*

With my first child I can recall screaming, 'Get this thing out of me! Get this thing out of me!' And that was the conception.

Joan Rivers

It feels like I'm shitting a knife!

Angie Ostrowiski, *Baby Mama*

Push. Push. Push.

Sign on a door in a hospital maternity wing

It was unbelievable. I ran outside to feed a meter, came back a few minutes later and I'm a father again!

Sylvester Stallone

I was so long in labour they had to shave me twice.

Saffy's midwife, *Absolutely Fabulous*

They held him up my son and I went, 'My God, he is hung like a bear.' They said, 'That's the umbilical cord.' I said, 'Don't cut that, let him dream for a while.'

Robin Williams

If newborns could remember and speak, they would emerge from the womb carrying tales as wondrous as Homer's.

Sharon Begley

Mother didn't make it to the hospital. I was born on the bus. She was furious when she had to open her purse the second time.

Jack Douglas

A degree in 'shit management' would be the best preparation for motherhood... Mothers are sewage workers.

Mum's the Word

You're not a mother until you've had nits.

Coleen Nolan

It sometimes happens, even in the best families, that a baby is born. This is not necessarily cause for alarm. The important thing is to keep your wits about you and borrow some money.

Elinor Goulding Smith

What is a baby? Nine months' interest on a small deposit.

Anon

A child is a grenade. When you have a baby, you set off an explosion in your marriage, and when the dust settles, your marriage is different from what it was.

Nora Ephron, *Heartburn*

What's the difference between couplehood and babyhood? In a word? Moisture.

Paul Reiser

Changing a diaper is a lot like getting a present from your grandmother: you're not sure what you've got but you're pretty sure you're not going to like it.

Jeff Foxworthy

Things a father should know: how to change a nappy – and dispose of the old one.

Katharine Whitehorn

A father is a man who has photos in his wallet where his money used to be.

Anon

People show you pictures of their babies on their phone now, and it looks like a cashew with some hair coming out of it. The thing to say is: 'Nice phone!'

Rich Hall, *QI*

When I ask how old your toddler is, I don't need to know in months: 'Twenty-seven months.' 'He's two,' will do just fine. He's not a cheese. And I don't really care in the first place.

Bill Maher

Having a baby is like suddenly sprouting a second head: the attention you get at the start is nice, but at the end of it, it's just another mouth to feed.

John Scalzi

There are three reasons for breast-feeding: the milk is always at the right temperature; it comes in attractive containers; and the cat can't get it.

Irena Chalmers

Christenings can be howling bad affairs, but of one which went off in a seemly and quiet way the mother explained afterwards that it was because 'my husband and I have been practising on him with a watering can for a whole week'.

Gerald Findler

I wouldn't say my father hated me, but at my christening, he tipped the vicar a fiver to hold me under.

Bob Monkhouse

My brother was adopted. Somebody left him on the back doorstep when he was a baby. We found him when he was 16. We didn't use that door.

Wendy Liebman

I carried eggs for lesbian couples who couldn't have children. I had 18 children in 3 years. I had to have my pelvic floor laminated.

Lily Savage, *The Parkinson Show*

I was at a dinner party where one actress had adopted a child from Africa and she was saying: 'I want my children to know their heritage.' I said: 'Lock them in a room and throw them a jar of flies.'

Joan Rivers

You kids are disgusting, standing here all day, reeking of popcorn and lollipops.

W.C. Fields

People ask me: 'Dave, what is the essence of parenthood?' I always answer: 'Lowering your standards.'

Dave Barry

I used to hear that song that talks about believing that children are our future and think it was a trite song. Now I realise it's a warning.

Jon Stewart

—If you had your life to live over would you still have children?
—Yes, but not the same ones.

Interviewer and Bill Miller

My kids? Have you seen *The Brady Bunch*? Well, picture them with knives.

Carla Tortelli, *Cheers*

Children can age an adult faster than ten years in prison. Parents can have the same effect on children.

David Brown, film producer

Alligators have the right idea. They eat their young.

Ida Corwin, *Mildred Pierce*

A two-year-old is like having a blender, but you don't have a top for it.

Jerry Seinfeld

Hanging out with any two-year-old is basically one big suicide watch. Their mission is to find one new way after another of offing themselves – piss in an electric socket, lick a pit bull's nose...and your job as a parent is to stop it before it happens.

Michael J. Fox

When I was 8 I ran away with a circus. When I was 9 they made me bring it back.

Eric Morecambe

Children are like farts – people quite like their own.

Graham Norton

Pamela Anderson has two gorgeous sons. They're actually the only two guys that have ever come *out* of Pam.

Sarah Silverman

Every son raised by a single mom is pretty much born married... Until your mom dies it seems like all the other women in your life can never be more than just your mistress.

Chuck Palahniuk, *Choke*

When I was married I had a stepson, which was great because that way I didn't have to hit my kids.

Rich Vos

Never raise your hands to your kids. It leaves your groin unprotected.

Red Buttons

I still remember Nanny pulling down my trousers and giving me a good spanking. Never did me any harm. Although it did make me late for the show this evening.

Humphrey Lyttelton, *I'm Sorry I Haven't a Clue*

When your children are teenagers, it's important to have a dog so that someone in the house is happy to see you.

Nora Ephron

Caron is fifteen, to put it mildly.

Joan Hess, *A Really Cute Corpse*

My parents said, 'Why can't you be like the girl next door?' We lived next to a cemetery.

Joan Rivers

—Kids, get down here!
—Dad, why are you yelling at us? We were way upstairs – just text me.

Phil and Haley Dunphy, *Modern Family*

The other night I told my kid, 'Someday you'll have children of your own.' He said, 'So will you.'

Rodney Dangerfield

The rights of teenagers to loaf at the end of the street smoking cigarettes, scowling, swearing and spitting are inalienable. They have been doing it ever since street corners were invented.

Keith Waterhouse

Like its politicians and its wars, society has the teenagers it deserves.

J.B. Priestley

Everyone talks about deadbeat dads. What about the kids who just aren't worth the child support?

David Feldman

I used to go on those field trips in school and gave my dad a permission slip. It's got that question: 'In case of emergency...' My dad would write: 'Do not resuscitate.'

Moody McCarthy

I went up to Dad when I was 13 or 14 and told him I was gay. Dad just looked at me and said, 'It's okay, son, I've had men before, too.'

Alexis Arquette

I would have loved to have had a gay dad. Do you remember at school, there were always kids saying, 'My dad's bigger than your dad,' 'My dad will batter your dad!' So what? 'My dad will shag your dad. And your dad will enjoy it.'

Frankie Boyle, *Mock the Week*

'John, your father wants you to build a boat at once,' she said. 'Where is Father?' inquired John. 'In the middle of the lake, drowning.'

Spike Milligan

I'm very protective of my daughters. 'No, Jenny isn't home right now. She's on the space shuttle.'

Billy Crystal

Every father's daughter is a virgin.

Tagline, *Goodbye Columbus*

Well, it's 1am. Better go home and spend some quality time with the kids.

Homer Simpson

SEX EDUCATION

—Mummy, where do babies come from?
—Why, the stork brings them, of course.
—So who fucks the stork?

Anon

What a kid I got! I told him about the birds and the bees, and he told me about the butcher and my wife.

Rodney Dangerfield

—I was 14 before I realised I was a Jew.
—That's nothing. I was 16 before I realised I was a boy.

Friend and George S. Kaufman

I actually learned about sex watching the neighbourhood dogs... I think the most important thing I learned was: never let go of the girl's leg no matter how hard she tries to shake you off.

Steve Martin

I didn't know the full facts of life until I was 17. My father never talked about his work.

Martin Freud, son of Sigmund

I didn't know how babies were made until I was pregnant with my fourth child.

Loretta Lynn, country music star

I'm a virgin and I brought up all my children to be the same.

Shirley Bassey

HOUSE & HOME

Democracy is buying a big house you can't afford with money you don't have to impress people you wish were dead.

Johnny Carson

A 30-year mortgage at his age essentially means that he's buying a coffin.

Dwight Schrute, *The Office (USA)*

—What's the top priority for a single man buying a house?
—Is it a kitchen sink that flushes?

Jimmy Carr and Sean Lock, *8 Out of 10 Cats*

Many a man who thinks to found a home discovers that he has merely opened a tavern for his friends.

Norman Douglas

The live in a beautiful little apartment overlooking the rent.

Anon

I sold my house this week. I got a pretty good price for it, but it made my landlord mad as hell.

Garry Shandling

The worst of taking a furnished house is that the articles in the rooms are saturated with the thoughts and glances of others.

Thomas Hardy

The house feels tired, even the furniture exhausted from old marital battles, the old green sofa looks like it has been awake sobbing all night.

Garrison Keillor

During his years of poverty Balzac lived in an unheated and almost unfurnished garret. On one of the bare walls the writer inscribed the words: 'Rosewood panelling with commode'; on another: 'Gobelin tapestry with Venetian mirror.' And in the place of honour over the empty fireplace: 'Picture by Raphael.'

E. Fuller

It is ridiculous to rent things if you are a gardener; it fidgets you. Even a very long lease is upsetting. I once owned a house with a 999 years lease, and it gave me an unbearable sense of being a sort of weekend guest; it hardly seemed worth while planting the hyacinths.

Beverley Nichols

We are but tenants and...shortly, the great Landlord will give us notice that our lease has expired.

Joseph Jefferson

Come live in my heart and pay no rent!

Samuel Lover

HOUSEWORK

True or false: Jeremy Irons?

Vic Reeves and Bob Mortimer, Shooting Stars

—Just look at the state of this place! I could write my name in the dust on that piano.
—Ain't education a wonderful thing!

Ted Ray and Mrs Mosseltoff, the cleaner (Harold Berens)

—Mummy, where does dust come from?
—Cremated fairies.

Five-Year-Old Child and Jil Evans

—That is *the* most disgusting bathroom I have ever seen!
—Well, we tried to clean it once, but the bacteria ate our sponge.

Kate O'Brien and Lewis Kiniski, *The Drew Carey Show*

Do you know you can get Apple and Mango Toilet Duck now when all you want to do is sluice the bog with it, not make a fruit salad.

Roger Lewis

Brave is the man who brushes the lavatory clean, but braver still the man who cleans the lavatory brush.

Miles Kington

I call my neighbour Mrs Clean. I finally found out why her laundry looks so much whiter than mine. She washes it.

Phyllis Diller

I am allergic to domestic goddesses. Men would prefer a woman with a dirty mind to a clean house.

Kathy Lette

The only day I enjoyed ironing was the day I accidentally put gin in the steam iron.

Phyllis Diller

He's fanatically tidy. Do you know, after he takes a bath he washes the soap.

Hugh Leonard

Show me a man who lives alone and has a perpetually clean kitchen, and eight times out of nine I'll show you a man with detestable spiritual qualities.

Charles Bukowski

That kind of so-called housekeeping where they have six bottles and no corkscrew.

Mark Twain

DIY

—How many birds does it take to screw in a light bulb?
—Two. One to run around screaming, 'What do I do?' and one to shag the electrician.

DCI Gene Hunt, *Ashes To Ashes*

Did you hear about the hundred Irish carpenters? One held the screw, one held the screwdriver, and 98 turned the wall.

Jackie Hamilton

Hammer: an instrument for smashing the human thumb.

Ambrose Bierce

Having a multiplicity of screwdrivers reminds me of the old Irish saying, 'It will come in handy, even if you never use it.'

Frank P. Dilkes

The roof leaked over our bedroom. When I told my husband to take care of it, he bought me a pair of all-weather pyjamas.

Phyllis Diller

Do you remember the first time I asked you to build something and you came in the kitchen wearing nothing but a tool belt?

Tanya Branning, to her husband, *EastEnders*

Don't sleep with a drip. Call your plumber.

Sign on a plumber's van

CHEATING

If you marry a man who cheats on his wife, you'll be married to a man who cheats on his wife.

Ann Landers

—What would you do if you found a man in bed with your wife?
—I'd kick his dog and break his white stick!

Ernie Wise and Eric Morecambe

A man returns home and finds his best friend in bed with his wife. He looks at them and says to his friend: 'I have to, but *you*?'

Larry Adler

A man comes home early and finds a naked guy hiding behind the shower curtain. He says, 'What are you doing in there?' The guy says, 'Voting.'

Lou Jacobi

Bought my wife one of those new water beds. Come home 4 o'clock in the morning, there's a guy in the middle of the floor. I said, 'Who's that?' She said, 'Lifeguard.'

Slappy White

The bed of Sir Christopher Dilke was so large that he was alleged to be able to keep his wife in one part of the bed and his mistress in another, and neither knew the other was there.

Anthony O'Reilly

—Have you been sleeping with Rose Flamsteed?
—Not a wink.

Peter De Vries

If I caught him in bed with my wife, I'd probably tuck him in.

Mike Stephenson, sports reporter, on 6ft 2" Kiwi rugby
player, Paul Rauhihi, who weighs 19 stones

My girlfriend had sex with my agent? I thought he only took 10 per cent.

Harris T. Telemacher, *L.A. Story*

It's hard to put a glutton permanently in front of cakes without him eating two or three of them.

Francine Distel, wife of Sacha, on his womanising

All my men cheated on me... All I ever got out of marriage, except my daughter, was some jewellery and a recipe for ravioli.

Shelley Winters, on divorcing her Italian husband

Men cheat for the same reason that dogs lick their balls: because they can.

Samantha Jones, *Sex and the City*

If we have a married employee who has a girlfriend, we terminate him. He's got a lifetime contract with his wife, and if she can't trust him, how can I?

Ross Perot, when head of EDS (Electronic Data Systems)

Adultery is much worse than homosexuality.

Margaret Thatcher

Middle-aged couples are five times more likely to fantasize about owning a dog than dream of an extra-marital affair.

Poll for *Reader's Digest*

SEPARATION & DIVORCE

Divorce is the future tense of marriage.

Anon

Married by Elvis. Divorced by Friday.

G.M. Rouse

One minute you're newlyweds, making love on the floor of Concorde, and the next your lawyers are fighting over who gets to keep the box your dog defecates in.

Jack Donaghy, *30 Rock*

It helps to label the books.

Juan Antonio del Rosario

My first wife divorced me on grounds of incompatibility. And besides, I think she hated me.

Oscar Levant

—What are the grounds for your divorce?
—Marriage is sufficient.

Judge and Wilson Mizner

—Oh, John, once we had something that was pure and wonderful and good. What happened to it?
—You spent it all.

Mary and John, *I'm Sorry, I'll Read That Again*

Divorce is only less painful than the need for divorce.

Jane O'Reilly, *The Girl I Left Behind*

Divorce is a system whereby two people make a mistake and one of them goes on paying for it.

Len Deighton

My wife made me a millionaire. I used to have three million.

Bobby Hull

Alimony is like putting a dime in the parking meter after they towed your car away.

Lenny Kent

My biggest regret? Not arranging a hit man to take out my ex-wife's divorce lawyer.

Pat Cash, tennis player

In our family we don't divorce our men – we *bury* 'em.

Stella Bernard, *Lord Love a Duck*

REMARRIAGE

After divorcing his first wife, Mark Thatcher has married again. And who's the lucky lady? Well, the first wife, obviously.

Clive Anderson

Many a man owes his success to his first wife and his second wife to his success.

Jim Backus

In Biblical times, a man could have as many wives as he could afford. Just like today.

Abigail Van Buren

Nigella finds it rather common to be my third wife, and would have found it more chic to be my fifth.

Charles Saatchi, *Charles Saatchi: Question*

I know a couple that got remarried. He missed two alimony payments and she repossessed him.

Bill Barner

I don't understand couples who divorce and remarry. That's like pouring milk on a bowl of cereal, tasting it, and saying: 'This milk is sour. Well, I'll put it back in the refrigerator – maybe it will be okay tomorrow.'

Larry Miller

I married William Saroyan the second time because I couldn't believe how terrible it was the first time.

Carol Saroyan, on her remarriage
(they divorced a year later and she married Walter Matthau)

The room was filled with people who hadn't talked to each other in years, including the bride and groom.

Dorothy Parker, on her remarriage to Alan Campbell

I planned on having one husband and seven children, but it turned out the other way around.

Lana Turner

—Can you tell me the names of your former spouses?
—What is this, a memory test?

Justice of the Peace and Elizabeth Taylor (married 8 times to 7 husbands)

Always a bride, never a bridesmaid.

Oscar Levant, on Elizabeth Taylor

I hope you've finally found the happiness you've been looking for because, quite frankly, I'm exhausted.

Melanie Cantor, matron of honour to Ulrika Jonsson at her third wedding

The others were only my wives. But you, my dear, will be my widow.

Sacha Guitry, reassuring his fifth wife, *attrib.*

COMMUNICATION

CONVERSATIONAL ICE-BREAKERS

Knock, knock.

Lee A. Davis

Did they capture it yet?

S. Kirschner

That's funny, I've been to bed with everyone in this room.

Tom Morrow

Oh, by the way, did you know I'm wearing Hitler's old shoes?

Pat McCormick

Didn't you used to be a woman?

Anon

Pardon me, but don't you think you've had enough to drink?

Steven B. Black

I found the rectal thermometer – what should I do with it?

Jack Ryan

CONVERSATION

The first human statement is a scream.

Robin Skelton

There's a curious statistic I came across recently. The average married couple converse for 20 minutes every week. What do they find to talk about?

Dave Allen

—Homer, I'd like to talk to you.
—But then I won't be watching TV. You can see the bind I'm in.

Marge and Homer Simpson

If a man speaks in the heart of a forest and no woman is there to hear him, is he still wrong?

Glen Cook

A foolish man tells a woman to stop talking, but a wise man tells her that her mouth is extremely beautiful when her lips are closed.

Anon

If you want all the conversation you can handle, put a bandage on your forehead.

Bill Vaughn

I have never heard a dull story about an actor, a parrot or a Negro preacher.

Arthur Krock

Wilfred Blunt used to say that you could put ten per cent on to any story by making its leading figure a bishop.

Edward Mars

E.F. Benson's idea of a good conversation: when neither party remembers a word of what was said afterwards.

A.C. Benson

Why can't anybody in this family talk in front of me? For years I went around thinking a surprise party was being planned for me.

Billy Tate, *Soap*

I can't stand whispering. Every time a doctor whispers in the hospital, the next day there's a funeral.

Evy, The Gingerbread Lady

One of the best rules in conversation is never to say a thing which any of the company can reasonably wish we had rather left unsaid.

Jonathan Swift

After eating an entire bull, a mountain lion felt so good he started roaring. He kept it up until a hunter came along and shot him. The moral: when you're full of bull, keep your mouth shut.

Will Rogers

There are very few people who don't become more interesting when they stop talking.

Mary Lowry

Howl! You will feel a few million years younger.

Stanislaw J. Lec

CONVERSATION- STOPPERS

Listen, could you do me a *really* big favour?

Steven Black

I hardly recognized you; how did you gain so much weight?

Bill Phillips

Do you think you could eat another human being?

C. Bruce Gordon

I think my colostomy bag just broke.

Jack Ryan

Paul here can whistle the entire score of *Oklahoma!*

Corinee Gillick

Hitler was right about a lot of things.

Thomas Van Steenbergh

Who left *this* in the bathroom?

Linda Quirini

Did I show you all the apps on my iPhone?

Anon

My real name is Jon Venables.

Anon

I do.

Jules Shumacher

GOSSIP

I always say, a problem shared is… gossip!

Graham Norton

Gossip is just news running ahead of itself in a red satin dress.

Liz Smith

A rabbit can't break wind round here without her knowing about it.

Brian Aldridge, *The Archers*

The story's everywhere – spreading faster than a rent boy's cheeks.

Malcolm Tucker, *The Thick Of It*

People keep telling us about their love affairs, when what we really want to know is how much money they make and how they manage on it.

Mignon McLaughlin

Men have always detested women's gossip because they suspect the truth: their measurements are being taken and compared.

Erica Jong

Men gossip less than women, but mean it.

Mignon McLaughlin

When a man tells you what people are saying about you, tell him what people are saying about him; that will immediately take his mind off your troubles.

Edgar Watson Howe

SECRETS

What is the most dangerous possession in the world? Someone else's secret.

Marjorie Bowen

I'm hoping you can keep the secret, because normally you're about as secure as a hymen in a south London comprehensive.

Jamie, *The Thick Of It*

Love, a cough, and the itch cannot be hid.

English proverb

The cat which isn't let out of the bag often becomes a skeleton in the cupboard.

Falconer Madan

—Do you have any skeletons in your cupboard?
—Dear boy, I can hardly close the door.

Interviewer and Alan Clark, MP

There are no secrets better kept than the secrets that everybody guesses.

George Bernard Shaw

An empty envelope that is sealed contains a secret.

Stanislaw J. Lec

LETTER

If you want to discover your true opinion of anybody, observe the impression made on you by the first sight of a letter from him.

Arthur Schopenhauer

I love getting mail. Just the fact that someone licked a stamp just for you is very reassuring.

Thomas Magnum, *Magnum P.I.*

A shocking thing to admit, but I begin to value my correspondents according to whether the stamps on their envelopes are cancelled or not. A handy tip... don't peel the stamp from the envelope, peel the envelope away from the stamp.

D.J. Enright

Always serve letters with a cup of tea and a footstool. Celebrate 'the reading' slowly. It is irreverent to read a letter fast.

Macrina Wiederkehr, *A Tree Full of Angels*

He'd hold a letter up to the light to see if there was a cheque inside; if not, he'd toss it into the wastebasket.

Robert N. Linscott, on William Faulkner

This is a free country. Folks have a right to send me letters, and I have a right not to read them.

William Faulkner

I would rather lay a pipeline or dig a grave than write a letter.

Edna St Vincent Millay

It is well to write love letters. There are certain things for which it is not easy to ask your mistress for face to face, like money, for instance.

Henri de Régnier

I just wish, when neither of us has written to my husband's mother, I don't feel so much worse about it than he does.

Katharine Whitehorn

Excuse me for not answering your letter sooner. I have been so busy not answering letters lately that I couldn't get around to not answering yours in time.

Groucho Marx

Never ask two questions in a business letter. The reply will discuss the one in which you are least interested and say nothing about the other.

Brian J. Weed

There ought to be a law against computers writing letters to people.

Lewis Grizzard

The post-office is a wonderful establishment! The regularity and dispatch of it! If one thinks of all that it has to do, and all that it does so well, it is really astonishing!

Jane Austen, *Emma*

—How does a funeral director sign his correspondence?
—Yours eventually.

Anon

TELEPHONE

Telephone? It's three-thirty in the blessed AM! Even the roosters are comatose!

Colonel Sherman T. Potter, *M*A*S*H*

[*on the phone*] You want to know where you can get a hold of Mrs Potter? I don't know, she's awfully ticklish.

Groucho Marx

The telephone is a good way to talk to people without having to offer them a drink.

Fran Lebowitz

Imagine how weird phones would look if your mouth was nowhere near your ears.

Steven Wright

Having a mobile phone is the technological equivalent of lying on the bed with your legs wide open all the time.

Anon

Today the ringing of the telephone takes precedence over everything. It reaches a point of terrorism, particularly at dinnertime.

Niels Diffrient

You never know, it could be somebody important.

Queen Elizabeth II, to a woman whose mobile rang as they chatted

The marvellous thing about mobile phones is that, wherever you are, whatever you are doing, you can keep them switched off so no one will bother you.

Guy Browning

Bluetooth headset users...you're not the Chief Communications Officer of the Starship *Enterprise*. You're a shoe salesman asking your mom if you can bring over your laundry.

Bill Maher

The First Law of Mobile Phone Etiquette: the volume with which an individual speaks into the phone is in inverse proportion to that individual's personal importance.

Geoffrey Horton

The Second Law of Mobile Phone Etiquette: the length of the call is in inverse proportion to the meaningful content.

Richard Polkinghorne

Never say anything on the phone that you wouldn't want your mother to hear at your trial.

Sydney Biddle Barrows

My relationship remains stable. Just me, the boyfriend and his BlackBerry. It's a bit like having a 'To do' list as your love rival.

Julian Clary

I use phone boxes. I think that it's only me and pimps that still do... You never have to queue.

Carolyn Braby

There are worse things than getting a call for a wrong number at 4am. It could be a right number.

Doug Larson

This bloke I met texted me, and I texted him back, but then he didn't text me again till the next day. 'Sorry I didn't text you back earlier,' he said, 'but my bat died.' I said, 'Really? I didn't know you had a bat.' He said, 'I don't. I was talking about my battery.'

Chantelle Houghton, *Celebrity Big Brother 4*

Personally, I'm waiting for Caller IQ.
Sandra Bernhard

Oh, how often I wished that Thomas A. Watson had laid a restraining hand on Alexander Graham Bell's arm and said to him: 'Let's not and say we did.'

Jean Mercier

By inventing the telephone, we've damaged the chances of telepathy.

Dorothy M. Richardson

PUBLIC SPEAKING

Ladies and gentlemen – and I guess that takes in most of you...

Groucho Marx

Ladies, gentlemen, and any transgendered species.

Data, *Star Trek Nemesis*

Desperately accustomed as I am to public speaking...

Noël Coward

This speech is a bit like my tee shot. I don't know where it's going.

José María Olazábal

Speeches are like babies – easy to conceive but hard to deliver.

Pat O'Malley

There are only two things more difficult than making an after-dinner speech: climbing a wall which is leaning toward you, and kissing a girl who is leaning away from you.

Winston Churchill

I have just got a new theory of eternity.

Albert Einstein, listening to a long-winded speech

The shortest distance between two jokes makes a perfect speech.

O.A. Battista

On occasions of this kind there are two speeches which I can make; one is short and one is long. The short one is 'Thank you', the long one is 'Thank you very much'. Now that I have acquainted you with the content of both speeches I see no reason for making either.

Gordon Hewart

Ian McEwan…rose to make his speech: 'Hegel said that at the age of 50 no man should speak for longer than he can make love.' He then sat down.

Steve Bird

NEWS – GENERAL

News isn't news anymore. It's hour-by-hour warnings.

Paul Harvey

It's not the world that's got so much worse but the news coverage that's got so much better.

G.K. Chesterton

If a tree falls in the forest and it isn't on the six o'clock news, did it actually fall?

Kevin Sweeney

If it's in the news, don't worry about it. The very definition of 'news' is 'something that hardly ever happens'.

Bruce Schneier

The news on an ordinary day is a strange assembly that swoops down on one's life like cousins from Oslo one has never seen before, will never see again, and who, between planes, thought they would call to say hello.

Roger Rosenblatt

To a philosopher all news, as it is called, is gossip, and they who edit and read it are old women over their tea.

Henry David Thoreau

Speculation: news you can use, eventually.

Jon Stewart

When we hear news we should always wait for the sacrament of confirmation.

Voltaire

NEWSPAPERS & JOURNALISM

—What do you do for a living?
—I work for the United Press.
—Do you do trousers?

Groucho Marx and Journalist

I call 'journalism' everything that will be less interesting tomorrow than today.

André Gide

Marmalade dropper: a news item in a morning paper which is so shocking that it causes the reader to drop their morning toast. The US equivalent was a *muffin choker*.

Susie Dent, *The Language Report*

POPE ELOPES

A marmalade dropper

Heard a report about Lindsay Lohan getting busted with coke in her car. That's a story? Call me when they find a book in her car.

Dave Attell

Read the sports section first every morning. It talks more about mankind's successes, while other parts of the paper talk about mankind's problems or failures.

Michael Milken

You ever read an article and at the bottom, it says 'continued on page 6'? I'm, like, 'Not for me! I'm done. Why don't you stop bossing me around?'

Jim Gaffigan

Lyndon B. Johnson scrutinized the daily papers like a playwright for whom each night of his life was a new opening.

Dick Goodwin

Mrs Thatcher never read a newspaper... She did not think she had the time.

Kenneth Clarke

I sometimes think our Minister doesn't believe that he exists unless he reads about himself in the paper.

Sir Humphrey Appleby, Yes, Minister

Lady Middleton...exerted herself to ask Mr Palmer if there was any news in the paper. 'No, none at all,' he replied, and read on.

Jane Austen, Sense and Sensibility

—Mr Coward, have you anything to say to *The Sun*?
—Shine!

Reporter and Noël Coward

My press relations will be minimum information given with maximum politeness.

Jacqueline Kennedy

He will eat you up, sick you out and grout his fucking wet room with you!

Jamie, preparing a junior government minister for
an interview with Jeremy Paxman, The Thick of It

The trouble with interviewers is that they actually *listen* to you. All your life you grapple for the other person's attention, and when you finally get it, it's alarming.

Cynthia Buchanan

I don't mind a microscope but, boy, when they use a proctoscope, that's going too far.

President Richard Nixon, on the press

TELEVISION NEWS

Who do you support? Mark's Israel. I'm Palestine. Makes the news more interesting.

Jeremy Osborne, *Peep Show*

News anchors used to be just pretty enough that you could spend a half hour a night getting informed, but now they're so hot I just wanna stay home, draw a steamy bath and inform the shit out of myself.

Samantha Bee, *The Daily Show*

Here is the news: a man who was attempting to walk around the world drowned today on the first leg of his journey, which would have taken him from San Francisco to Honolulu.

George Carlin

Television is to news what bumper stickers are to philosophy.

President Richard Nixon

If TV had covered the crucifixion, the cameras would have packed it in just before the third day.

Oliver Pritchett

When there was a disaster, it used to be that people went to church and all held hands... Now the minute anything happens they run to CNN.

Don Hewitt

Just because your voice reaches halfway around the world doesn't mean you are wiser than when it reached only to the end of the bar.

Edward R. Murrow, US broadcaster

[*angry TV executive to news broadcaster*] When you quote a Presidential candidate, Gorman, you do not – I repeat – do not roll your eyes.

James Stevenson, cartoon caption

We don't just have egg on our face. We have omelette all over our suits.

Tom Brokaw, NBC broadcaster, after the network prematurely broke the results of the US Election in 2000

In 1990, when *The Antiques Roadshow* was dropped for live coverage of the release of Nelson Mandela, more than 500 disgusted antiques lovers called the BBC to register their displeasure at being forced to watch history in the making.

Neil Armstrong, reporter

You know the really great thing about television? If something important happens, anywhere in the world, night or day, you can always change the channel.

Rev. Jim Ignatowski, *Taxi*

CHARACTER & HUMAN NATURE

CHARACTER
– GENERAL

—Can you tell me anything about yourself that might make me like you?
—But why would I care whether you like me?

Tessa Corbyn and Charles Saatchi

He's really a very nice guy. He'd give you the scales right off his back.

Alex Reiger, *Taxi*

He's the kind of guy who can brighten a room by leaving it.

Milton Berle

He reminded me of the Irishman's description of soda water: 'It was a tumbler of piss with a fart in it.'

Abraham Lincoln

He left a bad taste in my mind.

Geraldine Endsor Jewsbury

I'll tell you what kind of guy I was. If you ordered a boxcar full of sons-of-bitches and opened the door and only found me inside, you could consider the order filled.

Robert Mitchum

You can't please everyone, or you'd be Cat Deeley.

Alan Carr

There are people whose society I find delicious; but when I sit alone and think of them, I shudder.

Logan Pearsall Smith

I can safely say Michael Winner was one of the most bombastic, offensive, bloody-minded, arrogant pains in the backside imaginable. Which is probably why we get on so well.

Piers Morgan

He's such a quiet person that the night the Dodgers won the World Series he went out and painted the town beige.

Vin Scully, on Burt Hooton, Los Angeles Dodger

I've read that Dirk Bogarde's cruel streak can be attributed to his fight for acceptance as an actor, as a homosexual man, and as a writer. And all the time I thought it was just because he's quite an unpleasant fellow.

Michael Hordern

Your opinion of others is apt to be their opinion of you.

B.C. Forbes

Eighteen holes of match play will teach you more about your foe than will 18 years of dealing with him across a desk.

Grantland Rice

EGO

When I think of me, I smile.

Jim Ignatowski, *Taxi*

The capacity to admire others is not my most fully developed trait.

Henry Kissinger

Egotism is the anaesthetic that dulls the pain of stupidity.

Frank Leahy

We're all here for the same reason: to love me.

Barry Manilow, to fans at a concert in New York

An ego that can crack crystal at a distance of twenty feet.

John Cheever, on Yevgeny Yevtushenko

Marginally cockier than Idi Amin.

Jasper Gerard, on Piers Morgan

—You think you're God!
—I gotta model myself after someone.

Yale and Isaac Davis, *Manhattan*

Part of me suspects I'm a loser, and part of me thinks I'm God Almighty.

John Lennon

I'm not like John Lennon, who thought he was the great Almighty. I just think I'm John Lennon.

Noel Gallagher

The height of conceit: a flea, floating down the river with a hard-on, whistling for the drawbridge to open.

Anon

We go on fancying that each man is thinking of us, but he is not; he is like us: he is thinking of himself.

Charles Reade

It is more fun contemplating somebody else's navel than your own.

Arthur Hoppe

BORES & BOREDOM

If you have anything to tell me of importance, for God's sake begin at the end.

Sara Jeannette Duncan

Frank, you are the ten most boring people I know.

Captain John 'Trapper' McIntyre, *M*A*S*H*

Listening to him is like lying in your own coffin, hearing rainwater seep through the cracks.

Charlie Brooker

He is so dull that even ditchwater is thinking of lodging a libel action.

Ann Treneman, on Des Browne, MP

That man is such a bore. I haven't had my hearing aid open to him for years.

Bernard Baruch

I find that a most effective way of quelling bores is simply to say, suddenly and irrelevantly 'Now, Singapore – does that mean anything to you?'

Peter Ustinov

Everybody is somebody's bore.

Osbert Sitwell

ANGER & ARGUMENT

I had an interesting morning; I got into an argument with my Rice Krispies. I distinctly heard, 'Snap, crackle, fuck you!'

George Carlin

He loses his temper on Monday and doesn't find it again until Friday.

Civil Servant, on John Prescott

He's a guy who every now and then loses it so badly he needs sat nav to find his own nipples.

Jamie, *The Thick Of It*

I am righteously indignant; *you* are annoyed; *he* is making a fuss about nothing.

New Statesman magazine

Never start an argument at a dinner table; the person who isn't hungry is sure to win.

Evan Esar

—I was a bit short with Pauline – bit her head off.
—She'll grow a new one.

Sharon and Dennis Rickman, *EastEnders*

There are two theories to arguing with a woman. Neither one works.

Anon

Women are repeatedly accused of taking things personally. I cannot see any other honest way of taking them.

Marya Mannes

Unlike your thighs, your argument doesn't retain water.

Jack McFarland, to Karen Walker, *Will and Grace*

—We might consider trying to reach a compromise.
—Do I look French to you ?

Francis and Otto, *Malcolm in the Middle*

She held grudges till they died of old age, then had them stuffed and mounted.

David Weber, *Field of Dishonor*

I've had a few arguments with people, but I never carry a grudge. You know why? While you're carrying a grudge, they're out dancing.

Buddy Hackett

Never pick a quarrel – even when it's ripe.

Arnold H. Glasow

Do not argue with a spouse who is packing your parachute.

Anon

—When I get mad at you, you never fight back. How do you control your anger?
—I clean the toilet bowl.
—How does that help?
—I use your toothbrush.

Husband and Wife

RIGHT & WRONG

If you're going to do something wrong, at least enjoy it.

Leo Rosten

Most of the trouble on this planet is caused by people who must be right.

William Burroughs

The more you are in the right, the more natural that everyone else should be bullied into thinking likewise.

George Orwell

It grieves me deeply to find out how frequently and how violently wrong I can be – it doesn't seem reasonable somehow.

Dorothy Parker

It infuriates me to be wrong when I know I'm right.

Molière

If there is one thing worse than being wrong, it's being right with nobody listening.

Flo Capp

It is easier to forgive a nation for being wrong than to forgive a man for being right.

Stanislaw J. Lec

My father...never told me the difference between right and wrong; now, I think that's why I remain so greatly in his debt.

John Mortimer

People don't ever seem to realise that doing what's right's no guarantee against misfortune.

William McFee

Always do right. This will gratify some people, and astonish the rest.

Mark Twain

GOOD & BAD

People are divided into the goods and the bads. The thing is not to be caught with the goods.

Mae West

Good girls go to heaven – bad girls go everywhere.

Helen Gurley Brown

On the whole, human beings want to be good, but not too good, and not quite all the time.

George Orwell

In my family, goodness is just badness before it had something to drink.

Christopher Titus, *Titus*

I knew a man who neither drank, smoked, nor rode a bicycle. Living frugally, saving his money, he died early, surrounded by greedy relatives. It was a great lesson to me.

John Barrymore

If I repent of anything, it is very likely to be my good behaviour.

Henry David Thoreau

I have always found that so-called bad people gain in one's estimation when one gets to know them better, and good people decline.

Georg Christoph Lichtenberg

To be good is noble; but to show others how to be good is nobler and no trouble.

Mark Twain

They say the good die young. Generalissimo Francisco Franco was 82.

Richard Aregood

BELIEFS

There are two things that will be believed of any man whatsoever, and one of them is that he has taken to drink.

Booth Tarkington

We believe that electricity exists, because the electric company keeps sending us bills for it.

Dave Barry

There is no proposition, no matter how foolish, for which a dozen Nobel signatures cannot be collected.

Daniel S. Greenberg

You've gotta be a little sceptical, otherwise you end up believing in everything – UFOs, elves, income tax rebates.

Adrian Monk, *Monk*

I believe everything. It saves one such a world of bore from intelligent people who are anxious to explain things you doubt about.

Shirley Brooks

I doubt everything, even my own doubt.

Gustave Flaubert

He who believes in nothing still needs a girl to believe in him.

Eugen Rosenstock-Huessy

ASTROLOGY

Gypsy: a person who is willing to tell your fortune for a small portion of it.

Ambrose Bierce

—The medium will look at your aura. She'll say, 'Is there anybody there?' And then there's usually an eerie silence.
—It's like when I try to call the Gas Board.

Cissie and Ada, aka Roy Barraclough and Les Dawson

A belief in astrology is based on two premises: 1) That a small handful of the infinite number of gravitational masses of cosmic gas, billions of light years away... exert a direct influence on the lives...of one of the 50 million species...on one planet, in one solar system... 2) That the best person to interpret the effects is Russell Grant.

The Mary Whitehouse Experience

Groucho Marx was once coaxed into attending a séance. He sat, quiet and respectful, as the Swami stared into a crystal ball... After a long spell of omniscience the sorcerer intoned: 'There is time for one more question.' Groucho asked it: 'What is the capital of North Dakota?'

Leo Rosten

A banker's wife was having her fortune told. The fortune-teller gazed into her crystal ball and said solemnly: 'Prepare yourself for widowhood. Your husband is about to meet a violent end.' The wife sighed heavily and said: 'Will I be acquitted?'

Anon

TRUTH & LIES

Mother always said that honesty was the best policy, and money isn't everything. She was wrong about other things too.

Gerald Barzan

Yes, even I am dishonest. Not in many ways, but in some. Forty-one, I think it is.

Mark Twain

The ability to tell lies varies with the individual. For example, a short-armed fisherman isn't nearly as big a liar as a long-armed one.

Anon

Bullshit? Or bullfact?

John Oliver

Express a mean opinion of yourself occasionally; it will show your friends that you know how to tell the truth.

Ed Howe

All cruel people describe themselves as paragons of frankness.

Tennessee Williams

The only appropriate reply to the question, 'Can I be frank?' is 'Yes, if I can be Barbara.'

Fran Lebowitz

In human relations kindness and lies are worth a thousand truths.

Graham Greene

To reach the truth, the French subtract, the Germans add, and the English change the subject.

Peter Ustinov

No one ever tells the truth about fornication or cash. In these two fields, the ego is too deeply involved for truthfulness to be possible.

Malcolm Muggeridge

He sometimes told the truth – when his invention flagged.

Max Beerbohm

The truth is more important than the facts.

Frank Lloyd Wright

A sexually frustrated young girl sat on Pinocchio's nose and said, 'Now lie to me. Now tell me the truth. Now lie to me. Now tell me the truth.'

Paul Krassner

The secret of life is to appreciate the pleasure of being terribly, terribly deceived.

Oscar Wilde

SMELLS

I saw this nature show about how the male elk douses himself in urine to smell sweeter to the opposite sex. What a coincidence!

Jack Handey

—Eureka!
—You donna smella so good yourself!

Friend and Chico Marx

A hint of raw sourdough dough in a vat of mayonnaise that was in a trunk of a 70s car for the summer.

Sarah Silverman, sniffing Richard Christy's scrotum

—This perfume costs $400 an ounce.
—For that price it oughta smell like money.

Bob Hope and Jimmy Durante

'Where should one use perfume?' a young woman asked. 'Wherever one wants to be kissed.'

Coco Chanel

She smelled the way the Taj Mahal looks by moonlight.

Raymond Chandler, *The Little Sister*

My cologne is distilled from the bilge-water of Rupert Murdoch's yacht.

Jack Donaghy, *30 Rock*

Hay smells different to lovers and horses.

Stanislaw J. Lec

If you want to get rid of stinking odours in the kitchen, stop cooking.

Erma Bombeck

VOICE

The voice is a second face.

Gerard Bauer

Anthony Hopkins's voice is beautiful, mellifluous; when he talks it's like being dusted with deeply perfumed talcum powder.

Sally Weale

If marble could speak, it would have sounded like John Gielgud.

The Times obituary

If a swamp alligator could talk, he would sound like Tennessee Williams. His tongue seems coated with rum and molasses as it darts in and out of his mouth, licking at his moustache like a pink lizard.

Rex Reed

Everybody knows that if female genitalia could speak, it would sound exactly like Enya.

Dylan Moran

The tympanic resonance of Richard Burton's voice is so rich and overpowering that it could give an air of verse to a recipe for stewed hare.

John McPhee

His voice was intimate as the rustle of sheets.

Dorothy Parker

Mae West had a voice like a vibrating bed.

John Kobal

That wonderful voice of hers – strange, fey, mysterious, like a voice singing in the snow.

Louise Brooks, on Margaret Sullavan, actress

Any actress *with a deep voice* is always hailed by male critics for her wit, shrewdness, intellectuality – simply because she *sounds like a man*. Example, Bacall, Kate Hepburn, Marlene – all of them nice women but by no stretch of the imagination mental giants.

Kenneth Tynan

Men are attracted to a woman with a raspy voice. We think, 'Hey, maybe she's all done yelling.'

Moody McCarthy

My vocal cords are made of tweed – I give off an air of Oxford donnishness and old BBC wirelesses.

Stephen Fry

Prince Charles's vocal chords are plainly trying to strangle him. He may well become the first monarch to lose his head from the inside out.

A.A. Gill

I've been having elocution lessons. We learned to say: 'Peter Piper picked a peck of pickled pepper'. What a waste! How often does that sentence crop up in conversation?

Beryl Reid

OPTIMISM & PESSIMISM

—How's life treating you, Norm?
—Like it caught me in bed with its wife.

> Ernie 'Coach' Pantusso and Norm Peterson, *Cheers*

Things are going to get a lot worse before they get worse.

> Lily Tomlin

Far be it from me to rain on anybody's parade. That's my mother's job.

> Fran Fine, *The Nanny*

I'm one of the more pessimistic cats on the planet. I make Van Gogh look like a rodeo clown.

> Dennis Miller

Samuel Beckett was walking through a London park with a friend on a glorious day and seemed, most uncharacteristically, happy. The friend said it was the kind of sunny day that made one glad to be alive.
'I wouldn't go that far,' replied Beckett.

> John Heilpern

He must have read too many of his own plays. It gets him down, I expect.

> Noël Coward, when told of Samuel Beckett's pessimism

An optimist is a man who tells you to cheer up when things are going his way.

> Evan Esar

If ever I murdered someone, it might well be an optimist.

> G.K. Chesterton

I am an optimist. It does not seem too much use being anything else.

Winston Churchill

Being an optimist after you've got everything you want doesn't count.

Kin Hubbard

Things are going well, but my blood type is still very negative.

Richard Lewis

I'm a total pessimist. It's not that the glass is half empty. Someone stole the glass.

Joan Rivers

—God. How does a woman get so bitter?
—Observation.

Dedee Truitt and Lucia DeLury, *The Opposite of Sex*

She looked like something that might have occurred to Ibsen in one of his less frivolous moments.

P.G. Wodehouse, *Summer Lightning*

I don't consider myself a pessimist. I think of a pessimist as someone who is waiting for it to rain. And I feel soaked to the skin.

Leonard Cohen

I'd like to leave you with something positive, but I can't think of anything positive to say. Would you take two negatives?

Woody Allen

Then you reach the final torment: utter despair poisoned still further by a shred of hope.

Stendhal

That light we can see at the end of the tunnel... I think it's the taxman's torch.

Stu Francis

LUCK

'What are you so happy about?' a woman asked the 98-year-old man.
'I broke a mirror,' he replied. 'But that means 7 years of bad luck.'
'I know,' he said, beaming, 'Isn't it wonderful?'

Bob Monkhouse

He's very superstitious. He thinks it's unlucky to walk under a black cat.

Max Kauffmann

Luck? If the roof fell in and he was sitting in the middle of the room, everybody else would be buried and a gumdrop would drop in his mouth.

Leo Durocher, on Dizzy Dean

The novelist was in his late forties, tall, reddish, and looked as if life had given him an endless stream of two-timing girlfriends, five-day drunks and cars with bad transmissions.

Richard Brautigan, Revenge of the Lawn

If Dolly Parton had triplets, he'd be the one on the bottle.

Bernard Manning

He is so unlucky that he runs into accidents which started to happen to somebody else.

Don Marquis

You know it's going to be a bad day if you wake up with your water bed busted – and you ain't got a water bed.

Jan Murray

The rabbit's foot is a more efficient lucky charm if it comes from a rabbit that's been fed four-leaf clover.

Pierre Légaré

Depend on the rabbit's foot if you will, but remember it didn't work for the rabbit.

R.E. Shay

HAPPINESS & SADNESS

—What has four legs and one arm?
—A happy pit bull.

Anon

My idea of happiness is buying a piece of land large enough where I can shoot my .22 and not hit my neighbour's dog.

John Steinbeck

Happiness? A good cigar, a good meal, a good cigar and a good woman – or a bad woman; it depends on how much happiness you can handle.

George Burns

This obnoxious happiness has to end. It's just intolerable to live with.

Luke Marsden, *Big Brother 9*

If you were happy every day of your life you wouldn't be a human being. You'd be a game-show host.

Veronica Sawyer, Heathers

A person will be called to account on Judgement Day for every permissible thing he might have enjoyed but did not.

The Talmud

The secret to a happy life is to run out of cash and air at the same time.

Bobby Layne

You may speak of love and tenderness and passion, but real ecstasy is discovering you haven't lost your keys after all.

The Optimist magazine

I asked my girlfriend to tell me something that would make me happy and sad at the same time. She said I've got a bigger dick than my dad.

Popbitch.com

Never cry over spilt milk. It could've been whiskey.

Pappy Maverick, Maverick

Off-screen, Humphrey Bogart cried easily – Mary Philips once said that 'he cried at card tricks'.

Ann M. Sperber

Beware of men who cry. It's true that men who cry are sensitive to and in touch with their feelings, but the only feelings they tend to be sensitive to and in touch with are their own.

Nora Ephron

There, there, don't cry. Don't make the atmosphere damp – you know how it affects your succulents.

Pat Brandon, I Didn't Know You Cared

I've had a good snivel...and you do feel a bit better afterwards, like a radiator that has been bled.

Julie Burchill

If you're looking for sympathy you'll find it between 'shit' and 'syphilis' in the dictionary.

David Sedaris, *The Last Time You'll Hear From Me*

Remember you must die whether you sit about moping all day long or whether on feast days you stretch out in a green field, happy with a bottle of Falernian wine from your innermost cellar.

Horace, *Odes*

We're fools whether we dance or not, so we might as well dance.

Japanese proverb

MANNERS & BEHAVIOUR

MANNERS & ETIQUETTE – GENERAL

[*a knock at his door*] Come the fuck in or fuck the fuck off!

Malcolm Tucker, *The Thick of It*

—Mrs Blair…
—Oh, please call me Cherie.
—I'd rather not. It's not the way I've been brought up.

Princess Anne and Cherie Blair, *Speaking For Myself*

There goes a woman who knows all the things that can be taught and none of the things that cannot be taught.

Coco Chanel

Feet off the furniture, you Oxbridge twat, you're not in a punt now.

Malcolm Tucker, *The Thick of It*

Knickers: a definite yes, but not on show, please, ladies.

Dress code instruction for Royal Ascot, 2008

It's a myth that the British stand in orderly queues. Try getting the Number 159 outside Brixton station. It's like the last helicopter leaving Saigon. We queue until the bus arrives and then we stab and kill each other to get on.

Jeremy Hardy, *The News Quiz*

Never give up your seat for a lady. That's how I lost my job as a bus driver.

Milton Jones

In my mind, there is nothing so illiberal and so ill-bred, as audible laughter.

Lord Chesterfield

It is unusual to meet a working-class Liverpudlian who dresses for dinner, other than in the sense of putting on a shirt.

Terry Eagleton

Mr Phillips watches the inhabitant of a dark blue Vauxhall Astra...pick his nose, consider the product of his excavation, and then, with a decisive gourmandly air, eat it.

John Lanchester, *Mr Phillips*

—Do zombies eat popcorn with their fingers?
—No, they eat the fingers separately.

Anon

It is disgusting to pick your teeth; what is vulgar is to use a gold toothpick.

Louis Kronenberger

A man ought to carry himself in the world as an orange tree would if it could walk up and down in the garden, swinging perfume from every little censer it holds in the air.

Henry Ward Beecher

One sign of good manners is being able to put up with bad ones.

Texas Bix Bender

In America, people down South are incredibly polite. Even their war was civil.

Dudley Moore

In America, Southerners will be polite until they are angry enough to kill you.

John Shelton Reed

A general rule of etiquette is that one apologizes for the unfortunate occurrence, but the unthinkable is unmentionable.

Miss Manners

Only servants apologise.

Alan Clark, MP

Never thank anybody for anything, except a drink of water in the desert – and then make it brief.

Gene Fowler

Country manners dictate that even if someone phones you up to tell you your house is on fire, first they ask you how you are.

Alice Munro

Never ask old people how they are if you have anything else to do that day.

Joe Restivo

On receiving a detailed reply from a female student to the question of, 'How are you?' my somewhat Victorian Latin tutor explained: 'A lady is very well or dead.'

Katie Jarvis

A man asked an acquaintance how his wife was; then, suddenly remembering that she had died, he blurted out: 'Still in the same cemetery?'

Mauro Alves

GENTLEMAN

Good morning, gentlemen both.

Elizabeth I, addressing a group of 18 tailors

A gentleman is someone who always takes off his hat before striking
a lady.

Anon

An Australian gentleman is someone who gets out of the bath to piss in
the sink.

Anon

A gentleman should know how to carve, how to play the Stock Exchange
and how to spot a soft-centred chocolate at 100 yards.

Alastair Stewart, quoting his commanding officer

I always think of the Frenchman's answer when asked if a gentleman
must know Greek and Latin: 'No, but he must have forgotten them.'

Oliver Wendell Holmes

There were gentlemen and there were
seamen in the navy of Charles II.
But the seamen were not gentlemen;
and the gentlemen were not seamen.

Thomas Babington Macaulay

I may be a liar, but at least I'm a gentleman.

W.C. Fields

Make money and the whole world will conspire to call you a gentleman.

Mark Twain

LADY

I was taught three essentials for being a lady: no whisky before six, no diamonds before dinner and never go out with men in Jaguars. Believe me, it has stood me in very good stead.

Catherine Money

I was taught that a lady never bites bread, never cuts string and only ever wears white knickers.

David Morris-Marsham

One man's lady is another man's woman; sometimes, one man's lady is another man's wife.

Russell Lynes

A lady is someone whose name only appears in the newspapers three times in her life; when she is born, when she marries and when she dies.

Unidentified Correspondent to _The Times_

POLITE EUPHEMISMS FOR RELIEVING A WEDGIE

Attending to a debriefing

Sandra Hull

Saying no to crack

Tara Kennedy

Quelling the Boxer Rebellion

Chuck Smith

Helping a jockey come from behind

Ralph Scott

Pickin' cotton in the Deep South

Jean Sorensen

PUNCTUALITY

—In *Alice in Wonderland* who kept crying, 'I'm late, I'm late!'
—Alice – and her mother is sick about it.

Peter Marshall and Paul Lynde

—Hey, I'm finally here. Better late than never!
—That wouldn't be my choice.

Diane Chambers and Carla Tortelli, *Cheers*

I am a believer in punctuality though it makes me very lonely.

E.V. Lucas

I'm never on time for an appointment in England or America. In France I'm always on time because everybody else is always late; but in Spain, where nothing starts until midnight, I'm always early.

Peter Ustinov

I cannot cure myself of punctuality.

Rev. Sydney Smith

Punctuality is sacred at Buckingham Palace, but it is the height of bad manners to look at your watch while talking to someone. With a clock in every room, you don't need to.

Robert Hardman, on the 630 royal clocks

I almost had to wait.

Louis XIV

COMPLIMENTS & FLATTERY

What I should have said: Thank you.
What I did say: It's really a mousey brown, but I use Stardust Blonde No.4 and henna for body.

Anne Scott

When a man makes a woman his wife, it's the highest compliment he can pay her, and it's usually the last.

Helen Rowland

Try praising your wife – even if it does frighten her at first.

Billy Sunday

I think the world of you – and you know what condition the world is in today.

Henny Youngman

K.: You don't say many nice things to me.
M.: Mm. But I mean all the things I don't say.

Kenneth Tynan

Nowadays we are all of us so hard up, that the only pleasant things to pay *are* compliments. They're the only things we *can* pay.

Oscar Wilde

I have always thought that if I were a rich man I would employ a professional praiser.

Osbert Sitwell

Flattery is never so agreeable as to our blind side; commend a fool for his wit, or a knave for his honesty, and they will receive you into their bosoms.

Henry Fielding

The most beautiful compliment I received was when a lady ran into me on a bicycle and said, 'I'm so sorry. I didn't see you.'

Luciano Pavarotti

Try not to be one of those people who find a slight in every compliment.

Max Rothman

—Basil!
—Coming, my little piranha fish.

Sybil and Basil Fawlty, *Fawlty Towers*

SWEARING

—What do fish say when they hit a concrete wall?
—Dam!

Dustin Godsey

Damn, blast, and two extra slices of buttered damn.

Stephen Fry, *A Bit of Fry and Laurie*

—I'm a bastard, the biggest bastard in the whole world.
—Julian, please, you're starting to make it sound like bragging.

Julian Winston and Toni Simmons, *Cactus Flower*

Christ on a bendy bus! Don't be such a fucking faff arse!

Malcolm Tucker, *In the Loop*

I cannot bear the language TV chefs use – they don't seem able to look at a plate of vegetables without accusing it of sexual activity.

Ann Widdecombe

Ineffable: describes someone you absolutely cannot swear in front of, such as the Queen Mum, or Martha Stewart.

Jessica Henig

I shall never use profanity except in discussing house-rent and taxes.

Mark Twain

My old man worked in profanity the way other artists might work in oils or clay. It was his true medium.

Ralphie Parker, *A Christmas Story*

—Is it not a bad example to your children and my children to swear as much as you do in public?
—Fuck, no.

Ben Hoffman and Bob Geldof

Pay Up or Fuck Off

Inscription on the swear-box of artists, Gilbert & George

When we use the F-word today, we are almost always expressing hostility toward somebody who has taken our parking space.

Dave Barry

With just the change of vowel his second favourite term of abuse was cant.

Patrick Garland, on Rex Harrison

My wife loves the c-word. Sometimes, when the children are listening, she combines it with 'bastard' to create the word 'custard'.

Jeremy Clarkson

—What's your favourite swear word?
—Fuck.
—Fuck.
—Fuck.
—Douche-bag.

Interviewer and Ozzie, Sharon, Jack and Kelly Osbourne

Life's disappointments are harder to take when you don't know any swear words.

Calvin, *Calvin and Hobbes*

No one is ever capable of swearing properly in any language other than their own.

Ben Elton, *Stark*

To tell a man to go to hell and to make him go are two different propositions.

President Lyndon B. Johnson

MODERN CURSES

May you never see your eye doctor again, after your laser surgery.

Tom Witte

May Fox TV devote a half-hour show to you called *When Colonoscopies Go Bad*.

Bird Waring

May your elderly billionaire father marry a young woman with huge breasts.

Helene Haduch

May your therapist name his yacht after you.

Jonathan Alen Marks

May that ridiculous Internet urban legend about the stolen organs actually happen to you in Guatemala.

Stephen Dudzik

May your mother be the only respondent to your personal ads.

Roy Highberg

May your doctors say: 'Well, the *good* news is that you have a fatal disease...'

Dot Yufer

May it be that wherever you are, whatever you do, you can't get the song 'Seasons in the Sun' out of your head. Not the Jacques Brel original, the one by the idiot Terry Jacks. You know the one.

Rosemary Walsh

May you die a rock star's death, without a rock star's life.

Tom Witte

INSULTS

If a man's character is to be abused, say what you will, there's nobody like a relation to do the business.

William Makepeace Thackeray

Without being unduly vulgar, my ex-husband was so far up his own ass, he could polish his own ulcers.

Hermione Gingold

You think I'm an asshole now? You should've seen me when I was drunk.

John Cougar Mellencamp

He accused me of the thing men think is the most insulting thing they can accuse you of – wanting to be married.

Nora Ephron, *Heartburn*

Hearst married a prostitute, and then gradually dragged her down to his own level.

Moorfield Storey, on William Randolph Hearst

How *Sex and the City* are we three right now? I'm Samantha, you're Charlotte, and you're the lady at home who watches it.

Jenna Maroney, *30 Rock*

What an interesting person you probably are.

Dame Edna Everage

'Ha!' I said. And I meant it to sting.

P.G. Wodehouse, *Very Good, Jeeves!*

I'd love to stop and chat to you but I'd rather have Type 2 diabetes.

Malcolm Tucker, *The Thick of It*

SPORTS – GENERAL

Man, I'm so bad at sports, they used to pick me after the white kids.
Caretaker (Chris Rock), *The Longest Yard*

If there's one thing the British can still do well it is run sporting events – run them but not win them, of course.
Ravi Tikoo

It is a curious fact that you can give a...man some kind of ball and he will be thoroughly content.
Judson P. Philips

I look at Colin Meads and see a great big sheep farmer who carried the rugby ball in his hands as though it was an orange pip.
Bill McClaren

My goodness, that wee ball's gone so high there'll be snow on it when it comes down.
Bill McClaren, commentating during a rugby match

I'm no hod carrier but I would be laying bricks if Jonah Lomu was running at me.
Bill McClaren, on the New Zealand rugby player

Cockfighting has always been my idea of a great sport – two armed entrées battling to see who'll be dinner.
P.J. O'Rourke

Playing snooker gives you firm hands and helps to build up character. It is the ideal recreation for dedicated nuns.
Archbishop Luigi Barbarito

Snooker's not a sport really, is it? It's just standing around with a wooden stick.
Lemmy Kilmister, of heavy metal band, Motörhead

Watching gymnastics is just like paedophilia for cowards.

Frankie Boyle, *Mock the Week*

Driving a racing car is like dancing with a chainsaw.

Cale Yarborough

To achieve anything in this game, you must be prepared to dabble on the boundary of disaster.

Stirling Moss, on motor racing

Elite sports people are a fascinating breed: they are brilliant at what they do, but they have to be stupid enough to think it matters.

Beverley Turner, wife of James Cracknell, Olympic gold medallist

Who would want to watch a sport where the slow-motion replays are actually faster than the original action?

Jasper Carrott, on crown green bowling

I wasn't a very athletic boy. I was once lapped in the long jump.

Ronnie Corbett

The New York City Marathon is the only marathon in the world where the starter's gun gets return fire.

David Letterman

Six of us collapsed on top of each other, with a rhinoceros at the bottom. To cap it all, I was overtaken by a Womble.

Peregrine Armstrong-Jones, on his London marathon run

HORSE RACING

Is it just me or does John McCririck look a bit like a Womble?

Charlie Brooker

The Grand National is a moment when the whole nation comes together – like the opening of a Richard Curtis movie or the manhunt for a serial killer.

Manny Bianco, *Black Books*

I went to Huntingdon and took my grandson, Jake, who is 8; he sat in my car…reading form. 'What was I going to back?' Favourites, I explained. 'I confidently expect at least four favourites to win and shall have ten four-horse accumulators at £20. Then, on the way home, we can stop and use the winnings to buy a hotel and have afternoon tea in it.'

Clement Freud

Anybody who finds it easy to make money on the horses is probably in the dog food business.

Franklin P. Jones

Owning a racehorse is probably the most expensive way of getting on to a racecourse for nothing.

Clement Freud

The way his horses ran could be summed up in a word. Last. He once had a horse who finished ahead of the winner of the 1942 Kentucky Derby. Unfortunately, the horse started running in the 1941 Kentucky Derby.

Groucho Marx

If Sun Pageant were human, she'd be a model on page three of *The Times*, not *The Sun* – she's got class, you see.

Mark Rimmell

French filly, Shawanda is the equine equivalent of the woman with a hat over one eye, a cigarette holder, and revolver in her stocking top.

Richard Edmondson

Trainer, Vincent O'Brien was meticulous in his attention to detail...
When he thought that The Minstrel, winner of the 1977 Derby, would be upset by the noise of the Epsom crowd, he had cotton wool stuffed in the horse's ears.

Daily Telegraph

Vincent O'Brien once said that the real beauty of having Lester Piggott ride for you in the Derby was that it got him off the other fellow's horse.

John Karter

A volcano trapped in an iceberg.

Hugh McIlvanney, on Lester Piggott

I learned from Lester Piggott's great discipline. He would lock away his Yorkie bars and cigars and when he unlocked the cupboard he would take out one piece of Yorkie at a time.

Walter Swinburn, fellow jockey

That is the first time she has had 14 hands between her legs.

John Francombe, watching Sarah Ferguson, the Duchess of York, compete in a horse race marathon in Qatar

Jockey, author, broadcaster, *Sun* newspaper columnist, womaniser – the man must be scared to unzip his flies in case the next thing he touches also turns to gold.

John Anthony, on John Francombe

Had he been on the rails at Balaclava he would have kept pace with the Charge of the Light Brigade, listing the fallers in precise order and describing the riders' injuries before they hit the ground.

Hugh McIlvanney, on Peter O'Sullevan, commentator

CRICKET

The aim of English cricket is, in fact, mainly to beat Australia.

Jim Laker

I'm not interested in sport. I'm interested in cricket. I'm always surprised to find cricket books in the library in the sports section, next to football.

John Minnion

How can you tell your wife you are just popping out to play a match and then not come back for five days?

Rafael Benitez

Of course it's frightfully dull – that's the whole point. Any game can be exciting – football, dirt track racing, roulette… To go to cricket to be thrilled is as stupid as to go to a Chekhov play in search of melodrama.

Alexander Whitehead, *The Final Test*

The Sri Lankan batsmen found the spin bowler harder to read than *Finnegan's Wake*.

Peter Roebuck

Clive Lloyd hits him high away over mid-wicket for four, a stroke of a man knocking a thistle top off with a walking stick.

John Arlott

There was a slight interruption there for athletics.

Richie Benaud, after a streaker invaded the field at Lord's

I thought they were only allowed two bouncers in one over.

Bill Frindall, on a female streaker at Lord's

Watching the Aussies at cricket is like a porn movie: you always know what's going to happen in the end.

Mick Jagger

The traditional dress of the Australian cricketer is the baggy green cap on the head and the chip on the shoulder. Both are ritualistically assumed.

Simon Barnes

Merv Hughes's mincing run-up resembles someone in high heels and a panty girdle chasing after a bus.

Martin Johnson

Shane Warne is thicker than a complete set of Wisden yearbooks.

Matt Price

Why is Phil Tufnell the most popular man in the team? Is it the Manuel factor, in which the most helpless member of the cast is most affectionately identified with?

Mike Brearley

Richie Benaud has the watchfulness of a gentlemanly salamander…
To see him in the flesh is to appreciate the extent to which the voice is an extension of the man.

Steve Jacobi

If I knew I was going to die today, I'd still want to hear the cricket scores.

J.H. Hardy

FOOTBALL

One perishing morning, as the sleet stretched horizontally across Liverpool's training ground, Bill Shankly glanced up at the leaden Merseyside sky and told a group of shivering players: 'It's great to be alive. The grass is green and there's a ball. What more could a man want?'

Stephen Kelly

Football is a simple game; 22 men chase a ball for 90 minutes and at the end, the Germans win.

Gary Lineker, *attrib.*

The first ninety minutes are the most important.

Bobby Robson

Why is there only one ball for 22 players? If you gave a ball to each of them, they'd stop fighting for it.

Football Widow

It's very strange, isn't it, that you can't really tell the difference between the bar and the gents at most clubs?

Peter Cook

It was a very simple team talk. All I used to say was: 'Whenever possible, give the ball to George.'

Matt Busby, on George Best, while managing Manchester United

If you aren't sure what to do with the ball, just stick it in the net and we'll discuss your options afterwards.

Bill Shankly, to a striker

I'm not giving away any secrets to Milan; if I had my way I wouldn't even tell them the time of the kick-off.

Bill Shankly

In my time at Liverpool we always said we had the best two teams in Merseyside: Liverpool, and Liverpool Reserves.

Bill Shankly

Becoming promotions consultant to Wolverhampton Wanderers is like being asked to join the *Titanic* in mid-voyage.

Rachael Heyhoe-Flint

A football team is like a piano. You need 8 men to carry it and 3 who can play the damn thing.

Bill Shankly

Can you imagine what it would be like living in London if that bunch of precious, overpaid tossers win the World Cup?

John Humphrys, on England's football squad, 2002

—What would you be if you weren't a footballer?
—A virgin!

Reporter and Peter Crouch

I can't remember anything about my first-ever goal. It was against Oldham, Andy Goram was in goal, Alan Irvine crossed it for me and we won 3–2.

Ian Wright

There are kids out there who'd chop their legs off to play football for Brighton.

Robbie Savage

Dumfries is a lovely town but it has traditionally been to football what Reykjavik is to camel racing.

Michael Gove, on the successes of Queen of the South

I went to watch Spurs at White Hart Lane last week. I stayed until the very end of the game to avoid the traffic.

Frank Skinner

It's like a toaster, the ref's shirt pocket. Every time there's a tackle, up pops a yellow card.

Kevin Keegan

I never got booked because I never made a single tackle in my career.

Gary Lineker

The most intelligent bit of spectator violence I ever heard of happened at a football match in Brazil. An enraged spectator drew his gun and shot the ball.

John Cohen

—You've got to say that Tony Hateley's good in the air, Bill.
—Aye, so was Douglas Bader – and he had a wooden leg.

Tommy Docherty and Bill Shankly

Tom Finney would have been great in any team, in any match and in any age...even if he had been wearing an overcoat.

Bill Shankly

I shall continue to give Luton my support. In fact, I'm wearing it at this very moment. Some people think it's just the way I walk.

Eric Morecambe

I know this is a sad occasion, but I think that Dixie would be amazed to know that even in death he could draw a bigger crowd to Goodison than Everton on a Saturday afternoon.

Bill Shankly, Liverpool manager, at the funeral of legendary Everton player, Dixie Dean

God must have had a big game coming up.

Inscription on a wreath at Bobby Moore's funeral

GOLF

Have you ever noticed what golf spells backwards?

Al Boliska

They call it golf because all the other four-letter words were taken.

Ray Floyd

Golf is a game in which a ball – 1½ inches in diameter – is placed on a ball – 8,000 miles in diameter. The object being to hit the small ball…but not the larger.

John Cunningham

A golf ball is like a clock. Always hit it at 6 o'clock and make it go toward 12 o'clock. Just be sure you're in the same time zone.

Chi Chi Rodriguez

Imagine the ball has little legs, and chop them off.

Henry Cotton

Woodrow Wilson was a rather fidgety player who addressed the ball as if to reason with it.

Anon

Jim Furyk's swing is like an octopus falling out of a tree, or a man trying to kill a snake in a telephone booth.

David Feherty

My swing is so bad I look like a caveman killing his lunch.

Lee Trevino

I can make divots in which a small boy could get lost.

Lewis Grizzard

Golf...is not particularly a natural game. Like sword-swallowing, it has to be learned.

Brian Swarbrick

My goal is to play 72 holes someday without changing expression.

Jack Renner

The uglier a man's legs are, the better he plays golf – it's almost a law.

H.G. Wells

I can airmail the golf ball, but sometimes I don't put the right address on it.

Jim Dent

Golf tips are like aspirin. One may do you good, but if you swallow the whole bottle, you will be lucky to survive.

Harvey Penick

Keep on hitting it straight until the wee ball goes in the hole.

James Braid

—How can I get more distance on my tee shots?
—Hit it – and run backwards.

Amateur Golfer and Ken Venturi

I've hit more balls than Sir Elton John's chin this year, and still missed 16 cuts in a row.

David Feherty

I'm not saying my golf game went bad, but if I grew tomatoes, they'd come up sliced.

Miller Barber

—What should I take here?
—Well, sir, I recommend the 4:05 train.

Harry Vardon and Caddie

Once when I was golfing in Georgia, I hooked the ball into the swamp. I went in after it and found an alligator wearing a shirt with a picture of a little golfer on it.

Buddy Hackett

Two balls in the water. By God, I've got a good mind to jump in and make it four!

Simon Hobday

One of the advantages bowling has over golf is that you seldom lose a bowling ball.

Don Carter

At 15 we put down my bag to hunt for the ball, found the ball, lost the bag.

Lee Trevino, at Royal Birkdale

Tiger Woods hit a dangerous 3-wood approach to the green on the 18th, which runs along the Pacific at Pebble Beach. David Feherty stops him walking off and says, 'Tiger, great shot. But didn't you see that big blue thing to your left?'

Lance Barrow

I could never believe in a game where the one who hits the ball least wins.

Winston Churchill

Golf is like sex. Trying your hardest is the worst thing you can do.

Rick Reilly

I tried for years to slow my swing. Then all of a sudden it came – like whistling.

Tony Jacklin

That shot on eight just sort of landed on the green like a snowflake.

Sam Snead

I think golf is the hardest sport to play. One day you're up on Cloud Nine, and the next day you couldn't scratch a whale's belly.

Sam Snead

Some guys get so nervous playing for their own money, the greens don't need fertilizing for a year.

Dave Hill

I am so tense at times that I can hear the bees farting.

Mick O'Loughlin

Never bet with anyone you meet on the first tee who has a deep suntan, a one-iron in his bag, and squinty eyes.

Dave Marr

You can always spot an employee who's playing golf with his boss. He's the fellow who gets a hole-in-one and says, 'Oops!'

Bob Monkhouse

Your playing partner took more strokes than an eighth-grade schoolboy with a Victoria's Secret catalogue.

David Feherty

My golfing partner couldn't hit a tiled floor with a bellyful of puke.

David Feherty

I used to play golf with a guy who cheated so badly that he once had a hole in one and wrote down zero on the scorecard.

Bob Bruce

It is as easy to lower your handicap as it is to reduce your hat size.

Henry Beard

I got down to a nine handicap. The day I became a single digit, I called my agent and said: 'You have to look harder. I shouldn't be this good at golf.'

Jason Bateman, actor

That putt was so fast I don't think they mow the greens, I think they bikini wax 'em!

Gary McCord, at The Masters in Augusta

Some players would complain if they had to play on Dolly Parton's bedspread.

Jimmy Demaret

You can't trust anybody these days.

Peter Allis, after a player made the sign of the cross
before playing a bunker shot only to miss the ball completely

Golf: I hate it. No wonder Hitler died in a bunker.

Alan Coren, noted by Sandi Toksvig

If every golfer in the world, male and female, were laid end to end, I, for one, would leave them there.

Michael Parkinson

GOLF TERMS

BALL-STRIKING

An Arthur Scargill – a great strike but a poor result
A Paris Hilton – an expensive hole
A Princess Grace – should have taken a driver
A Princess Di – shouldn't have taken a driver
A Robin Cook – just died on the hill

An Adolf Hitler – taking two shots in a bunker
A Sally Gunnell – not pretty but a good runner
A Ladyboy – looks like an easy hole but all is not what it seems
A Glenn Miller – didn't make it over the water
An O.J. Simpson – somehow got away with it

PUTTING

A Dennis Wise – a nasty 5 footer
A Salman Rushdie – an impossible read
A Rock Hudson – thought it was straight, but it wasn't
A Cuban – need one more revolution
A Douglas Bader – nae legs
An Elton John – big bender that lips the rim
A Gynaecologist's assistant – just shaves the hole

BOXING

Boxing is…a celebration of the lost religion of masculinity all the more trenchant for its being lost.

Joyce Carol Oates

It's gonna be a thrilla, a chilla, and a killa, when I get the gorilla in Manila.

Muhammad Ali, on Joe Frazier

I'm so fast I could hit you before God gets the news.

Muhammad Ali

Not only do I knock 'em out, I pick the round.

Muhammad Ali

Everybody's got a plan – until he gets hit.

Mike Tyson

I'll never forget my first fight. All of a sudden I found someone I knew in the fourth row. It was me.

Henny Youngman

Sure the fight was fixed. I fixed it with a right hand.

George Foreman

The stubble on his chin even hurts you.

Glenn McCrory, on Mike Tyson

If only one of them would just say, 'I'm sorry.'

Joe Ancis, watching a boxing match on TV

The last time Frank Bruno fought Mike Tyson I had a bet on Frank, but I also had a bet on Elvis Presley sitting at ringside.

John H. Stracey

—Are you going to retire from boxing?
—It depends – just throw a punch at me.

Reporter and Lennox Lewis

—Prizefighter Stanley Ketchel's been shot!
—Tell 'em to start counting ten over him, and he'll get up.

Friend and Wilson Mizner

TENNIS

—What time does Sean Connery get to Wimbledon?
—Tennish.

Popbitch.com

If God had wanted me to play tennis, He would have given me less leg and more room to store the ball.

Erma Bombeck

Tennis: a middle-class version of professional wrestling.

John Ralston Saul

I always thought Tim Henman's racket had more personality than he did.

Edwina Currie

Like a Volvo, Björn Borg is rugged, has good after-sales service, and is very dull.

Clive James

—Who is the best doubles team in history?
—John McEnroe and anyone.

Reporter and Peter Fleming, who partnered
McEnroe to 7 Grand Slam doubles titles

Tennis should be played only in the long grass in the meadows – and in the nude.

George Bernard Shaw

It's not really a shorter skirt, I just have longer legs.

Anna Kournikova

Female tennis players must be able to control their grunting. Can't they just try and pretend that their parents are in the next room?

Jeremy Hardy, *The News Quiz*

—What's the key to the final?
—Win the last point.

Reporter and Jim Courier

BASEBALL

Baseball, it is said, is only a game. True. And the Grand Canyon is only a hole in Arizona. Not all holes, or games, are created equal.

George F. Will

I don't think I can be expected to take seriously a game which takes less than three days to reach its conclusion.

Tom Stoppard

Baseball is violence under wraps.

Willie Mays Jr.

Baseball is the only time a black man can wave a stick at a white man without starting a riot.

Rupert Anderson, *Mississippi Burning*

It isn't really the stars that are expensive. It's the high cost of mediocrity.

Bill Veeck, owner of the Chicago White Sox

Robert 'Lefty' Grove was a moody guy, a tantrum thrower like me, but when he punched a locker or something he always did it with his right hand. He was a careful tantrum thrower.

Ted Williams, on the left-handed pitcher

Robert 'Lefty' Grove only had one pitch – a fastball – but that's like saying that when Fred Astaire arrived in Hollywood, all he could do was dance.

Anon

Robert 'Lefty' Grove could throw a lamb chop past a wolf.

Bugs Baer

If Mike Scioscia raced his pregnant wife, he'd finish third.

Tommy Lasorda

If we hadn't won I would have jumped off a tall building. But the way I'm hitting, I wouldn't have hit the ground anyway.

Phil Garner

Hitting against Steve Carlton is like trying to drink coffee with a fork.

Willie Stargell

Being with a woman all night never hurt no professional baseball player. It's staying up all night looking for a woman that does him in.

Casey Stengel

Talking to Yogi Berra about baseball is like talking to Homer about the Gods.

A. Bartlett Giamatti

I never saw a ball hit so hard before or since. He was fat and old, but he still had that great swing. I can't forget that last one he hit off me. It's probably still going.

Guy Bush, pitcher, on Babe Ruth's last ever game

BASKETBALL

Any American boy can be a basketball star if he grows up, up, up.
Bill Vaughan

The rule was: 'No autopsy, no foul.'
Stewart Granger, on the pick-up games of his childhood

When I dunk, I put something on it. I want the ball to hit the floor before I do.
Darryl Dawkins, aka 'Chocolate Thunder'

A pressure game: when you look at a cheerleader and don't notice her body.
Al McGuire, basketball coach

Basketball, a game which won't be fit for people until they set the basket umbilicus-high and return the giraffes to the zoo.
Ogden Nash

WORK & BUSINESS

WORK

—What's the difference between your wife and your job?
—After three years your job still sucks.

Anon

I'm not really a cab driver. I'm just waiting for something better to come along. You know, like death.

Alex Rieger, *Taxi*

—Do you have a job?
—I'm an accountant.
—Chartered?
—Turf.

Penny Warrender and Vince Pinner, *Just Good Friends*

I was a house painter for five years. Five years. I didn't think I'd ever finish that damn house.

John Fox

I was a shepherd once, but I got fired because I always fell asleep during inventory.

John Mendoza

I used to have a job in the Kotex factory. I thought I was making mattresses for mice.

Ray Scott

Ninety-nine point nine per cent of the work of a professional bodyguard consisted of one activity: frowning.

Martin Amis, *Yellow Dog*

Vocation: any badly-paid job which someone has taken out of choice.

Mike Barfield, *Dictionary for our Time*

Never buy anything with a handle on it. It means work.

H. Allen Smith

I went for a job at one of the airlines. The interviewer asked me why I wanted to be a stewardess, and I told her it would be a great chance to meet men... She looked at me and said: 'But you can meet men anywhere.' I said, 'Strapped down?'

Martha Raye

I'm a poor candidate for espionage.

Dolly Parton

A lot of people complain about their dumb boss. What they don't realize is that they'd be out of a job if their dumb boss were any smarter.

Joey Adams

I hate my supervisor. Behind her desk it says, 'You don't have to be mad to work here, but it helps.' Mind you, she's written it in her own shit.

Alan Carr

—Griffin! Are you sleeping on the job?
—No. There's a bug in my eye and I'm trying to suffocate him.

Mr Weed and Peter Griffin, *Family Guy*

My husband always felt that marriage and a career don't mix. That is why he's never worked.

Phyllis Diller

My toughest job was being married to Barbra Streisand.

Elliott Gould

My theory is that the hardest work anyone ever does in life is to appear normal.

Edtv

IDLENESS

Laziness: the habit of resting before fatigue sets in.

Jules Renard

Believe me, you gotta get up early if you want to get out of bed.

Groucho Marx

I am not an early riser. The self-respect which other men enjoy in rising early I feel due to me for waking up at all.

William Gerhardie

I always like to have the morning well-aired before I get up.

Beau Brummell

He had once asked...what the old boy most liked in the morning. The reply was: 'Lying in bed on a summer morning, with the window open, listening to the church bells, eating buttered toast with cunty fingers.'

Henry Green

No man who is in a hurry is quite civilized.

Will Durant

I have seen slower people than I am – and more deliberate people than I am – and even quieter, and more listless, and lazier people than I am. But they were dead.

Mark Twain

I like the word 'indolence'. It makes my laziness seem classy.

Bern Williams

Few women and fewer men have enough character to be idle.

E.V. Lucas

I'm kind of lazy. I'm dating a pregnant woman.

Ron Richards

Never put off till tomorrow what you can do today. It may be made illegal by then.

Anon

PROBLEMS

It has been a nervous year and people have begun to feel like a Christian Scientist with appendicitis.

Tom Lehrer

Why can't life's problems hit us when we're 17 and know everything?

A.C. Jolly

If a man can see both sides of a problem, you know that none of his money is tied up in it.

Verda Ross

I have often wanted to drown my troubles, but I can't get my wife to go swimming.

President Jimmy Carter

The Queen rather likes things to go a bit wrong – then she copes.

Lady-in-Waiting, on Queen Elizabeth II

Many a problem will solve itself if you forget it and go fishing.

Olin Miller

Don't tell your problems to people: 80 per cent don't care, and the other 20 per cent are glad.

Lou Holtz

Personally, I always tell my troubles to my enemies. They're the only ones who really want to hear them.

Robert Orben

Remember that every life is a special problem which is not yours but another's and content yourself with the terrible algebra of your own.

Henry James

Sometimes the best you can do is move the turd to another pocket.

Scott Adams

That which does not kill us, only makes us stranger.

Æon Flux, *Æon Flux*

MISTAKES

Life is a maze in which we take the wrong turning before we have learned to walk.

Cyril Connolly

Doctors bury their mistakes. Lawyers hang them. But journalists put theirs on the front page.

Anon

To err is human, but to really screw things up requires a financial adviser.

Kathy Lette

All men make mistakes, but married men find out about them sooner.

Red Skelton

If I had to live my life again, I'd make all the same mistakes – only sooner.

Tallulah Bankhead

One of the blessings of being a humorist is that all your mistakes pass off as jokes.

Peter McArthur

—Tiny mistake? £75,000 wasted? Give me an example of a big mistake.
—Letting people find out about it.

Jim Hacker and Sir Humphrey Appleby, *Yes, Minister*

If life had a second edition, how I would correct the proofs.

John Clare, poet

Correction: the following typo appeared in our last bulletin: 'Lunch will be gin at 12:15.' Please correct to read: '12 noon.'

California Bar Association Newsletter

SUCCESS & FAILURE

My mother said: 'You won't amount to anything because you procrastinate.' I said: 'Just wait.'

Judy Tenuta

—What would you like to achieve before you die?
—World peace and a diet pill that really works.

Interviewer and Joan Rivers

I like when a woman has ambition. It's like seeing a dog wearing clothes.

Jack Donaghy, *30 Rock*

My goal is to be able to say, 'Fame and fortune just didn't bring me happiness.'

Lotus Weinstock

You've got a goal. I've got a goal. Now all we need is a football team.

Groucho Marx

If women can sleep their way to the top, how come they aren't there?

Ellen Goodman

You can only sleep your way to the middle.

Dawn Steel

I got what I have now through knowing the right time to tell terrible people when to go to hell.

Leslie Caron

You don't have to be nice to people on the way up if you're not planning to come back down.

Dan G. Stone

I'm a self-made man. Who else would help?

Oscar Levant

Leroy is a self-made man, which shows what happens when you don't follow directions.

Bill Hoest, cartoon caption

I was a pit bull on the pant leg of opportunity. I wouldn't let go.

George W. Bush

That's the way to get on in the world – by grabbing your opportunities. Why, what's Big Ben but a wrist-watch that saw its chance and made good.

P.G. Wodehouse, *The Small Bachelor*

Don't listen to those who say, 'You're taking too big a chance.' Michelangelo would have painted the Sistine floor, and it would surely be rubbed out by today.

Neil Simon

When eating an elephant, take one bite at a time.

Creighton W. Abrams

The secret of success is to know something nobody else knows.

Aristotle Onassis

The secrets of success are a good wife and a steady job. My wife told me.

Howard Nemerov

If at first you don't succeed... buy her another beer.

Slogan on T-shirt

If at first you do succeed – try to hide your astonishment.

Harry F. Banks

Success makes life easier. It doesn't make living easier.

Bruce Springsteen

On every summit you are on the brink of an abyss.

Stanislaw J. Lec

One evening when we were in Gerry's, which was predominantly a bar for journalists who liked a drink and actors who were out of work, somebody said: 'What is that terrible smell?' And Keith Waterhouse replied: 'Failure.'

Michael Parkinson

I got a sister who's got me beat in every way. She's 5ft 2". Her husband never has a drink until noon. And she's a beautician. I mean how do you compete with that?

Carla Tortelli, *Cheers*

I don't have any leadership qualities. In high school I was president of the German Club; nobody would listen to me. If you can't get Germans to follow orders, who will?

Felix Unger, *The Odd Couple*

Some people are so far behind in a race that they actually believe they're leading.

Corrado 'Junior' Soprano, *The Sopranos*

I feel about as useless as a mom's college degree.

Kenneth Parcell, *30 Rock*

Every man has one thing he can do better than anyone else – and usually it's reading his own handwriting.

G. Norman Collie

The penalty of success is to be bored by the attentions of people who formerly snubbed you.

Mary W. Little

—'To the victor belongs the spoils'.
—Why don't you get the fuck out of here before I shove your quotations book up your fat fuckin' ass!

Bobby Baccalieri and Tony Soprano, *The Sopranos*

AWARDS

Tonight is Oscars night... The night of nights. The nightiest night of them all.

Ben Elton, *Popcorn*

The Oscars are like having sex with someone on coke: it all starts out very exciting but, several hours in, you really just want them to finish.

Bill Maher

Awards are, of course, a lot of crap, but they awe the simple.

Robertson Davies

There are many people I should thank, but the truth is I did it all myself.

Martin Short, winning a Tony award

Man of the Year? I wouldn't vote him Jew of the Block.

Jan Murray, on Jerry Lewis

The cross of the Legion of Honour was been conferred upon me. However, few escape that distinction.

Mark Twain

Doctor of Letters? You haven't even written us a bloody postcard in three months!

Albert Finney Sr., when his son told him that he had been made an Honorary D.Litt

You can't ask a fantasy writer not to want a knighthood. You know, for two pins I'd get myself a horse and a sword.

Sir Terry Pratchett, on being knighted

The idea of pennants as prizes was absurd... Like Olympic medals and tennis trophies, all they signified was that the owner had done something of no benefit to anyone more capably than everyone else.

Joseph Heller, *Catch-22*

All anybody needs to know about prizes is that Mozart never won one.

Henry Mitchell

The only authors who are worthy of the Nobel Prize are those who are impossible to read. It is they who constantly renew the language.

Arthur Lundkvist

Stop babbling man! How much?

W.B. Yeats, on receiving a telephone call telling him that he had won the Nobel Prize for Literature, *attrib.*

BUSINESS

Business is the combination of war and sport.

André Maurois

An executive is an ulcer with authority.

Fred Allen

A 10,000-aspirin job.

Japanese term for executive responsibility

An entrepreneur…is a born schemer and thinker up of things.

Sir Alan Sugar

You and I are such similar creatures. We both screw people for money.

Edward Lewis, businessman, to a hooker, *Pretty Woman*

I want to please every woman, every time.

Stuart Rose, CEO of M&S

A swivel chair has ruined more men than chorus girls or liquor.

Fiorello LaGuardia

Willy was a salesman… He's a man way out there in the blue, riding on a smile and a shoeshine.

Charley, *Death of a Salesman*

—How many calls would you make on a prospect before you'd give up?
—Depends on which one of us dies first.

Sales Associate and Harvey Mackay

An appetite for haggling that would put a Turkish carpet salesman to shame.

Des Dearlove, on Richard Branson

Telephone, telegram and tell-a-woman.

Estée Lauder, maxim for promoting new products

What do you do when your competitor is drowning? Get a live hose and stick it in his mouth.

Ray Kroc, founder of McDonald's

I don't like to hire consultants. They're like castrated bulls – all they can do is advise.

Victor Kiam

Consultants are people who borrow your watch to tell you what time it is and then walk off with it.

Robert Townsend

A consultant's client is someone with a very expensive watch who doesn't know what time it is.

Robert J. Lewis

A monopolist is a fellow who manages to get an elbow on each arm of his theatre chair.

Herbert V. Prochnow

Decision: what a man makes when he can't find anybody to serve on a committee.

Fletcher Knebel

A committee is an animal with four back legs.

John Le Carré

A conference is just an admission that you want somebody to join you in your troubles.

Will Rogers

—How did your meeting go?
—Worse than a dentist. Better than a proctologist.

Catherine Willows and Conrad Ecklie, *CSI*

Five Stages of a Corporate Action: 1) Wild enthusiasm;
2) Disillusionment; 3) Search for the guilty; 4) Conviction of the
innocent; 5) Promotion of the uninvolved.

Anon

If you want something done, give it to a busy man – and he'll have his
secretary do it.

Anon

—You can't do shorthand, I suppose?
—I don't know. I've never tried.

P.G. Wodehouse, *Eggs, Beans and Crumpets*

You can teach 'em how to type, but you can't teach 'em how to grow tits.

**Charlie Wilson, Texan Democrat, who staffed his Washington office
with beautiful girls know as 'Charlie's Angels'**

If I had ever learned to type, I never would have made brigadier general.

Brigadier General Elizabeth P. Hoisington

Fire her. And don't ever make me talk to a woman that old again.

Jack Donaghy, *30 Rock*

I think that maybe in every company today there is always at least one
person who is going crazy slowly.

Joseph Heller

ADVERTISING

Advertising makes you think you've wanted something all your life that you've never heard of.

Anon

Advertisements are now so numerous that they are very negligently perused, and it is therefore become necessary to gain attention by magnificence of promises.

Dr Samuel Johnson, c.1759

Everyone in advertising is ex-something. Ex-actors, ex-artists, ex-writers, and quite a few ex-people too.

Charlotte Bingham

Creativity often consists of merely turning up what is already there. Did you know that right and left shoes were thought up only a little more than a century ago?

Bernice Fitz-Gibbon, advertising executive

We've taken your personality and translated it into bed linen.

Marketing Man, to Katie Price, *Katie and Peter: The Next Chapter*

The only reason I made a commercial for American Express was to pay for my American Express bill.

Peter Ustinov

The two infallible powers: The Pope and Bovril.

Advertising slogan, *c.* 1890

There are few things more destructive than an unsound idea persuasively expressed.

Bill Bernbach

INSURANCE

We were walking on air...till we tripped on a cloud.

Insurance advert

Insurance: an ingenious modern game of chance in which the player is permitted to enjoy the comfortable conviction that he is beating the man who keeps the table.

Ambrose Bierce

The Act of God designation on all insurance policies...means roughly that you cannot be insured for the accidents that are most likely to happen to you. If your ox kicks a hole in your neighbour's Maserati, however, indemnity is instantaneous.

Alan Coren

I have a cousin who became a mutual fund salesman. His wife has orgasmic insurance: if her husband fails to satisfy her sexually, Mutual of Omaha has to pay her every month.

Woody Allen

Some con men sell life insurance; the Church sells afterlife insurance. It's brilliant! Everyone thinks you might need it, and no one can prove you don't.

Brian Hope, *Nuns on the Run*

Insurance is no substitute for a good alarm system and a 12-gauge shotgun.

Bill, *Cagney and Lacey*

HOBBIES
& LEISURE

HOBBIES &
RECREATIONS

—When I touch my tongue to aluminium foil wrapped around a walnut while holding a toaster oven, I feel a peculiar tingling in my toes – what's wrong with me, Doctor?
—You have too much spare time.

Daniel Pirar, cartoon caption

Recently, I began to feel this void in my life…and I said to myself: 'Dave, all you do with your spare time is sit around and drink beer. You need a hobby.' So I got a hobby. I make beer.

Dave Barry

Twelve kids? What other hobbies have you got?

Groucho Marx

—I've joined the Ramblers' Club.
—Walking or talking?

Listener, *Wake Up to Wogan*

I still have two abiding passions. One is my model railway, the other – women. But the age of 89, I find I am getting a little too old for model railways.

Pierre Monteux

Ambrose Flood had a model railway, but none of us ever saw it, for it was under the floorboards of his bedroom. It was a Tube train, and Ambrose, who was literal-minded, believed that it should accordingly be kept underground.

Hugh Leonard

I'm very bad at Sudoku and crossword puzzles, any kind of pen and paper trivia. I started doing a word search once and then I realised it was a Will Self column.

Jo Caulfield

My favourite crossword clue is: '   ' (3,3,3,1,4). The solution is: Has not got a clue.

Val Gilbert, cruciverbalist

There is nothing that disgusts a man like getting beaten at chess by a woman.

Charles Dudley Warner

I see only one move ahead, but it is always the correct one.

José Raúl Capablanca, Cuban World Chess Champion

There is a new version of Trivial Pursuit. It's called 'The Economist's Edition'. There are 100 questions and 3,000 answers.

President Ronald Reagan

I wanna make a jigsaw puzzle that's 40,000 pieces. And when you finish it, it says 'go outside'.

Demetri Martin

Sailing: the fine art of getting wet and becoming ill while slowly going nowhere at great expense.

Henry Beard

Scuba diving is the closest you can come to going through the back of the wardrobe into a more fabulous world.

Norman Tebbit

I bought one of those frogman suits...jumped in the water and went down about 155 feet... All of a sudden I saw a man walking towards me in a sports jacket and grey flannels...I went up to him, took out a pad and wrote on it: 'What are you doing down here walking about in sports jacket and grey flannels?' And he wrote on the pad: 'I'm drowning.'

Tommy Cooper

Nothing spoils fun like finding out it builds character.

Calvin, *Calvin and Hobbes*

'WHO'S WHO' RECREATIONS

Book collecting, staring silently into space

Frank Muir

Skiing; teasing bureaucrats

Dudley Seers

Painting, sleeping

Beryl Bainbridge

Mending punctures, rehabilitating Clementi's piano works, falsifying personal records to mystify potential biographers

Miles Kington

Reading, loitering

Denis Norden

Letting the mind wander

Terry Pratchett

Living in Argyll

Sir Hugh Campbell Byatt

Lunch

Keith Waterhouse

FISHING

Give a man a fish, feed him for a day. Teach a man to fish, and he'll want to come along and drink all your beer.

Bob Ward

Fishing is a passion. I often think that when you are fishing, wildlife comes to you, because you are a peculiarity – a quiet human being.

Iain Duncan Smith

All you need to be a fisherman is patience and a worm.

Herb Shriner

Fishing trip: journey undertaken by one or more anglers to a place where no one can remember when the black flies arrived so early, the ice melted so late, or it rained so much.

Henry Beard

There is no use in your walking five miles to fish when you can depend on being just as unsuccessful nearer home.

Mark Twain

Somebody just back of you while you are fishing is as bad as someone looking over your shoulder while you write a letter to your girl.

Ernest Hemingway

Fly fishing is to fishing as ballet is to walking.

Howell Raines

There are two distinct kinds of visits to tackle-shops: the visit to buy tackle, and the visit which may be described as platonic when, being for some reason unable to fish, we look for an excuse to go in and waste a tackle dealer's time.

Arthur Ransome

This fishing tackle manufacturer I knew had all these flashy green and purple lures. I asked, 'Do fish take these?' 'Charlie,' he said, 'I don't sell these lures to *fish*.'

Charles T. Munger

My biggest worry is that my wife (when I'm dead) will sell my fishing gear for what I said I paid for it.

Koos Brandt

GAMBLING

—What has six balls and screws the poor?
—The lottery.

Anon

I know nothing about racing and any money I put on a horse is a sort of insurance policy to prevent it winning.

Frank Richardson

Gambling promises the poor what property performs for the rich – something for nothing.

George Bernard Shaw

Gosh, I just love gambling here in Vegas. Sure, I may lose $100,000, but the drinks are free, so it evens out!

Karen Walker, *Will and Grace*

Never bet odds-on. If you could buy money, they would sell it at the shop down the road.

Barry Hills

It is surely the epitome of pointlessness to gamble within your limits.

Clement Freud

Bookie: a pickpocket who lets you use your own hands.

Henry Morgan

My favourite occupation is gin rummy – but not together.

W.C. Fields

No wife can endure a gambling husband – unless he is a steady winner.

Lord Dewar

My wife made me join a bridge club. I jump off next Tuesday.

Rodney Dangerfield

AMUSEMENT PARKS

—Why is Disneyland like Viagra?
—The both make you wait an hour for a 2-minute ride.

Anon

He knew he'd have to go to Disney World eventually. It's middle class America's version of a pilgrimage to Mecca... the opportunity to gawk at a six-foot duck in a blue jacket.

Caryl Rivers

When I was a kid I never went to Disneyland. My ol' man told me Mickey Mouse died in a cancer experiment.

Rodney Dangerfield

I like Disney World. The rest rooms are clean enough for neurosurgery.

Dave Barry

I worked at Disneyland. I was one of the rides.

Willow Black, *Day of the Warrior*

—What's a country fair?
—It's like Disneyland for poor people.

Catalina and Randy Hickey, *My Name is Earl*

—Does 'Dollywood' have rides like Disneyland's Space Mountain?
—Space Mountain? I got twin peaks!

David Letterman and Dolly Parton

Walt Disney must be turning in his fridge.

Lily Savage, *The Parkinson Show*

CONSUMERISM

There must be more to life than having everything.

Maurice Sendak

The only reason a great many American families don't own an elephant is that they have never been offered an elephant for a dollar down and easy weekly payments.

Mad **magazine**

Marie Antoinette should be living in such an age!

Will Self, on the price of a Jane Asher birthday cake

Just before consumers stop doing something, they do it with a vengeance.

Faith Popcorn, *attrib.*

A lady once offered me a mat, but as I had no room to spare within the house, nor time to spare within or without to shake it, I declined it, preferring to wipe my feet on the sod before my door. It is best to avoid the beginnings of evil.

Henry David Thoreau

If I can't have too many truffles, I'll do without truffles.

Colette

The cost of a thing is the amount of what I call life which is required to be exchanged for it, immediately or in the long run.

Henry David Thoreau

I have the simplest tastes. I am always satisfied with the best.

Oscar Wilde

SHOPPING

—Where does a one-armed man shop?
—At a second-hand store.

Anon

One must choose, in life, between making money and spending it. There's no time to do both.

Edouard Bourdet

In their hearts women think that it is men's business to earn money and theirs to spend it.

Arthur Schopenhauer

My wife will buy anything marked down. She brought home two dresses and an escalator.

Henny Youngman

When it comes to plastic surgery and sushi, never be attracted by a bargain.

Graham Norton

I love to freak out shop assistants. They ask what size I need, and I say, 'Extra medium.'

Steven Wright

We're all going into the fitting room to have a fit.

Wanda, *Rose Marie*

I was shopping at IKEA and I decided to grab a ham sandwich from the kiosk. They gave me two slices of bread, a chunk of ham, an Allen key and told me to construct it myself. It was nice. The key was gritty but went down okay.

Darren Casey

There is only one thing for a man to do who is married to a woman who enjoys spending money, and that is to enjoy earning it.

Ed Howe

UNSEEMLY GREETINGS CARDS FOR UNLIKELY OCCASIONS

Watched your smoke! Now you're Pope! Congrats!

Charles Maguire

Hats off to your new hairpiece!

Harvey Sheirr

So you've had a penis enlargement!

Anon

Thank you for the one-night stand

Lee Powell

Sorry about last night

Li Hoffman

So, you've been chosen Thane of Cawdor!

David Deutsch

Thank you for the giant sea tortoise

Tom Morrow

The gang at the office will miss you except for the business manager

Henry Levinson

Our sympathy on the death of your giant sea tortoise

Len Elliott

Best wishes for a happy and successful first marriage

Marc Rosen

Happy Anniversary! It would have been a year today!

Lori Pearson

Congratulations on getting the children

Mark Sherman

Condolences on the loss of your shirt

Carol Drew

Sorry I missed your wake

J. Hawkes

GIFT

A man walks into a store and says, 'This is my wife's birthday, and I'd like to buy her a beautiful fountain pen.' The clerk looks up and says, 'A little surprise, huh?' 'Right,' said the man, 'she's expecting a Cadillac.'

Henny Youngman

I got my wife a vibrator for her birthday. She's done nothing but moan ever since.

Popbitch.com

When I was 16 years old, the morning of my birthday, my parents tried to surprise me with a car – but they missed.

Tom Cotter

I was looking for a wedding present for two of my friends… I was going to get them a dinner service, but I'm not actually convinced their marriage will last, so I settled for two picnic baskets.

Victoria Wood

A great birthday gift for a woman you don't like who's about to turn forty? Magnifying mirror.

Carol Leifer

I don't accept flowers. I take nothing perishable.

Paulette Goddard

One should never give a woman anything that she can't wear in the evening.

Oscar Wilde

If a man ever bought me a necklace like that, not only would I have sex with him, but I would enjoy it.

Florence Maybelle, *Isn't She Great*

It was once reported that he had been given a monogrammed straitjacket as a birthday gift.

Linda H. Davis, on Charles Addams, creator of *The Addams Family*

This must be a gift book. That is to say, a book which you wouldn't take on any other terms.

Dorothy Parker

The ideal present for someone you are not wild about, but cannot overlook.

Robin Day, on his book, *Speaking For Myself*

HOLIDAY

Vacation: two weeks on the sunny sands, the rest of the year on the financial rocks.

Sam Ewing

We hit the sunny beaches where we occupy ourselves keeping the sun off our skin, the saltwater off our bodies, and the sand out of our belongings.

Erma Bombeck

A friend of mine said, 'You want to go to Margate, it's good for rheumatism.' So I did and I got it.

Tommy Cooper

A vacation is having nothing to do and all day to do it in.

Robert Orben

The alternative to a vacation is to stay home and tip every third person you see.

Anon

I've found out what I don't like about family holidays: family.

Anon

A lot of parents pack up their troubles and send them off to a summer camp.

Raymond Duncan

A Jew on a vacation is just looking for a place to sit. A Jew sees a chair, it's a successful vacation.

Jackie Mason

Sunburn is very becoming – but only when it is even – one must be careful not to look like a mixed grill.

Noël Coward

A bikini is not a bikini unless it can be pulled through a wedding ring.

Louis Reard

Speedo? Speedon't!

Dr John Becker, *Becker*

When I go to a nude beach, I always take a ruler, just in case I have to prove something.

Rodney Dangerfield

Nudists are like people who do amateur dramatics: those who are most enthusiastic are those who should do it least.

Jeremy Hardy, *The News Quiz*

—Who's the most popular guy at the nudist camp?
—The one who can carry two cups of coffee and a dozen doughnuts at the same time.

Anon

With me a change of trouble is as good as a vacation.

David Lloyd George

HOTEL

—How do you know you're in a bad hotel?
—When you call reception and say, 'I've got a leak in my sink,' and they say, 'Go ahead.'

Anon

It used to be a good hotel, but that proves nothing – I used to be a good boy.

Mark Twain

My room's so small I put my key in the lock last night and broke a window.

David Feherty

Room service? Send up a larger room!

Groucho Marx

I'm staying in a strange hotel. I called room service for a sandwich and they sent up two hookers.

Bill Maher

When I came into my hotel room last night I found a strange blonde in my bed. I would stand for none of that nonsense! I gave her exactly 24 hours to get out.

Groucho Marx

Why do they put the Gideon Bibles only in the bedrooms, where it's usually too late?

Christopher Morley

A vicar books into a hotel and says to the hotel clerk: 'I hope the porn channel in my room is disabled?' She says: 'No sir, it's just regular porn. You sick bastard.'

Popbitch.com

Those bellhops in Miami are tip-happy. I ordered a deck of playing cards and the bellboy made fifty-two trips to my room.

Henny Youngman

DINNER PARTY

What I should have said: It's an old family recipe.
What I did say: Heinz soup and Kraft dip.

Anon

Drop in for drinks and brace yourself.

Tagline, **Who's Afraid of Virginia Woolf?**

A dinner invitation, once accepted, is a sacred obligation. If you die before the dinner takes place, your executor must attend.

Ward McAllister

Invited by vegetarians for dinner? As you'd no doubt be made aware of *their* special dietary requirements, tell them about *yours* – ask for a nice steak.

Top Tip, **Viz** magazine

There is a vegetarian option: you can fuck off!

Frankie Boyle, *Mock the Week*

I don't like having parties; the toilet always backs up.

Homer Simpson

*Words Heard on Stepping Over the Threshold That Make You Wish
You'd Never Come to Dinner*: 'All the children are eating with us tonight!'

Diane Eden

Never give a party if you will be the most interesting person there.

Mickey Friedman

One of a hostess's duties is to serve as a procuress.

Marcel Proust

When a woman's knee is touched, however delicately, that lady knows
infallibly whether the gentleman is really caressing her or whether he is
only wiping his greasy fingers on her stocking.

George Moore

—Isn't the party wonderful?
—Yes, if you see the essential horror of it all.

Fellow Party-goer and T.S. Eliot

The sixteenth Duke of Norfolk was heard to turn to a lady guest on his
right and say: 'I have only two topics of conversation – cricket and
drains. Choose.'

Brian Masters

She talked the entire time about colonic irrigation and matters of that sort.
Rabbiting on about rock stars and colonic irrigation. And hairdressers.

Norman Stone, dining with Diana, Princess of Wales

Never name-drop at the dinner table. The only thing worse than a fly in
one's soup is a celebrity.

Fran Lebowitz

If conversation is flagging, I ask the gentleman on my right: 'Are you a bed-wetter?'

Virginia Faulkner

A dinner party was presided over by Sylvia Brooke, then newly married to the last White Rajah of Sarawak, in Borneo. A lull in the conversation occurred, but, to her relief, she was able to announce to her guests, 'Listen, it's started to rain at last.' The guests remained dumb in silent horror as she turned to see the Rajah blithely relieving himself over the verandah.

Robert Morley

In dinner talk it is perhaps allowable to fling on any faggot rather than let the fire go out.

J.M. Barrie

Topics absolutely taboo: suicide, money, operations, one's illustrious ancestors or connections, religion, incurable diseases, dreams, illegitimacy, bright sayings of one's children or grandchildren.

Joseph Bryan

Don't ask about politics or religion, talk to them about how they get their duvet cover on because they'll all have opinions and they'll all have experience.

Guy Browning

…from politics it was an easy step to silence.

Jane Austen, *Northanger Abbey*

This was a good dinner enough, to be sure; but it was not a dinner to *ask* a man to.

Dr Samuel Johnson, who expected 'better than a plain dinner'
if invited to dine, even with a close friend

She was reckless in her use of fat which she poured over her food, straight from the pan, treating it as a sauce.

Caroline Blackwood, *Corrigan*

The lard starts forming on the guest even before he gets out of his car, and by the time he rises flushed from the table, he can be used to baste an ox.

S.J. Perelman

He had a Way of turning Things over with his Fork, as if to say, 'Well, I don't know about this.'

George Ade

Just as Americans don't make good gigolos, neither do they make good gourmets.

Ludwig Bemelmans

Gourmet: anyone who, when you fail to finish something strange and revolting, remarks that it's an acquired taste and that you're leaving the best part.

Henry Beard

It's all right, Arthur, the white wine came up with the fish.

Herman Mankiewicz, after throwing up at the dinner table of his gourmet host

Popularity is exhausting: the life of the party always winds up in a corner with an overcoat over him.

Wilson Mizner

Never be the first to arrive at a party or the last to go home, and never, ever be both.

David Brown

If they went to a wedding, they'd stay for a christening.

Patrick O'Keefe, on guests who outstay their welcome

The Arnolds feign death until the Wagners, sensing the sudden awkwardness, are compelled to leave.

Gary Larson, cartoon caption

British hosts often see you to the door at the end of social occasions and then stand on the steps, waving, until your car is out of sight. It is friendly, but it also might be because they want to be sure that you have genuinely left.

Sarah Lyall, *A Field Guide to the British*

He left us and we rejoiced; then an even more unbearable person came.

Arab proverb

CHRISTMAS

'Merry Christmas!' 'Merry Christmas!' Why does everyone keep saying that? It's only one day! God was born – move on!

Brian Hackett, *Wings*

There are two kinds of people in this world: those who count the days to December 25 and those who count the days to December 26.

Larenda Lyles Roberts

Legend has it that every time you say 'Happy Holidays', an angel gets AIDS.

Jon Stewart

I was coming out of my off-licence with four crates of lager and two crates of wine, and a bottle of brandy, and a bottle of vodka, and I said to the guy: 'Christmas is really about the children, isn't it?'

Barry Cryer

It is sad a lot of youngsters don't know the meaning of Christmas. They don't know that it is the time to celebrate the birth, the life and the work of Morecambe and Wise.

Alistair McGowan

Religions are getting multicultural, as they consider combining Christmas with Yom Kippur, the Jewish Day of Atonement. The resulting holiday would be called 'Yule be Sorry'.

Bill Kilner

I was brought up by atheists and as a kid I used to tell my parents about Christmas; I really wanted to celebrate Christmas. They'd look at me and say: 'Old man breaks into the house, creeps into your bedroom and empties his sack? You're not having Christmas.'

Shappi Khorsandi

If a kid ever asks you how Santa Claus can live forever, I think a good answer is that he drinks blood.

Jack Handey

Christmas, my daddy went in the alley and shot the rifle and came back in the house and told all the kids Santa Claus just committed suicide.

Redd Foxx

Father Christmas may not exist, but I believe in Noddy Holder.

Andrew Collins

'So here it is, Merry Christmas, everybody's having fun,' grunted the carol singers at my door. When I asked for a proper carol, they just looked at me blankly. I gave them some money out of pity.

Listener, *The Jeremy Vine Show*

I saw Daddy Kissing Santa Claus

Kip Addotta, song title

I went to the producer's Christmas party. He's very charming – took his teeth out to entertain the children. It was a bit messy really – he hasn't got false teeth.

Ronnie Corbett

Christmas comes but once a year. Thank God I'm not Christmas.

Graffiti

Isn't it just like Jesus to be born on Christmas morning?

Spike Milligan

I don't know what to get my nephew for Christmas. Last year his parents gave him a gun. I wonder what the little orphan wants this year?

Alan Young

This year I thought I'd give all my friends a book, but I don't know when they'd get together to read it.

Bob Hope

Don't talk to me about Christmas... All that sticky, phony goodwill. I'd like to get a giant candy cane and beat the wings off a sugar plum fairy.

Oscar Madison, *The Odd Couple*

—Where's your Christmas spirit?
—I drank it.

Jack Benny and Phil Harris

When having a family Christmas, always include an outsider. It is amazing how well people behave when they feel they have to make an effort.

Robin Stemp

By 6pm I'm usually hiding out in my shed, drunk on self-pity.

Christian O'Connell

Merry Syphilis and a Happy Gonorrhoea!

Australian festive greeting

Abi Titmuss, and a Happy New Year!

Giles Smith

Peace, harmony, comfort and joy... Maybe next year.

Tagline, *A Christmas Story*

POWER

I was allowed to ring the school-bell for five minutes until everyone was in assembly. It was the beginning of power.

Jeffrey Archer

The wrong sort of people are always in power because they would not be in power if they were not the wrong sort of people.

Jon Wynne-Tyson

Power corrupts; absolute power is really neat!

Donald Regan, President Reagan's Chief of Staff

Lyndon B. Johnson's instinct for power is as primordial as a salmon's going upstream to spawn.

Theodore H. White

Power is the ultimate aphrodisiac.

Henry Kissinger

Power is like a woman you want to stay in bed with forever.

Patrick Anderson

The thing women have yet to learn is nobody gives you power. You just take it.

Roseanne

I was a Playboy Bunny for three months. It was a good experience because it taught me pussy power.

Lauren Hutton

Many a man that could rule a hundred million strangers with an iron hand is careful to take off his shoes in the front hallway when he comes home late at night.

Finlay Peter Dunne

She Tarzan, he Jane.
> Andrew Morton, on the relationship between Victoria and David Beckham

There is no greater human power on earth than the tremendous indignation of the people.
> Daniel Webster

GOVERNMENT

Government is nothing but who collects the money and how do they spend it.
> Gore Vidal

In general, the art of government consists in taking as much money as possible from one party of the citizens to give to the other.
> Voltaire

—Is it possible that Caesar, the conqueror of the world, has time to occupy himself with such a trifle as our taxes?
—My friend: taxes are the chief business of a conqueror of the world.
> Pothinus and Caesar, *Caesar and Cleopatra*

Government's view of the economy could be summed up in a few short phrases: If it moves, tax it. If it keeps moving, regulate it. And if it stops moving, subsidise it.
> Ronald Reagan

A welfare state is one that assumes responsibility for the health, happiness and general well-being of all its citizens except the tax-payer.
> Boyle's Observation

Governments last as long as the under-taxed can defend themselves against the over-taxed.
> Bernard Berenson

A little government and a little luck are necessary in life, but only a fool trusts either of them.

P.J. O'Rourke

ELECTION

Do you ever get the feeling that the only reason we have elections is to find out if the polls were right?

Robert Orben

General or local election: rare opportunity for parents to learn the location of their children's school.

Mike Barfield, Dictionary for our Time

In elections, the undecided vote is usually the deciding factor.

Evan Esar

Come canvassing with me and you'll find more cold shoulders than in all the fridges of Smithfield.

Michael Gove, MP

—I can't stop to talk, I just lost my dog!
—Can I help look for it?
—No, it just died.

Elderly Lady and David Cameron, campaigning in Witney, 2001

Oh, great. Meeting my constituents. It's like being Simon Cowell, only without the ability to say, 'Fuck off, you're mental.'

Simon Foster, In the Loop

I did enjoy campaigning, up to a point. Some things I never learned to like. I didn't like to kiss babies, though I didn't mind kissing their mothers.

Pierre Trudeau

Michael Heseltine has been canvassing like a child molester hanging around the lavatories and waiting to pounce on people.

Norman Lamont

Receiving support from Ted Heath is like being measured by an undertaker.

George Gardiner, when the prime minister went to speak for him during a by-election

Don't do anything that indicates that you know you're going to lose. My wife actually wanted to put our house in the constituency up for sale *during* the election campaign. I said that will actually be a little bit revealing.

Gyles Brandreth, before losing his seat as MP for Chester

Things on the whole are much faster in America; people don't *stand for election*, they *run for office*.

Jessica Mitford

The race is as hot and tight as a too-small bathing suit on a too-long car ride back from the beach.

Dan Rather, broadcaster, on US election night, 1996

George McGovern couldn't carry the South if Rhett Butler were his running mate.

Spiro Agnew

We'd all like to vote for the best man, but he's never a candidate.

Kin Hubbard

Vote for the man who promises least; he'll be the least disappointing.

Bernard Baruch

Voters will always go for Santa not Scrooge.

Rachel Sylvester

When I was in the third grade, there was a kid running for office.
His slogan was: 'Vote for me and I'll show you my wee-wee.' He won by
a landslide.

Dorothy Zbornak, *The Golden Girls*

POLITICS – GENERAL

You campaign in poetry. You govern in prose.

Mario Cuomo

When we got into office, the thing that surprised me most was to find
that things were just as bad as we'd been saying they were.

John F. Kennedy

Politics is economics in action.

Robert M. La Follette

What's good politics is bad economics; what's bad politics is good
economics.

Eugene W. Baer

Politics: a Trojan horse race.

Stanislaw J. Lec

Politics is like football; if you see daylight, go through the hole.

John F. Kennedy

A politician...one that would circumvent God.

William Shakespeare, *Hamlet*

Politicians are not born; they are excreted.

Cicero

To be successful a British politician must be like a clergyman or like a bookmaker. Sanctimoniousness and sport are...our two great national pursuits... Sir Winston Churchill...merges comfortably into the landscape at a race meeting, whereas when Sir Anthony Eden orates a pulpit seems to rise from the ground to enfold him.

Malcolm Muggeridge

To succeed in modern politics you should take care to be a bland, self-preserving, sober, drugless, funless, dull-witted bore for years beforehand.

Libby Purves

There are only two ways to the top in British politics. One way is to crawl up the staircase of preferment on your belly; the other way is to kick them in the teeth. But for God's sake, Dick, don't mix the two methods.

Aneurin Bevan, to Richard Crossman

In politics, guts is all.

Barbara Castle

The double pleasure of pulling down an opponent, and of raising oneself, is the charm of a politician's life.

Anthony Trollope

Don't worry about your enemies, it's your allies who will do you in.

James Abourezk

Shafted by a shower of shits.

Mike Hancock, on the resignation of Ming Campbell
as leader of the Liberal Democrats

Never murder a man who is committing suicide.

President Woodrow Wilson, political maxim

They could not organise a colostomy bag in a sewage works.

**Unidentified Labour MP, on the failed coup by some Labour MPs
to oust the prime minister, Gordon Brown, June 2009**

It was a storm in a teacup, but in politics we sail in paper boats.

Harold Macmillan

The biggest political club contains ex-future prime ministers. And we all know for certain we would have done the job brilliantly.

Norman Tebbit

I'd be a terrible prime minister. I think on my first day I'd probably lose the keys to the country.

Chris Addison

Above any other position of eminence, that of prime minister is filled by fluke.

Enoch Powell

In politics, as in life or love, a lot depends on being in the right place at the right time. That's certainly what happened to me.

Senator Edward Kennedy

It is true that we had ten years of record growth when I was prime minister. I have, unfortunately, come to the conclusion that it was luck.

Tony Blair

Will Rogers once said it is not the original investment in a Congressman that counts; it is the upkeep.

John F. Kennedy

Two ducks sitting on a pond. One duck says: 'Time for parliamentary reform.' The other says: 'Well, at least I got a duck house out of it.'

Anon

Public money is like holy water; everyone helps himself.

Italian proverb

Nobody who has wealth to distribute ever omits himself.

Leon Trotsky

That most delicious of all privileges − spending other people's money.

John Randolph of Roanoke

I like the idea of Gordon Brown causing the credit crunch, and then making it better. It's like Bomber Harris going to Dresden and offering to put a few windows back in.

Frank Skinner, *Have I Got News For You*

There is no point in the Cabinet questioning the Treasury. On the rare occasions when the Treasury understands the question, the Cabinet does not understand the answer.

Sir Humphrey Appleby, *Yes, Minister*

The Treasury could not, with any marked success, run a fish and chip shop.

Harold Wilson

When I arrived [as chancellor of the exchequer], a very senior civil servant pointed out to me three envelopes that had been left by a previous chancellor. Each letter contained advice that, if things went wrong, the chancellor might choose to consult. When the first crisis arrived he would open the first envelope and the advice would be: 'Blame your predecessor.' And, of course, we did something of that. When the crisis got worse, he would open the second envelope, which said: 'Blame the statistics.' And we did a bit of that as well. And when things got really bad and the disastrous proportions were clear, the advice in the third envelope was clear: 'Start writing three envelopes to your successor.'

Gordon Brown

Balancing the budget is like going to heaven. Everybody wants to do it, but nobody wants to do what you have to do to get there.

Phil Gramm

Turning national economic policy around is like turning the Queen Mary around in a bathtub.

E. Gerald Corrigan

Three groups spend other people's money: children, thieves, politicians. All three need supervision.

Dick Armey

Nothing is easier than spending the public money. It does not appear to belong to anybody. The temptation is overwhelming to bestow it on somebody.

Calvin Coolidge

The government deficit is the difference between the amount of money the government spends and the amount it has the nerve to collect.

Sam Ewing

The debt is like a crazy aunt we keep down in the basement. All the neighbours know she's there, but nobody wants to talk about her.

H. Ross Perot, 1992

—What do you think of the national debt?
—We ought to be proud of it – it's the biggest in the world, isn't it?

Reporter and Gracie Allen, USA, 1940

California no longer has low-hanging fruits. As a matter of fact, we don't have any medium-hanging fruits. We also don't have any high-hanging fruits. We literally have to take the ladder away...and shake the whole tree.

Arnold Schwarzenegger, Governor of California,
proposing deep cuts in spending, 2010

Arkansas? Sell it.

Bob Dole, on balancing the US federal budget

I will consider selling off the Crown Jewels, but I am not absolutely sure that they are the property of Her Majesty's government.

Denis Healey, Chancellor of the Exchequer, on the economic crisis, 1976

No country has ever been ruined on account of its debts.

Adolf Hitler

When a problem is too difficult, ministers set up a Royal Commission... This bequeaths it to the next generation.

Sir Humphrey Appleby, *Yes, Minister*

Blessed are the young, for they shall inherit the National Debt.

President Herbert Hoover

Emile Zola launched into a violent attack on politicians, saying with some truth that they were our natural enemies and that he could see their hatred of us in their wives' eyes.

Edmond and Jules de Goncourt

Politicians and diplomats and public servants ought to feel the people breathing down the backs of their necks; and ought to be glad to feel it too.

A.J.P. Taylor

The minute I get cancer I'm killing all of Britain's politicians.

Frankie Boyle

I mostly like politicians. Very few of them are evil, although quite a lot are delusional.

Gavin Esler

The mistake a lot of politicians make is in forgetting they've been appointed and thinking they've been anointed.

Mrs Claude Pepper

Politicians. Little Tin Gods on Wheels.

Rudyard Kipling

Politicians, like prostitutes, are held in contempt. But what man does not run to them when he needs their services.

Brendan Francis

Politicians – power itself – are abject because they merely embody the profound contempt people have for their own lives.

Jean Baudrillard

The people trust you rich boys, figurin' since you got a lot of money of your own you won't go stealin' theirs.

Gore Vidal

History has taught me that rulers are much the same in all ages, and under all forms of government; they are as bad as they dare to be.

Samuel Taylor Coleridge

Politics is not the art of the possible. It consists in choosing between the disastrous and the unpalatable.

J.K. Galbraith

When anyone tells you that he belongs to no party you may at any rate be sure that he does not belong to yours.

Anne-Sophie Swetchine

If you want to find a politician free of any influence, you can find Adolf Hitler, who made up his own mind.

Eugene McCarthy

An Englishman has to have a Party, just as he has to have trousers.

Bertrand Russell

A conservative is a man who wants the rules changed so that no one can make a pile the way he did.

Gregory Nunn

The Tory mind has throughout history been rendered uneasy by the unknown, and has sought to restore equanimity by dismissing the incomprehensible either as ridiculous or wicked.

Harold Nicholson

A conservative is a liberal who's been mugged; a liberal is a conservative who's been arrested.

Old political joke

A liberal is a man who leaves the room when the fight starts.

Heywood Broun

As usual the Liberals offer a mixture of sound and original ideas. Unfortunately none of the sound ideas is original and none of the original ideas is sound.

Harold Macmillan

I am become a socialist. I love Humanity; but I hate people.

Edna St Vincent Millay

—Why do socialists drink herbal tea?
—Because proper tea is theft.

Anon

Bishops, financiers, lawyers and all the polite spongers up on the working classes know that this is the beginning of the end.

David Kirkwood, on the formation of the first Labour government, 1924

The working class can kiss my arse,
I've got the foreman's job at last.
And now that he is on the dole
You can stuff the red flag up your hole.

Lampoon of the socialist anthem, 'The Red Flag'

Politics makes estranged bedfellows.

Goodman Ace

Jumping into bed with people too quickly, I am told, makes any liaison far less satisfying when it is eventually achieved.

Simon Hughes MP, on flirtations between political parties

This coalition, led by David Cameron, is going to be a cross between a bulldog and a Chihuahua.

Boris Johnson, on the Tory–Lib Dem coalition, 2010

England does not love coalitions.

Benjamin Disraeli, 1852

A pantomime horse.

Sir Max Hastings, on the Tory–Lib Dem coalition, 2010

I, Nick, take you, Dave, to be my leader, for better, for worse, for richer, for poorer, in sickness and in health... till debt us do part.

The Independent, on the Tory–Lib Dem coalition, 2010

Compromise makes a good umbrella, but a poor roof; it is a temporary expedient, often wise in party politics, almost sure to be unwise in statesmanship.

James Russell Lowell

When a group of Cabinet Ministers begins to meet separately and to discuss independent actions, the death-tick is audible in the rafters.

Lord Curzon, 1922, just before the fall of Lloyd George's coalition government

Damn your principles! Stick to your party.

Benjamin Disraeli, to Edward Bulwer-Lytton, *attrib.*

Party men always hate a slightly differing friend more than a downright enemy.

Samuel Taylor Coleridge

The more you read and observe about the Politics thing, you got to admit that each party is worse than the other. The one that's out always looks the best.

Will Rogers

All political parties die at last of swallowing their own lies.

John Arbuthnot

POLITICIANS

Harold Wilson: all facts, no bloody ideas.

Aneurin Bevan

Better George Brown drunk than Harold Wilson sober.

The Times

Clement Attlee brings to the fierce struggle of politics the tepid enthusiasm of a lazy summer afternoon at a cricket match.

Aneurin Bevan

Neville Chamberlain – a good Lord Mayor of Birmingham in a lean year.

Lloyd George

Benjamin Disraeli – a flamingo in a farmyard.

Desmond McCarthy

There is nobody in politics I can remember and no case I can think of in history where a man combined such a powerful political personality with so little intelligence.

Roy Jenkins, on James Callaghan

A second-class intellect but a first-class temperament.

Oliver Wendell Holmes, on President Theodore Roosevelt, *attrib.*

John Gummer looks like a tax clerk. By which I suppose I mean he looks somehow like a paper clip, a bit like a going out tray loosely jammed into a coming in tray, a bit like a cold cup of instant coffee at 10.20, a bit like a neon light in a windowless office etc., etc...

Ted Hughes

Stephen Byers is the talking equivalent of invisible ink. Within seconds of his speaking you cannot recall a word he has said: he simply wipes himself from your consciousness.

Matthew Parris

R.A. Butler would have been marvellous in medieval politics, creeping about the Vatican; a tremendous intriguer, he always had some marvellous plan...and he loved the press.

Harold Macmillan

Peter Mandelson is a pussycat. By which I mean he is a sleek and mean carnivore who should never be rubbed up the wrong way.

Martin Rowson

Half the time Peter Mandelson was like one of those people who shout at strangers on buses; the other half he resembled a slightly creepy uncle reading a bedtime story.

Simon Hoggart, listening to a speech by Peter Mandelson

If either of them had anything to say, it would matter less that neither has the gift of language. If either had the gift of language, it would matter less that neither has anything to say.

Matthew Parris, listening to a debate between John Major and Neil Kinnock

John Major always came across as the sort of man your granny would knit a cardigan for. Honest John. Nice John. A good man, sadly fallen among Eurosceptics.

Caroline Daniel

If John Major was drowning, his whole life would pass in front of him, and he wouldn't be in it.

Dave Allen

John Major put the 'er' back into Conservative, David Cameron's put the 'con' into Conservative, and Norman Lamont put the VAT into Conservative.

David Miliband

Woody Allen without the jokes.

Simon Hoggart, on Sir Keith Joseph

Jeffrey has a gift for inaccurate precis.

Mary Archer, on her husband

The best way to think about Jeffrey Archer is to treat him as if he comes from another planet. He will drive over a cliff and then be amazed that he's falling. He thinks he's Peter Pan, and he'll never die.

Sheridan Morley

John Prescott – for years we had a deputy prime minister who looked liked a National Express coach-driver.

Rory Bremner

Everything John Prescott touches turns to sewage.

Simon Carr

Tony Benn has had more conversions on the road to Damascus than a Syrian long-distance lorry driver.

Jimmy Reid

David Steel's passed from rising hope to elder statesman without any intervening period whatsoever.

Michael Foot

Margaret Thatcher is the Sybil Fawlty of British Conservatism.

P.D. Morris-Morgan

Margaret Thatcher has no imagination and that means no compassion.

Michael Foot

I would suggest as a memorial to Mrs Thatcher that instead of the usual headstone or statue, a dance floor should be erected over her grave.

Ann Graham

Tony Blair has pushed moderation to extremes.

Robert Maclennan

Describing Tony Blair as Middle East peace envoy is like asking a mosquito to find a cure for malaria.

Rory Bremner

Tony Blair looks like a multi-millionaire playboy, a George Hamilton. That's what happens to Bambi when he gets old.

Lord Tim Bell, 2010

Gordon Brown has, ridiculously, been compared to Stalin. He is no Stalin. He lacks the grip of a leader.

William Rees-Mogg

Gordon Brown...would have been a great statesman in the 19th century, but in this televisual age, with his glowering demeanour, his blind eye and his introversion, he is out of time.

A.C. Grayling

He doesn't do limelight.

Ed Boyle, on Gordon Brown

Like a ticket inspector recently retrained in the art of customer relations, Gordon Brown was all smiles and small talk.

Matthew Parris

Where did Gordon Brown learn to smile? Watching *The Shining*?

Frankie Boyle, *My Shit Life So Far*

Gordon Brown sounds like a Dalek with about three stock phrases... Remember, Daleks always want world domination but they always lose.

Peter Bazalgette

David Miliband always has one expression on his face – it's a mixture of puzzlement and aggression. Which makes me think that he lives in a cul-de-sac. You know when you walk down a cul-de-sac by mistake and you see someone and they sort of look at you like, 'You don't live in a cul-de-sac...'

Frankie Boyle, Mock the Week

Boris Johnson's personality is like a hunt ball held in a cricket pavilion.

Clive James

The utensil that scraped Ken Livingstone from the soles of Londoners.

Boris Johnson, Mayor of London, describing himself

The blondest suicide note in history.

Ming Campbell, on Boris Johnson

If you said to most people on the Tube, 'Iain Duncan Smith?' they'd probably say, 'Oh, it's the next stop but one.'

Antony Jay

Iain Duncan Smith: two surnames in search of a hyphen.

Keith Waterhouse

John Redwood is not in fact a human being at all, but a Vulcan, recently landed from the planet of the same name, where merciless logic rules.

Matthew Parris

Theresa May: Lynda Bellingham's serious sister.

The Guardian

A politician with the persona of a sanctimonious Leeds undertaker on a day trip to Bridlington.

Roy Hattersley, on Vince Cable

David Cameron is a bum-faced southern ponce with a tiny washer for a mouth.

Armando Iannucci, *The Audacity of Hype*

The baby face doesn't worry me. It's the baby mind that does.

John Prescott, on David Cameron

It is easy to build a Cameron lookalike. Just simulate the smuggest estate agent you can think of. Or some interchangeable braying twit in a rugby shirt, ruining a local pub just by being there.

Charlie Brooker

If David Cameron hadn't gone to Eton, he'd be managing a Pizza Hut.

Frankie Boyle

Prime Minister, do you now regret, when once asked what your favourite joke was, you replied: 'Nick Clegg.'

Andy Bell, journalist, to David Cameron, after the 2010 election

I met Nick Clegg the other day, and he said, 'Can you do me?' I said, 'No, can you?'

Rory Bremner, impressionist

HOUSE OF LORDS

If you think there are some rum folk in the Commons, wait until you see who fetches up in a directly elected Lords.

George Walden

I may be here because my forefather got pissed with Pitt, but that's better than those newcomers who are just Blair's tennis partners.

Earl of Onslow, on the composition of the House of Lords, 2003

Obviously you do get one or two people in the Lords who are a bit odd, but you get nutters everywhere.

Baroness Strange

Ministers moving to the House of Lords receive approbation, elevation and castration, all in one stroke.

Sir Humphrey Appleby, *Yes, Minister*

The other night I dreamed that I was addressing the House of Lords. Then I woke up and, by God, I was!

Duke of Devonshire

I will be sad, if I look up or down after my death and don't see my son asleep on the same benches on which I slept.

Lord Onslow, opposing reforms

When I'm sitting on the Woolsack in the House of Lords I amuse myself by saying 'Bollocks' *sotto voce* to the bishops.

Lord Hailsham

The reason the bishops' benches in the House of Lords are the only ones in the chamber which have arms to them is to stop drunken bishops rolling off the seats and onto the floor, thus causing a scandal.

Jo Grimond, MP

POLITICAL SPEECHES

Speechwriting is to writing as Muzak is to music.

Aram Bakshian, political speechwriter

When Nelson Rockefeller buys a Picasso, he doesn't hire four housepainters to improve it.

Henry Kissinger, to Hugh Morrow, who had asked Rockefeller's speechwriting staff to edit Kissinger's draft of a speech

A good political speech is not one in which you can prove that the man is telling the truth; it is one where no one else can prove he is lying.

Sir Humphrey Appleby, *Yes, Minister*

All great soundbites happen by accident...as part of the natural expression of the text. They are part of the tapestry, they aren't a little flower somebody sewed on.

Peggy Noonan

It just shows, what any member of Parliament will tell you, that if you want real oratory, the preliminary noggin is essential. Unless pie-eyed, you cannot hope to grip.

P.G. Wodehouse, *Right Ho, Jeeves*

I noticed first the verb-free sentences, which Tony Blair still uses today: 'Our people, prosperous and secure. Our children, meeting the challenge...' He might use up to 200 in one speech, making it sound like oratorical Muzak, conveying little but a sense of wellbeing.

Simon Hoggart

William Hague makes rather good speeches. They've got verbs in them.

Douglas Hurd

I stand up when he nudges me. I sit down when they pull my coat.

Ernest Bevin

FOREIGN AFFAIRS & DIPLOMACY

Vladimir Putin doesn't have a foreign policy. He has a price.

Orlando Figes

Having a friend doesn't mean you are kneeling in front of him.

Gilles Duceppe, on the relationship between Canada and the USA, *attrib.*

No nation has friends – only interests.

Charles de Gaulle

Two nations which have never fought each other can never be real friends.

Miles Kington

There is only one thing worse than fighting with allies, and that is fighting without them.

Winston Churchill

Alliance: in international politics, the union of two thieves who have their hands so deeply inserted in each other's pockets that they cannot separately plunder a third.

Ambrose Bierce

Gratitude, like love, is never a dependable international emotion.

Joseph Alsop

Love for the same thing never makes allies. It's always hate for the same thing.

Howard Spring

Treaties are like roses and young girls. They last while they last.

Charles de Gaulle

The United Nations is the accepted forum for the expression of international hatred.

Sir Humphrey Appleby, *Yes, Prime Minister*

Ultimatum: in diplomacy, a last demand before resorting to concessions.

Ambrose Bierce

Diplomat: a man who thinks twice before saying nothing.

Frederick Sawyer

There is nothing more likely to start disagreement among people or countries than an agreement.

E.B. White

Forever poised between a cliché and an indiscretion.

Harold Macmillan, on the life of a Foreign Secretary

Just fucking do it! Otherwise you'll find yourself in some medieval war zone in the Caucasus with your arse in the air, trying to persuade a group of men in balaclavas that sustained sexual violence is not the fucking way forward!

Malcolm Tucker, to the British Ambassador to the United Nations, *In the Loop*

BUREAUCRACY

—How many bureaucrats does it take to change a light bulb?
—Two. One to assure us that everything possible is being done while the other screws the bulb into a hot water tap.

Voice for Health magazine

I came to Number 11 reluctantly, I can tell you, but after I'd lined up all the former staff and shot them I felt a good deal better. 'Start as you mean to go on,' has always been good advice.

Newly appointed Chancellor of the Exchequer, in a satirical article written for *Punch* magazine by Alan Hackney

Poor fellow, he suffers from files.

Aneurin Bevan, on administrator, Sir Walter Citrine

This place needs a laxative.

Bob Geldof, on red tape at the European Parliament, Strasbourg

The Pentagon is like a log going down the river with 25,000 ants on it, each thinking he's steering the log.

Henry S. Rowen

The Pentagon was so huge people were said to spend days and even weeks wandering its endless corridors trying to find their way out. One woman was said to have told a guard she was in labour and needed help in getting to a maternity hospital. He said: 'Madam, you should not have come in here in that condition.' 'When I came in here,' she answered, 'I wasn't.'

David Brinkley

Asking a town hall to slim down its staff is like asking an alcoholic to blow up a distillery.

Sir Humphrey Appleby, *Yes, Minister*

I confidently expect that we shall continue to be grouped with mothers-in-law and Wigan Pier as one of the recognized objects of ridicule.

Edward Bridges, on civil servants

The only thing that saves us from bureaucracy is its inefficiency.

Eugene McCarthy

The British created a civil service job in 1803 calling for a man to stand on the Cliffs of Dover with a spyglass. He was supposed to ring a bell if he saw Napoleon coming. The job was abolished in 1945.

Robert Sobel

US POLITICS

One useless man is a shame, two is a law firm, and three or more is a congress.

John Adams

Harry, don't you go to the Senate with an inferiority complex. You'll sit there about six months, and wonder how you got there. But after that you'll wonder how the rest of them get there.

Old Judge, to Harry S. Truman on his election to the senate

At one time, Washington actually meant something. But now, it's about as relevant as Bob Dylan's tuning fork.

Dennis Miller

I am not a member of any organized party. I am a Democrat.

Will Rogers

He's racist, he's homophobic, he's xenophobic, and he's a sexist. He's the perfect Republican candidate.

Bill Press, on Pat Buchanan

Tax hatred is what holds the Republican Party together.

Bill Schneider

The difference between Republicans and Democrats is the difference between syphilis and gonorrhoea.

Rita Mae Brown

There they were, See No Evil, Hear No Evil, and Evil.

Bob Dole, on Gerald Ford, Jimmy Carter and Richard Nixon
at a reunion of former US presidents

Richard Nixon always seemed ill at ease. His suits – he never wore anything else – didn't fit quite right; his sense of humour was non-existent; he had no capacity whatsoever for small talk. He was the boy you let play only if it was his ball.

Arthur Hoppe

I've often thought with Richard Nixon that if he'd made the football team, his life would have been different.

Adela Rogers St Johns

He is a man of splendid abilities, but utterly corrupt. He shines and stinks like rotten mackerel by moonlight.

John Randolph, on Edward Livingston

He was as cool as an undertaker at a hanging.

H.L. Mencken, on Henry Cabot Lodge

John-Boy Walton grown up.

Jack Temple Kirby, on Jimmy Carter

President Reagan was either a brilliant visionary who won the Cold War, or a walking cabbage that happened to be in office when the Soviet Union crumbled on its own. Pick one.

Scott Adams

The battle for the mind of Ronald Reagan was like the trench warfare of World War I: never have so many fought so hard for such barren terrain.

Peggy Noonan

Monica Lewinsky walks into the dry cleaner's and asks the guy to get a stain out of her dress. 'Come again?' he asks. 'No, it's ketchup.'

Anon

L'enthousiasme de M. le President

Le Figaro, French newspaper's tactful description of the stain on Monica Lewinsky's dress

Clinton's sole crime was a disinclination to confess to a grand jury that he likes the odd blow job, a taste he shares with most of the male population.

Gore Vidal

Freddie Roman wanted to get President Clinton impeached. Why should he be the only man in history to ever get a blow job from a Jewish girl?

Joy Behar

The Corleones of American politics.

Michael Ignatieff, on the Bush family

Barack Hussein Obama, not the best name to have in American politics; in fact, perhaps the most unfortunate name in American politics since World War II presidential candidate, Gaydolph Hitler.

Jon Stewart

The reason I'm running for president is because I can't be Bruce Springsteen.

Barack Obama

Barack Obama is a combination of Martin Luther King and Spock.

Robin Williams

The man with the best job in the country is the vice-president. All he has to do is get up every morning and say: 'How's the president?'

Will Rogers

I am nothing but tomorrow I may be everything.

John Adams, when US vice-president

Hillary Clinton says she's the most qualified because she was married to a president for 8 years. Now let me ask you, if a brain surgeon quit his job, would everyone in the operating room say, 'Wait, let's get his wife.'

Jackie Mason

The aunt no one can stand.

John Cleese, on Hillary Clinton

One advantage of electing a woman president is we wouldn't have to pay her as much.

Anon

—Have you considered running for office?
—Don't you think we've had enough boobs in the White House?

Interviewer and Dolly Parton

A president doesn't have to be smart. All he has to do is point the army and shoot.

Homer Simpson

LEAVING POLITICAL OFFICE

They asked Abraham Lincoln how he felt once after an unsuccessful election. He said he felt like a little boy who had stubbed his toes in the dark... too old to cry, but it hurt too much to laugh.

Adlai Stevenson, after his own 1952 defeat

Politics would be a helluva good business if it weren't for the goddamned people.

President Richard Nixon

Today a rooster, tomorrow a feather duster.

Arthur Calwell

At one moment Michael Portillo was polishing his jackboots and planning the advance. Next thing he shows up as a TV presenter. It is rather like Pol Pot joining the Teletubbies.

Tony Banks

It would be humane to shoot all Presidents on the expiration of their terms, as I long ago proposed that every unsuccessful candidate for the Presidency be hanged. They dodder along in a truly obscene manner, and always end as public nuisances.

H.L. Mencken

My esteem in this country has gone up substantially... It's very nice now that when people wave at me, they use all their fingers.

Jimmy Carter

Never was astonishment equal to that produced by the dismissal of the Whigs. I thought it better at first to ascertain whether the common laws of nature were suspended; and to put this to the test, I sowed a little mustard and cress seed, and waited in breathless anxiety the event. It came up. By little and little I perceived that, as far as the outward world was concerned, the dismissal of Lord Melbourne has not produced much effect.

Rev. Sydney Smith, on the general election of 1835

MPs, ministers or otherwise, do not resign because of their integrity. They do so because they have been found out.

David Axson

Leaving government is like coming off heroin.

Jonathan Powell, Tony Blair's chief of staff

If ever I left the House of Commons it would be because I wanted to spend more time on politics.

Tony Benn

I left Westminster to spend more time with my money.

Steven Norris, MP

I most certainly won't miss the constituency work... All you were was a sort of high-powered social worker and perhaps not even a good one.

Tony Banks

Politics is not a bad profession. If you succeed, there are many rewards; if you disgrace yourself, you can always write a book.

Ronald Reagan

Sarah Palin's autobiography is called *Going Rogue*. She got $1 million for the book. She's got a sequel coming out: *Going Shopping*.

David Letterman

ARTS & ENTERTAINMENT

MUSIC

—How do you make a bandstand?
—Take away their chairs.

Anon

A music lover is one who when told that Pamela Anderson sings in the bath, puts his ear to the keyhole.

Anon

Whatever music sounds like, I am glad to say that it does not sound in the smallest degree like German.

Oscar Wilde

Music is the only language in which you cannot say a mean or sarcastic thing.

John Erskine

Making music is like making love: the act is always the same, but each time it's different.

Arthur Rubinstein

Some people can carry a tune, but they seem to stagger under the load.

Richard Armour

—You sing like the Spice Girls.
—Thanks.
—Unfortunately, it wasn't a compliment.

Simon Cowell and Contestant, *Pop Idol*

Did anyone ever tell you, you have the voice of a songbird…slowly dying in tar?

Captain Benjamin 'Hawkeye' Pierce, *M*A*S*H*

The first Sunday I sang in the church choir, 200 people changed their religion.

Fred Allen

Y'know, I could sing like Caruso if I wanted to...but he's already done it.

Tom Waits

Once men sang together round a table in chorus; now one man sings alone for the absurd reason that he can sing better. If scientific civilization goes on...only one man will laugh, because he can laugh better than the rest.

G.K. Chesterton

A young composer had written two pieces of music and asked the great Rossini to hear them both and say which he preferred. He duly played one piece, whereupon Rossini intervened. 'You need not play any more,' he said, 'I prefer the other one.'

Kenneth Edwards

The next piece I composed was written in three flats – I moved three times while writing it.

Victor Borge

When you listen to Mozart, the silence that follows is still Mozart.

Sacha Guitry

Had Wagner been a little more human, he would have been truly divine.

Claude Debussy

Chopin's music is excellent on rainy afternoons in winter, with the fire burning, the shaker full, and the girl somewhat silly.

H.L. Mencken

Brahms feels with his head and thinks with his heart.

Louis Ehlert

Of Schubert I hesitate to speak... His merest belch was as lovely as the song of the sirens. He sweated beauty as naturally as a Christian sweats hate.

H.L. Mencken

If wind and water could write music it would sound like Benjamin Britten's.

Yehudi Menuhin

I am sure my music has a taste of codfish in it.

Edvard Grieg

One has in one's mouth the bizarre and charming taste of a pink sweet stuffed with snow.

Claude Debussy, on Edvard Grieg

Elgar – great gusts of roast-beef music...

Laurie Lee

My music is best understood by children and animals.

Igor Stravinsky

For Strauss, the composer, I take my hat off; for Strauss the man I put it on again.

Arturo Toscanini, on Johann Strauss Jr., the 'Waltz King'

I prefer the company of bankers to musicians, because musicians only want to talk about money.

Jean Sibelius, Finnish composer

Bach on the wrong notes.

Sergei Prokofiev, on Igor Stravinsky

At first I thought I should be a second Beethoven; presently I found that to be another Schubert would be good; then, gradually...I was resigned to be a Humperdinck.

Engelbert Humperdinck, composer

If the best thing a composer can be is dead, the next best thing he can be is German. One of the worst things he can possibly be, still, is American.

Milton Babbitt

John Cage was refreshing but not very bright. His freshness came from an absence of knowledge.

Pierre Boulez

There is no female Mozart because there is no female Jack the Ripper.

Camille Paglia

'Great' conductors, like 'great' actors, soon become unable to play anything but themselves.

Igor Stravinsky

The conductor has the advantage of not seeing the audience.

André Kostelanetz

I don't hire women for my orchestra because if they're pretty, they distract my musicians, and if they're not, they distract me.

Thomas Beecham

Listening to music on records is like being kissed over the telephone.

George Szell, conductor, and champion of live music

Having verse set to music is like looking at a painting through a stained glass window.

Paul Valéry, poet

If the music doesn't say it, how can the words say it for the music?

John Coltrane

Words make you think thoughts. Music makes you feel a feeling. But a song makes you feel a thought.

E.Y. Harburg

In writing songs I've learned as much from Cézanne as I have from Woody Guthrie.

Bob Dylan

The English language is a difficult tool to work with. Two of the hardest words in the language to rhyme are 'life' and 'love'. Of all words! In Italian, easy. But not English.

Stephen Sondheim, on writing lyrics

I was very proud to work with the great George Gershwin, and I would have done it for nothing, which I did.

Howard Dietz, lyricist

Ninety-nine per cent of the world's lovers are not with their first choice. That's what makes the jukebox play.

Willie Nelson

The test of a good song is, can you sing it around a campfire, or, could you imagine Elvis singing it?

Mark Ronson, music producer

I thought being a Beatle would be a great way to get out of Birmingham. I used to dream that Paul McCartney would marry my sister. That was going to be my ticket into the Beatles. Unfortunately, Paul wouldn't have liked my sister.

Ozzy Osbourne

Wings – they're the band the Beatles could have been.

Alan Partridge

Even John Peel used to pop by to see how I was getting on, pre-Womble, never post-Womble.

Mike Batt

Disco is from hell, okay? And not the cool part with all the murderers, but the lame-ass part where all the bad accountants live.

Steven Hyde, *That 70s Show*

Italians tend to break down into two kinds of people: Lucky Luciano or Michelangelo. Frank Sinatra's an exception. He's both.

Gene DiNovo

Frank Sinatra is a singer who comes along once in a lifetime, but why did he have to come in my lifetime?

Bing Crosby

To Sinatra, a microphone is as real as a girl waiting to be kissed.

E.B. White

I could go on stage and make a pizza and they'd still come to see me.

Frank Sinatra

Amy Winehouse is more famous for her drinking and drug-taking than her singing. If only the same were true of Céline Dion.

Sandi Toksvig, *The News Quiz*

Michael Jackson will be remembered for how he touched people.

Martine McCutcheon

Paul Weller is like Victor Meldrew with a suntan.

Noel Gallagher

They're usually very sweet underneath. But they look like some sort of wet dream of Himmler's.

Stephen Fry, on Emos and Goths

Glastonbury was very wet and muddy. There was trench foot, dysentery, peaches...all the Geldof daughters.

Sean Lock, *8 Out of 10 Cats*

Thank God the Spice Girls reunion is over. The only way I want to see Geri Halliwell draped in a Union Flag again is if she died in battle.

Frankie Boyle

—You haven't mentioned Elvis Presley.
—I seldom do unless I stub my toe.

Interviewer and Groucho Marx

Your last album sold 2.5 million copies. How come I don't know anybody who owns one?

Craig Kilborn, to guest, Joey Lawrence

It's like an act of murder: you play with intent to commit something.

Duke Ellington, on jazz

I think I had it in the back of my mind that I wanted to sound like a dry Martini.

Paul Desmond, saxophonist

You can taste a word.

Pearl Bailey, singer

—Your band must arrive on the film-set promptly at 8 o'clock in the morning.
—Jesus Christ, my boys don't even start vomiting till eleven.

Producer and Tommy Dorsey

I never really liked jazz. It always sounded to me like scribble.

Jac Naylor, *Holby City*

It's like living in a house where everything's painted red.

Paul Desmond, listening to the 'free jazz' of Ornette Coleman

Play us a medley of your hit.

Oscar Levant, to George Gershwin

Cabaret singer, Blossom Dearie...offers a tiny sound that without a microphone would not reach the second floor of a doll's house.

Whitney Balliett

I never knew how good our songs were until I heard Ella Fitzgerald sing them.

Ira Gershwin

Ella Fitzgerald had a vocal range so wide you needed an elevator to go from the top to the bottom.

Music Journalist

Ella Fitzgerald could sing the California telephone directory with a broken jaw and make it sound good.

Jazz Fan

'Did I Shave My Legs For This?'

Country music song title, Deana Carter & Rhonda Hart

You don't understand country and western music. It's about the real things in life – murder, train wrecks, amputations, faucets leakin' in the night...

Charlie Haggars, *Mary Hartman, Mary Hartman*

Play a country and western song backwards and what happens? You get your wife back, your dog back and you sober up.

James Woods

I had to get rich so I could afford to sing like I was poor again.

Dolly Parton

'If the Phone Doesn't Ring, It's Me'

Country music song title, Jimmy Buffett, Waylon Jennings & Michael Utley

MUSICAL INSTRUMENT

—What's the difference between a bagpiper and a terrorist?
—Terrorists have sympathizers.

Anon

I found Mr Shortis playing the banjo with a delicacy and conscientiousness that ought to have been devoted to some musical instrument.

George Bernard Shaw

What is a harp but an oversized cheese-slicer with cultural pretensions?

Denis Norden

Harpists spend 90 per cent of their lives tuning their harps and 10 per cent playing out of tune.

Igor Stravinsky

No one should be allowed to play a saxophone until he knows how.

Evan Esar

My father used to play the tuba as a young man. He tried to play 'Flight of the Bumblebee' and blew his liver out through the horn.

Woody Allen

—What's the difference between an accordion and a lawn mower?
—If you put both on eBay, you could sell the lawn mower.

Anon

—What's the definition of 'perfect pitch'?
—When you toss an accordion into a skip and it lands on a set of bagpipes.

Anon

Play a scale in C major metronomically and ask someone else to do the same. The difference in the playing is the proof of the presence of personality.

Igor Stravinsky

As I play, the piano comes alive like an organism... Sometimes when I'm practising it feels as if the piano might actually eat me!

Piotr Anderszewski, Polish concert pianist

The notes I handle no better than many pianists, but the pauses between the notes – ah, that is where the art resides!

Artur Schnabel

—Why are the keys of your piano so yellow?
—The piano's not so old, but the elephant was a heavy smoker.

Interviewer and Victor Borge

He played like he was in jail – behind a few bars and couldn't find the key.

Anon

To use a woman or a guitar, one must know how to tune them.

Spanish proverb

All you need to play is five strings, three notes, two fingers and one asshole.

Keith Richards, on 'open tuning' style of guitar-playing

The electric guitar was vital in helping what I've achieved... Where would I be without it? Playing awfully quietly, for a start.

Keith Richards

Cello players, like other great athletes, must keep their fingers exercised.

Julian Lloyd Webber

I never go to hear virtuosi if I can help it. Even Fritz Kreisler tires me after an hour. It offends me greatly to see a performer getting applause that belongs to the composer.

H.L. Mencken, on the violin virtuoso

It was loud in spots and less loud in other spots, and it had that quality which I have noticed in all violin solos, of seeming to last much longer than it actually did.

P.G. Wodehouse, *The Mating Season*

Difficult do you call it, Sir? I wish it were impossible.

Dr Samuel Johnson, when a solo violinist's technical virtuosity was pointed out to him during a concert

The telephone is my favourite musical instrument.

Quentin Crisp

An oboe is an ill-wind that nobody blows good.

Bennett Cerf

I wish the Government would put a tax on pianos for the incompetent.

Edith Sitwell

His cello playing is just terrible. He had no conception of the instrument. He was blowing into it.

Cello Teacher, *Take the Money and Run*

He couldn't even get a job wetting the thumb of the man who turns over the music for the triangle-player in Spike Jones's City Slickers.

Stewart MacPherson

A xylophone is an instrument used mainly to illustrate the letter X.

Anon

OPERA

And for my next trick I'm going to make my boyfriend disappear. I say the magic word: Opera!

Caroline Duffy, *Caroline in the City*

Opera is a form of entertainment where there is always too much singing.

Claude Debussy

To the opera one goes either for want of any other interest or to facilitate digestion.

Voltaire

Harrods' Food Hall had yielded up its dead.

Jonathan Miller, on Royal Opera House audiences

Opera in English is, in the main, just about as sensible as baseball in Italian.

H.L. Mencken

Sleep is an excellent way of listening to opera.

James Stephens

Every theatre is a madhouse, but an opera theatre is the ward for the incurables.

Franz Schalk, conductor

The tenor voice differs as much from all other human voices as the French horn differs from a piccolo. It has more wolf tones.

H.L. Mencken

Pavarotti's vocal cords were kissed by God.

Harold Schoenberg

—Are you a slave to your voice?
—Yes, but a slave in a golden cage.

Reporter and Luciano Pavarotti

One cracked top note will ruin the whole evening... It is exactly like a bullfight. You are not allowed one mistake.

Luciano Pavarotti

Pavarotti's greatest achievement: bringing football to the middle classes.

Gerry Bond

One fart from Caruso would drown out all the tenors on stage today.

Titta Ruffo

Regard your voice as capital in the bank. When you go to sing, do not draw on your bank account. Sing on your interest and your voice will last.

Lauritz Melchior

If you think you've hit a false note, sing loud. When in doubt, sing loud.

Robert Merrill

My voice is not so much *bel canto* as *can belto*.

Harry Secombe

A healthy sex life. Best thing in the world for a woman's voice.

Leontyne Price, soprano

The soprano sounded like the brakes on the Rome Express.

Charles Winthrop, *Serenade*

She was a singer who had to take any note above 'A' with her eyebrows.

Montague Glass

Her singing was mutiny on the high Cs.

Hedda Hopper

I don't like raised voices; they suggest domestic discord.

Laurie Lee, on his dislike of operatic voices

Stopera!

Graffiti outside a proposed opera house in Holland

DANCE

—Why do Morris Dancers wear bells?
—So they can annoy blind people as well.

Anon

I went to my little niece's tap-dance recital the other day after a few too many beers and I got thrown out cos apparently you're not supposed to stuff the dollar-bills into the leotards.

Tom Cotter

Dancing makes me look like a coma victim being stood up and zapped with a cattle prod.

Mark Corrigan, *Peep Show*

A good education is usually harmful to a dancer. A good calf is better than a good head.

Agnes de Mille, choreographer

There's half a millimetre of Lycra between dancing and sex.

Otto Bathurst

Cynthia was a burlesque queen. I used to love the cute way she'd throw her leg up in the air. Then catch it coming down!

Milton Berle

Fred Astaire was as born to the dance as some men are born to the priesthood.

Tom Shales

Watching the nondancing, nonsinging Astaire is like watching a grounded skylark.

Vincent Canby, on Fred Astaire

Ballroom dancing is the most marvellous business to be in because all the girls are beautiful and all the blokes are gay.

Len Goodman, judge, *Strictly Come Dancing*

Remember those magical nights, Cynthia? We'd dance cheek to cheek. I'd rub my stubble against yours.

Milton Berle

Poofs' football.

John Osborne, on ballet

I'm a guy who likes to keep score. With ballet I can't tell who's ahead.

Fiorella La Guardia

Even the ears must dance!

Natalia Makarova

There are some things it is foolish to try to indicate in a ballet: you cannot indicate your mother-in-law and be readily understood.

George Balanchine

ART

Art is a misquotation of something already heard. Thus, it becomes a quotation of something never heard.

Ned Rorem

I don't know what art is. If it's on the wall at Sotheby's by definition it is art.

Damien Hirst

Art is always the replacement of indifference by attention.

Guy Davenport

I can never pass by the Metropolitan Museum of Art in New York without thinking of it not as a gallery of living portraits but as a cemetery of tax-deductible wealth.

Lewis H. Lapham

All you learn from the art museum is how to keep your mouth shut and how to walk without making squeaky sounds with your shoes.

Curly Sue, *Curly Sue*

Impressionist paintings' prices have become so exorbitant that I can now only afford the frames.

Jeffrey Archer

John Constable observed a landscape so intently and quietly that, while he sat, a field-mouse entered his coat-pocket and fell asleep there.

C.R. Leslie

I have long held the view that Van Gogh's 'Letters to Theo' is a far greater work of art than all his canvases put together.

Henry Miller

You want to know how to paint a perfect painting? It's easy. Make yourself perfect, and then just paint naturally.

Robert Pirsig

Three things that are never drawn or painted the way they really look: a Christmas tree, a star in the sky, and a very rich but ugly person.

Miles Kington

The windmill was invented for the sole purpose of filling up the blank bits in the back of 16th-century Flemish paintings.

Alan Coren

Flesh was the reason why oil painting was invented.

Willem de Kooning

Nudity is to art what a ball is to football.

Antony Gormley

What is the difference between art and pornography? A government grant.

Peter Griffin, *Family Guy*

If you pay enough for pornography it becomes art.

Caller, *Stephen Nolan Show*, Radio 5 Live

Picasso had his blue period. And I'm in my blonde period.

Hugh Hefner

I have a predilection for painting that lends joyousness to a wall.

Pierre-Auguste Renoir

Part of what painting is, is something to look great over the sofa.

Damien Hirst

At one point I found myself standing before an oil of a horse that I figured was probably a self-portrait judging from the general execution.

Peter De Vries

It was touching to see Alma Tadema's delight at finding (in the Grafton Gallery) pictures demonstrably worse than his own.

Edward Marsh

An age is best revealed by its artists of the second rank.

Geoffrey Wolff

One of my dogs jumped through an Augustus John when I worked at Christie's. When we repaired it, it was marginally better than before.

Brian Sewell, art critic

Henri de Toulouse-Lautrec's paintings were almost entirely painted in absinthe.

Gustav Moreau

Let's go and get drunk on light again – it has the power to console.

Georges Seurat

Matisse was accused of doing things any child could do, and he answered very cheerfully, 'Yes, but not what *you* could do.'

Allan Kaprow

Isn't art which needs explaining as pointless as jokes which do?

Paul Whittle

Picasso was constantly upsetting the verb 'to see'.

Roberto Matta

They ought to put out the eyes of painters as they do goldfinches in order that they can sing better.

Pablo Picasso

Picasso would spit in people's eye but people would frame the spit and sell it.

Roberto Matta

Pop Art is the advertising art advertising itself as art that hates advertising.

Harold Rosenberg

A genius with the IQ of a moron.

Gore Vidal, on Andy Warhol

An artist cannot speak about his art any more than a plant can discuss horticulture.

Jean Cocteau

Damien Hirst... the artist who can transform a pickled bovine into a cash cow.

Rachel Campbell-Johnson

What he burned to do, as Velázquez would have burned to do if he had lived today, was to think of another Mickey Mouse and then give up work and watch the money roll in.

P.G. Wodehouse, *Buried Treasure*

It's always good to remember that people find it easier to name ten artists from any century than ten politicians.

John Heath-Stubbs

SCULPTURE

Sculpture is the stuff you trip over when you are backing up trying to look at a painting.

Jules Olitski

Sculpture is the art of the hole and the lump.

Auguste Rodin

We sculptors are generally less nervy than painters because we get a chance to hammer out our neuroses.

Henry Moore

He didn't like heads, did he?

John Prescott, opening an exhibition of Henry Moore's sculptures

To be a sculptor you need to be one part artist and nine parts navvy.

John Skeaping

For Alberto Giacometti, to sculpt is to take the fat off space.

Jean-Paul Sartre

I saw the angel in the marble and carved until I set him free.

Michelangelo Buonarroti

A great sculpture can roll down a hill without breaking.

Michelangelo Buonarroti

—A Hollywood statistician has found that you have the same dimensions as the Venus de Milo.
—I've got it on her. I've got two arms and I know how to use them. Besides, dearie, I'm not marble.

Reporter and Mae West

Marble and flesh look so different that nude statues need never bring a blush to anyone's cheek.

Francis Turner Palgrave

There cannot be another Michelangelo in today's society because our faith in man is too weak.

André Malraux

PHOTOGRAPHY

Do you think you can manage a smile? It's only for a fiftieth of a second.

Frank Modell

Photographing a cake can be art.

Irving Penn

Photography is not art. It's pressing buttons. People take it up because they can't draw.

Lord Snowdon

The photographer is like the cod, which produces a million eggs in order that one may reach maturity.

George Bernard Shaw

Eugène Atget couldn't have cared less about seeing the sights. Not once, in almost 40 years behind a camera, did he point it at the Eiffel Tower.

Anthony Lane, on the French photographer

FILM & HOLLYWOOD

We go to the movies to be entertained, not to see rape, ransacking, pillage and looting. We can get all that in the stock market.

Kennedy Gammage

A good film is when the price of the admission, the dinner and the babysitter was well worth it.

Alfred Hitchcock

People always ask me, 'Did you see Larry's latest movie?' I always say, 'No, but I flushed a ten dollar bill down the toilet, so I feel like I've seen it.'

Jeff Foxworthy

That movie left the theater so fast they held the premiere at Blockbuster.

Jeffrey Ross

If movie theatres had windows, I would have jumped out of one by the end of *Love Actually*.

Stephanie Zacharek

Don't Look Now was so boring I let my hand wander into the crotch of my companion and the only reaction was the line, 'Any diversion is welcome.'

Kenneth Williams

I've only actually sat through 4 movies in 10 years. There's nothing in my contract that says I have to see the stuff. I clocked in and clocked out.

Robert Mitchum

The only reason I went to Hollywood was to fuck that divine Gary Cooper.

Tallulah Bankhead

Hollywood is full of genius. All it lacks is talent.

Henri Bernstein

God felt sorry for actors so he created Hollywood to give them a place in the sun and a swimming pool. The price they had to pay was to surrender their talent.

Cedric Hardwicke

Hollywood is Disneyland staged by Dante. You imagine purgatory is like this, except that the parking is not so good.

Robin Williams

Hollywood is a place where they'll pay you a thousand dollars for a kiss and fifty cents for your soul.

Marilyn Monroe

You can't find true affection in Hollywood because everyone does the fake affection so well.

Carrie Fisher

Hollywood is a town that will nice you to death.

Mel Brooks

You are not allowed to be anything but completely polite in Hollywood. It is a comedy of manners. But it is a world of bed-wetters.

Rupert Everett

If you stay in Beverly Hills too long, you become a Mercedes.

Dustin Hoffman

—Would you do a *Rocky 5*?
—What am I gonna fight? Arthritis?

Jonathan Ross and Sylvester Stallone, *The Jonathan Ross Show*

The Rocky Horror Picture Show: A Sly Stallone retrospective.

Russell Beland

I prefer films to newspapers because papers tell lies about real people and films tell the truth about imaginary ones.

G.K. Chesterton

I like movie stills better than the movies. Movies are too long, it bores me after an hour.

Karl Lagerfeld

All you need to make a movie is a girl and a gun.

Jean-Luc Godard

There are just two stories: going on a journey and a stranger comes to town.

John Gardner

A story should have a beginning, a middle and an end – but not necessarily in that order.

Jean-Luc Godard

Being a writer is like having homework every night for the rest of your life.

Lawrence Kasdan, screenwriter

While in Europe, Eugene O'Neill received a cable on behalf of Jean Harlow, explaining that Miss Harlow wanted the best available American dramatist to write a screenplay for her. Would O'Neill please cable back, collect, confining his answer to 20 words. O'Neill cabled: 'No No No No No No No No No No No No No No No No No No O'Neill.'

Croswell Bowen

Who the fuck wants to see a movie about a little brown guy dressed in a sheet, carrying a beanpole?

Hollywood Executive, to Richard Attenborough
about *Gandhi*, which went on to win 8 Oscars

In this business we make movies. American movies. Leave the films to the French.

Sam Shepard

For some reason, I'm more appreciated in France than I am back home. The subtitles must be incredibly good.

Woody Allen

I don't write pictures about tomatoes that eat people. I write pictures about people who eat tomatoes.

Julius Epstein

It's a bit like leaving your teenage daughter on Jack Nicholson's doorstep; you know no good will come of it.

Unidentified British Author, on selling their novel to Hollywood

Studio heads have foreheads by dint of electrolysis.

S.J. Perelman

Metro-Goldwyn-Merde

Dorothy Parker

People ask me if I went to film school. And I tell them: No, I went to films.

Quentin Tarantino

At work, he is two people – Mr Hyde and Mr Hyde.

Harry Kurnitz, on Billy Wilder

I always thought the real violence in Hollywood isn't what's on the screen. It's what you have to do to raise the money.

David Mamet

Hollywood people don't like making movies. They like making deals.

Roman Polanski

—Movies cost millions of dollars to make.
—That's after gross net deduction profit percentage deferment 10 per cent of the net. Cash, every movie cost $2,184.

Dave and Bobby Bowfinger, Bowfinger

AGENT

Only agents last for ever.

William Goldman

You are the person I distrust least.

Terry Pratchett, taking on Colin Smythe as his agent

The trouble with this business is that the stars keep 90 per cent of my money.

Lord Lew Grade, agent

He is audibly tan.

Fran Lebowitz, listening to an agent phoning from Hollywood

This agent called the William Morris Agency and spoke to his boss. He said: 'I'm not coming in today; I'm sick.' The boss said: 'How sick are you?' The agent said: 'I'm lying in bed right now and I'm fucking my sister. Is that sick enough?'

Norm Crosby

Anybody can make an easy deal, but only a true agent can sell a dog.

Irving 'Swifty' Lazar

Harvey Korman, in honour of his former agent, is having a tree uprooted in Israel.

Daily Variety

MUSICAL

A Bonnie Langford concert? Hmm. I think I'd rather be gang-raped by the House of Lords.

Stephen Fry, *A Bit of Fry and Laurie*

Two things should be cut: the second act and the child's throat.

Noël Coward

If they'd stuffed the child's head up the horse's arse, they would have solved two problems at once.

Noël Coward, when a horse defecated on stage during a musical starring child-star, Bonnie Langford

Don't talk to me about working with kids. When I was in the musical *Annie*, I caught nits from Annie; we all did.

Paul O'Grady

When I saw *Annie* I had to hit myself on the head afterward with a small hammer to get that stupid 'Tomorrow' song out of my head.

Ian Shoales

Lestat is not a show from which you leave whistling anything, except for a taxi.

Anon, on the Elton John and Bernie Taupin musical

The mighty moral instrument, the voice of Paul Robeson, has been issuing gloriously from the radio, and I am knee-deep in its black, glutinous residue.

Kenneth Tynan

Broadway has been very good to me – but then, I've been very good to Broadway.

Ethel Merman

She stopped the show – but then the show wasn't really travelling very fast.

Noël Coward

THEATRE

The English theatre reminds me of a glorious pool table: great legs, a beautiful green felt top and no balls!

Kenneth Tynan

I am unable to pass a theatre without wanting to walk in, and am unable to listen to a single word from an actor without wanting to walk out again.

Howard Jacobson

One goes to the theatre mainly for the intermissions.

Antoni Slonimski

Long experience has taught me that in England nobody goes to the theatre unless he or she has bronchitis.

James Agate

Sore throat and headache; the responsibility, I'm sure, of the occupant of row A in the royal circle, seat no. 4, on Thursday night.

Alec Guinness, diary entry, 22 Oct. 1995

When you visit a West End theatre...it's like sitting in an Anderson shelter in the Imperial War Museum as part of the Blitz Experience.

Sir Richard Eyre, on the dilapidated state of British theatre buildings

The most famous building in the heart of Dublin is the architecturally undistinguished Abbey Theatre, once the city morgue and now entirely restored to its original purpose.

Frank O'Connor

I had no experience of going to the theatre before I became an actor. When I first got a job at the National, I told my dad and he thought I was working on the horse-race.

Eddie Marsan

I started at the Windmill Theatre in 1949. My father didn't want to me appear there. He said I would see things I shouldn't really see. He was correct. On my third day I saw my father sitting in the front row.

Arthur English

There are two kinds of director in the theatre. Those who think they are God, and those who are certain of it.

Rhetta Hughes

In the theatre, the director is God; unfortunately, the actors are atheists.

Žarko Petan

I was once watching the theatre director, John Dexter, rehearsing a piece, when one of the actors asked him how he should play a particular scene. 'Play it,' advised Dexter silkily, 'as if you could act.'

Keith Waterhouse

—I'm in an off-Broadway production of *The Vagina Monologues*. We talk a lot about vaginas.
—That's how I spent college.

Calista Flockhart and David Letterman

When Coral Browne attended the first night of a Peter Brook production, the opening scene revealed a huge phallus about 15 feet high. 'No one we know,' said Coral to her companion.

Spectator magazine

—Wake up you old fool, you slept through the show!
—Who's a fool? *You* watched it.

Stadler and Waldorf, *The Muppet Show*

You have to settle down to Eugene O'Neill like three day cricket: then the slowness becomes a virtue.

Peter Jenkins

When you leave the theatre, if you don't walk several blocks in the wrong direction, the performance has been a failure.

Edith Evans

Two white-haired ladies, wearing floral dresses, as they left the theatre after seeing Chekhov's *The Cherry Orchard*: 'Well, I thought it was very enjoyable, didn't you, Mary? But why on earth they had to set it in Russia is beyond me.'

Maureen Lipman, *overheard*

All I hope now is the dog hasn't been sick in the car.

**One Playgoer to another, leaving the Old Vic
after seeing Peter O'Toole in** *Macbeth*, *overheard*

PLAYWRIGHT

—Does Jeffrey Archer have a future as a popular playwright?
—He doesn't even have a past.

**Questioner and Hugh Leonard, after seeing
his first play,** *Beyond Reasonable Doubt*

Most of the greatest playwrights have been actors – Molière, Shakespeare, for instance. They know an actor's problems, even though few of them have been good actors.

Peter Ustinov

If the playwright is funny, the English look for a serious message, and if he's serious, they look for the joke – that's the English sense of humour.

Sacha Guitry

J.M. Barrie was inspired to write *Peter Pan* after spotting an urchin running down in the street. What a one-in-a-million chance that one should have escaped from the Marine Biology Aquarium that very day.

Humphrey Lyttelton, *I'm Sorry I Haven't a Clue*

I submit all my plays to the National Theatre for rejection. To assure myself I am seeing clearly.

Howard Barker

'Upon Her Play Being Returned to Her, Stain'd With Claret'

Molly Leapor, poem title, c.1740

No performance of a play that is halfway decent is ever as good as the performance the author saw when he wrote it.

Edward Albee

Shut up, Arnold, or I'll direct the play the way you wrote it.

John Dexter, to playwright, Arnold Wesker

If you want to see your plays performed the way you wrote them, become President.

Václav Havel, Czech playwright and president

SHAKESPEARE

Some people cry at weddings, some at funerals. I cry at performances of Shakespeare's comedies.

Russ McDonald

Anthony and Cleopatra is not a funny play. If Shakespeare had meant *Anthony and Cleopatra* to be funny, he would have put a joke in it.

Rowan Atkinson, as a schoolmaster, *The Secret Policeman's Ball*

In the 1890s, there was a touring company of *Hamlet* in the provinces and after a performance the audience said, 'Author! Author!' They pushed a stagehand onstage and someone shot him.

John Wood

I saw *Hamlet, Prince of Denmark* played; but now the old plays begin to disgust this refined age.

John Evelyn, diary entry, 26 Nov. 1661

Moan moan moan moan moan moan moan moan moan moan moan moan moan moan moan moan moan moan moan moan moan moan moan moan moan. Dead.

Winning entry in a competition to encapsulate the entire plot of *Hamlet* into 140 characters or fewer, for twitter.com

There is nothing lonelier than being on stage in pantaloons... I leave the Tudor verse to others.

Bill Nighy, actor, who has forsworn the Bard

After all, all he did was string together a lot of old, well-known quotations.

H. L. Mencken

No one can convince me that Shakespeare didn't make up words just to upset the actors.

Jack Lemmon, rehearsing Marcellus in *Hamlet*

I've always been a bit afraid of Shakespeare. I just thought it was for people with posh voices, middle class backgrounds and central heating.

Lenny Henry

After God, Shakespeare has created most.

Alexandre Dumas

Shakespeare is a reason to believe in aliens. Most authors have one idea per book. Shakespeare had two per sentence.

Lauren Hutton

Shakespeare, like David Beckham, is king of the set piece.

David Baddiel

Romeo and Juliet: William Shakespeare's 17th century interpretation of Leonardo DiCaprio's work of the same name.

Scott Wilson

I failed my audition as Romeo through a misunderstanding over a simple stage direction. My copy of the script clearly said: 'Enter Juliet from the rear.'

Lester Stevens

All of Stratford...suggests powdered history – add hot water and stir and you have a delicious, nourishing Shakespeare.

Margaret Halsey

If we wish to know the force of human genius we should read Shakespeare. If we wish to see the insignificance of human learning, we may study his commentators.

William Hazlitt

The remarkable thing about Shakespeare is that he is really very good – in spite of all the people who say he is very good.

Robert Graves

People simply do not read Shakespeare anymore, nor the Bible either. They read *about* Shakespeare.

Henry Miller

I heard someone tried the monkeys-on-typewriters bit trying for the plays of William Shakespeare, but all they got was the collected works of Francis Bacon.

Bill Hoest, cartoon caption

I heard that if you locked Shakespeare in a room with a typewriter for long enough, he'd eventually write all the songs by the Monkees.

Anon

ACTORS & ACTING

—Why did you go on stage?
—To get out of the audience.

Interviewer and Michael Blakemore

Acting is the most minor of gifts. After all, Shirley Temple could do it when she was four.

Katharine Hepburn

Players, Sir! I look on them as no better than creatures set upon tables and joint stools to make faces and produce laughter, like dancing dogs.

Dr Samuel Johnson

When he was a young boy, Sanjeev Bhaskar confided in his parents that he wanted to be an actor. His dad's response? 'We pronounce it *doctor*.'

Charlotte Civil

I always felt I was a nobody, and the only way for me to be somebody was to be – well, somebody else. Which is probably why I wanted to act.

Marilyn Monroe

I feel most like myself when I am playing someone else.

Ingrid Bergman

I realised I should try harder to be an actress because I'd never make it as a waitress.

Jane Krakowski

My sister wanted to be an actress. She never made it, but she does live in a trailer... so she got halfway. She's an actress, she's just never called to the set.

Mitch Hedberg

When people warned me there would be long periods out of work if I became an actor, I couldn't keep a straight face because that was exactly what I had in mind.

Bill Nighy

Making the rounds of auditions is like being a door-to-door brush salesman. Only you are the brush.

Robert Barton

—Make up your mind, dear heart. Do you want to be a great actor or a household word?
—Both.

Laurence Olivier and Richard Burton

I'm an actor, not a star. Stars are people who live in Hollywood and have heart-shaped swimming pools.

Al Pacino

The bad news is that Philip Seymour Hoffman won't be a $25 million star. The good news is that he'll work for the rest of his life.

Joel Schumacher

Q: Do actors need brains? A: If they can act, no. If they can't, yes.

James Agate

I always admired Katharine Hepburn's cheekbones. More than her films.

Bette Davis

Dramatic art in her opinion is knowing how to fill a sweater.

Bette Davis, about Jayne Mansfield, famous for her 40-inch bust

There are only two great actors in America. You are the other one.

President Franklin Roosevelt, to Orson Welles

I once asked a US writer why we Brits always get the bad-guy parts.
He explained that we are the only ethnic group left in the world that
doesn't mind.

Ian Ogilvy

—Dame Edith, how do you approach your parts? How do you go about
researching? How do you—
—I pretend, dear boy, I pretend.

Interviewer and Dame Edith Evans

I don't go in for that Method rubbish. Go into a room and pretend to be
a packet of Kellogg's or a tin of condensed milk. God, what crap.

Dirk Bogarde

I was in New York with Maggie Smith...and we were asked about the
Sanford Meisner Method school of acting, which is based on ruthless
self-exploration. Maggie said: 'Oh, we have that in England, too. We call
it wanking.'

Judi Dench

When an actor comes to me and wants to discuss his character, I say, 'It's
in the script.' If he says, 'But what's my motivation?', I say, 'Your salary.'

Alfred Hitchcock

If you give audiences a chance they'll do half your acting for you.

Katharine Hepburn

I speak, then some bullshit. I speak again, more bullshit. Then I speak again.

Unidentified Actor, describing his scene

If you haven't complete rapport with the actress with whom you are acting it is like being thrust into the middle of a particularly edgy bullfight.

Peter Ustinov

She has two expressions: joy and indigestion.

Dorothy Parker, on Marion Davies

I loved the way all the actresses smelt. I didn't realise until years after that it was gin.

Rhys Ifans, recalling his days as a stagehand

I can't do the same thing every night, the same gestures…it's like putting on dirty panties every day.

Brigitte Bardot, on acting in the theatre

The question actors most often get asked is how they can bear saying the same things over and over again night after night, but God knows the answer to that is, don't we all anyway; might as well get paid for it.

Elaine Dundy

FAME & CELEBRITY

Actor David Carradine has been found dead in a wardrobe in his Bangkok hotel room, after 'accidentally' hanging himself while attempting auto-erotic asphyxiation. He was best known for his role as Kwai Chang Caine in the TV series *Kung Fu*. Well, not anymore he's not.

Frankie Boyle

Fame means millions of people have a wrong idea of who you are.

Erica Jong

—Oh, Miss West, I've heard so much about you!
—Yeah, honey, but you can't prove a thing.

Fan and Mae West

I was in a bookshop in Ireland recently and a guy came up to me and said, 'Are you who you think you are?'

Paul Merton

You're never who you think you are. Sometime in the 1980s, an old lady approached me and asked, 'Mr Elton, may I have your autograph?' I told her that I wasn't Elton but David Bowie. She replied, 'Oh, thank goodness. I couldn't stand his red hair and all that make up.'

David Bowie

It's like having Alzheimer's disease. You don't know anybody, but they all know you.

Tony Curtis

What makes a star a star is not that 'indefinable something extra'...
What makes a star a star is that indefinable something MISSING.

Julie Burchill

—Is that a star over there?
—No, that's Ted Danson.

Nancy Lee and Hank Gordon, *Doc Hollywood*

People want to fuck movie stars and hug television stars.

Television adage

When rulers are ruthless and priests are randy, actors become role models.

Mavor Moore

Carroll Levis, the talent-scout, discovered me. He lifted up a manhole cover and there I was!

Harold Berens

One day you are a signature, next day you're an autograph.

Billy Wilder

Glamour girl Katie Price did a book signing last week that lasted nearly two hours. To be fair, she didn't take quite so long to sign the second book.

Frank Skinner

I don't sign parts of the body, even if they're still attached.

Terry Pratchett

Writing is my trade and I exercise it only when I am obliged to. It would never be fair to ask a doctor for one of his corpses to remember him by.

Mark Twain, declining a request for an autograph

A celebrity is a person who works hard all his life to become well known, and then wears dark glasses to avoid being recognized.

Fred Allen

Joan Collins is a proper celebrity. She sunbathes in a turban and red lipstick.

Victoria Beckham

The most intolerable people are provincial celebrities.

Anton Chekhov

I made quite a name for myself back home. I left when I found out what it was.

Herb Shriner

They've put a plaque on the wall of the house where I was born. It says: condemned.

Arthur Askey

With fame I become more and more stupid, which of course is a very common phenomenon.

Albert Einstein

My persona don't really work without fame. Without fame, this haircut could be mistaken for mental illness.

Russell Brand

In America I had two secretaries – one for autographs and the other for locks of hair. Within six months one had died of writer's cramp, and the other was completely bald.

Oscar Wilde

Posh and Becks will need more of a talent than just acting like air is absolutely delicious...

Mandy Stadtmiller, after the Beckhams' move to Los Angeles, 2007

If you put a brown jug of water on TV for five minutes a night, it will get fan mail.

Michael Aspel, *attrib.*

Fame is like V.D. Everybody wants to fuck you until they see what they get.

Sylvester Stallone

Being famous means that you can get a table in a restaurant. But then you've got to go past a line of people who can't get a table, and that's a bad feeling.

Hugh Laurie

The famous are balloons far up in the sky, to be envied for their quiet freedom or shot down as enemies.

Arthur Miller

Censure is the tax a man pays to the public for being eminent.

Jonathan Swift

When I hear a man applauded by the mob I always feel a pang of pity for him. All he has to do to be hissed is to live long enough.

H.L. Mencken

I was on a bus and I heard someone say: 'I saw one of those Two Fat ladies the other day – not the dead one.'

Kevin Ashman

PUBLICITY

One dreams of the goddess Fame and winds up with the bitch Publicity.

Peter De Vries

Hell hath no fury like a hooker with a press agent.

Frank Sinatra, on kiss-and-tell stories

Wooing the press is an exercise roughly akin to picnicking with a tiger. You might enjoy the meal, but the tiger always eats last.

Maureen Dowd

He doesn't do standing up parties – even the normal ones – so he is not a cocktail party goer. I am his representative on earth.

Nigella Lawson, on why her husband, Charles Saatchi, missed his own book launch

Live by publicity, you'll probably die by publicity.

Russell Baker

TELEVISION

There are three great moments in a man's life: when he buys a house, a car, and a new TV.

Archie Bunker, *All in the Family*

The human race is divided into two distinct groups: those who walk into rooms and automatically turn television sets on, and those who walk into rooms and automatically turn them off. The trouble is that they end up marrying each other.

Raymond Shaw, *The Manchurian Candidate*

My husband wanted one of those big-screen TVs for his birthday. I just moved his chair closer to the one we already have.

Wendy Liebman

Daddy, tell us again how when you were a boy you had to walk all the way across the room to change channels.

Anon

When I was your age, television was called books.

Grandpa, *The Princess Bride*

When I got my first TV set, I stopped caring so much about having close relationships with other people... I started an affair with my television.

Andy Warhol

Television's far more entertaining and much less trouble than a wife would be.

George Boar

Television: teacher... mother... secret lover!

Homer Simpson

Television is a method to deliver advertising like a cigarette is a method to deliver nicotine.

Bill Maher

Television – a medium, so called because it is neither rare nor well-done.

Ernie Kovacs

RADIO

We sauntered into the rumpus room and Diana turned on the radio. With a savage snarl the radio turned on her.

S.J. Perelman

If I wished to be awakened by Stevie Wonder I would sleep with Stevie Wonder.

Fran Lebowitz, on clock-radios

Radio lets people see things with their own ears.

New York Times

Radio – that wonderful invention by which I can reach millions of people who fortunately can't reach me.

Milton Berle

Chris Evans is not as good as he thinks he is, but then nobody has ever been as good as Evans thinks he is.

Chris Tarrant

George Lamb talks, like most radio presenters, as if chased by a pathological fear of dead air.

Laura Barton

All disc jockeys talk like cheeky sons-in-law chatting up mums-in-law.

Kenneth Tynan

COMEDY

There are three golden rules of comedy: 1) If in doubt, wobble about; 2) If that don't work, fall over; 3) If that don't work – knob out!

Malcolm Hardee

My favourite noise in comedy is the laugh followed by the sharp intake of breath.

Jimmy Carr

Bad Taste: the jokes about atrocities rather than those atrocities themselves, oddly.

Mike Barfield, *Dictionary for our Time*

Never forget that the following take themselves seriously: politicians, vegetarians, advanced thinkers and gentlemen in the care of warders and male nurses.

D.B. Wyndham-Lewis

A person reveals his character by nothing so clearly as the joke he resents.

Georg Christoph Lichtenberg

Say I make a 'joke' and it doesn't appeal to you, you are annoyed rather than amused. Annoyed, simply because you haven't found out how to unlaugh.

Flann O'Brien

Gay audiences will laugh at anything except Barbra Streisand. If you dare to say she's cross-eyed... I have one joke in my act that she can cross the street without looking to the right or the left. And they just go 'huh'.

Joan Rivers

What is this, an audience or a jury?

Johnny Carson, after a joke bombed

I don't mind when my jokes die because they go to Heaven and get 72 virgin jokes.

Omar Marzouk

To me, clowns aren't funny. In fact, they're kind of scary. I've wondered where this started, and I think it goes back to the time I went to the circus and a clown killed my dad.

Jack Handey

The only time Chevy Chase has a funny bone in his body is when I fuck him in the ass.

Richard Belzer, comedian

Humour is falling downstairs if you do it while in the act of warning your wife not to.

Kenneth Bird

Looking over old *Punche*s. Am struck with the frequent wrong direction of satire, and of commendation, when seen by the light of later days.

Thomas Hardy

If you crack a joke in London, people laugh. If you crack a joke in Hollywood, they say, 'You're funny.'

Rhys Ifans

A very little wit is valued in a woman, as we are pleased with a few words spoken plain by a parrot.

Jonathan Swift

Charlie Chaplin's genius was in comedy. He had no sense of humour, particularly about himself.

Lita Grey, his ex-wife

If you can't see the humour in yourself, you could be missing the joke of the century.

Dame Edna Everage

HECKLE

I did a show last week in another place where the act before me was so terrible that throughout my performance they kept booing *him*. They couldn't forget how lousy he was. Some people even walked out on him while *I* was still performing!

Jackie Mason

—They threw an apple at me!
—Well, watermelons are out of season.

Lassparri and Otis B. Driftwood (Groucho Marx), *A Night at the Opera*

It's kind of silly to heckle. You've spent big money to see the show, and you're ruining it for yourself. It's like going to the ballet and trying to trip up the dancers.

Jimmy Brogan

The house-lights should immediately be trained on hecklers. Like owls they cannot hoot comfortably when illuminated.

Peter Ustinov

My uncle was thrown out of a mime show for having a seizure. They thought he was heckling.

Jeff Shaw

I don't mind hecklers, because I know how to ignore people: I was an airline stewardess.

Jo Ann Deering

—Get your cunt out!
—I don't bring my cunt to work; I usually find there's at least one cunt in the audience already.

Male Audience Member and Donna McPhail

—I'm a schizophrenic.
—Well, you can both fuck off then!

Jim Tavare and Heckler

Get 'em on!

Audience Member, when Liza Minnelli, 62, tore off her black sequinned trousers during the finale of her concert at the London Coliseum, 2008

If your cock's as big as your mouth, honey, I'll see you after the show.

Mae West, to a heckler

—You'd make a good vice-president!
—That was the ultimate heckle.

Unidentified Student and Al Gore, when he was a presidential candidate

Get off, you bastard!...............Has he gone yet?

Blind Heckler, to Frank Skinner

TRANSPORT

TRANSPORT – GENERAL

A man walks into a bar in Ireland and says to the barman: 'What's the quickest way to Dublin?' Barman says, 'Are you walking or driving?' 'Driving,' says the man. Barman says, 'That's the quickest way.'

Anon

As Captain Oates said: 'There's never a minicab around when you need one.'

William Rushton

Cab drivers are living proof that practice does not make perfect.

Howard Ogden

I recently retraced on foot a famous journey that William Hazlitt made from Shropshire to Somerset to visit Wordsworth and Coleridge. I spent two weeks slogging through nettle beds before I realised the bastard had taken the coach.

A.C. Grayling

If God wanted us to walk he'd have given us pogo sticks instead of feet. Feet are made to fit car pedals.

Stirling Moss

No other form of transport in the rest of my life has ever come up to the bliss of my pram.

Osbert Lancaster

CAR

What I should have said: Look, there's a lot of traffic, and he's probably been stuck in a meeting all day and didn't get your message, or he'd have called. I'm sure there's nothing to worry about.
What I did say: Maybe he's dead.

Cynthia Harrison

Fear is being stuck in traffic and you just had two cups of coffee and a bran muffin.

John Mendoza

They have a sign on the freeway that says: 'Orange cones mean men at work'. What else could orange cones mean? Psychedelic witches embedded in asphalt?

Karin Babbitt

If you can read this, where the hell is my caravan?

Notice seen in a car in Norfolk by G. Wilford

Mother-in-law in Boot

Car bumper sticker

An Italian driver's reaction to any encounter with another vehicle is, first, stunned disbelief, then outrage.

Jack Burgess

—Why can't Helen Keller drive?
—She's a woman.

Anon

Who would give me a driver's licence? I got two tickets on my written test.
Phyllis Diller

One day my wife drove up the side of a building...and hit another woman driving down.

Milton Berle

My wife had her driver's test the other day. She got 8 out of 10. The other 2 guys jumped clear.

Rodney Dangerfield

I sailed through my driving test. That's why I failed it. Apparently, you're meant to use a car, and my yacht capsized in Balham High Road.

Arthur Smith, *The Smith Lectures*

I am the worst driver... I should drive a hearse and cut out the middleman.

Wendy Liebman

Oddly enough, all the bad drivers I have ever known died peacefully in their beds.

Paul Johnson

A man took his car to the garage for a service. The mechanic looked under the bonnet and said: 'I'd keep the oil and change the car.'

Anon

You might be a redneck if your car breaks down on the side of the road and you never go back and get it.

Jeff Foxworthy

My wife called me. She said, 'There's water in the carburettor.' I said, 'Where's the car?' She said, 'In the lake.'

Henny Youngman

My husband insists on fixing the car himself, even though he is so far from mechanical that I've seen him try to look at the engine through the ignition keyhole.

Phyllis Diller

I had a Rolls-Royce that ran so quiet, I didn't *know* it had broken down. But the trees weren't moving so I figured it had. Then I figured maybe for the $24,000 I had paid for it, the place I was going to would come to me!

Bill Cosby

Nothing tests your ethics like selling a used car.

Linda Holland

If you get a van, you're not just a man any more. You are a man with a van. You get a van, Jez, and we could be men with ven.

Super Hans, *Peep Show*

Eighty per cent of the people of Britain want more money spent on public transport in order that other people will travel on the buses so that there is more room for them to drive their cars.

John Gummer

Mass transportation is doomed to failure in North America because a person's car is the only place where he can be alone and think.

Marshall McLuhan

My idea of paradise is a perfect automobile going thirty miles an hour on a smooth road to a twelfth-century cathedral.

Henry Adams

Never take a cross-country trip with a kid who has just learned to whistle.

Jean Deuel

Like a lot of men, my boyfriend takes great pride in his car. Honey, this car is detailed, waxed and vacuumed weekly. My car, on the other hand, looks like a really big purse.

Diane Nichols

A friend of mine is a pilot, and we were going somewhere in his car, and for no reason at all he waited 45 minutes before pulling out of his driveway.

Steven Wright

The nicest thing about the Jaguar XJR is that you can pull up outside an expensive West End hotel and the doorman will scuttle out and open the door, and yet, in south London, it won't be touched because people assume you're a drug dealer.

Jeremy Clarkson

Sat nav? In no time at all you're up a lane staring at a herd of cows and wondering why this isn't inner Bristol.

Joan Bakewell

I was given a parking ticket. I said to the policeman, 'What do I do with this?' 'Keep it,' he said. 'If you manage to collect three of them, you get a bicycle.'

Denis Norden

BICYCLE

Get a bicycle. You will not regret it, if you live.

Mark Twain

The bicycle is a curious vehicle. Its passenger is its engine.

John Howard

The bicycle is the most efficient machine ever created: converting calories into gas, a bicycle gets the equivalent of 3,000 miles per gallon.

Bill Strickland

Bicycles are almost as good as guitars for meeting girls.

Bob Weir

When I go biking…I am mentally far far away from civilization. The world is breaking someone else's heart.

Diane Ackerman

The fresh air, the exercise, and the pleasure of a leather saddle between one's thighs. 'Bicycle smile' I believe they call it.

Virginia Cranehill, *Road to Wellville*

Being dangerous without being fun puts bicycles in a category with open-heart surgery, the South Bronx, and divorce.

P.J. O'Rourke

TRAIN

Tell me, porter, does this train clap at Stopham Junction?

Arthur Marshall

—Two return tickets, please.
—Where to?
—Why, back here, of course.

Oliver Hardy and Railway Station Clerk

We are sorry for the substantial delay. This is due to leaves on the lines, and further due to those leaves still being attached to the trees.

Local station announcement, noted by Mark Solon

It was then that we heard the words that strike fear into the heart of every God-fearing commuter: 'replacement bus service'.

David Lewis

I have talked to the Pope, the Queen, the Prime Minister and Mother Teresa, but the station master at Westbury is unavailable?

Ann Widdecombe, trying to ring the Wiltshire station from a broken-down train

Railway timetable: a triumph of hope over experience.

Mike Barfield, *Dictionary for our Time*

The train to Birmingham was in an ironical mood, for it ran into New Street to the very minute of the timetable.

Arnold Bennett, 1912

The tragedy of travelling first class is that however comfortable you are, and however many free drinks you get, you still arrive at your destination at the same time as the second-class passengers.

Miles Kington

AIR TRAVEL

A tomcat hijacked a plane, stuck a pistol into the pilot's ribs and demanded: 'Take me to the canaries.'

Bob Monkhouse

Airports like abattoirs are white.

Todd McEwen

At the airport they asked me if anybody I didn't know gave me anything. Even the people I know don't give me anything.

George Wallace

Checking in at Luton airport recently, I was asked: 'Has anyone put anything in your luggage without you knowing?'

Pauline Pearson

On a flight to Belfast, I was upgraded to business class. I was a bit scared. I thought, will I have to play golf?

Jeremy Hardy

The food on the plane was fit for a king. 'Here, King!'

Henny Youngman

Overly chatty airline captains are one of air travel's annoyances. But as a young pilot I often flew beside one captain, a taciturn Yorkshireman, who had perfected his passenger address, reducing it to slightly less than two words. In the middle of the flight he would announce to the cabin: ''alf way.'

Colwyn Lee

—How was your flight?
—Well, aeronautically, it was a great success. Socially, it left quite a bit to be desired.

Noël Coward

If you're travelling alone, beware of seatmates who by way of starting a conversation make remarks like: 'I just have to talk to someone – my teeth are spying on me.'

Miss Piggy

A child on a farm sees a plane fly overhead and dreams of a faraway place. A traveller on the plane sees the farmhouse and dreams of home.

Carl Burns

If you're ever on an airplane that's crashing, see if you can't organize a quick thing of group sex, because come on, you squares!

Jack Handey

I had an uncle who was afraid to fly. So he took a train and you know what happened? A plane fell on it.

Roger Miller

SEA TRAVEL

Cruising: if you thought you didn't like people on land...

Carol Leifer

I have smelled what suntan lotion smells like spread over 21,000 tons of hot flesh.

David Foster Wallace, on a cruise

A luxury liner is really just a bad play surrounded by water.

Clive James

I have in one week been the object of over 1,500 professional smiles.

David Foster Wallace, on a cruise

Remember when I met you on the high seas, Cynthia. How coy you were. You tried to get away from me and what a fight you put up! You bent four of my harpoons.

Milton Berle

I have now heard – and am powerless to describe – reggae elevator music.

David Foster Wallace, on a cruise

We all like to see people seasick when we are not, ourselves.

Mark Twain

I have heard a professional comedian tell folks, without irony, 'But seriously.'

David Foster Wallace, on a cruise

I was so seasick, my stomach was ejecting meals I had hoped to eat the following week.

Fred Allen

I have learned what it is to become afraid of one's own toilet.

David Foster Wallace, on a cruise

It is no mystery to me at all why so many people commit suicide on boats. There's nothing preferable to do.

Colin Thubron

TRAVEL & COUNTRIES

TRAVEL & TOURISM

When one realizes that his life is worthless he either commits suicide or travels.

Edward Dahlberg

I think that travel comes from some deep urge to see the world, like the urge that brings up a worm in an Irish bog to see the moon when it is full.

Lord Dunsany

People travel to faraway places to watch, in fascination, the kind of people they ignore at home.

Dagobert D. Runes

One never feels such distaste for one's countrymen and countrywomen as when one meets them abroad.

Rose Macaulay

We can go away right now. I pack light. Everything we need is right here in my pants.

Ryan Harrison, to Lauren Goodhue, *Wrongfully Accused*

STREETS FLOODED. PLEASE ADVISE.

Robert Benchley, telegram sent on his arrival in Venice

Come on in here and see our stuff, señorita! We rip you off less!

Junk-Jewellery Seller, Tijuana market, overheard by Tee

Nepal is the most fun place in the world. You've got monkeys roaming around, cremations and animal sacrifices... The country could have been invented by Beavis and Butt-head. Even the gods have nice breasts.

Emo Philips

—You know what I want to get while I'm here in India? A Sherpa. That would be so cool.

—What's a Sherpa?

—It's, like, a people endemic to the Himalayas. You can buy one, and they carry your stuff for you!

Two American Girls in Goa, India, overheard by wish I were Canadian

The tyrannical beauty of Hawaii, after a little while, becomes a little troubling. The beauty, the palm trees... It's like being hit over the head with a rainbow.

Russell Brand

Any sizable Portuguese town looks like a superstitious bride's finery – something old, something new, something borrowed, and something blue.

Mary McCarthy

Some years ago entering Stonehenge, I overheard a harassed mother say to her small daughter, 'Now, just you be careful and don't knock anything over.'

L. Markes

I reckon that Stonehenge was built by the contemporary equivalent of Microsoft, whereas Avebury was definitely an Apple circle.

Terry Pratchett

Asthmatics: avoid going on holiday to places where the scenery is described as breathtaking.

Top Tip, *Viz* magazine

Fortissimo at last!

Gustav Mahler, visiting Niagara Falls

Niagara Falls would be more impressive if it flowed the other way.

Oscar Wilde

I had this great idea to make the Great Wall of China into a handball court.

George Gobel

Noël Coward was once staying round the corner from the Taj Mahal and refused to see it. 'I'd seen it on biscuit boxes and didn't want to spoil the illusion.'

John Heilpern

Ruins, museums and cathedrals...leave no imprint whatsoever. In fact, many of the world's noblest antiquities have definitely irritated me. Perhaps the sheen on them of so many hundreds of years' intensive appreciation makes them smug.

Noël Coward

As for seeing the town, he did not even think of it, being of that breed of Britons who have their servants do their sightseeing for them.

Jules Verne, *Around the World in Eighty Days*

He who has seen one cathedral ten times has seen something; he who has seen ten cathedrals once has seen but little; and he who has spent half an hour in each of a hundred cathedrals has seen nothing at all.

Sinclair Lewis

Like all great travellers, I have seen more than I remember, and remember more than I have seen.

Benjamin Disraeli

Most of my treasured memories of travel are recollections of sitting.

Robert Thomas Allen

In Paris they just simply...stared when we spoke to them in French! We never did succeed in making those idiots understand their own language.

Mark Twain

—I just heard General de Gaulle has died. I wonder what he and God are talking about in heaven?
—That depends on how good God's French is.

Friend and Noël Coward

Why do you want to go Paris? There are parts of Reading you haven't seen yet.

Eva Gervais, to her son, Ricky

Travelling is the ruin of all happiness! There's no looking at a building here, after seeing Italy.

Fanny Burney

A blade of grass is always a blade of grass, whether in one country or another.

Dr Samuel Johnson, preferring people-watching to views

Do you know, if you took all the metal that it took to make the Eiffel Tower and laid it end to end…it would fall down.

Sandi Toksvig

—Coming up?
—What's up there?
—The view.
—The view of what? The view of down here? I can see that down here.
—Ray, you are about the worst tourist in the whole world.

Ken and Ray, *In Bruges*

I'm 73 years old, I've seen half the wonders of the world and I never laid eyes on a finer sight than the curve of Betty Browning's breasts.

Grandfather George, *Hope and Glory*

COUNTRIES – GENERAL

Austria is the most amazing place in Europe. We're all proud of our country and are raised to try and achieve the Austrian Dream – find a job, get a dungeon and raise a family in it.

Brüno Gehard, aka Sacha Baron Cohen

Americans go to France expecting to hear someone say, 'Sank heavens for leetle girls,' and instead they find some really sullen bureaucrat saying, 'Grandmoser's maiden name?' and they get irritated.

Calvin Trillin

I can't think much of a people who drew cats the same way for four thousand years.

Lord Kitchener, on Egypt

David Hasselhoff has gone on to sell more records in the reunified country of Germany than Madonna. Who says the Germans don't have a sense of humour?

David Batty

A German joke is no laughing matter.

Anon

One could almost believe that in this people there is a peculiar sense of life as a mathematical problem which is known to have a solution.

Isak Dinesen, on the Germans

—What's the capital of Iceland?
—About £3.50.

Anon

Charles is Viceroy of India, which means he can take over India when Roy retires.

Milton Jones, *The Unbelievable Truth*

We have often heard Cork called the Venice of Ireland, but have never heard Venice called the Cork of Italy.

John Betjeman

The Italians have a saying: 'Keep your friends close and your enemies closer,' and although they've never won a war or mass-produced a decent car, in this area they are correct.

Jack Donaghy, *30 Rock*

Men run the country, but women run men. Italy is, in reality, a crypto-matriachy.

Luigo Barzini

Italy ends up giving one a nostalgia for grey.

Edmond and Jules de Goncourt

We believed for fifty years that the Japanese are small Americans who wanted to be like us. They are not.

Lester Thurow

Japan: the land where they don't have time to let the trees grow tall.

Edina Monsoon, *Absolutely Fabulous*

In Japan everything is miniaturised. The women are none too pleased about it.

Ken Dodd

In Poland, people talk foolishly about important things, and in England intelligently about foolish things.

Leopold Infeld

The Swedes have their medical expenses taken care of, all of their welfare costs paid for, their rent subsidized, and so much done for them, that if they lose their car keys, they promptly commit suicide.

Godfrey Cambridge

Switzerland is a small, steep country, much more up and down than sideways, and is all stuck over with large brown hotels built in the cuckoo-clock style of architecture.

Ernest Hemingway

Since both its national products, snow and chocolate, melt, the cuckoo clock was invented solely in order to give tourists something solid to remember it by.

Alan Coren, on Switzerland

Switzerland... France to the right of 'em, Austrians to the left of 'em, Germans up above, Italians below. You'd never sell that flat would you?

Al Murray, *The Pub Landlord's Book of Common Sense*

I walked across Switzerland – and am cured of that little country for ever. The only excitement in it is that you can throw a stone a frightfully long way down – and that is forbidden by law.

D.H. Lawrence

As soon as I stepped off the plane, I became a Turkish nationalist! There was a man in a black uniform, smoking heavily underneath a 'No smoking' sign. I thought, 'That's my kind of place'.

Norman Stone, in Ankara

AMERICA

I am willing to love all mankind, except an American.

Dr Samuel Johnson

America: 20 Million Illegal Immigrants Can't Be Wrong!

Richard Jeni, slogan against anti-Americanism

I came to America because I heard the streets were paved with gold. When I got here I found out three things. First, they weren't paved with gold; second, they weren't paved at all; and third, I was expected to pave them.

Italian Immigrant, in a letter to his relatives, 1912

America is a place where Jewish merchants sell Zen love beads to Agnostics for Christmas.

John Burton Brimer

Americans may have no identity, but they do have wonderful teeth.

Jean Baudrillard

My niece married a Greek who had taken out his US naturalization papers, and was very proud of his new status. They recently purchased a home; and when the deed came, he looked it over solemnly, then grinned and broke into a little dance step. 'I'm a real American now,' he exclaimed, 'I'm in debt!'

R.M. Fee

The American way is the way most law-abiding, tax-paying Americans live – in debt. Does this make a balanced budget un-American?

Cullen Hightower

Un-American: wicked, intolerable, heathenish.

Ambrose Bierce

A Coke is a Coke and no amount of money can get you a better Coke than the one the bum on the corner is drinking. All the Cokes are the same and all the Cokes are good... The idea of America is so wonderful because the more equal something is, the more American it is.

Andy Warhol

In the United States there is more space where nobody is than where anybody is. That is what makes America what it is.

Gertrude Stein

Nothing that you say about the whole country is going to be true.

Alistair Cooke

America is a vast conspiracy to make you happy.

John Updike

The American people never carry an umbrella. They prepare to walk in eternal sunshine.

Alfred E. Smith

The happy ending is our national belief.

Mary McCarthy

If America leads a blessed life, then why did God put all of our oil under people who hate us?

Jon Stewart

Double – no triple – our troubles and we'd still be better off than any other people on earth.

Ronald Reagan

Asked if they think they are good at maths, Americans tend to answer yes when they are not, while Koreans answer no when they are.

Alan Wolfe

The British think they have a sense of irony. They also think they have a special relationship with America. But they cannot have it both ways.

Miles Kington

We are all American at puberty; we die French.

Evelyn Waugh

AMERICAN PLACES

I was born in Alabama, but I only lived there for a month before I'd done everything there was to do.

Paula Poundstone

The Deep South...Alabama. You talk about Darwin's waiting room, there are guys in Alabama who are their own father.

Dennis Miller

Don King started out in Cleveland and then he went to prison – which, if you are from Cleveland, is called upward mobility.

Colin Quinn

Montana's lovely, beautiful and flat... In fact it's so flat that if your dog runs away you can watch him go for three days.

Rich Hall

The only trouble with Spokane, Washington, as a city, is that there's nothing to do after 10 o'clock. In the morning.

Jim Murray

The town was so small, when I went to the public library there was a sign on the door that said: 'The book is out.'

Fred Allen

The only thing Californians read is the licence plate in front of them.

Neil Simon

This is California. Blondes are like the state flower or something.

Steve Sanders, *Beverly Hills 90210*

—I'd like to show you around town. You know, a kind of cultural tour of L.A.
—That's the first 15 minutes, then what?

Harris T. Telemacher and Sara McDowel, L.A. Story

One of the things I had a hard time getting used to when I came to California in '78 was Santa Claus in shorts.

Dennis Franz

California is a tragic country – like Palestine, like every Promised Land.

Christopher Isherwood

Living in California adds ten years to a man's life. And those extra ten years I'd like to spend in New York.

Harry Ruby

It is not that Los Angeles is altogether hideous, it is even by degrees pleasant, but for an Easterner there is never any salt in the wind; it is like Mexican cooking without the chilli.

Norman Mailer

Los Angeles is just New York lying down.

Quentin Crisp

I love New York. It's the only place where, if you look at anyone long enough, they'll eventually spit.

Caroline Rhea

New York is like living inside Stephen King's brain during an aneurysm.

Kevin Rooney

This giant asparagus bed of alabaster and rose and green skyscrapers.

Cecil Beaton

Every year when it's Chinese New Year in New York, there are fireworks going off at all hours. New York mothers calm their frightened children by telling them it's just gunfire.

David Letterman

There's no room for amateurs, even in crossing the street.

George Segal, on New York

Many people have not learned to enjoy the noise of New York as harmony. I'm surprised at that. They find it nerve-racking. And I have never found a sound to be nerve-racking; not even a burglar alarm.

John Cage, composer

Texas is a place where they barbecue everything but ice cream.

Anon

AUSTRALIA

The land that foreplay forgot.

Germaine Greer

Australia is still a male-chauvinist bastion and most of the women like it that way.

Paul Hogan

Where else in the world is a generous man defined as one who would give you his arsehole and shit through his ribs?

Germaine Greer

In Australia, not reading poetry is the national pastime.

Phyllis McGinley

Never do business with an Australian who says 'no worries' a lot.

Frank Moorhouse

CANADA

What a place, Canada! They started a country and no one showed up.

Wally Sparks, *Meet Wally Sparks*

Canada is like a loft apartment over a really great party. Like, 'Keep it down, eh?'

Robin Williams

The most parochial nationette on earth.

Wyndham Lewis

A Canadian is somebody who knows how to make love in a canoe.

Pierre Berton

I hear in Canada you only have sex doggy style; that way you can both see the hockey game.

Wally Sparks, *Meet Wally Sparks*

I have to spend so much time explaining to Americans that I am not English and to Englishmen that I am not American that I have little time left to be Canadian.

Laurence J. Peter

Americans are benevolently ignorant about Canada, while Canadians are malevolently well informed about the United States.

J. Bartlet Brebner

In the world menu, Canada must be considered the vichyssoise of nations – it's cold, half-French and difficult to stir.

Stuart Keate

I don't like living any place where I'm older than the buildings.

Joe Grundy, *The Archers*

The tragedy of Canada is that they had the opportunity to have French cuisine, British culture, and American technology, and instead they ended up with British cuisine, American culture, and French technology.

Will Shetterly, *overheard*

GREAT BRITAIN – GENERAL

The British have three qualities: humour, tenacity and realism.
I sometimes think we are still at the humour stage.

Georges Pompidou

Being British is about driving in a German car to an Irish pub where we imbibe copious amounts of Belgian or eastern European beer, then on the way home stopping to pick up an Indian curry or a Turkish kebab to consume as we sit on our Swedish furniture watching American shows on Japanese TVs.

Robert Readman

We have all got to be as British as Carry On films and scotch eggs and falling over on the beach while trying to change into your swimming trunks with a towel on. We should all feel the same mysterious pang at the sight of the Queen.

Boris Johnson

Does anyone else feel a tinge of British pride when they see people drinking pints of lager in the airport before it's turned 8am?

Richard Bacon

The passion to be left alone, if only to one's own foolishness, lies deep rooted in the British character.

Stephen Leacock

MOTTOS FOR MODERN BRITAIN

Dipso, Fatso, Bingo, Asbo, Tesco

JLC

Smile, you're on CCTV

Les

Once mighty empire, slightly used

J. Harris

At least we're not French

Sig

We apologise for the inconvenience

Matthew Bailey

Mathematically, we could still qualify
Wobbly

Sorry, is this the queue?

Mark Joint

Mind your own business!

Brian Clacey

Ne nostra in fundamenta subeamus
Let us not climb up our own bottoms

Matthew Parris

Sorry it's all our fault

Anon

Let's discuss it down the pub

Pete

Drinking continues till morale improves

Freddie

No motto please, we're British

David Bishop

ENGLAND

In order to appreciate England one has to have a certain contempt for logic.

Lin Yutang

We do not regard Englishmen as foreigners. We look on them only as rather mad Norwegians.

Halvard Lange, Norwegian politician

You can go sauntering along for a certain period, telling the English some interesting things about themselves, and then all at once it feels as if you have stepped on the prongs of a rake.

Patrick Campbell

I'm American... but I live in England with my English husband. By that I mean he eats pizza with a knife and fork. And sunburns under a 50-watt bulb.

Kit Hollerbach

It is, of course, a particularly British characteristic to think that every man is the same under the skin, and that Eskimos are really only would-be Old Etonians wearing fur coats.

John Harvey-Jones

He was born in Luton or, as EasyJet call it, London.

David Mitchell, *The Unbelievable Truth*

London, that *hot-plate* of humanity, on which we first sing, then simmer, then boil, then dry away to dust.

Thomas Hardy

That slowest and dreariest of boroughs...where the inhabitants are driven to ring their own door-bells lest they should rust from disuse.

Ouida, on Cantitborough (modelled on Bury St Edmunds)

Sir Clement Freud wanted to call a horse Bury St Edmunds but the local council turned it down. He called it Digup St Edmunds instead.

Michael Chapman

I spent a year in that town, one Sunday.

Warwick Deeping

The beautiful thing about Brighton is that you can buy your lover a pair of knickers at Victoria Station and have them off again at the Grand Hotel in less than two hours.

Keith Waterhouse

My apologies to the citizens of Chipping Sodbury for calling their town Chipping Sudbury last week. Fact is always stranger than fiction.

Stephen Glover

M3, car park, car park, roundabout, car park, roundabout, car park, tart, roundabout, M3.

Andy, on a drive through Basingstoke, *Crap Towns*

According to legend, Telford is so dull that the bypass was built before the town.

Victor Lewis-Smith

Jade went to Newcastle to do a film premiere and she went, 'Do I need euros, Mum?'

Jackiey Budden, on Jade Goody

I would never leave England. I am too fond of complaining about the government.

Julian Fellowes

He was inordinately proud of England and he abused her incessantly.

H.G. Wells

IRELAND

I am not an American, but I am the next worst thing – an Irishman.

George Bernard Shaw

A nation of masturbators under priestly instruction.

Brian Moore, *Fergus*

Ireland remains a deeply religious country, with the two main denominations being 'us' and 'them'.

Frank McNally

When I was in primary school we had a drawing on the wall of Northern Ireland with blue surrounding it. I thought Northern Ireland was an island until I was 12.

Anne Dunlop

I know I've got Irish blood because I wake up every day with a hangover.

Noel Gallagher

The famous drinking exists largely as material for anecdotes... The conversation hardly leaves a man time to swallow anything.

Wilfred Sheed

An Irishman will always soften bad news, so that a...near-hurricane that leaves thousands homeless is 'good drying weather'.

Hugh Leonard

If one could only teach the English how to talk and the Irish how to listen, society here would be quite civilized.

Oscar Wilde

SCOTLAND

Want to know what the world will be like after the Apocalypse?
Four pounds on National Express gets you to Glasgow.

Jimmy Carr, 8 Out Of 10 Cats

That garret of the earth – that knuckle-end of England – that land of Calvin, oatcakes and sulphur.

Rev. Sydney Smith

Get yer haggis, right here! Chopped heart and lungs boiled in a wee sheep's stomach. Tastes as good as it sounds.

Groundskeeper Willie, The Simpsons

I think most Scottish cuisine is based on a dare.

Charlie Mackenzie, So I Married an Axe Murderer

—Scotland is a very vile country to be sure.
—Well, Sir! God made it.
—Certainly he did, but we must always remember that he made it for Scotchmen.

Dr Samuel Johnson and Mr Strahan

The Scots are a very tough people. They have drive-by headbuttings. In Glasgow a sweatband is considered a silencer.

Emo Philips

Some place, Govan, eh? Where else can you get a fish supper at 9am? Simple, just steal it off a drunk that's been lyin' pished outside a close all night.

Rab C. Nesbitt

The most Scottish thing I've ever seen: I was going through a town called Bathgate at about half past eleven at night, and there was a guy pissing against a front door. He then took out his keys and went inside.

Frankie Boyle, Mock the Week

Glasgow is not a melting pot; it's closer to a chip pan in which you've attempted to boil cream, the ingredients have separated, and neither element is palatable.

Tom Lappin

For a while I did unite the Rangers and Celtic fans. There were people in both camps who hated me.

Mo Johnston, Scottish striker who played with both football teams

It's been said that Scotland is an argument. That's so true. It's where the enlightenment came from.

Elaine Smith

You must not look down on…Glasgow which gave the world the internal combustion engine, political economy, antiseptic and cerebral surgery, the balloon, the mariner's compass, the theory of Latent Heat, Tobias Smollett and James Bridie.

James Bridie

I think it possible that all Scots are illegitimate, Scotsmen being so mean and Scotswomen so generous.

Edwin Muir

If you unscotch us, you will find us damned mischievous Englishmen.

Sir Walter Scott

God help England if she had no Scots to think for her!

George Bernard Shaw

I went to Scotland and found nothing there that looks like Scotland.

Arthur Freed, on why the film *Brigadoon* was shot in MGM studios in Hollywood

The noblest prospect which a Scotsman ever sees is the high road that leads him to England!

Dr Samuel Johnson

WALES

What do you call a sheep tied to a lamp post in Cardiff? A leisure centre. No, no, don't laugh! It's an example of the institutionalized racism against the Welsh!

Rob Brydon, *QI*

First God made England, Ireland and Scotland. That's when he corrected his mistakes and made Wales.

Katharine Hepburn

Show a Welshman a dozen exits, one of which is marked 'Self-Destruction', and he will go right through that door.

Joseph L. Mankiewicz, after directing Richard Burton in *Cleopatra*

All the Welsh are natural actors. Only the bad ones become professionals.

Richard Burton

Welsh rain…descends with the enthusiasm of someone breaking bad news.

Saki

The Welsh are the Italians in the rain.

Anon

It was…controversially asked, 'What are the Welsh for?' I was brought up to believe that our purpose in God's scheme of things was to keep the Irish and the English apart.

Michael Bissmire

SCIENCE & TECHNOLOGY

COMPUTER

I think I bought a bad computer. The mouse bit me.

David Letterman

My Apple Mac is so high-tech it can do everything. I'm frightened to press a button in case I launch a space shuttle.

Kathy Lette

—How much should my computer cost?
—About $350 less than you will actually pay.

Dave Barry

There are only two industries that refer to their customers as 'users'.

Edward Tufte

User: the word that computer professionals use when they mean 'idiot'.

Dave Barry

Those parts of the system that you can hit with a hammer are called 'hardware'; those program instructions that you can only curse at are called software.

Anon

There is only one satisfying way to boot a computer.

J.H. Goldfuss

I always refer to any machine I work on as 'Annie'. This was the name of my first girlfriend. She was equally ungiving and unforgiving.

David P. Lintott

Don't anthropomorphize computers. They hate it.

Anon

I believe in the total depravity of inanimate things.

Katherine Kent Child Walker

The nice thing about Windows is, it does not just crash, it displays a dialog box and let's you press 'OK' first.

Arno Shaefer

Jesus saves! The rest of us better make backups.

Anon

I took a two-year-old computer in to be repaired, and the guy looked at me as though he was a gun dealer and I had brought him a musket. In just two years, I'd gone from cutting-edge to Amish.

Jon Stewart

It would take one hundred clerks working for one hundred years to make a mistake as monumental as a single computer can make in one thousandth of a second.

***Dental Economics* magazine**

They've finally come up with the perfect office computer. If it makes a mistake, it blames another computer.

Milton Berle

Computers make it easier to do a lot of things, but most of the things they make it easier to do don't need to be done.

Andy Rooney

Our new computer system is about as much use as a cat flap in a submarine.

Unidentified Employee at Tory HQ

Computers aren't very intelligent. On the evolutionary scale, they're on the same level as a sea-slug.

Computer Programmer

The computer was working fine when Rob started; after several hours of installation, it was a totally dysfunctional, muttering, potentially violent thing, and we had to take it outside and shoot it.

Dave Barry

Never trust a computer you can't throw out of a window.

Stephen Wozniak

The cause of the problem in 97.3 per cent of cases is a simple fault with the nut attached to the keyboard.

Steve Turner

This granny finds that spending ten hours a week on the keyboard helps to sustain and even improve one's waning powers of concentration, muscular co-ordination, aural attention, critical self-appraisal, finger dexterity and musical appreciation. The instrument in question is called a pianoforte.

Pauline M. Atkins

INTERNET

—Behold… the Internet.
—My God! It's full of ads!

Bender and Philip J. Fry, *Futurama*

I bought a novelty hot water bottle on Amazon for Christmas and in Amazon's infinite wisdom they suggested I buy an Andrea Bocelli CD to go with it.

Dan H., online shopper

The Internet is just a world passing around notes in a classroom.

Jon Stewart

The Internet: Transforming Society and Shaping the Future Through Chat.

Dave Barry

You can't define 'news' on the Web since everyone with a homepage is a global town crier.

Joshua Quittner

The trouble with the global village is all the global village idiots.

Paul Ginsparg

The Internet: absolute communication, absolute isolation.

Paul Carvel

My little sister got me on Facebook because I was on MySpace... So I joined both. But I keep muddling them up, so I keep asking people to come on MyFace. Still, 80,000 friends...

Shappi Khorsandi

I've joined an *anti*-social networking site. It's called Shutyerfacebook.

Anon

Too many twits might make a twat.

David Cameron, on Twitter

I think I'll live to see the end of capital letters.

Larry Gelbart, on the 21st century preference for using lower-case letters in email and on the Web

The Internet is not, actually, very much like a private correspondence which will be read by the addressee only. It is more like standing in the street, naked, shouting random secrets, forever.

Philip Hensher

You can't take something off the Internet – it's like taking pee out of a pool.

Anon

Computers can now keep a man's every transgression recorded in a permanent memory bank, duplicating with complex programming and intricate wiring a feat his wife handles quite well without fuss or fanfare.

Lane Olinghouse

It all boils down to just a bunch of ones and zeroes. I don't know how that enables me to see naked women, but however it works, God bless you guys.

Doug Heffernan, *The King of Queens*

Well, thanks to the Internet, I'm now bored with sex.

Philip J. Fry, *Futurama*

SCIENCE & SCIENTISTS

Does the name Pavlov ring a bell?

Anon

The white rat said to the other white rat: 'I've got that psychologist so well trained that every time I ring the bell he brings me something to eat.'

David Mercer

Scientists are peeping Toms at the keyhole of eternity.

Arthur Koestler

Scientists have odious manners, except when you prop up their theory; then you can borrow money off them.

Mark Twain

Carl often bragged that Chaos Theory was his moral and aesthetic code. What this actually meant was that he couldn't be bothered to clean up after himself.

Ellen Steiber, *The Cats of San Marino*

The scientific acquisition of knowledge is almost as tedious as a routine acquisition of wealth.

Eric Linklater

Most 'scientists' are bottle washers and button sorters.

Robert A. Heinlein

If you cannot – in the long run – tell everyone what you have been doing, your doing has been worthless.

Erwin Shrödinger

If we knew what it was we were doing, it would not be called research, would it?

Albert Einstein

If half the engineering effort and public interest that go into the research on the American bosom had gone into our guided-missile program, we would now be running hot-dog stands on the moon.

Al Capp

The simplest schoolboy is now familiar with truths for which Archimedes would have sacrificed his life.

Ernest Renan

—Mummy, how do airplanes fly?
—The airlines smushed up Tinker Bell and put a little of her in every plane.

Five-Year-Old Child and Elly Kugler

Since my 10-year-old got a microscope that she can connect to the PC for her birthday, she can't wait to have nits again.

Forum Member, *The Guardian*

Don't forget that the bacteria watch *us* from the other end of the microscope.

Stanislaw J. Lec

Objects are smaller and less alarming than they appear.

Warning on a microscope, J. Calvin Smith

Where the telescope ends, the microscope begins. Which of the two has the grander view?

Victor Hugo

Instead of troubling itself about sunspots, which nobody ever saw, or, if they did, ought not to speak about, why does not science busy itself with drainage and sanitary engineering? Why does it not clean the streets and free the rivers from pollution?

Oscar Wilde

Pollution is so bad that when I put air in my tyres two of them died.

Lee Tully

I think somebody should come up with a way to breed a very large shrimp. That way, you could ride him, then, after you camped at night, you could eat him. How about it, science?

Jack Handey

In my opinion, we don't devote nearly enough scientific research to finding a cure for jerks.

Calvin, *Calvin and Hobbes*

EVOLUTION & CREATIONISM

That ugly beast the ape's the very spit of us!

Quintus Ennius (c.239–169 BC)

How extremely stupid not to have thought of that!

Thomas Huxley, on first reading *The Origin of Species* by Charles Darwin

Ah, Corporal Klinger, my constant reminder that Darwin was right.

Major Charles Winchester, *M*A*S*H*

According to archaeologists, for millions of years Neanderthal man was not fully erect. That's easy to understand considering how ugly Neanderthal women were.

Anon

We have reason to believe that Man first walked upright to free his hands for masturbation.

Lily Tomlin

To introduce creationism into schools as a counterbalance to evolution would be like introducing the stork as a counterbalance to the study of conception, pregnancy and childbirth.

Brian P. Block

Science has proof without any certainty. Creationists have certainty without any proof.

Ashley Montagu, *attrib.*

Evolution was far more thrilling to me than the biblical account. Who would not rather be a rising ape than a falling angel?

Terry Pratchett

TIME

—What's the definition of an eternity?
—The time from when you come to when she leaves.

Anon

God, who winds up our sundials...

Georg Christoph Lichtenberg

I have a *carpe diem* mug and, truthfully, at six in the morning the words do not make me want to seize the day. They make me want to slap a dead poet.

Joanne Sherman

A femtosecond is a millionth of a billionth of a second... Put in comparative terms, a femtosecond is to a second as a second is to 32 million years.

Professor Ahmed Zewail

The femtosecond may be defined as the interval between the traffic light changing to green and the person in the vehicle behind sounding their horn.

John Thurston

The femtosecond is the time it takes for the smile to leave the face of an airline's chief flight attendant as he walks from Club Class to Economy Class.

John Bell

In our house, the femtosecond denoted the time which elapsed between putting on a fresh nappy, and its being filled by a grateful, gurgling infant.

Kieran Sweeney

For cruciverbalists...a femtosecond is the interval between a clue being utterly obscure and blindingly obvious.

Stanley Armstrong

In my street the shortest space of time is that between a car leaving a parking space and another occupying it.

Evan M. Davies

The shortest perceptible slice of time is the ohnosecond: that infinitely painful moment between shutting the front door and realizing that your keys are still inside the house.

David Colvin

The shortest recorded period of time lies between the minute you put some money away for a rainy day and the unexpected arrival of rain.

Jane Bryant Quinn

There is never enough time unless you're serving it.

Malcolm Forbes

MATHEMATICS

—How are you at mathematics?
—I speak it like a native.

Moriarty and Secombe, *The Goon Show*

One plus one is two. Two plus two is four. But five will get you ten if you know how to work it.

Mae West

There are three kinds of mathematicians: those who can count and those who cannot.

Anon

—How many grains of sand in the Sahara, then, d'you reckon?
—I lost count. It's quite a few. I got up to 17 and it's definitely more than that.

Alan Davies and Stephen Fry, *QI*

Round numbers are always false.

Dr Samuel Johnson

Five out of four people have trouble with fractions.

Steven Wright

I'm not very good with diagrams. I remember when I first saw the one in the Lil-lets packet...I thought, no, I'll just put a ship in a bottle each month, it'll be quicker.

Victoria Wood

Paralllels.

Professor Robert C. Art

G.H. Hardy, who was professor of pure mathematics...told me once that if he could find a proof that I was going to die in five minutes he would of course be sorry to lose me, but this sorrow would be quite outweighed by pleasure in the proof. I entirely sympathized with him and was not at all offended.

Bertrand Russell

Dreamt I solved the Poincaré Conjecture using a tennis racket, a teapot and a rubber sheet. It really worked but vital steps gone.

Stephen Fry

Do not worry about your difficulties in mathematics; I can assure you that mine are still greater.

Albert Einstein

STATISTICS

Three statisticians go deer hunting with bows and arrows. They spot a big buck and take aim. One shoots, and his arrow flies off 10 feet to the left. The second shoots, and his arrow goes 10 feet to the right. The third statistician jumps up and down yelling, 'We got him! We got him!'

Bill Butz

I could prove God statistically.

George Gallup, Jr.

Like dreams, statistics are a form of wish fulfilment.

Jean Baudrillard

[The War Office kept three sets of figures:] one to mislead the public, another to mislead the Cabinet, and the third to mislead itself.

Herbert Asquith

—Why were there not balance-of-payment crises in Queen Victoria's reign?
—Because there weren't any balance-of-payment statistics.

Interviewer and James Callaghan

Cheerios can lower cholesterol 4% in 6 weeks. To appreciate that number, give the Inland Revenue an extra 4%.

Advertisement for breakfast cereal

According to statistics, a man eats a prune every 20 seconds. I don't know who this fellow is, but I know where to find him.

Morey Amsterdam

Oh, people can come up with statistics to prove anything. Fourteen per cent of people know that.

Homer Simpson

Say you are standing with one foot in the oven and one foot in an ice bucket. According the percentage people, you would be perfectly comfortable.

Bobby Bragan

There must be at least 500 million rats in the United States; of course, I am speaking only from memory.

Edgar Wilson Nye

The statistician drowned in a lake of average depth 6 inches.

Anon

INVENTIONS

The printing press is either the greatest credit or the greatest curse of modern times, one sometimes forgets which.

J.M. Barrie

Some sad news from Australia... the inventor of the boomerang grenade died today.

Johnny Carson

I ran into Isosceles. He has a great idea for a new triangle!

Woody Allen

Do you suppose the inventor of the vibrator heard a voice that said: 'If you build it, they will come.'

Anon

—All you have to do is think of things which people need but which don't exist yet...or you could take something that already exists and find a new use for it, like—
—Hamburger earmuffs!

Professor Frink and Homer Simpson, The Simpsons

Probably the earliest fly swatters were nothing more than some sort of striking surface attached to the end of a long stick.

Jack Handey

What a lucky thing the wheel was invented before the automobile; otherwise, can you imagine the awful screeching?

Samuel Hoffenstein

Anything invented after you're 35 is against the natural order of things.

Douglas Adams

I would have preferred to invent something which helps people.
A lawnmower, for example.

Mikhail Kalashnikov, inventor of the AK-47 assault rifle

—What use is electricity?
—Why, sir, there is every possibility that you will soon be able to tax it!

William Ewart Gladstone and Michael Faraday, physicist

Thomas Edison spent years trying to invent the electric light... Finally, late one night, he got the bulb to glow. He ran out of his laboratory, through the house, up the stairs to his bedroom. 'Honey,' Edison called to his wife, 'I've done it!' She rolled over and said, 'Will you turn that light off and come to bed!'

Ron Dentinger

ASTRONOMY

The universe is merely a fleeting idea in God's mind – a pretty uncomfortable thought, particularly if you've just made a down payment on a house.

Woody Allen

In the beginning, there was nothing. God said, 'Let there be light.' And there was light. There was still nothing, but you could see it much better.

Ellen DeGeneres

The origin of the universe was, of course, the Big Bang, which happened about 14,700 billion years ago. I was away at the time.

Patrick Moore

—What existed before the Big Bang?
—That is like asking what is north of the North Pole. It is a meaningless question.
—Well I've asked a few of those in my time.

Richard Madeley and Professor Stephen Hawking

Being stuck between Rugby and Nuneaton in a broken-down train is bad enough. Being lost in space is probably marginally worse.

Michael Fabricant, on Virgin's plans to expand into space tourism

Space is only 80 miles from every person on earth – far closer than most people are to their own national capitals.

Daniel Deudney

We have a few clues as to what space smells like... Astronauts reported a smell of fried steak, hot metal and even welding a motorbike.

Steven Pearce

For years politicians have promised the moon. I'm the first one to be able to deliver it.

President Richard Nixon, *attrib*., on the first moon landing, 1969

—Forget the moon. Everybody goes to the moon. We'll go to the sun.
—We can't go to the sun. If we get within 13 million miles of it, we'll melt.
—So we go at night.

Two Aspiring Astronauts

The sun? That's the hottest place on Earth!

Homer Simpson

—Landing cameras on Mars is like hitting a hole in one, only you start in California and end in Australia...
—...and Australia's moving!

Two Scientists, on the Mars Polar Lander project

The Mars Polar Lander has been quieter than George W. Bush after a foreign policy question.

David Letterman, when the space exploration vehicle went missing in outer space

Put three grains of sand inside a vast cathedral, and the cathedral will be more closely packed with sand than space is with stars.

Sir James Jeans

There are more stars in the universe than there have ever been heartbeats in the whole of humankind.

Fact learned on a visit to the Royal Observatory, Greenwich, noted by Paul Milligan

[*gazing at the stars in the sky*] Let's go inside and watch television. I'm beginning to feel insignificant.

Charlie Brown

EXTRATERRESTRIAL LIFE

Why is it that all of the instruments seeking intelligent life in the universe are pointed *away* from Earth?

Anon

It's arrogant for humans to think they're alone in the universe. Earth is probably like Inverness. Inverness is in Britain, so Earth probably has the same relationship to the universe.

Geri Halliwell

I have spotted a UFO. I was in my observatory one night, looking at the Moon. Then I saw dozens of flying saucers swirling around. I thought: 'The Martians have arrived!' But then I realised I was looking at pollen slightly out of focus.

Patrick Moore

—Have you ever encountered aliens?
—No, only when I met members of New Labour.

Interviewer and Tony Benn

If aliens ever visit us, I think the outcome would be much as when Christopher Columbus first landed in America, which didn't turn out very well for the Native Americans.

Professor Stephen Hawking

If we actually find advanced life on another planet I wonder whether they'll be as obsessed with their own genitals as we are.

Albert Brooks

SOCIETY
& LAW

CLASS

An Englishman's social standing seems to depend on the number of people he can afford to despise.

Peter McArthur

Let me explain the order of things to you: there's the aristocracy, the upper class, the middle class, working class, dumb animals, waiters, creeping things, head lice, people who eat packet soup, then you.

Gareth Blackstock, Chef!

Put three Englishmen on a desert island and within an hour they'll have invented a class system.

Alan Ayckbourn

The English are like their beer: froth at the top, dregs at the bottom, and excellent in the middle.

Voltaire

The middle classes are rancid scraps in the middle of the luscious, bad-for-you bread of British life.

Julie Burchill

The middle classes will kill football. The middle classes kill everything they touch.

Matthew Parris

The upper class keeps all the money, pays none of the taxes. The middle class pays all of the taxes, does all of the work. The poor are there to scare the shit out of the middle class.

George Carlin

The only class you do *not* belong to and are not proud of at all is the lower-middle class. No one ever describes himself as belonging to the lower-middle class.

George Mikes

By and large, I've met a better class of person in the gutter than I have in the drawing room.

Jeffrey Bernard

You might be a redneck if...when your wife left you, she took the house with her; you take your dog for a walk and you both use the tree at the corner; you've ever unstopped a sink with a shotgun; you've ever worn a tube-top to a funeral home; you work with a shirt off... and so does your husband.

Jeff Foxworthy

In life there exist two classes: first class and no class.

Hugh Leonard

ROYALTY

Imagine the Queen meeting Camilla. 'You're my son's mistress? That must be interesting.'

Linda Smith, *I Think the Nurses are Stealing my Clothes*

Pat Boone met the Queen at a Royal Variety Performance. She said to him: 'We've met before, haven't we?' He said: 'Have we?'

Maureen Lipman

I only met the Queen briefly, at a party for World War II veterans, but I remember noticing what a good bra she was wearing.

Barbara Windsor

I met the Queen years ago at a Megastars Anonymous meeting. She was a quiet little thing in the corner with a little scarf over her tiara. I recognized her jewellery. My butler had sold it to her.

Dame Edna Everage

Former royal butler Paul Burrell – facially, a cross between Jamie Oliver and a simpering broad bean.

Charlie Brooker

I remember asking Diana who were the people she admired most in the world. She named three: Margaret Thatcher, Mother Teresa and Madonna.

Andrew Morton

It was the usual 'zoo tea'. You know, we eat – the others watch.

Princess Margaret, at a public reception

The food was memorable. Tiny fragments of nouvelle cuisine, everything tastefully decorated with crossed chives. I obviously stopped at McDonald's, Wandsworth, on the way home.

Charles Saatchi, dining at Windsor Castle with Prince Charles, *Charles Saatchi: Question*

I just didn't know what to do with the little bag.

Prince Charles, explaining to President Ronald Reagan why he didn't drink the cup of tea served to him at the White House, which contained a teabag

Prince Philip is a bloody-minded man with a temper as foul as an arthritic corgi.

Jean Rook

—How do you manage to act charming and not look bored at everyone's questions?
—A thousand years of breeding.

Questioner in New York and Prince Charles

To be Prince of Wales is not a position. It is a predicament.

Prince of Wales, *The Madness of King George*

Nobody but me can possibly understand how perfectly bloody it is to be Prince of Wales.

Prince Charles

We're all in line to succession to the throne. If 48 million people die, I shall become Queen.

Peter Cook

I'm doing pretty well considering. In the past, when anyone left the Royal family they had you beheaded.

Sarah Ferguson, Duchess of York

—Lord St John of Fawsley refuses to acknowledge the Royal Family are ever wrong about anything. If the Queen was found to practise cannibalism, the noble lord would fatten up a missionary in his back garden for her.
—No, I would offer myself as the main course.

Dr Piers Brendon and Lord St John of Fawsley

ARISTOCRACY

Take a good look: there are only 24 of these in the country.

The Duke of Marlborough, to an interested party
at the urinals of his gentleman's club

A title is really rather a nuisance in these democratic days. As George Hartford I had everything I wanted. Now I have merely everything other people want, which isn't nearly so pleasant.

Lord Illingworth, *A Woman of No Importance*

I was once naive enough to ask the late Duke of Devonshire why he liked Eastbourne and he replied with a self-deprecating shrug that one of the things he liked was that he owned it.

A.N. Wilson

[*filling out an official form*] Q: How long has your family lived at the present address?
A: 697 years.

Sir Thomas Ingilby, of Ripley Castle

I believe in inherited wealth. Society needs to have some people who are above it all.

Edward Digby Baltzell

The strength of England is that they have no real aristocracy. Anyone's blood can become blue for a lump sum down.

Nancy Astor

One has often wondered whether upon the whole earth there is anything so unintelligent, so unapt to perceive how the world is really going, as an ordinary young Englishman of our upper class.

Matthew Arnold

There is always more brass than brains in an aristocracy.

Oscar Wilde

To discard magnificence, and remain magnificent, is the inimitable privilege of aristocracy.

Falconer Madan

In England, having had money…is just as acceptable as having it, since the upper-class mannerisms persist, even after the bankroll has disappeared. But never having had money is unforgivable, and can only be atoned for by never trying to get any.

Margaret Halsey

Did you know that a peer condemned to death had the right to be hanged with a silken cord? A bit like insisting that the electric chair had to be Chippendale.

Charles Mosley

CLASS CONSCIOUSNESS

A lobster and a crab fell in love and wished to marry but the lobster's mother disapproved: 'Crabs are common, and what is more, they walk *sideways*!' 'Just meet him, Mother,' begged the lobster. She brought in the crab who walked in a perfectly straight line to greet the lobster's mother. 'But I thought crabs always walked sideways,' she said. 'They do,' replied the crab, 'but I'm drunk.'

Anon

Could someone please settle this: in a Rolls-Royce Corniche the bar opens from *left* to *right,* doesn't it?

Sylvia Pickel, Vibes

He's so snobbish he won't even travel in the same car as his chauffeur.

David Frost

I went to a party given for Noël Coward, and at those parties everybody tries to act so British. There was a dame there riding a Kotex sidesaddle.

Jack Benny

Good Lord, I can't believe I'm at a public pool. Why doesn't someone just pee on me directly?

Karen Walker, Will and Grace

I never look at price labels. Someone once told me it was common. That and sending mixed-coloured flowers.

Julie Burchill

Having photographs around the house is fine – if they're royal and on the piano.

Nicky Haslam, interior designer

There is no snob like a left-wing snob.

Andrew Neil

Before God and the bus driver we are all equal.

German proverb

LAW & LAWYERS

In the past when I've talked to audiences like this, I've often started off with a lawyer joke, a caricature of a lawyer who's been nasty, greedy and unethical. But I've stopped that practice. I gradually realized that the lawyers in the audience didn't think the jokes were funny and the non-lawyers didn't know they were jokes.

Chief Justice William Rehnquist, making a speech

—How many lawyers does it take to change a light bulb?
—How many can you afford?

Anon

Ninety-nine per cent of all lawyers give the rest a bad name.

Anon

You've heard about the man who got the bill from his lawyer, which said: 'For crossing the road to speak to you and discovering it was not you: $12.'

George S. Kaufman

And God said: 'Let there be Satan, so people don't blame everything on me. And let there be lawyers, so people don't blame everything on Satan.'

George Burns

—You're a lawyer?
—I prefer 'law stylist'.

Liz Lemon and Floyd, *30 Rock*

I didn't become a lawyer because I like the law. The law sucks. It's boring, but it can also be used as a weapon. You want to bankrupt somebody? Cost him everything he's worked for? Make his wife leave him, even make his kids cry... yeah, we can do that.

Richard Fish, *Ally McBeal*

Lawyers and tarts are the two oldest professions in the world. And we always aim to please.

Horace Rumpole, *Rumpole of the Bailey*

A lawyer is one who protects you against robbers by taking away the temptation.

H.L. Mencken

A peasant between two lawyers is like a fish between two cats.

Spanish proverb

Apologists for the profession contend that lawyers are as honest as other men, but this is not very encouraging.

Ferdinand Lundberg

If you can think about a thing that is inextricably attached to something else without thinking of the thing which it is attached to, then you have a legal mind.

Thomas Reed Powell

Now I realise what Mark Twain meant when he said, 'The more you explain it, the more I don't understand it.'

Justice Robert H. Jackson

One listens to one's lawyer prattle on as long as one can stand it and then signs where indicated.

Alexander Woollcott

I think the reason justice is blind is because lawyers are jerking off all the time.

Dennis Miller

I decided law was the exact opposite of sex: even when it was good it was lousy.

Mortimer Zuckerman

CRIME

Fellow walked up to me and said: 'You see a cop around here?' I said, 'No.' He said, 'Stick 'em up!'

Henny Youngman

Thieves! Thieves... O pray, sir, spare all I have, and take my life!

George Farquhar

I came from a pretty tough neighbourhood. Nothing but killings. I went out and bought a water bed – and there was a guy at the bottom of it.

Joey Adams

You think New York is bad? You ought to go to Detroit. You can go ten blocks and never leave the scene of the crime.

Red Skelton

New Orleans is the only city in the world you go in to buy a pair of nylon stockings and they want to know your head size.

Billie Holiday

When I approached the check-out counter of a Miami store, the clerk said, 'Cash, cheque or stick-up?'

Pat Williams

Freeze, mother-stickers, this is a fuck-up!

Would-be Robber, waving a gun in a Florida bank (the staff dissolved into hysterics and the humiliated robber fled, empty-handed)

—What goes clip clop, clip clop, bang bang, clip clop, clip clop?
—An Amish drive-by shooting.

Anon

—How do you explain this huge rise in crime?
—There's so much more to nick.

Interviewer and Douglas Hurd, MP

Some guy came running in the other night and said, 'Somebody stole my car!' I said, 'Did you see him?' He said, 'No, but I got his licence number.'

Bill Barner

I used to leave a pair of dirty underpants on the driver's seat of my car because I always thought anybody wanting to steal the car would look in and think, 'Oh dear, oh dear, look at that. There's bound to be another one round the corner, we'll take that instead.'

John Peel

There is no such thing as an unexpectedly pleasant ring on your doorbell in London. The only people who ring when you don't expect it are the police, religious maniacs, menacing youths selling products that are undoubtedly criminally acquired, bailiffs and your in-laws.

Michael Gove, MP

In England, if you commit a crime, the police say, 'Stop! Or I'll say 'stop' again!'

Robin Williams

Figures released today by the FBI show that for the first time there is now as much crime on the streets as there is on TV.

Joey Adams

Growing up in inner London somewhere today, I would possibly have been a hoodie.

Norman Tebbit

—It isn't fair what people say about him. They'd tell you he'd sell his own mother. I heard that on very good authority.
—Who from?
—The two blokes who bought his mother.

Ingrid and Norman Stanley Fletcher, Porridge

Nothing incites to money-crimes like great poverty or great wealth.

Mark Twain

Whenever he saw a dollar in another man's hands he took it as a personal grudge, if he couldn't take it any other way.

O. Henry

I like thieves. Some of my best friends are thieves. Why, just last week we had the president of the bank over for dinner.

W.C. Fields

What is robbing a bank compared with founding a bank?

Bertolt Brecht

—I would imagine the biggest problem in Uckfield is graffiti.
—It is. There's a river called the River Uck.

Nick Hancock and Contestant, Duel, TV quiz

Someone stole my identity. Now *he* has no life.

Larry Brown

'It restores your faith in natural justice,' said Pat McGillivray, of Carisbrooke, after a snatch-thief grabbed her plastic carrier bag which contained nothing more than the fresh droppings of Whisky, Mrs McGillivray's West Highland terrier.

Isle of Wight County Press

A man in Illinois is suing a woman, claiming she stole his sperm to have his baby without his knowledge. Now that's a good pickpocket.

Conan O'Brien

—What's the difference between a pickpocket and a peeping Tom?
—A pickpocket snatches watches.

Redd Foxx

My ex-wife claimed she was violated. Knowing my ex-wife, it wasn't a moving violation.

Woody Allen

Most paedophiles wear glasses and a beard. What is it about that look that kids find so attractive?

Frankie Boyle

A Jewish child molester: 'Hey, kid…wanna buy some candy?'

Jackie Martling

Should rapists be castrated at birth?

Twiggy Rathbone, *Hot Metal*

A man doesn't rape for sex any more than an alcoholic drinks because he's thirsty.

Dr A. Nicholas Groth

—I'm going to kill you!
—Oh, John, *please* – mind your blood pressure.

John and Meg, *Salvation*

A first killing is like your first love. You never forget it.

Alexander Pichushkin, Russia's 'Chessboard Killer', convicted of 48 murders

Do you know why it's so hard to solve a Redneck murder? Cos there's no dental records and all the DNA is the same.

Jeff Foxworthy

The criminal is the creative artist; the detective only the critic.

G.K. Chesterton

—How many cops does it take to throw a man down the stairs?
—None. He fell.

Anon

You know what I think is really wrong with the police in this country? Institutional sarcasm.

Frances Kapoor, *Criminal Justice*

If you really want to study police methods, do what I do: watch television.

Officer Gunther Toody, *Car 54, Where Are You?*

IN COURT

I go on jury duty Friday. And I'm telling you right now, I *want* to be tampered with.

David Letterman

Good morning, everybody. My name is Donald, and I'll be your judge today.

James Stevenson, cartoon caption

I think a judge should be looked on rather as a sphinx than as a person – you shouldn't be able to imagine a judge having a bath.

Judge H.C. Leon

The acme of judicial distinction means the ability to look a lawyer straight in the eyes for two hours and not hear a damned word he says.

Judge John Marshall

On my first day of law school, my professor said two things. First was: 'From this day forward, when your mother tells you she loves you – get a second opinion.' And: 'If you want justice, go to a whorehouse. If you wanna get fucked, go to court.'

Martin Vail, lawyer, *Primal Fear*

If you have the facts on your side, hammer the facts. If you have the law on your side, hammer the law. If you have neither the facts nor the law, hammer the table.

Lawyers' saying

Laughing juries don't convict.

F. Lee Bailey, one of the lawyers who defended O.J. Simpson

First rule of murder: never ask the client if they did it – in case they tell you.

Horace Rumpole, barrister, *Rumpole of the Bailey*

Attack the medical evidence. Remember, the jury's full of rheumatism and arthritis and shocking gastric troubles. They love to see a medical man put through it.

John Mortimer

Say you sue me because you say my dog bit you, well, now this is my defence: my dog doesn't bite. And second, in the alternative, my dog was tied up that night. And third, I don't believe you really got bit. And fourth, I don't have a dog.

Richard 'Racehorse' Haynes, US defence attorney

In Texas, they say Richard 'Racehorse' Haynes can get a charge of sodomy reduced to following too closely.

Kinky Friedman

Mr Justice Phillimore was trying a sodomy case and brooded greatly whether his judgement had been right. He went to consult Birkenhead. 'Excuse me, my lord, but could you tell me – what do you think one ought to give a man who allows himself to be buggered?' 'Oh, 30s or £2 – anything you happen to have on you.'

Evelyn Waugh

You'll find big, ugly, hairy, strong men who've got faces only a mother could love that will pay a lot of attention to you. And your anatomy.

Judge in a Sydney court, warning a 19-year-old of what he can expect in prison if he offends again

I think my mistake was yelling 'Hi' to the eyewitnesses as they filed into court.

Phil Interlandi

PRISON

Prison is like mime or juggling: a tragic waste of time.

Malcolm Hardee

Where would Christianity be if Jesus got 8 to 15 years, with time off for good behaviour?

James Donovan

The good thing about prison is that you never have to wonder what to wear.

Carol Siskind

Some zebras would love to sit behind bars if only to pretend they are white horses.

Stanislaw J. Lec

My prison would be walking through this world always having to listen to Eagles albums.

Kinky Friedman

—What do you call a clairvoyant midget who escaped from prison?
—A small medium at large.

Anon

HISTORY

I've gone back in time to when dinosaurs weren't just confined to zoos!

Homer Simpson

Stuff happens.

Donald Rumsfeld

I just adore history. It's so old.

Beulah (an American), *Romanoff and Juliet*

—If you could have dinner with anyone who lived in the history of the world, who would it be?
—That depends on the restaurant.

Interviewer and Rodney Dangerfield

I've always thought Alfred showed a marked lack of ingenuity over cakes – why didn't he cut off the burned bits, and ice the rest?

Madeleine Bingham

Tutankhamun looks like Tiger Woods eating a Cornetto.

Alan Davies, *QI*

J.P. Postgate was maintaining that the Roman Empire had to all intents everything we had. I asked whether they had asparagus (which we were eating). 'Oh yes.' 'What was it called?' 'Asparagus.'

John Edensor Littlewood

Twenty-two concubines, and a library of 62,000 volumes attested the variety of his inclinations, and from the productions which he left behind him, it appears that both the one and the other were designed for use rather than for ostentation.

Edward Gibbon, on Emperor Gordian the Younger

The best chance of reproducing the ancient Greek temperament would be to cross the Scots with the Chinese.

Hugh MacDiarmid

After the death of Nelson, English ladies were fond of wearing the Trafalgar garter, on which was inscribed the memorable signal: 'England expects every man to do his duty.'

Edmund Fuller

What if the French had successfully repelled the Germans in 1940? They would have become a vainglorious, pompous, rude people with a ridiculous sense of their importance in world affairs.

Jeff Chostner

—I slept through the 1960s.
—Don't worry, you didn't miss a thing.

Tennessee Williams and Gore Vidal

All the 'flower children' were as alike as a congress of accountants and about as interesting.

John Mortimer

History repeats itself – the first time as tragi-comedy, the second time as bedroom farce.

***Private Eye* magazine**

Those who don't study the past will repeat its errors; those who do study it will find other ways to err.

Charles Wolf, Jr.

Any event, once it has occurred, can be made to appear inevitable by a competent historian.

Lee Simonson

—What is the crucial virtue one requires of an historian – on or off television – the single, unequivocal demand that we make?
—That he wears a leather jacket?

Charles Prentiss and Martin McCabe, *Absolute Power*

The only entirely creditable incident in English history is the sending of £100 to Beethoven on his deathbed by the London Philharmonic Society; and it is the only one that historians never mention.

George Bernard Shaw

After you've heard two eyewitness accounts of a car accident, you begin to wonder about what passes for history.

H.R. Smith

WAR & PEACE

War is capitalism with the gloves off.

Tom Stoppard

I have never met anyone who wasn't against war. Even Hitler and Mussolini were, according to themselves.

Sir David Low

I detest war. It spoils armies.

Grand Duke Constantine of Russia

The belief in the possibility of a short decisive war appears to be one of the most ancient and dangerous of human illusions.

Robert Lynd

When you get into trouble 5,000 miles away from home, you've got to have been looking for it.

Will Rogers

Wars teach us not to love our enemies, but to hate our allies.

W.L. George

We should never fight a war unless we have been attacked and our country is in danger – or unless we are sure we can win.

Alex Ayres

You can no more win a war than you can win an earthquake.

Jeannette Rankin

The Romans never lost a war…because they never permitted a war to end until they won.

Louis D. Brandeis

The only war where the men knew what they were fighting for was the Trojan War: it was fought over a woman.

William Lyon Phelps

Remember, gentlemen, it's not just France we are fighting for, it's Champagne!

Winston Churchill, 1918, during World War I

In war, you win or lose, live or die – and the difference is just an eyelash.

General Douglas MacArthur

You can be killed just as dead in an unjustified war as you can in one protecting your own home.

Will Rogers

Soon after the American Revolution, Colonel Ethan Allen of the US army visited England. In the toilet of one of his hosts he found a portrait of George Washington. When he inquired why it had been hung there, he was told: 'Because there is nothing that will make an Englishman shit so quick as the sight of General Washington.'

Abraham Lincoln, *attrib.*

At Victoria Station the RTO gave me a travel warrant, a white feather and a picture of Hitler marked 'This is your enemy'. I searched every compartment but he wasn't on the train.

Spike Milligan, *Adolf Hitler, My Part in His Downfall*

Afghanistan is like you would imagine Colchester was like in Roman times.

Ray Winstone, 2009

Defence secretary, Geoff Hoon says that the city of Umm Qasr in Iraq is similar to Southampton. He's either never been to Southampton, or he's never been to Umm Qasr. There's no beer, no prostitutes and people are shooting at us. It's more like Portsmouth.

Unidentified British Soldier stationed in Iraq

I was at a field hospital in Basra. We went to speak to a squaddie who'd been blown up the day before, so I remarked: 'The only thing worse than being blown up on a Sunday is to be visited by politicians on a Monday,' to which he replied: 'Actually, it's on a par, sir.'

William Hague, in Iraq with David Cameron, 2006

You have to have a physical before you get into the army. A doctor looks in one ear, another doctor looks in the other ear, and if they can't see each other, you're in. And if they can see each other, you join the military police.

Joe E. Brown

Keep your bowels open, your mouth shut, and never volunteer.

Anon, advice to someone joining the army

All a soldier needs to know is how to shoot and salute.

General John Pershing

Whenever I see a fellow look as if he was thinking, I say that's mutiny.

Sir Thomas Troubridge, naval commander

When I first went into the active army, you could tell someone to move a chair across the room. Now you have to tell him why.

Major Robert Lembke, 1979

There is only one way for a young man to get on in the army. He must try and get killed in every way he possibly can!

Sir Garnet Wolseley

When I lost my rifle, the army charged me $85. That's why in the navy, the captain goes down with the ship.

Dick Gregory

My brother just got out of the Marines. They made a man out of him. Paid for the operation and everything.

Stu Trivax

Women make better soldiers than men. They always know where the real enemy is hidden.

José Yglesias

—Where was the soldier wounded?
—Ma'am, the bullet that wounded *him* would not have wounded *you*.

Unidentified Woman and Abraham Lincoln, during the American Civil War

In England, it is thought a good thing every now and then to shoot an admiral, to encourage the others.

Voltaire

The only thing more accurate than incoming enemy fire is incoming friendly fire.

Murphy's Military Law

The war situation has developed, not necessarily to Japan's advantage.

Emperor Hirohito, announcing Japan's surrender, 1945

A prisoner of war is a man who tries to kill you and fails, and then asks you not to kill him.

Winston Churchill

—Sometimes I ask myself how I'd stand up under torture.
—You kiddin'? If the Gestapo would take away your Bloomingdale's charge card, you'd tell 'em everything.

Annie Hall and Alvy Singer, *Annie Hall*

His brain has not only been washed, it has been dry-cleaned.

Dr Yen Lo, *The Manchurian Candidate*

If everyone demanded peace instead of another television set, then there'd be peace.

John Lennon

Peace is what we call that brief moment between wars when people stop to reload.

James W. Dobson

TERRORISM

—What's yellow and hides in Afghanistan?
—The Talibanana.

Popbitch.com

Iranians don't understand basic British joke construction. For you, an Englishman, an Irishman and a Scotsman, this is a joke. For us, it's a hostage situation.

Omid Djalili

A fanatic is a man that does what the Lord would do if he knew the facts of the case.

Finley Peter Dunne

Terrorists are high-minded idealists who assassinate innocent men, women and children for a good cause.

Alex Ayres

War upon rebellion was messy and slow, like eating soup with a knife.
T.E. Lawrence, on defeating guerrillas

Susan Boyle is an important weapon in the war on terror. Young extremists are thinking twice about blowing themselves up now because they now know what a virgin looks like.

Sean Lock, *8 Out of 10 Cats*

Apparently they're building a tower at the site of 9/11 but are worried about how to make it terrorist-proof. I think they should just build a big mosque.

Frankie Boyle

—Do you think there is room for forgiveness towards the people who have harboured and abetted the terrorists who perpetrated the 9/11 attacks on America?
—I believe that forgiving them is God's function. Our job is to arrange the meeting.

Interviewer and General Norman Schwarzkopf

VIOLENCE & WEAPONS

—What happened to your nose? Somebody slam a bedroom-window on it?
—Nope. Your wife got excited. She crossed her legs a little too quick.

Loach and Jake Gittes, *Chinatown*

Don't get sarcastic with me… You get sarcastic with me again and I will stuff so much cotton wool down your fucking throat it'll come out your arse like the tail on a Playboy bunny.

Malcolm Tucker, *In the Loop*

They do say that verbal insults hurt more than physical pain. They are, of course, wrong, as you will soon discover when I stick this toasting fork in your head.

Edmund Blackadder, *Blackadder*

The temperature inside this apple turnover is 1,000 degrees. If I squeeze it, a jet of molten Bramley apple is going to squirt out. Could go your way; could go mine. Either way, one of us is going down.

Alan Partridge

I can lick my weight in wildflowers.

W.C. Fields

I went out and caught that boy and shook him until his freckles rattled.

O. Henry

Nice people down South. They take their guns seriously. We passed a pickup truck. It had a bumper sticker: 'Guns don't kill people. I do.'

Jon Haymen

If I had time to clean up the mess, I'd shoot you.

J.R. Ewing, *Dallas*

—Sorry, the law requires a five-day waiting period before you can purchase a gun. We've got to run a background check.
—Five days? But I'm mad now!

Gun Shop Owner and Homer Simpson

But why do I need a gun licence? It's only for use around the house.

Charles Addams

Using another man's gun is like eating with another man's teeth.

Ben Maverick, *Maverick*

—Is that a gun in your pocket?
—Uh, no... it's my penis.

Emma and Simon Garden, *The Parole Officer*

I'd like to shoot a laser out of my cock. And when I'm empty, my balls glow.

Dane Cook

Instead of trying to build newer and bigger weapons of destruction, mankind should be thinking about getting more use out of the weapons we already have.

Jack Handey

No mode of warfare ever becomes truly obsolete. It always turns up again as an event in the Olympics.

Miles Kington

HEALTH, MEDICINE & DRUGS

WEIGHT

I have the body of a man half my age. Unfortunately, he's in terrible shape.

George Foreman, aged 48

You're getting so big I need double vision to take you in.

Peter De Vries

I think one reason they call them 'Relaxed Fit' jeans is that 'Ass The Size of Texas' jeans would not sell very well.

Jim Rosenberg

Due to the recent heat wave, doctors are warning obese people to stay indoors. Not for their health, but because no one wants to see them in short pants.

Conan O'Brien

We're all concerned about your weight. Bart said NASA called. They said that your gravity is pulling all the satellites out of orbit.

Marge Simpson, to Homer

I won't tell you how much I weigh, but don't ever get in an elevator with me unless you're going down.

Jack E. Leonard

My life today is tough. My wife, she's attached to a machine that keeps her alive – the refrigerator.

Rodney Dangerfield

Come into the front parlour, and mind your hips on the ornaments – this hall can be very tricky for women of your build.

Pat Brandon, *I Didn't Know You Cared*

This girl was fat. I hit her with my car. She asked me, 'Why didn't you go around me?' I told her, 'I didn't have enough gas.'

Rodney Dangerfield

I hear they're going to tear you down and put up an office building where you're standing.

Groucho Marx

When you have a fat friend there are no see-saws. Only catapults.

Demetri Martin

She needs to lose thirty pounds or gain sixty. Anything in between has no place on television.

Jack Donaghy, about an actress, *30 Rock*

DIET

Diet: a system of starving yourself to death so you can live a little longer.

Totie Fields

I once drove with friends from Cannes to Nice. It took about an hour, and we dieted all the way.

Elsa Maxwell

According to a brand new scientific study, more than 90 per cent of diet plans used by Americans do not work. The American scientists conducted this study by looking out a window.

Conan O'Brien

I've written a diet book. It's called: 'Put That Down, Fatty.'

Jimmy Carr, *The Jonathan Ross Show*

You could lose a lot of weight if you'd just carry all your diet books around the block once a day.

Bill Hoest, cartoon caption

—How on earth do you keep that figure? Is it some special diet?
—No, lady, by isometric farting.

Gina Lollobrigida and Robert Mitchum

A great way to lose weight is to eat naked in front of the mirror. Restaurants will almost always throw you out before you can eat too much.

Frank Varano

Another good reducing exercise consists of placing both hands against the table edge and pushing back.

Robert Quillen

You can't survive by sucking the juice from a wet mitten.

Charles M. Schulz

Ah, Charles! I wish I were allowed even the wing of a roasted butterfly!

Rev. Sydney Smith

If one doesn't have a character like Abraham Lincoln or Joan of Arc, a diet simply disintegrates into eating exactly what you want to eat, but with a bad conscience.

Maria Augusta Trapp

I never worry about diets. The only carrots that interest me are the number you get in a diamond.

Mae West

Food is like sex: when you abstain, even the worst stuff begins to look good.

Beth McCollister

It is harder to eat sparingly than to fast. Moderation requires awareness. Renunciation requires only the tyranny of will.

Sandor McNab

The problem with food, of course, is that we can't ever really break up with it.

Cathy Guisewite

I'm so compulsive about losing weight, I weigh myself after I cough.

Elayne Boosler

Forget about calories – everything makes thin people thinner, and fat people fatter.

Mignon McLaughlin

Lord, if you can't make me thin – can you make all my friends fat?

Judy Hampton

Don't worry about this fat. I'll fuck it off in three days.

Errol Flynn, to his cinematographer, before shooting on a film began

—Is it true that you went on a diet that involved eating 9 eggs a day?
—Yes, it's true. I was fat and ugly and now I'm thin and ugly.

Questioner and Charles Saatchi,
My Name is Charles Saatchi and I am an Artoholic

Bulimia is still, to me, the number one eating disorder if you want a great body.

Brüno Gehard, aka Sacha Baron Cohen

If Mama Cass had shared her ham sandwich with Karen Carpenter, they'd both be alive today.

Anon

Loretta's losing 5 pounds a week on her new diet. I figure I'll be rid of her completely in about 10 months.

Bill Hoest, cartoon caption

If you hear of 16 or 18 pounds of human flesh, they belong to me. I look as if a curate had been taken out of me.

Rev. Sydney Smith, after losing weight

Even the soul has to go on a diet sometimes.

Stanislaw J. Lec

HEALTHY EATING

STEAKS, MARTINIS & CIGARS: YOU GOT A PROBLEM WITH THAT?

Restaurant sign, cartoon caption by Lee Lorenz

I have a friend who's a macrobiotic. She doesn't eat meat, chicken, fish, white flour, sugar or preservatives. She can eat wicker.

Paula Poundstone

My whole family's lactose intolerant; when we take pictures we can't say 'Cheese'.

Jay London

I'm allergic to food. Every time I eat, it breaks out in fat.

Jennifer Greene Duncan

All these disorders. When I was a kid we just had crazy people.

Ellen DeGeneres

If you are what you eat, no wonder most healthy eaters have the mentality of vegetables.

Julie Burchill

How do you get your children to avoid fatty, greasy, disgusting, unhealthy food? Don't let them eat from your plate.

Bill Dodds

I am opposed to refined, processed foods... If you were put into a can to be eaten 12 months later, how would *you* taste?

Yehudi Menuhin

Health Food: any food whose flavour is indistinguishable from that of the package in which it is sold.

Henry Beard

Tofu – what is that stuff? It's like chickpeas and grout. Food should not caulk windows.

Billiam Coronel

What is 'organic'? Just another word for dirty fruit.

Ruby Wax

People on a diet should have a salad dressing called '250 Islands'.

George Carlin

The only time to eat diet food is when you're waiting for the steak to cook.

Julia Child

Health nuts are going to feel stupid someday, lying in hospitals dying of nothing.

Redd Foxx

EXERCISE

Are you getting fit or having one?

Captain Benjamin 'Hawkeye' Pierce, *M*A*S*H*

Fitness experts are encouraging Americans to make small New Year's resolutions this year that they can keep, like adding five minutes to their exercise routines. As a result, most Americans will now have a five-minute exercise routine.

Conan O'Brien

The average American would drive his car to the bathroom if the doors were wide enough.

Anon

I won't say I'm out of condition now, but I even puff going downstairs.

Dick Gregory

I bought an exercise bicycle two years ago… the most expensive coat hanger in New York.

Robert Klein

If you are seeking creative ideas, go out walking. Angels whisper to a man when he goes for a walk.

Raymond Inmon

My beauty routine is a mixture of aerobics, isometrics and a little bit of yoga. To the observer it would look as if I was merely lifting a cup of coffee to my lips and lighting a cigarette.

Peter Cook

One time I said, 'You should jog around the block.' He said, 'Why? I'm already here.'

Phyllis Diller

All that running and exercise can do for you is make you healthy.

Denny McClain

A friend of mine runs marathons. He always talks about this 'runner's high'. But he has to go 26 miles for it. That's why I smoke and drink. I get the same feeling from a flight of stairs.

Larry Miller

Exercise is the most awful illusion. The secret is a lot of aspirin and *marrons glacés*.

Noël Coward

For exercise, I wind my watch.

Robert Maxwell

—Your body is the only home you'll ever have!
—Yes, my home is pretty messy. But I have a woman who comes in once a week.

Mr Universe and Johnny Carson

HEALTH & MEDICINE

—Doctor, doctor, I have five penises!
—Crikey, how do your trousers fit you?
—Like a glove.

Anon

A smart doctor is one who can diagnose the ailment of a patient who doesn't smoke or drink and isn't overweight.

Al Haywood

My doctor grabbed me by the wallet and said, 'Cough'.

Henny Youngman

A doctor tells a guy, 'I have bad news. You have Alzheimer's, and you have cancer.' Guy says, 'Thank God I don't have cancer.'

Roseanne

My father died of cancer when I was a teenager. He had it before it became popular.

Goodman Ace

'My father's great dread was going senile,' said one aristocrat, apologizing for his father, who was happily exposing himself in the orangery. 'But now he has, he's enjoying himself enormously.'

Jilly Cooper

The great thing about Alzheimer's disease is that you never have to watch repeats on television.

Anon

I've got a great Alzheimer's joke.....but I can't remember it.

Pat Mulligan

We were at a party once and my husband said to a doctor, 'What should I do about this cough?' The doctor said, 'Put your hand over your mouth.'

Phyllis Diller

'Virus' is a Latin word used by doctors meaning 'your guess is as good as mine'.

Anon

—Doctor, are you sure it's pneumonia? I've heard of cases where a doctor treated a patient for pneumonia and he ended up dying of something else.
—Don't worry. When I treat a patient for pneumonia, he dies of pneumonia.

Winston K. Pendleton

—I though chicken soup was the universal cure-all?
—Not for flesh-wounds.

Janet Fowler and Cecilia Simon, *Simon & Simon*

I went to the doctor's for a check up. He said, 'I want a urine, stool and semen sample,' so I just left my underwear and went home.

Anon

Researchers at Yale University have found a connection between brain cancer and work environment. The number-one most dangerous job for developing brain cancer? Plutonium hat model.

Jimmy Fallon

The doctor said, 'Take off your clothes and stick your tongue out of the window.' I said, 'Why?' He said, 'I'm mad at my neighbour.'

Anon

The doctor looked my body over. I said, 'Is there any hope?' He said, 'Yes. Reincarnation.'

Phyllis Diller

A motto for hypochondriacs: There is no such thing as just a mole.

Fran Lebowitz

A bloke goes into the doctor's and says: 'I've got a mole on my dick, can you remove it, please?' ...The doc says: 'Yes sir, I can remove that mole, but I'm afraid I'm going to have to report you to the RSPCA.'

Popbitch.com

Every proctologist story ends in the same way: 'It was a million to one shot, Doc. Million to one.'

Cosmo Kramer, *Seinfeld*

My proctologist won't even see me anymore, he's so sensitive. The last time he saw me, I moaned the name of another doctor.

Dick Capri

—Are you allergic to anything?
—Country and Western music.

Nurse and Buddy Rich

—Why are you jumping up and down?
—I've just taken my medicine and I forgot to shake the bottle.

Anon

When you're 64, a doctor is someone you see in a soap opera. When you're 66, you see more of them than members of your family.

Eugene Shapiro

—Doc, what is the exact function of the prostate gland?
—Well, it's main function, when patients pass middle age, is to make money for urologists like me.

Anon

I thought I had PMS so I went to the doctor. The doctor said: 'I got good news and bad news. The good news is you don't have PMS. The bad news is you're just a bitch.'

Rhonda Bates

I had a girlfriend who told me she was in the hospital for female problems... I said, 'What? You can't parallel park?'

Pam Stone

An emergency exit in a local hospital is labelled: 'This door is alarmed.' Given the current state of the NHS, it's not alone.

Stuart Reed

—How long do you expect to be hospitalized?
—If all goes well, about a week. If not, about an hour and a half.

Reporter and Rodney Dangerfield, on going into hospital for heart surgery

My doctor promised he would have me walking within two months. He was right. When I got his bill I had to sell my car.

Anon

After what I've been through, I am happy just to be wearing clothes that open in the front.

David Letterman, after a quintuple bypass

Doctors think a lot of patients are cured who have simply quit in disgust.

Don Herold

Molière...detested doctors and when asked if he wanted the doctor to come, replied in his last breath: 'No, I'm too ill to see him.'

Earle P. Scarlett

Doctor Diaulus has changed his trade: he is now an undertaker – with the same results he got before as a practising physician.

Martial

DENTIST

A Texas oil millionaire had toothache, so he went to the dentist and the dentist said: 'Where does it hurt?' The oil man replied, 'I feel lucky today – drill anywhere.'

Barry Took

Drill, fill and bill.

Newsweek magazine

The dentist told me I grind my teeth at night, so now before I go to sleep I fill my mouth with hot water and coffee beans and set my alarm for 7:30.

Jeff Marder

Simon Cowell's smile seems extra-dazzling – I can't tell if he's had his teeth whitened or his mouth blackened.

Peter Serafinowicz

—Root canal work is expensive. It'll come to $600.
—Six hundred dollars? Why don't you just add a toll bridge and we'll go partners!

Dentist and Jack E. Leonard

Here's a dental plan. Chew on the other side.

Johnny Barnes, *Sleep When I'm Dead*

DISABILITY

Did you hear about the blind skunk? Fell in love with a fart.

Anon

A blind man and his guide dog go into a shop. He picks up his dog and swings it around his head. The shopkeeper cries, 'What are you doing? Can I help you?' Blind man says, 'No, thanks, just looking.'

Anon

A nun is having a bath and a knock comes on the door. She says, 'Who is it?' and the reply comes, 'It's the blind man! Can I come in?' She says, 'Er, yes, all right.' So the chap comes in and says, 'Nice tits! Where d'you want me to hang the blind?'

Rev. Geraldine Granger, *The Vicar of Dibley*

There is a wonder in reading Braille that the sighted will never know: to touch words and have them touch you back.

Jim Fiebig

I think I'd rather be blind than deaf. Blindness is like being in the dark all the time, but deafness is like being trapped on a planet full of mimes.

Doug Finney

Genesis drummer Phil Collins is partially deaf... That's terrible. To be in Genesis and only partially deaf.

Mark Lamarr, *Never Mind the Buzzcocks*

In this enlightened age, we don't do jokes about dyslexia because it's not clever and it's not furry.

Humphrey Lyttelton, *I'm Sorry I Haven't a Clue*

Whose cruel idea was it for the word 'lisp' to have an 's' in it?

George Carlin

In a country without the letter 's', nobody knows if you lisp or not.

Miles Kington

I used to have a speech impediment. I couldn't say 'no'.

Susan, *The Hard Way*

I used to have a speech impediment but we got divorced.

Bill Hoest, cartoon caption

I know Abu Hamza is a hate preacher but it must be terrible to go through life with two hooks for hands. Luckily, he likes corn on the cob.

Frank Skinner

That statement was as insensitive as a quadriplegic.

Washington Post

We have many more abilities and resources than we know. My advice is that you don't need to break your neck to find out about that.

Christopher Reeve

DRUGS & ADDICTION

They're selling crack in my neighbourhood. Finally.

Kevin Brennan

Everything I've ever loved was immoral, illegal or grew hair on your palms.

Steve Tyler, frontman of rock band, Aerosmith

Parents that use drugs have kids that use drugs. So there's an important lesson here: don't have kids!

Dave Gold, *The War at Home*

I used to have a drug problem, but now I make enough money.

David Lee Roth

I liked drugs. I was good at them.

Noel Gallagher

Having a wonderful time. Wish I were here.

Carrie Fisher

Taking cocaine is like being a haemophiliac in a razor factory.

Robin Williams

I'm not addicted to cocaine. I just like the way it smells.

Richard Pryor

According to a new report, in England cocaine is cheaper to buy than coffee. So apparently they have Starbucks, too.

Conan O'Brien

Marijuana is self-punishing; it makes you acutely sensitive and, in this world, what worse punishment could there be?

P.J. O'Rourke

She was on Valium and a Sainsbury's wine box a day... She'd lie naked on the kitchen floor at 7 o'clock in the morning, the fridge door open, and the wine box dripping on her head.

Dame Edna Everage

The Bishop of Stortford was talking to the local Master of Hounds about the difficulty he had in keeping his vicars off the incense.

P.G. Wodehouse, *Mr Mulliner Speaking*

Applause is an addiction, like heroin, or checking your email.

Sideshow Mel, *The Simpsons*

They used to tell me, 'Drugs can kill you.' Now that I'm 58, they are saying, 'Drugs can save your life.' I realise my doctor is my dealer now. He's a lot harder to get hold of.

Robin Williams

There were a lot of doctors in rehab. It's rather like being in a fat farm with nutritionists.

Robin Williams

Can you imagine walking through the Priory and seeing Robbie Williams coming over in a dressing gown? That's enough to drive you to heroin.

Noel Gallagher

There are no Chocoholics Anonymous because nobody wants to quit.

Anon

The sun is nature's Prozac.

Astrid Alauda

If you really want a mind-altering experience, look at a tree.

A.C. Grayling

SMOKING

The believing we do something when we do nothing is the first illusion of tobacco.

Ralph Waldo Emerson

I smoke 15 to 20 cigars a day. At my age I need something to hold on to.

George Burns, aged 85

A cigarette was like a little reward I gave myself twenty-five to forty times a day.

Lewis Grizzard

They threaten me with lung cancer, and still I smoke and smoke. If they'd only threaten me with hard work, I might stop.

Mignon McLaughlin

My neighbour asked me for a cigarette. I said, 'I thought you'd stopped smoking.' He said, 'Well, I've managed the first stage – I've stopped buying them.'

Joey Adams

I quit smoking and it was a very, very disappointing experience. I found out my teeth are really brown.

Bill Dana

I gave up smoking four years, two weeks and five days ago. But who misses it?

Sandra Scoppettone

Perfection is such a nuisance that I often regret having cured myself of using tobacco.

Emile Zola

I offered Dawn a cigarette. She refused. 'No thanks, I've already got cancer.'

Elaine Dundy

DEPRESSION

Depression is melancholy minus its charms.

Susan Sontag

The despair beyond despair.

William Styron

Tom Cruise says there's no such thing as depression, that you can get better with physical exercise. Well, maybe he's right – beating the shit out of Tom Cruise would be physical all right, and it would cheer me up.

David Feherty, who suffered from depression

Keep a box of sugar-plums on the chimney-piece and a kettle simmering on the hob.

Rev. Sydney Smith, recipe against melancholy

Depressives don't want to be happy. They want to be unhappy to confirm they're depressed. If they were happy they couldn't be depressed anymore. They'd have to go out into the world and live. Which can be depressing.

Larry, *Closer*

I saw a psychologist once because I thought I had depression. It cost me $100. When I left, I realised that there's nothing he could have said that would cheer me up as much as if I found a $100 bill on my way home.

Emo Philips

Most of us are pretty good at postponing our nervous breakdowns till we can afford them.

Mignon McLaughlin

I tend to treat my emotions like unpleasant relatives – a long-distance call once or twice a year is more than enough. If I got in touch with them, they might come to stay.

Molly Ivins

PSYCHIATRY & THERAPY

Two cows grazing in a field. One says: 'Aren't you worried about that mad cow disease?' The other says: 'Not me, I'm a squirrel.'

Anon

You know how when you're leaning back on a chair and you lean back too far and you're just about to fall and then at the last second you catch yourself? I feel like that all the time.

Steven Wright

I have an intense desire to return to the womb. Anybody's.

Woody Allen

I'm kind of paranoid. I often think the car in front of me is following me the long way around.

Dennis Miller

He would let me tell my dreams. That's the main difference between a husband and a psychoanalyst.

Lillian Day

Sometimes I get the feeling that the whole world is against me, but deep down I know that's not true. Some of the smaller countries are neutral.

Robert Orben

The poet Percy Bysshe Shelley, seized by one of his occasional neurotic hallucinations, screamed that he saw eyes staring at him from the breasts of his second wife, Mary Godwin.

Edward S. Gifford

Do not disturb. I'm disturbed enough already.

Sign on Spike Milligan's office door

When you think about it, attention deficit disorder makes a lot of sense. In this country there isn't a lot worth paying attention to.

George Carlin

I have obsessive compulsive disorder. I have to do everything in threes. That's kinda how I got my reputation in school as a slut.

Mimi Bobeck, *The Drew Carey Show*

Jesus, save a little craziness for menopause!

Larry Lipton, *Manhattan Murder Mystery*

People like *you* are the reason people like *me* need medication.

Tagline, *Charlie Bartlett*

Kleptomania is a strange disease; you can't take anything for it.

Anon

The most common last straw leading to admission to mental hospitals in the United States in 1972 was – what would you think? – smashing the television set.

Ross Speck

Everybody in Los Angeles is in therapy. It's a good thing they don't have parking spaces for the emotionally handicapped. There'd be no place to park.

Jackson Perdue

I've been seeing an analyst for 15 years. I'm gonna give him one more year and then I'm going to Lourdes.

Alvy Singer, *Annie Hall*

My psychiatrist and I have decided that when we both think I'm ready, I'm going to get my car and drive off the Verrazano Bridge.

Barney Cashman, *Last of the Red Hot Lovers*

You heard about the accountant who came in for treatment? He kept hearing strange invoices.

Anon

—How many psychiatrists does it take to fill a swimming pool?
—About 130, but the manufacturer recommends water.

Boo Blume

A psychiatrist is the next man you start talking to after you start talking to yourself.

Fred Allen

A psychiatrist is a person who owns a couch and charges you for lying on it.

Edwin Brock

My parents sent me to a child psychiatrist. The kid didn't help me at all.

Rodney Dangerfield

Satisfaction guaranteed or your mania back.

Sign on a psychiatrist's office

—Dr Crane has tunnelled his way into the very depths of my psyche.
—Well, let's hope he sent a canary down first.

Bebe Glazer and Niles Crane, *Frasier*

With therapy, one-third get better, one-third stay the same, and one-third get worse. Without therapy, one-third get better, one-third stay the same, and one-third get worse.

Jeremy Leven

—I'm pleased to say you're making excellent progress.
—Progress? Six months ago I was Napoleon Bonaparte! Today I'm nobody! Call that progress?

Psychiatrist and Patient

I went to this analyst. He's helped me a great deal. In fact, I am so much better now, I get to sit up.

Phyllis Diller

The psychiatrist said to the patient: 'You have nothing to worry about – anyone who can pay my bills is certainly not a failure.'

Lea Berner

They told me I had an unresolved Oedipus complex, which, according to them, meant I want to sleep with my mother. Which is preposterous. My father doesn't even want to sleep with my mother.

Dennis Wolfberg

—Oedipus is the one who killed his father and married his mother.
—Argh! Who paid for *that* wedding?

Lisa and Homer Simpson

The doc told me that I had a dual personality. Then he lays an $82 bill on me, so I give him 41 bucks and say, 'Get the other 41 bucks from the other guy.'

Julius Kelp (Jerry Lewis), *The Nutty Professor*

Roseanne had something like 27 personalities. Only 2 of them liked me.

Tom Arnold, ex-husband

Schizophrenia beats dining alone.

Oscar Levant

Who thinks Freud is how Brummies like their eggs?

Anne Robinson, *The Weakest Link*

Freud is the father of psychoanalysis. It had no mother.

Germaine Greer

—According to Freud, what comes between fear and sex?
—Fünf.

Anon

Freud put the 'anal' into psychoanalysis.

Graffiti

Psychiatrists are terrible ads for themselves, like a dermatologist with acne.

Mignon McLaughlin

My analyst didn't know what he was doing. He used to listen to my problems and write them down on a pad and mail them in to 'Dear Abby'.

Woody Allen

Therapist? Why can't you talk to your hairdresser like everyone else?

May, *The Mother*

I never know whether to pity or congratulate a man on coming to his senses.

William Makepeace Thackeray

EDUCATION & THINKING

EDUCATION & SCHOOLS

Free: Mon-Fri: Knowledge. Bring your own containers.

Sign in a school in Dallas, Texas

Isn't education a wonderful thing? If you couldn't sign your name you'd have to pay cash.

Rita Mae Brown

Good news, bad news... I went to 17 different schools in 17 different cities. Good news: I got really good at geography. Bad news: I couldn't spell 'geography'.

Lorna Luft

One of the first things schoolchildren in Texas learn is how to compose a simple declarative sentence without the word 'shit' in it.

Anon

One of our children's first schools was so posh that when a teacher asked the class, 'Who is Mohammed?' a small boy stuck up his hand and quietly answered, 'Our chauffeur.'

Charles Saatchi, *Charles Saatchi: Question*

The high school I went to, they asked a kid to prove the law of gravity, he threw the teacher out the window.

Thornton Melon, *Back to School*

As for helping me in the outside world, the convent taught me only that if you spit on a pencil eraser, if will erase ink.

Dorothy Parker

I never let my schooling interfere with my education.

Mark Twain

You know there is a problem with the education system when you realize that out of the three Rs only one begins with an R.

Dennis Miller

If we practised medicine like we practise education, we'd look for the liver on the right side and left side in alternate years.

Alfred Kazin

The primary purpose of a liberal education is to make one's mind a pleasant place in which to spend one's time.

Sydney J. Harris

Von Ribbentrop was the new German Ambassador in London, and as a good Nazi, hoped to send his son to Eton.

Peter Ustinov

A lot of public school boys are twits with polish. When I encounter expensive shirts and upper-class accents I have always presumed vacuity until offered firm evidence to the contrary.

Matthew Parris

In my opinion Hook was a good Etonian though not a great one... The proud, if detestable position he attained is another proof that the Etonian is a natural leader of men... In politics he was a Conservative... At Oxford he fell among bad companions – Harrovians.

J.M. Barrie, on his fictional creation, Captain Hook

[*noticing Churchill leave the bathroom without washing his hands*] —At Eton they taught us to wash our hands after using the toilet.
—At Harrow they taught us not to piss on our hands.

Unidentified Etonian and Winston Churchill, *attrib.*

At Harrow, you could have any boy for a box of Cadbury's milk chocolate.

John Mortimer, an Old Harrovian

There is a certain confidence about anyone who's been to Eton – or to
Borstal.

George Passmore, of Gilbert & George

It is a measure of how much the world has changed...that proud
Etonians and closet homosexuals have been replaced by proud
homosexuals and closet Etonians.

John Julius Norwich, *Trying to Please*

Britain cannot afford a schooling system where the most important book
is the cheque book.

Neil Kinnock, on private education

TEACHER

The main purpose of education is to keep them off the streets – the
teachers, I mean.

Katharine Whitehorn, quoting her father, a schoolmaster

The secret of teaching is to appear to have known all your life what you
learned this afternoon.

Anon

It doesn't matter what you teach a child as long as the child doesn't like it
– and does like you.

Collin Brooks

A schoolmaster should have an atmosphere of awe, and walk
wonderingly, as if he was amazed at being himself.

Walter Bagehot

Parent-Teacher Night: Let's Share the Blame.

Sign outside Springfield Elementary School,
attended by Bart Simpson, *The Simpsons*

The only reason I always try to meet and know the parents better is because it helps me to forgive the children.

Louis Johannot, teacher

If you promise not to believe everything your child says happens at this school, I'll promise not to believe everything he says happens at home.

Unidentified Schoolteacher

He has glaring faults and they have certainly glared at us this term.

Headmaster's report on Stephen Fry

The boy is every inch the fool, but luckily for him he's not very tall.

School report on Norman Wisdom

I will not yell 'She's dead' during roll call; Global warming did not eat my homework; A burp is not an answer; I am not authorized to fire substitute teachers; Funny noises are not funny; I am not my long-lost twin; I do not have diplomatic immunity; The class hamster isn't 'just sleeping'; I will not hide the teacher's Prozac.

Lines written on the blackboard by Bart Simpson

My teachers told me I would never make anything of myself if I sat staring into space during lessons; however, I had the last laugh as I am now the Astronomer Royal.

Martin Rees, *Viz* magazine

Teaching has ruined more American novelists than drink.

Gore Vidal

One teacher recently retired with $500,000 after 30 years of working hard, caring, dedicating herself and totally immersing herself in the problems of the students. That gave her $50. The rest came from the death of a rich uncle.

Milton Berle

EXAMS & TESTS

Next week I have to take my college aptitude test. In my high school they didn't even *teach* aptitude.

Tony Banta, Taxi

Had silicon been a gas, I would have been a major-general by now.

James McNeil Whistler, artist, on being found
'deficient in chemistry' in a West Point exam

I managed to get through the mining exams. They're not very rigorous. They only ask you one question. They say, 'Who are you?' and I got 75 per cent on that.

Peter Cook

Q: The estimated amount of the national debt of England in 1827 is said to have been £900000000; how long would it take to count this debt, supposing you counted $50 per minute, and 12 hours a day, during the whole time? (Sundays excepted.)
A: 354 years, 309 days, 1 hour and 20 mins.

Question from Conkling's Arithmetic,
text book of 1831 for children aged 8–10 years

Rufus is a pimp for three girls. If the price is $65 per trick, how many tricks per day must each girl turn to support Rufus' $800 per day crack habit?

Question in a Winnipeg maths exam for which a teacher was suspended, 2002

English Literature GCSE, Question 1: Discuss the use of imagery and metaphor in *My Story So Far* by Wayne Rooney.
Spell 'Mississippi', without looking at how we've spelt it in the question.
It takes 2 men 10 minutes to check in for their flight – how long will it take Ahmed and Imran?
Thunderbirds are what?

Rejected Exam Questions, Mock the Week

COLLEGE

—How do you get a philosophy major off your doorstep?
—Pay for the pizza.

Anon

—Do you think your boy will forget all he learned in college?
—I hope so. He can't make a living drinking.

Larry Wilde

The only thing you study is your navel. You even shave lying down.

Rupert Rigsby, to his student lodger, *Rising Damp*

—He's at Oxford, technically.
—Yes, I met him. Brideshead Regurgitated.

Hannah and Bernard, *Arcadia*

Trinity dons in Hall looking less where they shall sit than where they shall *not* sit.

A.C. Benson

I recollect an acquaintance saying to me that 'the Oriel Common Room stank of Logic'.

John Henry Newman, on the Oxford college

I find the three major administrative problems on a campus are sex for the students, athletics for the alumni, and parking for the faculty.

Clark Kerr

Four years of Harvard College, if successful, resulted in an auto-biographical blank, a mind on which only a watermark had been stamped.

Henry Adams

You want either a first or a fourth. There is no value in anything between.

Evelyn Waugh, *Brideshead Revisted*

KNOWLEDGE

This would be a great time in the world for some man to come along that knew something.

Will Rogers

I think this is the most extraordinary collection of talent, of human knowledge, that has ever been gathered together at the White House — with the possible exception of when Thomas Jefferson dined alone.

John F. Kennedy, at a dinner for 49 American Nobel Prize Winners, 1962

You can swim all day in the Sea of Knowledge and still come out completely dry. Most people do.

Norman Juster

It wasn't until quite late in life that I discovered how easy it is to say, 'I don't know.'

W. Somerset Maugham

The dumbest people I know are those who know it all.

Malcolm Forbes

A weekday edition of the *New York Times* contains more information than the average person was likely to come across in a lifetime in 17th century England.

Richard Saul Wurman

Knowledge consists of knowing that a tomato is a fruit, and wisdom consists of not putting it in a fruit salad.

Miles Kington

We are here and it is now. Further than that all human knowledge is moonshine.

H.L. Mencken

INTELLIGENCE

My cat is very intelligent. I asked her what two minus two was and she said nothing.

Brian Johnston

The first time I ever talked to Jonathan Miller his greeting remark was: '*The Times*'s review of my *Tosca* production this morning was disgracefully impertinent – and I use the word in the 17th-century sense.'

Richard Morrison, music critic of *The Times*

He not only overflowed with learning but stood in the slop.

Rev. Sydney Smith, on Thomas Macaulay

When I left the dining room after sitting next to Mr Gladstone, I thought he was the cleverest man in England. But after sitting next to Mr Disraeli, I thought I was the cleverest woman in England.

Princess Marie Louise

The greatest good you can do for another is not just to share your riches but to reveal to him his own.

Benjamin Disraeli

I am so clever that sometimes I don't understand a single word of what I am saying.

Oscar Wilde

The two biggest myths about me are that I'm an intellectual, because I wear these glasses and that I'm an artist because my films lose money.

Woody Allen

—What do you think of intellectual women?
—Are there any?

Reporter and George Sanders

Educating a beautiful woman is like pouring honey into a fine Swiss watch. Everything stops.

Kurt Vonnegut

A man likes his wife to be just clever enough to appreciate his cleverness, and just stupid enough to admire it.

Israel Zangwill

Hide your learning, daughter, as if it were a physical defect.

Lady Mary Wortley Montagu

Diamonds are a girl's best friend. Dogs are a man's best friend. Now you know which sex is smarter.

Nancy Gray

STUPIDITY

It would be easier to pay off the national debt overnight than to neutralise the long-range effects of national stupidity.

Frank Zappa

Think of how stupid the average person is, and then realize half of them are even stupider.

George Carlin

Your brain's so minute that if a hungry cannibal cracked your head open, there wouldn't be enough to cover a small water biscuit.

Edmund Blackadder, *Blackadder*

Think donkey, then take it down a few notches.

David Sedaris

I'll tell you how smart he is. When they had a blackout in New York, he was stranded 13 hours on an escalator.

Joe Nuxhall

Now I may be an idiot, but there's one thing I am not sir, and that sir, is an idiot.

Peter Griffin, *Family Guy*

A man may be a fool and not know it, but not if he is married.

H.L. Mencken

No one can make a man look a fool quite so successfully as a woman. Any man: any woman.

Ray Connolly

—I've changed my mind.
—Yeah, does it work any better?

Bill Barton and Tira (Mae West), *I'm No Angel*

Never call a man a fool. Borrow from him.

Addison Mizner

THINKING

Data, data, everywhere, but not a thought to think.

Theodore Roszak

The human animal resists thinking. You never think until you come to a crossroads.

Philip M. Hauser

I vill a little t'ink.

Albert Einstein, the phrase he used in his broken English
when he needed more time to consider a problem

I prefer thinking to understanding, for thinking is active and continuous, like composing, while to understand is to bring to an end.

Igor Stravinsky

Our best friends and our worst enemies are our thoughts. A thought can do us more good than a doctor or a banker or a faithful friend. It can also do us more harm than a brick.

Frank Crane

The species of whale known as the black right whale has 4 kilos of brains and 1,000 kilos of testicles. If it thinks at all, we know what it is thinking about.

Jon Lien

Cats think about three things: food, sex, and nothing.

Adair Lara

Certain thoughts are better left unthunk.

Woody Allen

It is not merely that Johnny can't read, or even that Johnny can't think. *Johnny doesn't know what thinking is*, because thinking is so often confused with feeling.

Thomas Sowell, on American educational standards

You might very well think that. I couldn't possibly comment.

Francis Urquhart, Chief Whip, *House of Cards*

Think Tank: an organization which invents disinterested intellectual justifications for the policies of the corporate groups that fund it. The result is an unfortunate confusing of knowledge and power.

John Ralston Saul

Let us go down to Covent Garden and look at the roses. Come! I am tired of thought.

Oscar Wilde

PHILOSOPHY

—Life is like a bowl of tuna fish.
—Why is life like a bowl of tuna fish?
—How should I know? Am I a philosopher?

Jewish joke

You could read Kant by yourself, if you wanted; but you must share a joke with someone else.

Robert Louis Stevenson

You would not enjoy Nietzsche, Sir. He is fundamentally unsound.

P.G. Wodehouse, *Carry On, Jeeves*

Whenever Westerners don't understand something, they simply think it's Zen.

Yasujiro Ozu

If a tree falls in the forest and nobody is around, the firewood is yours for the taking.

Oleg Vishnepolsky

If a tree falls in a forest and lands on a politician, even if you can't hear the tree or the screams, I'll bet you'd at least hear the applause.

Paul Tindale

It is a safe rule to apply that, when a mathematical or philosophical author writes with a misty profundity, he is talking nonsense.

Alfred North Whitehead

Every professor of philosophy needs a nine-year-old daughter. Mine has a habit of saying, 'Daddy, that is a very silly idea.' She is always right.

A.C. Grayling

I have studied many philosophers and many cats. The wisdom of cats is infinitely superior.

Hippolyte Taine

LIFE, AGEING & DEATH

LIFE

—How's life, Norm?
—Not for the squeamish, Coach.

Ernie 'Coach' Pantusso and Norm Peterson, *Cheers*

I was born in 1957. I have a wife, a child, a mortgage, two dogs and gum disease.

Dave Barry

Clock on. Do as little as you can. Clock off. Live beyond your means. Then die.

Eileen Grimshaw, *Coronation Street*

Be, beget, begone.

William Saroyan

I wish life were like *Spooks* where everything is a) knowable, and b) soluble by six people.

Dame Eliza Manningham-Buller, Director General of MI5

Life and death are two locked caskets, each of which contains the key to the other.

Isak Dinesen

Life is better than death, I believe, if only because it is less boring, and because it has fresh peaches in it.

Alice Walker

LIVING

—What happened to you? What's with the bandages and the crutch?
—I was living the life of Riley.
—Then what?
—Riley came home.

Anon

A human lifespan is less than a thousand months long. You need to make some time to think how to live it.

A.C. Grayling

—I've wasted half my life, Marge. Do you know how many memories I have? Three! Standing in line for a movie, having a key made, and sitting here talking to you. Thirty-eight years and that's all I have to show for it.
—You're 39.

Homer and Marge Simpson

Groucho Marx at the end of his life was asked if he had it to do all over again what he would do differently: 'Try another position.'

Gore Vidal

Life is a banquet, and most poor sons-of-bitches are *starving* to death! Live!

Auntie Mame, *Auntie Mame*

I intend to live the first half of my life. I don't care about the rest.

Errol Flynn, who died aged 50

There's more to life than getting drunk, being naked and having sex.

Alex Sibley, *Big Brother 3*

—If you had it all to do over, would you change anything?
—Yes, I wish I had played the black instead of the red at Cannes and Monte Carlo.

Questioner and Winston Churchill

Hope for the best. Expect the worst. Life is a play. We're unrehearsed.

Mel Brooks

—How's life, Mr Peterson?
—Oh, I'm waiting for the movie.

Woody Boyd and Norm Peterson, *Cheers*

AGE & AGEING

First thing I do when I wake up in the morning is breathe on a mirror and hope it fogs.

Early Wynn

My older son who is, I think, here tonight, is 41 years old. Which is odd because so am I.

Robert Parker

Is anyone else here getting older?

Maria Bamford

I am becoming like the Irish Census, I am broken down by age, sex and religion.

Seán MacRéamoinn

—You shouldn't let it get to you. You don't look your age.
—Don't I?
—No. You can never tell how old fat people are. The fat pushes the wrinkles out.

Penny Neville and Lindsay Pearce, *Teachers*

I told my wife a man is like wine, he gets better with age. She locked me in the cellar.

Rodney Dangerfield

The first sign of getting old is listening to Radio 2 and thinking it's Radio 1.
Matthew Parris

I've reached an age where I wake up in the morning, look in the obituary column, and if I don't see my name, I call a hooker.

George Jessel

I recently turned 50, which is young for a tree, midlife for an elephant, and ancient for a quarter-miler, whose son now says, 'Dad, I just can't run the quarter with you anymore unless I bring something to read.'

Bill Cosby

Middle age... the time of a man's life when, if he has two choices for an evening, he takes the one that gets him home earlier.

Alvan L. Barach

Another sign of middle age: questions begin with the words, 'Are you still...'
D.C. Burrows

Middle age was that period of life when parents and children caused equal amounts of worry.

Romy Halliwell

Once you pass 35, your age becomes part of the first sentence of anything written. It's a form of...putting you in your place. For women, naturally. Men still get a free pass, more or less.

Madonna

My wife never lies about her age. She just tells everyone she's as old as I am. Then she lies about *my* age.

Anon

Nothing makes a woman feel as old as watching the bald spot daily increase on the top of her husband's head.

Helen Rowland

You know you're getting older when by the time you've lit the last candle on your cake, the first one has burned out.

Jeff Rovin

You know you're getting old when... your favourite pastime is surfing the Internet medical sites; the senior citizens in television commercials look 20 years younger than you do; you say, 'Over my dead body!' and people aren't sure if you're kidding.

Joey Green and Alan Corcoran

A characteristic of old age is thinking that our own ruin should coincide precisely with that of the universe.

Santiago Ramón y Cajal

An elderly woman in a nursing home declined her pastor's suggestion that she get a hearing aid. 'At 91, I've heard enough,' she said.

Catherine Hall

I did a gig at an old people's home. Tough crowd. They wouldn't respond to my knock-knock jokes until I showed ID.

Frank Skinner

There is no point in growing old unless you can be a witch.

Germaine Greer

A person is always startled when he hears himself seriously called an old man for the first time.

Oliver Wendell Holmes

—You're not the man I knew ten years ago.
—It's not the years, honey, it's the mileage.

Marion Ravenwood and Indiana Jones, Raiders of the Lost Ark

I have reached an age when I look just as good standing on my head as I do right side up.

Frank Sullivan

You know when you're really old? When your testicles tell you it's time to mow the lawn.

Rodney Dangerfield

I was actually walking around downtown not too long ago, and I saw Milton Berle in an antique shop – 800 bucks.

Jeffrey Ross, on Milton Berle, aged 87

The older you get, the more important it is not to act your age.

Ashleigh Brilliant

Aztec law… gave the death sentence for all sorts of things – fornication, indignity even – until a man was sixty. Then all the laws were suspended, and he could be as ridiculous as he wanted. I've always wanted to be silly if I felt like it, and now I can.

John Steinbeck, aged 60

I'm not sixty, I'm *sexty*.

Dolly Parton, on reaching the milestone birthday

The great thing about turning 75 is you don't get any more calls from insurance salesmen.

Soupy Sales

—What is the secret of your enduring vigour?
—The saliva of beautiful women.

Interviewer and Tony Curtis, aged 83

I have enjoyed great health at a great age because every day since I can remember, I have consumed a bottle of wine except when I have not felt well. Then I have consumed two bottles.

Bishop of Seville

People are living longer than ever before, a phenomenon undoubtedly made necessary by the 30-year mortgage.

Doug Larson

According to actuarial tables, people who live the longest are rich relatives.

Bob Monkhouse

Death only ever happens to someone ten years older than you, however old you get.

Tim Lott

I think all this talk about age is foolish. Every time I am one year older, everyone else is too.

Gloria Swanson

We are always the same age inside.

Gertrude Stein

Happy Birthday! P.S. If you keep having birthdays, you'll eventually die. Love, Groucho.

Groucho Marx, greetings to a good friend

At whatever age, I hope to die young.

Jean Lemoyne

MEMORY

I remember a lot of things before I was even born. I remember going to a picnic with my father and coming home with my mother.

Foster Brooks

I've a grand memory for forgetting.

Robert Louis Stevenson

To improve your memory, lend people money.

Anon

You are never more than 10 days away from forgetting someone's birthday.

Miles Kington

Women forget injuries but never forget slights.

T.C. Haliburton

Elephants and grandchildren never forget.

Andy Rooney

RETIREMENT

My, my – 65! I guess this marks the first day of the rest of our life savings.

H. Martin

It's nice to get out of the rat race, but you have to learn to get along with less cheese.

Gene Perret

Gone today, here tomorrow.

Catherine Crook de Camp, on retirement savings

My assistant asked me when I was going to retire. I said, 'When I can no longer hear the sound of laughter.' He said, 'That never stopped you before.'

Bob Hope

When I retire, I'm going to grow a juniper forest and tap the trees every morning for my daily gin.

W.C. Fields

My Maryland farm is where I'll finally sit on the porch with a shotgun across my knee and aim at anything that looks like it's going to make me work.

Robert Mitchum

Most people perform essentially meaningless work. When they retire that truth is borne upon them.

Brendan Francis

I wanted to spend more time with my family, but I found my family didn't want to spend more time with me.

Greg Dyke, former director general of the BBC

I married him for better or worse, but not for lunch.

Hazel Weiss, on her husband's retirement

Mario Andretti has retired from motor racing. That's a good thing. He's getting old. He ran his entire last race with his left indicator on.

Jon Stewart

When a jockey retires he becomes just another little man.

Eddie Arcaro, US jockey

DEATH & DYING

Think of death as a pie in the face from God.

Tagline, *The End*

—How do you feel about death?
—I don't think it's right for me.

Christopher Howse and Alan Whicker

He's terrified of dying. His theory is that he can't possibly die if he has tickets to the ball game.

George Axelrod, on Irving 'Swifty' Lazar

Dying's not so bad. At least I won't have to answer the telephone.

Rita Mae Brown

Untimely deaths seem common – but I don't remember hearing of a timely one.

Frank A. Clark

I regard it as a matter of honour not to expire before my passport.

Peter Ustinov

The greatest thing about your last journey is that you don't have to pack.

Tony Benn, quoting his grandmother

—I'm settling my estate.
—What estate? Your bus pass and loofah-sponge?

Sophia Petrillo and Dorothy Zbornak, *The Golden Girls*

—Jack is dead.
—Don't be ridiculous. Jack would never die without telling me.

Omar and Joan Wilder, *The Jewel of the Nile*

When they found Michael Jackson lying face down next to the bed they assumed he was looking for the other glove.

Frank Skinner

In an interview, Matthew McConaughey said that he wants to die the same way his father did, right after having sex. McConaughey's mother has said, 'Absolutely not.'

Tina Fey

You don't die in the United States, you underachieve.

Jerzy Kosinski

The man who invented the taser has passed away at the age of 88. I understand his relatives were stunned.

Conan O'Brien

When a humorist dies, you should go somewhere that has a piano and drink until they throw you out.

Robert Benchley, noted by Alan Coren

My Auntie Eileen's getting on a bit now, and she's always going on about who just died: 'D'you remember Arthur? He's just died. D'you remember Mervyn? He's just died.' I said, 'Auntie, get off the roof and give me the gun!'

Milton Jones, *The News Quiz*

I don't like to cross dead people out of my address book. I put them in square brackets.

Julian Barnes

First you are, then you are not. This I find deeply satisfying.

Ingmar Bergman

LAST WORDS

When I was a little kid, I wished the first words I ever said was the word, 'Quote…' so right before I died I could say, '…unquote.'

Steven Wright

When she was dying, she let out a loud fart. 'Good,' she said, looking around her, 'a woman who farts is not dead.' These were the last words she spoke.

Jean-Jacques Rousseau, on the Countess de Vercellis

—If there is anything you'd care to say to me, I shall be only too happy to oblige.
—Much obliged, Padre, but why bother? I'll be seeing your boss in a few minutes.

Minister and Wilson Mizner, on his deathbed

Put out that bloody cigarette!

Saki, to a fellow officer in a trench during World War I,
fearing the smoke might give away their positions.
A German sniper overheard the remark and shot him.

For Christ's sake, can't you get them to turn off the television!

Bob Brown

Doctor, do you think it could have been the sausage?

Paul Claudel

Let down the curtain; the farce is over.

François Rabelais

SUICIDE

Without the possibility of suicide I would have killed myself long ago.

E.M. Cioran

Doesn't it seem a little like going where you haven't been invited?

Richard Eberhart

The first thing I did when I made the decision to kill myself was to stop dieting. Let them dig a wider hole.

Gail Parent

No one is promiscuous in his way of dying. A man who has decided to hang himself will never jump in front of a train.

A. Alvarez

Sylvia Brooke made two attempts at suicide by the time she was 12: she first tried ptomaine poisoning, buying a tin of sardines from the village shop, opening it and leaving it on top of her cupboard for 7 days before eating it; when that failed, she sought to catch pneumonia by lying naked in the snow.

Philip Eade

I have always thought the suicide should bump off at least one swine before taking off for parts unknown.

Ezra Pound

How many people have wanted to kill themselves, and have been content with tearing up their photograph!

Jules Renard

FUNERAL

At 90, my mother has taken out a funeral plan with Age Concern...
She has specified that she wants cremation. The letter of confirmation...
offers her 'a very warm welcome'.

Jo Dean

I would like to be scattered on the pitch at Elland Road. If the board of
Leeds United object, my solicitor may consent to have me cremated first.

D.A. Barham

At the funeral of the crossword puzzle guru they announced that he
would be buried 6 feet down and 3 across.

Professor Robert C. Art

In her will, my grandmother stipulated that she wanted to be buried with
all of her favourite possessions. Her cat was not happy.

Tom Cotter

To my nephew, Irving, who still keeps asking me to mention him in my will: 'Hello, Irving!'

Henny Youngman

A son can bear with composure the death of his father, but the loss of his
inheritance might drive him to despair.

Machiavelli

I do like Italian graves; they look so much more lived in.

Elizabeth Bowen

Eulogy: too much – too late.

Arnold H. Glasow

In grief one turns either to the monastery or the brothel.

Roman Polanski

When her third husband died, her hair turned quite gold from grief.

Oscar Wilde

If, after I depart this vale, you ever remember me and have thought to please my ghost, forgive some sinner and wink your eye at some homely girl.

H.L. Mencken

What's the average man's life but a succession of cars? When he dies, we should carve on his tombstone simply the makes and years.

Richard Needham

When I die, my epitaph should read: *She paid the bills.* That's the story of my life.

Gloria Swanson

RELIGION

RELIGION – GENERAL

—What do you get when you cross an insomniac, a dyslexic and an agnostic?
—Someone who lies awake all night wondering if there really is a dog.

Anon

It's a god eat god world.

Maurice Yacowar

Religion. It's given people hope in a world torn apart by religion.

Jon Stewart

Religion is what people had before television.

Dylan Moran

There are many different religions in this world, but if you look at them carefully, you'll see that they all have one thing in common: they were invented by a giant, superintelligent slug named Dennis.

Homer Simpson

The more I study religions the more I am convinced that man never worshipped anything but himself.

Richard Francis Burton

We must respect the other fellow's religion, but only in the sense and to the extent that we respect his theory that his wife is beautiful and his children smart.

H.L. Mencken

Many people think they have religion when they are troubled with dyspepsia.

Robert G. Ingersoll

My faith is a bit like Magic FM in the Chilterns, in that the signal comes and goes.

Boris Johnson

Isn't an agnostic just an atheist without balls?

Stephen Colbert

You are not an agnostic... You are just a fat slob who is too lazy to go to Mass.

Conor Cruise O'Brien, *attrib.*

Atheism – a religion dedicated to its own sense of smug superiority.

Stephen Colbert

—What do you get if you cross an atheist with a Jehovah's Witness?
—Someone who rings your doorbell for no reason.

Anon

A Mormon told me that they don't drink coffee. I said, 'A cup of coffee every day gives you wonderful benefits.' He said, 'Like what?' I said, 'Well, it keeps you from being Mormon.'

Emo Philips

My impression of a Mormon comedian: 'Take my wife, take my wife, take my wife...'

Stewie Stone

I went to see the Dalai Lama once. I was surprised at the number of things he said which my dad had already told me at the kitchen sink.

Julia Sawalha

A lot of people ask, 'What would Jesus do?' It's harder when your role model is Zeus. You see a pretty girl and ask, 'What would Zeus do? Turn into a swan and rape her?'

Seán Cullen

The various modes of worship, which prevailed in the Roman world, were all considered by the people as equally true; by the philosopher, as equally false; and by the magistrate, as equally useful. And thus toleration produced not only mutual indulgence, but even religious concord.

Edward Gibbon

GOD

An eminent doctor recently said that after decades of work on the human ear, he had come to believe in God. I asked why, and he replied: 'God is the only explanation for ear wax.'

William O. Douglas

I cannot believe in a God who wants to be praised all the time.

Friedrich Nietzsche

I guess I began to doubt the existence of God after I had been married about three years.

Brian Savage

It is much more difficult to believe in marriage than to believe in God.

Eugen Rosenstock-Huessy

If there is a God, give me a sign!... See, I told you that the klmpt smflrrt glptnrf...

Steve Martin

Flaubert told the story of a man who was taken fishing by an atheist friend. They fished up a stone on which was carved: 'I do not exist. *Signed*: God.' 'What did I tell you?' said the friend.

Edmond and Jules de Goncourt

I get just as upset thinking that God exists as thinking that he doesn't. That's why I'd rather not think about it.

Gabriel García Márquez

—What's God?
—Well, you know when you want something really bad and you close your eyes and wish for it? God's the guy that ignores you.

Tom Lincoln and James McCord, *The Island*

A little boy is drawing at his desk. His teacher asks, 'What are you drawing?' The child says, 'I'm drawing a picture of God.' Teacher replies, 'But how can you do that? Nobody knows what God looks like.' 'They will when I've finished.'

Anon

All your Western theologies...are based on the concept of God as a senile delinquent.

Tennessee Williams

It has occurred to me that God has Alzheimer's and has forgotten we exist.

Lily Tomlin

Imagine the Creator as a low comedian, and at once the world becomes explicable.

H.L. Mencken

What if God's a woman? Not only am I going to hell, I'll never know why!

Adam Ferrara

Oh God, if there is one, save my soul, if I have one.

Voltaire

God is silent, now if only we can get Man to shut up.

Woody Allen

JEW

A Jewish male, who starts life by receiving the unkindest cut of all, expects the worst from then on and is rarely disappointed.

Larry Gelbart

I suppose the nearest equivalent to a Bar Mitzvah in terms of emotional build-up would probably not even be one's wedding day, but one's coronation.

Maureen Lipman

I'm Jewish but we're not religious. My mother had a menorah on a dimmer.

Richard Lewis

I believe that a Jew can always tell another Jew. It's just like black people. Black people can pick each other out of a crowd like that!

Judy Gold

An adult was converting and becoming a Jew. When asked if he minded being circumcised, he replied, 'Why not, it's no skin off my nose.'

Red Buttons

After I decided to become a Jew, only then did I learn the Jews don't really have all the money. When I found out Rockefeller and Ford were *goyim* I almost resigned.

Sammy Davis, Jr.

My dad said I couldn't be a comic. He said: 'You're kosher. You can't be a ham.'

Billy Crystal

My father rationalized a fondness for pork chops by saying Mother's cooking rendered them unrecognizable by God.

Michael Feldman

—What's the ultimate Jewish dilemma?
—Pork on sale.

Anon

A rabbi is praying in a synagogue: 'God, no one but you can help me in my terrible predicament – my only son is about to turn Christian.' God replies: '*Your son*!'

Larry Adler

CHRISTIAN

There has been only one Christian. They caught and crucified him – early.

Mark Twain

I was walking through the woods, thinking about Christ. If he was a carpenter, I wondered what he charged for bookshelves.

Boris Grushenko, *Love and Death*

She was a woman of singular piety, whose birth gem was the brimstone.

Peter De Vries

Confirmation – one of the sacraments of the Church of England – tends to be a sort of spiritual sheep dip.

Lord Altrincham

I was recently born-again. I must admit it's a glorious and wonderful experience. I can't say my mother enjoyed it a whole lot.

John Wing

Born-again Christians seldom blink. A blink marks the mind's registration of a new idea. Converts have no intention of receiving new ideas. They know already all they want to know.

Fay Weldon

Why do born-again people so often make you wish they'd never been born the first time?

Katharine Whitehorn

I don't think Jews can be born-again. A makeover, yes...

Michael Feldman

I said I was into porn again, not born-again.

Billy Idol

There is a rumour going around that I have found God. I think this is unlikely because I have enough difficulty finding my keys.

Terry Pratchett

A Sunday school is a prison in which children do penance for the evil conscience of their parents.

H.L. Mencken

MIRACLES THIS WAY

Sign in the car-park of a building used for evangelical services

—Only 2 per cent of people go to church in this country.
—And they're priests!

Sean Lock and Paul Merton, *Have I Got News For You*

My twins were conceived on Easter Sunday. Don't tell my mom. I was supposed to be in church. But you know what? I was saying, 'Oh, God,' the entire time.

Kerri Louise

If I had been the Virgin Mary, I'd have said, 'No!'

Stevie Smith

Jesse Jackson is a man of the cloth. Cashmere.

Mort Sahl

I'm not coming to your Baptist church! They always get people when they're down.

Alan Partridge

Churchyard: a place where teenagers can smoke undisturbed.

Mike Barfield, *Dictionary for our Time*

St Hilda's Church at Ellerburn in North Yorkshire…has a colony of bats living inside the building… Bats are fiercely protected by law…so the problem is what to do about them. A local Yorkshireman has advised the vicar to baptise the bats and then confirm them, after which he will never see them again.

Nicholas Rhea

I hate going to church. Why can't I worship the Lord in my own way, by praying like hell on my death bed.

Homer Simpson

CATHOLIC

Just saw the Pope on TV. Anyone else get nervous watching a German guy on a balcony addressing a crowd of 200,000?

Nick DiPaolo

—What happened to the Pope when he went to Mount Olive?
—Popeye almost killed him.

Anon

The priest shortage is so bad that today in Brooklyn an altar boy had to grope himself.

David Letterman

Last time I went to confession I said: 'You first.'

Dennis Miller

—How do you get a nun pregnant?
—Dress her up as an altar boy.

Anon

Sister Augustine, you must be all the talk around the holy water cooler.

Dr Gregory House, *House*

A celibate clergy is an especially good idea, because it tends to suppress any hereditary propensity toward fanaticism.

Carl Sagan

Cardinal O'Connor revealed he's coming out with an exorcize tape.

Michael Feldman

I'm not Catholic, but I gave up picking my belly button for lint.

Emo Philips

MUSLIM

—Why do Arab women wear veils?
—So they can blow their noses without getting their hands dirty.

Anon

Until the Iraq War, most of us thought Sunni and Shia were that duo who had a hit in the Sixties with 'I Got You Babe.'

Richard Littlejohn

God created women to look like women; he didn't create them to look like parrot cages with a nightshade chucked over it.

Julie Burchill, on the burkha

If it's men's uncontrollable sexual urges that are the problem, then instead of Islamic women having to veil themselves in public, Islamic men should have to blindfold themselves in public, and have the women lead them around.

Ebonmuse

If they make it illegal to wear the veil at work beekeepers are gonna be furious.

Milton Jones

The Muslims are the new Irish. But give them 30 years and there'll be Muslim theme pubs everywhere and Osama Bin Laden will be education minister.

Patrick Kielty

Islam will only be truly acculturated to our way of life when you could expect a Bradford audience to roll in the aisles at Monty Python's 'Life of Mohammed'.

Boris Johnson

IMMORTALITY

Most men think they are immortal – until they get a cold, when they think they are going to die within the hour.

Norman Cousins

Sadly, the immortal Jackie Milburn died today.

Cliff Morgan

One dies only once, and it's for such a long time!

Molière

He had had enough of being dead.

> Anne Darwin, on her husband, John, who faked his own death
> in a canoe only to return from the 'dead' five years later

What man is capable of the insane self-conceit of believing that an eternity of himself would be tolerable even to himself.

> George Bernard Shaw

If my decomposing carcass helps nourish the roots of a juniper tree or the wings of a vulture – that is immortality enough for me. And as much as anyone deserves.

> Edward Abbey

HEAVEN & HELL

A Yorkshireman reached the Pearly Gates and gave one of those sniffs they use in the Ridings as a form of social comment. 'From Yorkshire, eh?' said the Recording Angel, unlocking the gates wearily. 'Well, you can come in, but you won't like it.'

> John Sandilands

At the very door of St Peter of the Keys, I shall stipulate that I will only go into Heaven on condition that I am never in a room with more than ten people.

> Edward Lear

I don't see Heaven in the sense of fat babies with wings playing compact harps for other fat babies with wings. But I do have a strong sense of Hell, where people who have been mean to me personally will suffer terribly. And that brings me joy.

> Alan Partridge

'Heaven seems vera little improvement on Glesga,' a good Glasgow man is said to have murmured, after death, to a friend who had predeceased him. 'Man, this is no Heaven,' the other replied.

C.E. Montague

Welcome to hell. Here's your accordion.

Gary Larson, cartoon caption

In hell the auto mechanics have to drive the cars they 'fixed' on earth.

Peter Kreft

Yes, there is life after death. But please don't tell the Inland Revenue.

Alex Ayres

INDEX

Abbey, Edward 155, 540
Abbott, Sidney 139
Abourezk, James 321
Abrams, Creighton W. 285
Absolute Power 465
Absolutely Fabulous 21, 184, 413
Ace, Goodman 328, 482
Ackerman, Diane 401
actors & acting 381–4
Adams, Douglas 443
Adams, Franklin Pierce 156
Adams, Henry 399, 505
Adams, Joey 7, 56, 59, 73, 74, 75, 174, 279, 456, 458, 490
Adams, John 341, 344
Adams, Scott 282, 342
Addams Family, The 34, 305, 472
Addams, Gomez (*The Addams Family*) 34
Addison, Chris 322
Addotta, Kip 313
Ade, George 311
Adler, Grace (*Will and Grace*) 52
Adler, Larry 12, 196, 535
Adolf Hitler, My Part in His Downfall (Milligan) 467
Adorno, Theodor 151
Adventures of Ford Fairlane, The 91
advertising 291
Æon Flux (*Æon Flux*) 282
Aerosmith 488
After the Thin Man 13

After You With the Pistol (Bongfiglioli) 12
Agate, James 160, 375, 383
age & ageing 516–20
agent 373
Agnew, Spiro 319
agriculture 125
Agutter, Jenny 33
Aherne, Caroline 135
Aikman, Leo 106
air travel 402–5
Airey, Sir Lawrence 53
Aitken, Jonathan 30
Alauda, Astrid 490
Albee, Edward 168, 378
alcohol 13–21
Aldridge, Brian (*The Archers*) 205
Aleichem, Sholom 103
Ali, Muhammad 270
All in the Family 389
Allan, Colonel Ethan 467
Allen, Dave 203, 331
Allen, Fred 83, 288, 349, 386, 405, 417, 495
Allen, Gracie 16, 94, 325
Allen, Robert Thomas 410
Allen, Ted 71
Allen, Vanessa 157
Allen, Woody 9, 40, 55, 61, 96, 100, 235, 292, 356, 372, 442, 443, 459, 493, 497, 508, 510, 533
Allis, Peter 269
Ally McBeal 78, 455
Alsop, Joseph 338
Altrincham, Lord 535

Alvarez, Al 526
Alves, Mauro 244
America 414–16
American Pie 36
American places 417–19
Amies, Hardy 122
Amis, Martin 142, 278
Amsterdam, Morey 441
amusement parks 299–300
Ancis, Joe 271
Anderson, Clive 199
Anderson, Pamela 88
Anderson, Patrick 316
Anderson, Rupert (*Mississippi Burning*) 273
Anderszewski, Piotr 357
Andrews, Andy 102
anger & argument 223–5
animals & nature 105–25
Anne, Princess 242
Annie Hall 469, 494
anonymous 2, 5, 6, 12, 13, 15, 20, 27, 33, 35, 39, 42, 43, 50, 61, 64, 66, 69, 71, 73, 74, 86, 88, 90, 93, 108, 109, 110, 111, 113, 114, 116, 120, 122, 125, 128, 129, 133, 146, 147, 148, 149, 152, 155, 164, 180, 185, 191, 192, 198, 202, 205, 209, 222, 224, 225, 229, 237, 243, 245, 256, 265, 273, 278, 281, 282, 290, 291, 294, 298, 299, 301,

303, 306, 307, 308, 323, 328, 343, 348, 356, 357, 359, 361, 381, 389, 396, 397, 398, 412, 419, 422, 428, 430, 431, 433, 434, 437, 438, 439, 442, 445, 453, 454, 457, 460, 463, 468, 474, 477, 480, 481, 482, 483, 484, 485, 486, 490, 492, 494, 496, 500, 502, 505, 515, 518, 521, 530, 531, 533, 535, 537, 538
Anthony and Cleopatra (Shakespeare) 378
Anthony, John 259
appearance & fashion 81–103
Apple Jr., R.W. 5
Appleby, Sir Humphrey (*Yes, Minister*) 107, 215
Arbuthnot, John 329
Arcadia 505
Arcaro, Eddie 522
Archer, Jeffrey 316, 363
Archer, Mary 332
Archer, William 168
Archers, The 173, 205, 420
Aregood, Richard 227
aristocracy 451–3
Arlen, Michael 30
Arlott, John 260
Armey, Dick 52, 324
Armour, Richard 135, 348
Armstrong, Neil 217
Armstrong, Stanley 438
Armstrong-Jones, Peregrine 257

Arnold, Kevin (*The Wonder Years*) 54
Arnold, Matthew 452
Arnold, Tom 496
Around the World in Eighty Days (Verne) 410
Arquette, Alexis 190
art 363–6
Art, Professor Robert C. 121, 440, 527
arts & entertainment 347–94
Ashes To Ashes 195
Ashman, Kevin 388
Askey, Arthur 387
Asnas, Max 50
Aspel, Michael 387
Asquith, Herbert 441
Astaire, Fred 362
Astor, Nancy 75, 452
astrology 228–9
astronomy 443–4
Atget, Eugène 368
Atkins, Dame Eileen 99
Atkins, Pauline M. 432
Atkinson, Rowan 378
Atkinson, S. 154
Attell, Dave 15, 19, 214
Attenborough, David 107
Attenborough, Richard 371
Attlee, Clement 330
Atwood, Margaret 132
Aubernon, Madame 87
Auden, W.H. 149
Auntie Mame 515
Austen, Jane 177, 209, 215, 310
Australia 419
Australian festive greeting 314
autobiography & biography 161–3
awards 286–7
Axelrod, George 523
Axson, David 345
Ayckbourn, Alan 448
Ayres, Alex 466, 470, 541
Ayres, Pam 173

Babbitt, Milton 351
Babel, Isaac 151

Baby Mama 184
Baccalieri, Bobby (*The Sopranos*) 286
Back to School 500
Backus, Jim 199
Bacon, Richard 421
Baddiel, David 380
Baer, Bugs 273
Baer, Eugene W. 320
Bagehot, Walter 64, 502, 511
Bailey, David 139
Bailey, F. Lee 461
Bailey, Matthew 422
Bailey, Pearl 354
Bainbridge, Beryl 296
Baker, Russell 166, 388
Baker, Stephen 111
Baker-Finch, Ian 266
Bakewell, Joan 400
Bakken, Jim 2
Bakshian, Aram 336
Balanchine, George 362
Balckstock, Gareth (*Chef!*) 448
Ballard, J.G. 163
Balliett, Whitney 355
Baltzell, Edward Digby 452
Bamford, Maria 516
Bankhead, Tallulah 282, 369
bankruptcy 59
banks & borrowing 65–6
Banks, Harry F. 285
Banks, Heywood 73
Banks, Tony 345, 346
Banta, Tony (*Taxi!*) 504
Barach, Alvan L. 19, 517
Barbarito, Archbishop Luigi 256
Barber, Miller 266
Barbirolli, Sir John 3
Bardot, Brigitte 384
Barfield, Mike 6, 116, 279, 318, 391, 402, 537
Barham, D.A. 527
Barker, Harvey Granville 5
Barker, Howard 378
Barner, Bill 200, 457
Barnes, Djuna 91
Barnes, Jimmy 121

Barnes, Johnny 486
Barnes, Julian 10, 524
Barnes, Simon 261
Barnett, Joel 64
Baron, Glenn 154
Barraclough, Roy 228
Barrie, J.M. 161, 310, 378, 380, 442, 501
Barrow, Lance 267
Barrows, Sydney Biddle 210
Barry, Dave 17, 37, 54, 72, 119, 187, 250, 294, 300, 430, 432, 433, 514
Barrymore, John 58, 227
Barton, Laura 390
Barton, Lewis 129
Barton, Robert 382
Baruch, Bernard 223, 319
Barzan, Gerald 229
Barzini, Luigo 413
baseball 273–4
Bashevis, Isaac 167
basketball 275
Bassey, Shirley 191
Bateman, Jason 269
Bates, Rhonda 484
Batchelder, Ann 6
Bathurst, Otto 362
Batt, Mike 353
Battista, O.A. 212
battle of the sexes 135–7
Batty, David 412
Baudrillard, Jean 66, 85, 168, 326, 415, 441
Bauer, Gerard 232
Bazalgette, Peter 333
Beard, Henry 3, 9, 120, 268, 295, 297, 311, 479
Beaton, Cecil 418
Beatty, Warren 79
Beaumont & Fletcher 45
beauty 96–7
beauty treatments 101–2
Becker 306
Beckett, Samuel 234
Beckham, David 317, 380, 387

Beckham, Victoria 183, 386, 387
Bee, Samantha 216
Beecham, Thomas 351
Beecher, Henry Ward 243
Beerbohm, Max 152, 230
Begley, Sharon 184
Behan, Brendan 180
Behar, Joy 84, 343
Beland, Russell 129, 130, 371
beliefs 227–8
Bell, Andy 335
Bell, John 438
Bell, Lord Tim 333
Bellingham, Lynda 334
Belzer, Richard 392
Bemelmans, Ludwig 311
Benaud, Richie 260
Benchley, Robert 113, 165, 408, 524
Bender, Texas Bix 3, 243
Benitez, Rafael 260
Benjamin, Walter 169
Benn, Tony 346, 446, 523
Bennett, Arnold 402
Benny, Jack 314, 453
Benson, A.C. 203, 505
Bentley, Dick 152
Berens, Harold 386
Berenson, Bernard 317
Bergman, Ingmar 524
Bergman, Ingrid 382
Berle, Milton 8, 94, 220, 362, 390, 398, 404, 431, 503, 519
Bernard, Jeffrey 39, 449
Bernard, Stella 199
Bernbach, Bill 291
Berner, Lea 496
Bernhard, Sandra 211
Bernstein, Henri 370
Berton, Pierre 420
Best, George 262
Betjeman, John 413
Bevan, Aneurin 321, 330, 340
Beverly Hills 90210 417
Bevin, Ernest 337

Beyond Reasonable Doubt (Leonard) 377
Bhaskar, Sanjeev 381
Bianco, Manny (*Black Books*) 258
bicycle 400–1
Bierce, Ambrose 163, 195, 228, 292, 338, 339, 415
Big Brother 138, 211, 237, 515
Biggins, Roy (*Wings*) 32, 38
Biggs, David 54
Bilmes, Alex 94
Bingham, Charlotte 291
Bingham, Madeleine 463
Bird and Fortune 67
Bird, Steve 212
birds 114–15
Bishop, David 423
Bishop, Jim 167
Bisset, Jackie 37
Bissmire, Michael 428
Bit of Fry and Laurie, A 102, 167, 249, 374
Black Books 258
Black, Lewis 124
Black, Steven 202, 204
Black, Willow 300
Blackadder 471, 509
Blair, Cherie 242
Blair, Tony 322, 333, 335
Blakemore, Michael 381
Blier, Bernard 143
Block, Brian P. 437
Bluestone, Ed 38
Blune, Boo 495
Blunkett, David 85
Boar, George 389
Bobeck, Mimi (*The Drew Carey Show*) 494
Bogarde, Dirk 383
Boliska, Al 265
Bombeck, Erma 8, 179, 231, 272, 305
Bonaparte, Napoleon 103
Bond, Gerry 360
Bondy, Caroline 176
Bonfiglioli, Kyril 12, 129

Book of Shadows, The (Paterson) 41
books & language 145–69
Boosler, Elayne 22, 183, 458, 477
Borden, Jane 141
bores & boredom 222–3
Borge, Victor 349, 357
Borman, Frank 59
Boulez, Pierre 351
Bourdain, Anthony 23, 26
Bourdet, Edouard 301
Bowen, Croswell 371
Bowen, Elizabeth 527
Bowen, Marjorie 206
Bowfinger 373
Bowie, David 385
boxing 270–1
Boyd, Woody (*Cheers*) 14, 21
Boylan, Clare (*Black Baby*) 83
Boyle, Ed 333
Boyle, Frankie 190, 257, 308, 326, 333, 334, 335, 354, 384, 427, 459, 470
Boyle's Observation 317
Braby, Carolyn 210
Bracken, Peg 9, 51
Bradley, Mary Hastings 13
Bradshaw, Carrie (*Sex and the City*) 181
Bragan, Bobby 442
Braid, James 266
Brand, Christianna 84
Brand, Russell 92, 387, 409
Brandeis, Louis D. 466
Brandon, Les (*I Didn't Know You Cared*) 98
Brandon, Pat (*I Didn't Know You Cared*) 474
Brandreth, Gyles 157, 161, 319
Brandt, Koos 298
Branning, Tanya (*EastEnders*) 195
Branson, Richard 75, 288
Brault, Robert 124

Brautigan, Richard 85, 236
Bravman, Danny 130
Brearley, Mike 261
breasts 87–8
Brebner, J. Bartlet 420
Brechlin, Jeff 130
Brecht, Bertolt 458
Bremner, Rory 332, 333, 335
Brendon, Dr Piers 451
Brennan, Kevin 488
Brideshead Revisited (Waugh) 506
Bridges, Arthur 111
Bridie, James 427
Brigadoon 428
Brilliant, Ashleigh 130, 519
Brimer, John Burton 415
Brinkley, David 340
Britt's Green Thumb Postulate 121
Brock, Edwin 495
Brockman, Karen 73
Brogan, Jimmy 393
Brokaw, Tom 11, 217
Bronfman, Edgar 75
Brook, Peter 376
Brooker, Charlie 5, 10, 76, 99, 119, 223, 258, 335, 450
Brooks, Albert 446
Brooks, Collin 502
Brooks, Foster 521
Brooks, Louise 233
Brooks, Mel 370, 516
Brooks, Shirley 228
Broun, Heywood 298, 327
Brown, Bob 525
Brown, Charlie 445
Brown, Dan 157
Brown, David 187, 311
Brown, George 330
Brown, Gordon 322, 324, 333
Brown, Helen Gurley 226
Brown, Joe E. 468
Brown, Larry 44, 459, 481, 483
Brown, Rita Mae 342, 500, 523
Browne, Coral 376

Browning, Guy 122, 152, 210, 310
Bruce, Bob 268
Bruce, Lenny 115
Brummell, Beau 280
Bruno, Frank 271
Bryan, Daniel 138
Bryan, Joseph 3, 108, 310
Brydon, Rob 428
Buchanan, Cynthia 215
Buchanan, Pat 341
Buchwald, Art 62
Buckler, Ernest 159
Budden, Jackiey 424
Buffett, Jimmy 356
Buffett, Warren 69, 70
Bukowski, Charles 194
Bulwer-Lytton, Edward 329
Bundy, Al (*Married With Children*) 2
Bunker, Archie (*All in the Family*) 389
Buonarroti, Michelangelo 367
Burchill, Julie 44, 123, 133, 239, 385, 448, 453, 478, 538
bureaucracy 339–44
Buren, Abigail Van 199
Burgess, Anthony 83
Burgess, Jack 397
Buried Treasure (Wodehouse) 366
Burke, Edmund 53
Burney, Fanny 411
Burns, Carl 403
Burns, George 16, 43, 94, 137, 166, 181, 237, 454, 490
Burroughs, William 225
Burrows, D.C. 517
Burton, Richard 18, 382, 428
Burton, Richard Francis 530
Busby, Matt 262
Bush, George W. 284, 445
Bush, Guy 274
business 288–90
Butler, R.A. 331
Buttons, Red 79, 188, 534
Butz, Bill 441

Byatt, Sir Hugh
  Campbell 297
Byers, Stephen 330
Byron, Lord 181

Cable, Vince 334
Cactus Flower 249
Cadbury, George 120
Caesar and Cleopatra
  317
Cage, John 419
Cagney and Lacey 292
Cajal, Santiago Ramón
  y 518
California Bar
  Association
  Newsletter 283
Callaghan, James 330,
  441
Calvin and Hobbes
  251, 296, 436
Calwell, Arthur 345
Cambridge, Godfrey
  413
Cameron, David 95,
  318, 328, 331, 335,
  433, 467
Campbell, Alan 200
Campbell, Ming 321,
  334
Campbell, Naomi 159
Campbell, Patrick 423
Campbell-Johnson,
  Rachel 366
Camus, Albert 46, 158
Canada 420–1
Canby, Vincent 362
Canetti, Elias 108
cannibal 12
Cantitborough 424
Cantor, Eddie 149
Cantor, Melanie 200
Cap, Flo 226
Capablanca, José Raúl
  295
Čapek, Karel 113
capitalism &
  communism 60–1
Capone, Al 60
Caponera, John 35
Capp, Al 435
Capri, Dick 112, 484
*Captian's Corelli's
  Mandolin* (de
  Bernières) 155
car 397–400

*Car 54, Where Are
  You?* 460
Caras, Roger 113
Caravella, Johnny 141
Carey, Drew (*The
  Drew Carey Show*)
  37, 72, 86, 194, 494
Carey, Peter 83
Carlin, George 89, 123,
  146, 149, 216, 223,
  448, 479, 487, 493,
  508
Carlton, Mike 62
Carlyle, Thomas 61,
  162
Carnahan, Elden 130
Caroline in the City 32,
  359
Caron, Leslie 284
Carr, Alan 220, 279
Carr, Jimmy 37, 123,
  192, 391, 426, 475
Carr, Simon 332
Carradine, David 384
Carré, John Le 289
Carroll, Jean 31, 100,
  113
Carry on, Jeeves
  (Wodehouse) 511
Carson, Johnny 128,
  192, 392, 442, 481
Carter, Billy 16
Carter, Deana 355
Carter, Don 267
Carter, Jack 42, 97
Carter, Jimmy 281,
  342, 345
Cartland, Barbara 139
Carvel, Paul 433
Carver, George
  Washington 120
Casey, Darren 302
Cash, Pat 199
Cashman, Barney (*Last
  of the Red Hot
  Lovers*) 494
Cassel, Sir Ernest 67
Casson, Hugh 7
Castle, Barbara 321
Castro, Fidel 92
cat 110–11
Cat, The (*Red Dwarf*)
  82
Catholic 537–8
*Cats of San Marino,
  The* (Steiber) 435

Caulfield, Jo 295
Cavett, Dick 87
Cavey, Dana 123
Cebrian, Katherine 9
Celebrity Big Brother 4
  211
Cerf, Bennett 358
Chalmers, Irena 186
Chamberlain, Neville
  330
Chance, The (Carey)
  83
Chandler, Raymond 15,
  85, 92, 154, 231
Chanel, Coco 231, 242
Chapel, Helen (*Wings*)
  34
Chapman, Michael 424
character & human
  nature 219–39
charity 78–9
*Charles Saatchi:
  Question* (Saatchi)
  199, 500
Charles, Nick 13
Charles, Prince 450,
  451
Charlie (*Caroline in the
  City*) 32
Charlie Bartlett 494
Chase Manhattan Bank
  57
Chase, Chevy 30, 84
cheating 196–7
*Cheech & Chong's The
  Corsican Brothers* 2
Cheers 14, 21, 22, 97,
  187, 234, 285, 514,
  516
Cheever, John 158, 222
Chef! 448
Chekhov, Anton 169,
  386
Cher 135, 172
Chesterfield, Lord 242
Chesterton, G.K. 213,
  234, 349, 371, 460
Child, Julia 27, 479
children 182–90
Childs, Toni
  (*Girlfriends*) 93
Chinatown 471
*Chocolate and Cuckoo
  Clocks* (Coren) 165
*Choke (*Palahniuk) 188
Chopia, Dan 17

Chostner, Jeff 464
Christian 535–7
Christie, Agatha 69
Christmas 312–14
Christmas Story, A 250,
  314
Christy, Richard 231
Churchill, Winston
  212, 235, 267, 338,
  466, 469, 501, 516
Cicero 321
Cincinnati Symphony
  Orchestra 351
Cioran, E.M. 162, 526
Citibank 72
Clacey, Brian 422
Clare, John 283
Clark, Alan 207, 244
Clark, Frank A. 523
Clarke, Kenneth 215
Clarkson, Jeremy 250,
  400
Clary, Julian 139, 210
class 448–9, 453–4
Claudel, Paul 16, 525
Clegg, Nick 335
Cleopatra 428
Cleveland, Don 91
Clinton, Bill 343, 344
Clinton, Hilary 344
Closer 39, 492
Cobb, Irvin S. 17, 91
Cobbett, William 58
Cocoanuts, The 51
Cocteau, Jean 165,
  169, 366
Cody, Buffalo Bill 95
Cohen, John 264
Cohen, Leonard 235
Cohen, Myra 179, 182
Cohen, Sacha Baron 3,
  94, 106, 154, 412,
  477
Colbert, Stephen 65,
  531
Colegate, Isabel (*The
  Shooting Party*) 160
Coleman, Ornette 355
Coleridge, Samuel
  Taylor 327, 329
Colette 301
college 505–6
Collie, G. Norman 286
Collins, Andrew 313
Collins, Joan 386
Collins, Phil 487

Coltrane, John 352
Colvin, David 439
comedy 391–3
communication 201–17
compliments & flattery 248–9
computer 430–2
Condell, Pat (*The Store*) 179
Conkling's Arithmetic 504
Connelly, Ray 509
Connolly, Cyril 116, 155, 282
Connor, Grant (*The Simpsons*) 106
Conrad, Joseph 133
Constable, John 363
Constantine of Russia, Grand Duke 465
consumerism 300–1
conversation 202–4
  ice-breakers 202
  stoppers 204–5
Cook, Dane 143, 178, 472
Cook, Glen 203
Cook, Peter 262, 451, 480, 504
Cooke, Alistair 416
cooking 7–12
Coolidge, Calvin 65, 324
Cooper, Gary 369
Cooper, Jilly 482
Cooper, Thomas 122
Cooper, Tommy 138, 296, 305
Coquelin, Ernest 181
Corbett, Ronnie 257, 313
Corbyn, Tessa 220
Corcoran, Alan 518
Cord, Jonas (*The Carpetbaggers*) 174
Coren, Alan 20, 165, 269, 292, 364, 414, 524
Coren, Giles 24
Corey, Irwin 174
Coronation Street 514
Coronel, Billiam 479
Corrigan, E. Gerald 324
Corrigan, Mark (*Peep Show*) 44, 361
Corso, Rick 100

Cort, David 48
Corwin, Ida 187
Cosby, Bill 89, 182, 399, 517
cosmetic surgery 98–9
Cotter, Tom 112, 304, 361, 527
Cotter, Wayne 110
Cotton, Henry 265
countries 412–28
Country Girl, The (Dodd) 134
Coupling 139
Courier, Jim 272
court, in 460–2
Cousins, Norman 539
Coward, Noël 98, 211, 215, 234, 306, 374, 403, 410, 411, 453, 481
Cowdray, Lord 69
Cowell, Simon 348
Crabbe, Buster 89
Crane, Frank 510
Crane, Niles (*Frasier*) 495
Cranehill, Virginia (*Road to Wellville*) 401
Crap Towns 424
Crews, Harry 160
cricket 260–1
crime 456–60
Criminal Justice 460
Crisp, Quentin 138, 358, 418
critic 166–9
Crosby, Bing 353
Crosby, Norm 373
Crossman, Richard 321
Crouch, Peter 263
Cruise, Tom 491
Cryer, Barry 312
Crystal, Billy 190, 534
Crystal, David 150
CSI 290
Cukor, George 76
Cullen, Seán 531
Cunningham, John 265
Cuomo, Mario 320
Cuppy, Will 164
Curly Sue 363
Current Comedy 68
Currie, Edwina 272
Curtis, Danny 110
Curtis, Tony 385, 520

Cushman, Wilhela 90
Cutler, Carl 11

da Vinci, Leonardo 167
Daché, Lilly 95
Dahlberg, Edward 408
Daily Show, The 216
Daily Telegraph 259
Daily Variety 373
Dalai Lama 531
Dallas 472
Dana, Bill 89, 490
dance 361–2
Dangerfield, Rodney 8, 33, 43, 77, 98, 178, 189, 191, 299, 306, 398, 463, 474, 475, 485, 495, 517, 519
Daniel, Caroline 331
Darian, Ron 115
Darwin, Anne 540
Darwin, Charles 437
Davenport, Guy 363
David Copperfield (Dickens) 57
David, Elizabeth 5
Davies, Alan 6, 439, 463
Davies, Evan M. 439
Davies, Marlon 384
Davies, Robertson 287
Davis Jr., Sammy 534
Davis, Bette 383
Davis, Lee A. 202
Davis, Linda H. 305
Dawkins, Darryl aka 'Chocolate Thunder' 275
Dawson, Les 228
Day, Lillian 493
Day, Robin 305
de Bernières, Louis 155
de Camp, Catherine Crook 522
de Gaulle, Charles 338, 339, 411
de Gramont, Sanche 9
de Kooning, Willem 364
de la Mare, Walter 157
de Montherlant, Henri 45
De Palma, Louis (*Taxi*) 30
de Vercellis, Countess de 525

Cushman, Wilhela 90
De Voto, Bernard 16
De Vries, Peter 42, 96, 118, 148, 196, 365, 388, 535
Dean, Dixie 264
Dean, Dizzy 236
Dean, Jo 527
Dearlove, Des 288
death & dying 523–4
Death of a Salesman (Miller) 288
debt 57–8
Debt to Pleasure, The (Lanchester) 11
Debussy, Claude 349, 350, 359
Deeping, Warwick 424
Deering, Jo Ann 394
DeGeneres, Ellen 26, 444, 478
Deighton, Len 199
Del Boy (*Only Fools and Horses*) 9
del Rosario, Juan Antonio 198
Demaret, Jimmy 269
Dench, Judi 383
Denson, Neville 122
Dent, Susie 214
Dental Economics 431
Dentinger, Ron 4, 443
dentist 485–6
depression 491–2
Designing Women 82
Desmond, Paul 354, 355
Deudney, Daniel 444
Deuel, Jean 399
Deutsch, David 303
Devonshire, Duke of 336
Dewar, Lord 70, 299
Dewar, Thomas R. 93
Dexter, John 378
Diana, Princess of Wales 309
diary 160–1
DiCaprio, Leonardo 380
Dickens, Charles 11, 57, 165
Dictionary for our Time (Barfield) 6, 116, 279, 318, 391, 402, 537
diet 475–8

Dietrich, Marlene 96
Dietz, Howard 352
Diffrient, Niels 209
Dilkes, Frank P. 195
Diller, Phyllis 59, 88, 97, 175, 194, 195, 279, 397, 398, 480, 483, 495
Dinesen, Isak 412, 514
dinner party 308–12
DiNovo, Gene 353
Dion, Céline 353
DiPaolo, Nick 537
disability 486–8
Disraeli, Benjamin 329, 330, 410, 507
Distel, Francine 197
Distel, Sacha 197
Ditka, Mike 74
DiTullio, Janine 115
DIY 195
Djalili, Omid 470
Dobson, James W. 469
Doc Hollywood 385
Dodd, Bernie (*the Country Girl*) 134
Dodd, Ken 413
Dodds, Bill 479
dog 112–14
Dole, Bob 342
Dom Ruinart champagne, advert for 16
Don't Look Now 369
Donaghy, Jack (*30 Rock*) 136, 173, 198, 231, 283, 290, 413, 475
Donnay, Maurice 156
Donovan, Jason 462
Dornan, Paul 123
Dorsey, Tommy 354
Douglas, Jack 184
Douglas, Norman 164, 192
Douglas, William O. 532
Douglas-Home, Sir Alex 63
Dowd, Maureen 388
Drew Carey Show, The 37, 72, 86, 194, 494
Drew, Carol 303
drugs & addiction 488–90
Duceppe, Gilles 338

Dudzik, Stephen 252
Duel 458
Duffy, Caroline (*Caroline in the City*) 359
Dukes, Carol Muske 91
Dumas, Alexandre 379
Duncan, Isadora 39
Duncan, Jennifer Greene 478
Duncan, Raymond 306
Duncan, Sara Jeannette 222
Dundy, Elaine 384, 491
Dunne, Dan (*Half Nelson*) 103
Dunne, Finlay Peter 316, 470
Dunsany, Lord 408
Dunslop, Anne 425
Durant, Will 280
Durante, Jimmy 231
Durocher, Leo 236
Durst, Will 117
Duse, Eleanora 86
Dworkin, Andrea 47, 135
Dyke, Greg 522
Dylan, Bob 352

Eade, Philip 526
Eagleton, Terrry 243
Earl of Onslow 335, 336
EastEnders 183, 195, 224
Eastman, George 79
Eastwood, Clint 97
eating, healthy 478–9
Eberhart, Richard 526
Ebonmuse 539
Eco, Umberto 158
economics 61–4
Edison, Thomas 443
Edmondson, Richard 259
Edtv 279
education & thinking 499–512
Education of an Editor, The (Giroux) 164
Edwards, Jimmy (*Take it From Here*) 152
Edwards, Jonathan 257
Edwards, Kenneth 349

Eggs, Beans and Crumpets (Wodehouse) 290
ego 221–2
Ehlert, Louis 349
8 Out of 10 Cats 192, 354, 426, 470
Einstein, Albert 212, 387, 435, 440, 510
election 318–20
Eliot, T.S. 3, 101, 309
Eliscu, Margery 9
Elizabeth I, Queen 245
Elizabeth II, Queen 210, 281
Ellington, Duke 354
Elliott, Len 303
Ellis, Alice Thomas 10
Elton, Ben 251, 286, 385
Emerson, Ralph Waldo 2, 50, 117, 143, 162, 490
Emma (Austen) 177, 209
End, The 523
England 423–5
English, Arthur 376
Ennius, Quintus 437
Enright, D.J. 207
environment & green issues 123–5
Ephron, Nora 173, 185, 189, 238, 253
Epstein, Julius 372
Erskine, John 348
Esar, Evan 57, 75, 116, 117, 146, 224, 234, 318, 356
Esler, Gavin 326
Evans, Dame Edith 377, 383
Evans, Florida (*Maude*) 99
Evans, Jill 193
Evdokimov, Paul 172
Evelyn, John 379
Everage, Dame Edna 47, 92, 101, 253, 393, 450, 489
Everett, Rupert 370
evolution & creationism 437
Ewing, Sam 305, 324
exams & tests 504–5
exercise 480–1

extraterrestrial life 445–6
Eyre, Hermione 25
Eyre, Sir Richard 375

Fabricant, Michael 444
fame & celebrity 384–8
Family Guy 18, 279, 364, 509
family life 178–9
Faraday, Michael 443
Farewell, My Lovely (Chandler) 92
Farmer, Philip José 27
Farquhar, George 456
fashion & dress 90–5
Faulkner, William 208
Fawlty Towers 249
Feather, William 71, 178
Fechtner, Leopold 69
Fee, R.M. 415
Feherty, David 265, 266, 268, 307, 491
Feldman, David 136, 189
Feldman, Michael 534, 535, 538
Fellowes, Julian 100, 425
Female Eunuch (Greer) 135
Ferber, Edna 11, 177
Ferguson, Sarah 259, 451
Ferrara, Denis 181, 533
Ferreiro, Antonio 84
Fey, Tina 524
Fez (*That 70s Show*) 30
Fiebig, Jim 487
Fiedler, Edgar R. 62, 64
Field Guide to the British, A (Lyall) 312
Fielding, Henry 248
Fields, Totie 475
Fields, W.C. 4, 17, 18, 20, 100, 114, 187, 245, 299, 458, 471, 522
Figes, Orlando 338
film & Hollywood 369–73
Final Test, The (Whitehead) 260
Findler, Gerald 186
Fine, Sylvia (*The Nanny*) 37

Finishing School, The (Spark) 25
Finney Sr., Albert 287
Finney, Doug 487
Firestein, Les 35, 36
Firth, Peter 33
Fish, Richard (*Ally McBeal*) 78, 455
Fisher King, the (Lucas) 161
Fisher, Carrie 370, 488
fishing 297–8
Fitzgerald, Ella 355
Fitzgerald, F. Scott 21
Fitz-Gibbon, Bernice 291
Flammarion, Camille 172
Flaubert, Gustave 228
Fleming, Peter 272
Fletcher, Norman Stanley (*Porridge*) 458
Flockhart, Calista 376
Floyd, Ray 265
Flynn, Errol 33, 477, 515
Foch, Marshal Ferdinand 181
Fonseca, Chris 180, 183
food and drink 1–27
Foot, Michael 332
football 261–4
Forbes, B.C. 221
Forbes, Malcolm 439, 506
Forbes, Steve 56
Ford, Gerald 342
foreign affairs & diplomacy 338–9
Foreman, George 271, 474
Forman, Milos 39
Fowler, Gene 244
Fowler, Janet (*Simon & Simon*) 483
Fowles, John 141
Fox, John 278
Fox, Michael J. 188
Foxworthy, Jeff 121, 149, 185, 369, 398, 449, 460
Foxx, Redd 48, 77, 313, 459, 479
Francis, Brendan 35, 47, 326, 522

Francis, Steven 182
Francis, Stu 236
Francombe, John 259
Frankenfield, Philip J. 73
Franz, Dennis 418
Fraser, Benton (*Due South*) 44
Frasier 34, 495
Freddie 423
Freed, Arthur 428
French Leave (Wodehouse) 163
Freud, Clement 258, 299, 424
Freud, Martin 191
Freud, Sigmund 191
Friedman, Kinky 111, 462, 463
Friedrich, Otto 147
friends & enemies 142–3
Frindall, Bill 260
Frink, Professor (*The Simpsons*) 442
Front Row 161
Frost, David 453
Frost, Robert 163, 165, 172
Frost, William Henry 160
Fry, Stephen 102, 156, 167, 233, 249, 354, 374, 439, 440, 503
Fuller, Edmund 193, 464
funeral 527–8
Fuoss, Robert 340
Fussman, Cal 160
Futurama 432, 434

Gable, Clark 45
Gabor, Zsa Zsa 30
Gaffigan, Jim 214
Gagnière, Claude 146
Galbraith, J.K. 50, 61, 62, 63, 327
Galifianakis, Zach 183
Gallagher, Noel 78, 222, 353, 425, 488, 489
Gallup, Jr., George 441
gambling 298–9
Gammage, Kennedy 369
Gandhi 371

garden & flowers 120–2
Garden, Simon (*The Parole Officer*) 472
Gardiner, George 319
Gardner, John 371
Garfield, Elliot (*The Goodbye Girl*) 96
Garland, Patrick 250
Garner, Phil 274
Garrett, Brad 22, 98
Garrett, Todd (*Girlfriends*) 93
Gehard, Brüno 3, 94, 106, 154, 412, 477
Gelbart, Larry 84, 433, 534
Geldof, Bob 250
gender 138–40
Genesis 487
gentleman 245
George, David Lloyd 307, 330
George, Eddie 53
George, W.L. 466
Gerard, Jasper 222
Gerhardie, William 280
Gershwin, George 355
Gershwin, Ira 355
Gervais, Eva 411
Gervais, Ricky 15, 18, 85, 99, 411
Getty, John Paul 75
Getz, Tiffany 129
Ghostbusters 20
Giacometti, Alberto 48
Giamatti, A. Bartlett 274
Gibbon, Edward 464, 532
Gide, André 214
Gielgud, John 232
Gifford, Edward S. 493
gift 304–5
Gilbert & George 250, 502
Gilbert, Val 205
Gill, A.A. 4, 25, 26, 147, 233
Gillick, Corinee 205
Gingerbread Lady, the 204
Gingold, Hermione 252
Ginsparg, Paul 433
Giraldo, Greg 98

Girl I Left Behind, The (O'Reilly) 198
Girlfriends 93
Giroux, Robert 164
Gladstone, William Ewart 443, 507
Glasow, Arnold H. 21, 55, 225, 527
Glass, Montague 361
Glazer, Bebe (*Frasier*) 495
Glover, Stephen 424
Glums, The 92
Gobel, George 410
God 532–3
Godard, Lean-Luc 371
Goddard, Paulette 304
Godsey, Dustin 249
Gold, Dave (*The War at Home*) 488
Gold, Judy 44, 534
Golden Girls, The 320, 523
Golden Globe Awards 15, 99
Golden, Harry 23
Goldfuss, J.H. 430
Goldsmith, Warren H. 174
golf 265–60
golf terms 269–70
Goncourt, Edmond de 97, 326, 413, 532
Goncourt, Jules de 97, 326, 413, 532
Gone With the Wind (Mitchell) 183
good & bad 226–7
Good Housekeeping 99
good name…bad name 129–30
Goodbye Columbus 190
Goodbye Girl, The 96
Goodman, Ellen 284
Goodman, Len 362
Goodwin, Dick 214
Goodwin, Rachel 91
Goody, Jade 424
Goon Show, The 439
Gordon, C. Bruce 205
Gordon, Hank (*Doc Hollywood*) 385
Gore, Al 394
Gorky, Maxim 174
Gormley, Antony 364

Gorodetsky, Eddie 36
gossip 205–6
Gottfried, Gilbert 36, 44
Gould, Elliott 279
Gove, Michael 263, 318, 457
government 317–18
Gowers, Ernest 150
Grade, Lord Lew 373
graffiti 313, 361, 497
Graham, Ann 332
Grahame, Kenneth 108
Gramm, Phil 324
grammar & punctuation 150–1
grandparents 179–80
Granger, Reverend Geraldine (*The Vicar of Dibley*) 486
Granger, Stewart 275
Graves, Robert 380
Gray, Nancy 508
Gray, Serena 133
Gray, Spalding 95
Grayling, A.C. 117, 333, 396, 490, 512, 515
Great Britain 421–5
Green, Henry 280
Green, Joey 518
Greenberg, Daniel S. 228
Greene, Graham 230
Greer, Germaine 35, 40, 135, 140, 419, 496, 518
Gregory, Dick 55, 141, 468, 480
Greiner, Diana 45
Grenfell, Joyce 7, 82
Gretchen, John 119
Grey, Lita 393
Grieg, Edvard 350
Grierson's Law of Minimal Self-Delusion 74
Griffin, Peter (*Family Guy*) 18, 279, 364, 509
Grigson, Jane 6
Grimond, Jo 336
Grimshaw, Eileen (*Coronation Street*) 514
Grizzard, Lewis 39, 113, 208, 265, 490

Groth, Dr A. Nicholas 459
Grundy, Joe (*The Archers*) 420
Grushenko, Boris 535
Guardian, The 334, 436
Guccione, Bob 37
Guest, Katy 158
Guinness, Alec 375
Guisewite, Cathy 477
Guitry, Sacha 200, 349, 377
Gummer, John 330, 399
Guthrie, Woody 60, 352
Gypsy Rose Lee 159

H., Dan 432
Hacker, Jim (*Yes, Prime Minister*) 63
Hackett, Buddy 224, 267
Hackett, Joe (*Wings*) 34
Hackney, Alan 340
Haduch, Helene 251
Hagman, Larry 16
Hague, William 89, 337, 467
hair 88–90
Half Nelson 103
Haliburton, T.C. 521
Halisham, Lord 336
Hall, Annie (*Annie Hall*) 469
Hall, Catherine 518
Hall, Rich 186, 417
Hall, William 85
Halliwell, Geri 446
Halliwell, Romy 517
Halsey, Margaret 380, 452
Hamilton, Jackie 195
Hamlet (Shakespeare) 320, 379
Hampton, Christopher 148
Hampton, Judy 477
Hamza, Abu 487
Hancock, Mike 321
Hancock, Nick 458
Hancock, Tony 4
Handey, Jack 95, 106, 107, 128, 231, 313, 392, 404, 436, 443, 472

happiness & sadness 237–9
Harburg, E.Y. 352
Hard Way, The 487
Hardee, Malcolm 391, 462
Hardin, Patrick 31
Harding, Gilbert 26
Hardman, Robert 247
Hardwicke, Cedric 370
Hardy, J.H. 261
Hardy, James 57
Hardy, Jeremy 242, 272, 306, 403
Hardy, Oliver 401
Hardy, Thomas 96, 114, 192, 392, 424
Hardy, W.S. 31
Harling, Robert 98
Harlow, Jean 371
Harman, Harriet 69
Harper, Alan (*Two and a Half Men*) 114
Harriman, Margaret Case 50
Harris, J. 422
Harris, Phil 314
Harris, Roy 128
Harris, Sydney J. 501
Harrison, Cynthia 397
Harrison, Elizabeth 174
Harrison, I.S. 6
Harrison, Rex 250
Harry Hill's TV Burp 102, 113
Hart, Jennifer 118
Hart, Moss 166
Hart, Rhonda 355
Harvey, Paul 213
Harvey-Jones, John 423
Haslam, Nicky 92, 454
Hasselhoff, David 412
Hastings, Sir Max 329
hate 46
Hattersley, Roy 113, 334
Hauser, Philip M. 510
Have I Got News For You 323, 536
Havel, Václav 378
Hawkes, J. 303
Hawking, Stephen 444, 446
Hayman, Jon 472
Haynes, Homer 91

Haynes, Richard 'Racehorse' 461, 462
Hayridge, Hattie 86
Hazlitt, William 380, 396
Healey, Denis 56, 325
health, medicine & drugs 473–97
healthy eating 478–9
Healy, Father 82
Hearst, William Randolph 253
Heartburn (Ephron) 185, 253
Heath, Edward 54
Heath, Ted 319
Heathcoat-Amory, Derick 64
Heathers 238
Heath-Stubbs, John 366
Heat-Moon, William Least 6
heaven & hell 540–1
heckle 393–4
Hedberg, Mitch 4, 23, 94, 149, 164, 382
Heddy, Julian 90
Hefferman, Doug (*The King of Queens*) 434
Hefner, Hugh 364
Heilpern, John 234, 410
Heimel, Cynthia 45
Heine, Heinrich 143, 147
Heinlein, Robert A. 20, 147, 435
Heller, Joseph 287, 290
Hello Darlin' 16
Hemingway, Ernest 59, 297, 414
Henahan, Donal 161
Henig, Jessica 249
Henry, Lenny 379
Henry, O. 458, 471
Hensher, Philip 433
Hepburn, Audrey 87
Hepburn, Katharine 381, 383, 384, 428
Herbert, Jack 146
Herold, Don 133, 485
Herriot, James 110
Heseltine, Michael 319
Hess, Joan 189
Hewart, Gordon 212

Hewitt, Don 216
Hewitt, Jennifer Love 87
Heyhoe-Flint, Rachel 262
Hicks, Bill 18
High Window, The (Chandler) 85
Highberg, Roy 252
Hightower, Cullen 50, 415
Hill, Dave 268
Hill, Harry 107, 115
Hillis, Chuck 70
Hills, Barry 299
Hirohito, Emperor 469
Hirst, Damien 363, 364
history 463–5
Hitchcock, Alfred 369, 383
Hitler, Adolf 325, 392
Hobbes, Miranda (Sex and the City) 181
hobbies & leisure 293–314
Hobday, Simon 267
Hodges, Vicky (The Archers) 173
Hoest, Bill 284, 381, 476, 478, 487
Hoffenstein, Samuel 443
Hoffman, Arthur S. 62
Hoffman, Ben 250
Hoffman, Dustin 370
Hoffman, Li 303
Hoffman, Monty 36
Hoffman, Philip Seymour 382
Hogan, Paul 419
Hoggart, Simon 89, 164, 331, 332, 337
Hoisington, Brigadier General Elizabeth P. 290
Holby City 355
holiday 305–7
Holland, Linda 399
Hollerbach, Kit 423
Holliday, Billie 457
Holmes, Oliver Wendell 245, 330, 519
Holtz, Lou 281
Hoon, Geoff 467
Hooton, Burt 221
Hoover, Herbert 65, 325

Hope and Glory 411
Hope, Bob 8, 65, 79, 101, 178, 231, 314, 522
Hopkin, Mary 161
Hopkins, Anthony 232
Hopkinson, Simon 5, 25
Hoppe, Arthur 222, 342
Hopper, Hedda 361
Horace 239
Hordern, Michael 221
horse racing 258–9
Horton, Geoffrey 210
Hot Shots! 39
hotel 307–8
Houghton, Chantelle 211
house & home 192–3
House 538
House of Cards 511
House of Lords 335–6
housework 193–4
How to Murder Your Wife (Mayehoff) 176
Howard, John 400
Howe, Ed 4, 89, 206, 229, 302
Howse, Christopher 523
Hubbard, Kin 8, 235, 319
Hughes, Rhetta 376
Hughes, Simon 328
Hughes, Ted 330
Hugo, Victor 436
Hull, Bobby 199
Hull, Sandra 246
Humperdinck, Engelbert 351
Humphrys, John 263
Huneker, James 166
Hunt, DCI Gene (Ashes To Ashes) 195
Hunt, James 3
Hunt, Leigh 5
Hurd, Douglas 337, 457
Hurka, Thomas 132
Hurrah at Last 52
Hutchence, Michael 30
Hutton, Lauren 316, 380
Huxley, Thomas 437
Hyde, Steven 353

hygiene, personal 102–3

I Didn't Know You Cared 98, 109, 238, 474
I Think the Nurses are Stealing my Clothes (Smith) 94, 449
I'm No Angel 509
I'm Sorry I Haven't a Clue 4, 189, 378
I'm Sorry I'll Read That Again 112, 198
Iannucci, Armando 335
idleness 280–1
Idol, Billy 536
Ifans, Rhys 119, 384, 392
Ignatieff, Michael 343
Ignatowski, Jim (Taxi) 217, 221
Illingworth, Lord (A Woman of No Importance) 451
immortality 539–40
In Bruges 411
In the Loop 249, 318, 339, 471
Independent, The 329
Indiscretions of Archie, The (Wodehouse) 24, 128
Infeld, Leopold 413
Ingersoll, Robert G. 530
Ingilby, Sir Thomas 452
Inmon, Raymond 480
insects 115–16
insults 252–3
insurance 292
intelligence 507–8
Interlandi, Phil 462
internet 433–4
inventions 442–3
investing & the stock market 69–72
investment banks 67–9
Ireland 425–6
Irish toast v
Irrera, Dom 33
Isherwood, Christopher 154, 418
Island, The 533
Isle of Wight County Press 459

Ivins, Molly 60, 492

Jacklin, Tony 267
Jackson, 'Junior' (That's My Boy) 83
Jackson, Michael 353
Jackson, Robert H. 455
Jacobi, Lou 196
Jacobi, Steve 261
Jacobson, Howard 375
Jagger, Mick 260
James, Clive 25, 272, 334, 404
James, Henry 46, 150, 158, 282
Jamie (The Thick Of It) 206
Jarman, Derek 138
Jarrett, Beverly 164
Jarvis, Alan S. 118
Jarvis, Katie 244
Jay, Antony 334
Jeans, Sir James 445
Jefferson, Joseph 193
Jefferson, Thomas 17, 67
Jeni, Richard 414
Jenkins, Dan 19
Jenkins, Peter 377
Jenkins, Roy 330
Jennings, Waylon 356
Jeremy Vine Show, The 313
Jerrold, Douglas 125
Jessel, George 517
Jessica (American Pie) 36
Jew 534–5
Jewel of the Nile, The 153, 523
Jewsbury, Geraldine Endsor 220
Jie, Xu Ying 7
Jitterbug Perfume (Robbins) 119
JLC 422
Joe (Some Like it Hot) 71
Johannot, Louis 503
John XXIII, Pope 125
John, Augustus 365
John, Elton 374
Johnson, Barbara 102
Johnson, Boris 66, 328, 334, 421, 531, 539

Johnson, Dr Samuel 167, 291, 310, 358, 381, 414, 426, 428, 440
Johnson, Lyndon B. 251
Johnson, Martin 261
Johnson, Paul 398
Johnson, Robert A. 174
Johnston, Mo 427
Joint, Mark 422
Jokes, Jewish 511
Jolly, A.C. 281
Jonathan Ross Show, The 370, 475
Jones, Allen 32
Jones, Bill 78
Jones, Clinton 52
Jones, Franklin P. 154, 258
Jones, Indiana (*Raiders of the Lost Ark*) 519
Jones, Milton 153, 242, 412, 524, 539
Jones, Samantha (*Sex and the City*) 197
Jong, Erica 134, 385
Jonhston, Brian 507
Jonsson, Ulrika 200
Just Good Friends 13, 278
Juster, Norman 506

Kalashnikov, Mikhail 443
Kaliban, Bob 74
Kallen, Lucille 83
Kane, Charles 140
Kaplan, Myq 114
Kapoor, Frances (*Criminal Justice*) 460
Kaprow, Allan 365
Karr, Alphonse 34
Karter, John 259
Kasdan, Lawrence 371
Katie and Peter: The Next Chapter 291
Kauffman, Max 58, 236
Kaufman, George S. 58, 106, 191, 454
Kavanagh, Patrick 159
Kazin, Alfred 501
Keate, Stuart 420
Keating, H.R.F. 163
Keegan, Kevin 263

Keenan, Jeff 129
Keillor, Garrison 192
Keller, Sheldon 95
Kelly, Bill 138
Kelly, Gene 95
Kelly, Stephen 261
Kelp, Julius (Jerry Lewis) (*The Nutty Professor*) 496
Kennedy, Edward 322
Kennedy, Jacqueline 129, 215
Kennedy, John F. 320, 323, 506
Kennedy, Tara 246
Kent, Eddie 62
Kent, Katherine 431
Kent, Lenny 199
Kenyon, Shirlee 140
Kerr, Clark 505
Keynes, John Maynard 56, 70, 71
Keynes, William Maynard 60
Khorsandi, Shappi 120, 313, 433
Kiam, Victor 289
Kielty, Patrick 539
Kilborn, Craig 119, 180, 354
Kilmister, Lemmy 121, 178, 256
Kilner, Bill 313
Kilpatrick, James J. 151
Kimmel, Jimmy 54
King of Queens, The 434
King, Stephen 160
Kingsmill, Hugh 142
Kington, Miles 66, 93, 131, 132, 194, 296, 338, 364, 402, 416, 472, 487, 507, 521
Kiniski, Lewis (*The Drew Carey Show*) 194
Kinnock, Neil 331, 502
Kipling, Rudyard 326
Kirkby, Jack Temple 342
Kirkwood, David 328
Kirschner, S. 202
Kissinger, Henry 221, 316, 336, 339
Kitchener, Lord 412
Kitching, R.E. 19

Klein, Robert 480
Knave 172
Knebel, Fletcher 289
Knoebel, Steven M. 68
knowledge 506–7
Kobal, John 232
Kocak, Paul 89
Koestler, Arthur 434
Koncius, Jura 131
Kondis, Paul 130
Koontz, Dean 156
Korman, Harvey 373
Kosinski, Jerzy 524
Kostelanetz, André 351
Kournikova, Anna 272
Kovacs, Ernie 390
Krakowski, Jane 382
Kramer, Kosmo (*Seinfeld*) 483
Krassner, Paul 230
Krasus, Karl 151
Kreft, Peter 541
Kroc, Ray 289
Krock, Arthur 203
Kronenberger, Louis 243
Kugler, Elly 435
Kurnitz, Harry 372

L.A. Story 140, 197, 418
La Follette, Robert M. 320
La Guardia, Fiorella 362
Ladies of the Corridor, The 112
Ladman, Cathy 86
Lady 246
Lagerfeld, Karl 48, 371
LaGuardia, Fiorello 288
Lahr, Chris 46
Laker, Jim 260
Lamarr, Mark 487
Lamb, Charles 132
Lambert, Madame de 162
Lamont, Norman 319, 331
Lancaster, Osbert 396
Lanchester, John 11, 243
Landers, Ann 196
Lane, Anthony 368
Lange, Halvard 423

Langford, Bonnie 374
languages 146–8
Lapham, Lewis H. 65, 66, 363
Lapides, Beth 38
Lappin, Tom 427
Lara, Adair 510
Lardner, Ring 118, 157
Larkin, Philip 166
Larson, Doug 148, 211, 520
Larson, Gary 312, 541
Laski, H.J. 148
Lasorda, Tommy 274
Last Days of Lehman Brothers, The (Warner) 67
Last of the Red Hot Lovers 494
Last Time You'll Hear From Me (Sedaris) 239
last words 525
Laud, Derek 138
Lauder, Estée 289
Laurel, Stan 72
Laurie, Hugh 387
law & lawyers 454–6
Lawrence, D.H. 414
Lawrence, Joey 354
Lawrence, T.E. 470
Lawson, Mark 161
Lawson, Nigella 10, 388
Layne, Bobby 238
Lazar, Irving 'Swifty' 373, 523
Le Figaro 343
Leacock, Stephen 65, 109, 150, 421
Leahy, Frank 221
Leapor, Molly 378
Lear, Edward 540
Learning to Fly (Beckham) 183
Lease, Mary E. 65
Lebowitz, Fran 61, 92, 209, 230, 309, 373, 390, 410, 483
Lec, Stanislaw J. 93, 108, 125, 150, 204, 207, 226, 231, 285, 320, 436, 463, 478
Lecoat, Jenny 19, 41
Lee, Colwyn 403
Lee, Laurie 350, 361

Lee, Nancy (*Doc Hollywood*) 385
Lefevre, Jr., William M. 67
Légaré, Pierre 237
Lehrer, Tom 281
Leibling, A.J. 24
Leibovich, Kathryn 131
Leifer, Carol 24, 31, 182, 304, 404
Leitsch, Dick 138
Lembke, Major Robert 468
Lemmon, Jack 379
Lemon, Liz (*30 Rock*) 136
Lemoyne, Jean 520
Lenin, Vladimir Ilich 61
Lennon, John 222, 469
Leon, H.C. 461
Leonard, Elmore 151, 160
Leonard, Hugh 15, 21, 96, 110, 194, 294, 377, 425, 449
Leonard, Jack E. 486
Les 422
Leslie, C.R. 363
Lette, Kathy 101, 153, 194, 282, 430
letter 207–9
Letterman, David 22, 118, 140, 257, 300, 346, 376, 419, 430, 460, 485, 537
Leunig, Michael 45, 120, 156
Levant, Oscar 97, 198, 200, 284, 355, 496
Leven, Jeremy 495
Levenson, Sam 55
Levin, Bernard 47
Levinson, Henry 303
Levis, Carroll 386
Lévy, Paul 7
Lewinsky, Monica 343
Lewis, David 402
Lewis, Edward 288
Lewis, Jerry 181
Lewis, Joe E. 15, 21, 173
Lewis, Lennox 271
Lewis, Richard 235, 534
Lewis, Robert J. 289

Lewis, Roger 194
Lewis, Sinclair 410
Lewis-Smith, Victor 15, 25, 77, 424
Lichtenberg, Georg Christoph 111, 227, 391, 438
Liddle, Rod 162
Liebman, Wendy 173, 186, 389, 398
Lien, Jon 510
life, ageing & death 513–28
Lincoln, Abraham 220, 344, 467, 469
Lineker, Gary 262, 263
Linklater, Eric 435
Linscott, Robert N. 208
Lintott, David P. 430
Lipman, Maureen 377, 449, 534
Lipton, James 18
Lipton, Larry (*Manhattan Murder Mystery*) 494
Lister, Dave (*Red Dwarf*) 108
Little, Mary W. 286
Little Richard 103
Little Sister, the (Chandler) 231
Littlewood, John Edensor 464
living 515–16
Livingstone, Ken 334
Livington, Edward 342
Llewellyn, Caroline 76
Lock, Sean 192, 354, 470, 536
Lodge, Henry Cabot 342
Lollobrigida, Gina 476
London, Jay 32, 38, 478
Loos, Anita 85
Loose Ends 182
Loose Women 32
Lopokova, Lydia 116
Lord Love a Duck (Bernard) 199
Lord St John of Fawsley 451
Lord, Graham 18
Lorenz, Lee 478
Lott, Tim 520
Louis XIV, King 247
Louis, Joe 51

Louise, Anita 37
Louise, Kerri 536
Louise, Princess Marie 507
love 44–5
Love and Death (Grushenko) 5353
Love, Barbara 139
Lover, Samuel 193
Low, Sir David 465
Lowell, James Russell 329
Lowry, Mary 204
Lucas, E.V. 97, 280
Lucas, F.L. 161
Lucas, Jack 161
luck 236–7
Luckett, Bernadette 142
Lucy (*Peanuts*) 8
Luft, Lorna 500
Lumley, Joanna 119
Lundberg, Ferdinand 455
Lundkvist, Arthur 287
Lungu, Mircea 34
Lyall, Sarah 311
Lynch, Peter 70, 71, 72
Lynd, Robert 466
Lynde, Paul 88, 90, 247
Lynes, Russell 246
Lynn, Loretta 191
Lyttelton, Humphrey 4, 189, 378

M*A*S*H 14, 16, 17, 209, 223, 340, 348, 437, 480
MacArthur, General Douglas 466
Macaulay, Rose 408
Macaulay, Thomas 245, 507
MacDiarmid, Hugh 464
MacHale, D.J. 132
Machiavelli 527
machismo 34–5
Mackay, Harvey 288
MacKenzie, Alistair 17
Mackenzie, Charlie (*So I Married an Axe Murderer*) 426
Maclennan, Robert 333
Macmillan, Harold 63, 322, 328, 331, 339
MacPherson, Ian 358, 538

MacPherson, Stewart 359
MacRéamoinn, Seán 516
MAD 99, 300
Madan, Falconer 207, 452
Madeley, Richard 444
Madison, Oscar (*The Odd Couple*) 314
Madness of King George, The 451
Madonna 181, 517
Magnum P.I. 207
Magnum, Thomas (*Magnum P.I.*) 207
Maguire, Charles 302
Maher, Bill 22, 86, 186, 210, 286, 307, 390
Mahler, Gustav 409
Mahy, Margaret 420
Mailer, Norman 158, 418
Major, John 331
Makarova, Natalia 362
make-up 86–7
Malcolm in the Middle 95, 224
Malcolm X 142
Maldonado, Linda 183
Mallet, Robert 98
Malraux, André 368
Mamet, David 372
Manchurian Candidate, The 388, 469
Mandelson, Peter 331
Manhattan 222
Manhattan Murder Mystery 8, 4943
Manilow, Barry 221
Mankiewicz, Herman 311, 428
Mankoff, Robert 128
manners & behaviour 241–53
manners, Miss 244
Mannes, Marya 137, 224
Manning, Bernard 236
Manningham–Buller, Dame Eliza 514
Manoukian, Dan 22
Mansfield, Jayne 383
Mansfield, Katherine 177
Manson, Marilyn 131

Mantel, Henriette 87
Marder, Jeff 486
Margaret, Princess 450
Markes, L. 409
Marks, Jonathan Alen 251
Marlborough, Duke of 451
Marquand, John 77
Marquette, 'Pee Wee' 84
Márquez, Gabriel García 174, 533
Marquis, Don 21, 236
Marr, Dave 268
marriage & family life 171–200
married life 174–6
Married With Children 2
Mars, Edward 203
Marsan, Eddie 376
Marsden, Luke 237
Marsh, Edward 365
Marshall, Alfred 63
Marshall, Arthur 401
Marshall, John 461
Marshall, Peter 88, 90, 247
Marskon, Elaine 78
Martin, Demetri 47, 93, 146, 295
Martin, H. 521
Martin, Roxanne 117
Martin, Steve 39, 191, 532
Martling, Jackie 40, 459
Marx, Chico 51, 231
Marx, Groucho 8, 31, 51, 69, 72, 116, 151, 155, 157, 167, 208, 209, 211, 214, 258, 280, 283, 294, 307, 354, 393, 475, 520
Marx, Karl 60, 71, 159
Mary Hartman, Mary Hartman 355
Mary Whitehouse Experience, The 228
Marzouk, Omar 392
Mason, Jackie 23, 72, 306, 344, 393
Masters, Brian 309
mathematics 439–40

Mating Season, The (Wodehouse) 358
Matta, Roberto 365, 366
Matthau, Walter 176
Maude 99
Maugham, W. Somerset 506
Maurois, André 153, 288
Maverick 238, 472
Maxwell, Elsa 97, 475
Maxwell, Robert 481
Mayehoff, Eddie 176
Mays Jr., Willie 273
McAllister, Ward 308
McArthur, Peter 283, 448
McBride, Jeannie 183
McCabe, Martin (Absolute Power) 465
McCarthy, Charlie 100
McCarthy, Desmond 330
McCarthy, Eugene 327, 341
McCarthy, Mary 409, 416
McCarthy, Moody 190, 233
McCartney, Paul 352
McClain, Denny 481
McClaren, Bill 256
McCollister, Beth 476
McCord, Gary 269
McCormick, Pat 22, 202
McCourt, Malachy 21
McCrory, Glenn 271
McCrum, Mark 162
McCutcheon, Matine 353
McDonald, Russ 378
McDowel, Sarah (L.A. Story) 418
McEwan, Ian 212
McEwen, Todd 402
McFarland, Jack (Will and Grace) 224
McFarlin, Steve 173
McFee, William 226
McGiffin, Carol 32, 173
McGillivray, Pat 459
McGinley, Phyllis 419
McGland, Gowan 87

McGovern, George 319
McGowan, Alistair 312
McGuire, Al 275
McIlvanney, Hugh 259
McIntyre, Captain John 'Trapper' (M*A*S*H) 223
McLaughlin, Mignon 15, 56, 206, 477, 490, 492, 497
McLean, Andrea 32, 175
McLenna, Rebecca 132
McLuhan, Marshall 399
McNab, Sandor 477
McNally, Frank 425
McPhail, Donna 394
McPhee, John 232
McQueen, Alexander 94, 138
meanness 73–4
Medici, Catherine de 101
Meeks, Dodie 150
Meet Wally Sparks 420
Meir, Golda 124
Melchior, Lauritz 360
Mellencamp, John Cougar 253
Melly, George 142
Melon, Thornton 500
Melville, Elizabeth 165
Memoirs of a Mangy Lover (Marx) 157
memory 521–2
men 132–3
Men Behaving Badly 183
Mencken, H.L. 342, 345, 349, 350, 358, 359, 360, 379, 388, 455, 507, 509, 528, 530, 533, 536
Mendoza, John 278, 397
Meneve, Russ 108
Menuhin, Yehudi 350, 479
Mercer, David 434
Mercier, Jean 211
Meredith, George 24
Merman, Paul 374
Merrill, Robert 360
Merton, Mrs 135
Merton, Paul 6, 7, 385, 536

Metalious, Grace 153, 160
Meyer, F.V. 61
Michener, James 159
Mickey Mantle's Country Cooking Restaurant Chain 23
Mickler, Ernest Matthew 9
Midler, Bette 41, 137
Midsummer Night's Sex Comedy, A 38
Mikes, George 95, 449
Milburn, Jackie 539
Mildred Pierce 187
Miliband, David 331, 334
Milken, Michael 214
Millay, Edna St Vincent 208, 328
Mille, Agnes de 361
Mille, Larry 200
Miller, Arthur 288, 388
Miller, Bill 187
Miller, Dennis 123, 234, 341, 417, 456, 493, 501, 537
Miller, George 136
Miller, Harlan 175
Miller, Henry 2, 159, 363
Miller, Jonathan 359
Miller, Larry 481
Miller, Mick 4
Miller, Olin 281
Miller, Roger 404
Milligan, Paul 445
Milligan, Spike 56, 106, 119, 190, 314, 467, 493
Minnelli, Liza 394
Minnion, John 260
Miss Piggy 27, 45, 86, 403
Mississippi Burning 273
mistakes 282–3
Mitchell, David 424
Mitchell, Henry 287
Mitchell, Margaret 183
Mitchum, Robert 85, 220, 369, 476, 522
Mitford, Jessica 319
Mizner, Addison 509
Mizner, Wilson 100, 153, 168, 198, 271, 311, 525

Mock the Week 190, 257, 308, 334, 427, 504
Modell, Frank 368
modern curses 251–2
Modern Family 189
Molière 225, 377, 539
money matters 49–79
Money, Catherine 246
Monk 228
Monkhouse, Bob 42, 54, 109, 112, 175, 186, 236, 268, 402, 520
Monroe, Marilyn 370, 381
Monsoon, Edina (*Absolutely Fabulous*) 413
Montagu, Ashley 437
Montagu, Lady Mary Wortley 508
Montague, C.E. 541
Monteux, Pierre 294
Moore, Bobby 264
Moore, Brian 425
Moore, Dudley 243
Moore, George 309
Moore, Henry 367
Moore, Mavor 385
Moore, Patrick 444, 446
Moorehouse, Agnes (*Yes, Minister*) 107
Moorhouse, Frank 419
Moran, Caitlin 41
Moran, Dylan 232, 530
Moreau, Gustav 365
Morecambe and Wise 11, 102, 178, 196
Morecambe, Eric 120, 175, 178, 188, 196, 264
Morgan Stanley Financial Services 56
Morgan, Cliff 539
Morgan, Henry 299
Morgan, J.P. 72
Morgan, Piers 221, 222
Morley, Christopher 94, 308
Morley, Robert 310
Morley, Sheridan 332
Morny, Duc de 43
Morris-Marsham, David 246

Morris-Morgan, P.D. 332
Morrison, Richard 507
Morrissey 13
Morrow, Lance 95
Morrow, Tom 202, 303
Mortimer, Bob 140, 193
Mortimer, John 156, 226, 461, 464, 501
Morton, Andrew 317, 450
Morton, J.B. 166
Mosley, Charles 453
Moss, Stirling 257, 396
Mother, The 497
mother-in-law 181–2
mottos for Modern Britain 422–3
Mowrer, Paul Scott 117
Mr Mulliner Speaking (Wodehouse) 20, 489
Mr Phillips (Lanchester) 243
Mrmić, Marijan 121
Mueller, Robert 136
Muggeridge, Malcolm 47, 230, 321
Muir, Edwin 427
Muir, Frank 296
Mulligan, Pat 103, 482
Mulroy, Terry 36
Mum's the Word 184
Munger, Charles T. 298
Munro, Alice 244
Muppet Show, The 376
Murdock, Jeff (*Coupling*) 139
Murphy's Military Law 469
Murray, Al (The Pub Landlord) 53, 135, 414
Murray, Jan 237
Murray, Jim 417
Murrow, Edward R. 216
music 348–56
musical 374
Musical Courier 129
musical instrument 356–9
Muslim 538–9
my dick is so big... 35–6
My Favorite Year (Silver) 19

My Name is Charles Saatchi and I am an Artoholic (Saatchi) 10, 477
My Name is Earl 300
My Shit Life So Far (Boyle) 333
Mystic Masseur, The (Naipaul) 152

Nabokov, Vladimir 158
Nagy, Bernadette 74
Naipaul, V.S. 152
Naked Jape, The (Carr) 123
names 128–9
Nanny, The 37, 234
Nash, Monica 7
Nash, Ogden 67, 275
Nathan, George Jean 76, 134, 168
nature & country life 116–17
Naylor, Jac (*Holby City*) 355
Nealon, Kevin 42
Needham, Richard 528
Negulesco, Jean 161
Neil, Andrew 454
Nelms, Cynthia 38
Nelson, Willie 40, 352
Nemerov, Howard 285
Nesbitt, Rab C. 427
Never Mind the Buzzcocks 487
Neville, Penny (*Teachers*) 516
New Statesman 224
New York Times 390
Newman, John Henry 505
news – general 213
News Quiz, The 242, 272, 306, 353, 524
newspapers & journalism 214–15
Newsweek 485
Newton, Isaac 70
Nichols, Beverly 117, 120, 121, 122, 193
Nichols, Diane 400
Nicholson, Harold 327
Nicholson, Jack 372
Nietzsche, Friedrich 133, 532

A Night at the Opera 393
Nighy, Bill 379, 382
Nixon, Julie 46
Nixon, Pat 46
Nixon, Richard 46, 215, 342, 345, 444
Noe, Booker 17
Nolan, Coleen 185
Noonan, Peggy 337, 343
Norden, Denis 83, 296, 356, 400
Norris, Steven 346
Norton, Graham 188, 205, 302
Norwich, John Julius 502
nose job 99–100
Now Show, The 178
Nunn, Gregory 327
Nuns on the Run 292
Nutley, Buzz 159
Nutty Professor, The 496
Nuxhall, Joe 509
Nye, Edgar Wilson 442
Nyman, Marian 148

O'Brien, Conan 118, 459, 474, 475, 480, 489, 524
O'Brien, Conor Cruise 531
O'Brien, Flann 391
O'Brien, Kate (*The Drew Carey Show*) 194
O'Connell, Christian 314
O'Connor, Frank 375
O'Connor, Joseph 57
O'Donoghue, Michael 5
O'Grady, Paul 374
O'Keefe, Patrick 74, 311
O'Loughlin, Mick 268
O'Malley, Pat 212
O'Neill, Eugene 371, 377
O'Neill, Molly 20
O'Reilly, Anthony 196
O'Reilly, Jane 198
O'Rourke, P.J. 11, 13, 32, 40, 58, 91, 117,

178, 179, 256, 318, 401, 489
O'Sullevan, Peter 259
O'Toole, Peter 377
Oates, Joyce Carol 270
Obama, Barack 140, 343
Odd Couple, The 286, 314
Odes (Horace) 239
Odets, Clifford 176
Office, the (USA) 192
Ogden, Howard 396
Ogilvy, Ian 383
Olazábal, José Maria 212
Olinghouse, Lane 123, 434
Olitski, Jules 367
Oliver, John 229
Olivier, Laurence 128, 382
Onassis, Aristotle 52, 285
Only Fools and Horses 9
opera 359–61
Opposite of Sex, The 235
optimism & pessimism 234–6
Optimist, The 238
Orben, Robert 51, 58, 282, 305, 318, 493
Origin of Species, the (Darwin) 437
Orwell, George 225, 226, 227
Osborne, Jeremy (*Peep Show*) 44, 216
Osborne, John 362
Osbourne, Jack 250
Osbourne, Kelly 250
Osbourne, Ozzy 250, 352
Osbourne, Sharon 250
Out to Lunch (Lévy) 7
Outnumbered 73
Overmyer, Eric 132
Overstone, Lord 70
Ozu, Yasujiro 512

Pacino, Al 382
Paglia, Camille 351
Palahniuk, Chuck 188

Palgrave, Francis Turner 368
Palin, Sarah 346
Paphitis, Theo 75
Parent, Gail 526
Parfait, Paul 182
Park, Brad 100
Parker, Alan 142
Parker, Dorothy 3, 15, 31, 82, 100, 112, 114, 200, 225, 232, 305, 372, 384, 500
Parker, Ralphie 250
Parker, Robert 516
Parkinson Show, The 187, 300
Parkinson, Michael 269, 285
Parole Officer, The 472
Parris, Matthew 330, 331, 333, 334, 422, 448, 501, 517
Partington, Mrs (*I Didn't Know You Cared*) 109
Parton, Dolly 30, 87, 98, 124, 279, 300, 344, 356, 519
Partridge, Alan 96, 150, 162, 353, 471, 537, 540
Passmore, George 502
Patchen, Kenneth 152
Paterson, Don 41
Patorelli, Tammy 125
Patterson, Sir Les 14
Pattinson, Iain 155
Pavarotti, Luciano 249, 360
Peanuts 8, 131
Pearce, Lindsay (*Teachers*) 516
Pearce, Steven 444
Pearson, Lord 303
Pearson, Pauline 403
Peck, Gregory 110
Peel, John 353, 457
Peep Show 44, 131, 216, 361, 399
Pelletier, Jerry 22
Pendleton, Winston K. 124, 482
Penick, Harvey 266
Penn, Irving 368
people 127–43

Pepper, Mrs Claude 326
Percy, Walker 14
Perdue, Jackson 494
Perelman, S.J. 125, 311, 372, 390
Perkins, Ray 102
Perot, Ross 67, 197, 325
Perret, Gene 180, 521
Perry, Graham (*Just Good Friends*) 13
Pershing, General John 468
Petan, Žarko 376
Pete 423
Peter, Laurence J. 420
Peterson, Norm (*Cheers*) 14, 21, 234, 514, 516
Peterson, Peter 124
Petrillo, Sophia (*The Golden Girls*) 523
pets 109–10
Peyser, Jerry (*The In–Laws*) 26
Peyton Place (Metalious) 153, 160
Phelps, William Lyon 466
Philip, Duke of Edinburgh, Prince 16, 450
Philips, Bill 204
Philips, Emo 22, 408, 426, 492, 531, 538
Philips, Judson P. 256
Philips, William Lyon 152
Phillips, Larry 130
philosophy 511–12
photography 368
Picasso, Pablo 134, 366
Pichushkin, Alexander 460
Pickel, Sylvia (*Vibes*) 453
Pickwick Papers, The (Dickens) 11
Pierce, Captain Benjamin 'Hawkeye' (*M*A*S*H*) 14, 16, 348, 480
Pierce, David Hyde 84
Piggott, Lester 259

Pigs Have Wings (Wodehouse) 14
Pinner, Vince (*Just Good Friends*) 13
Pirar, Daniel 294
Pirsig, Robert 364
Pitt, Brad 215
playwright 377–8
Plimpton, George 154
Poe, Edgar Allan 111
Poehler, Amy 128
poetry 164–6
Polanski, Roman 372, 528
polite euphemisms for relieving a wedgie 246–7
political office, leaving 344–6
political speeches 336–7
politicians 330–5
politics 315–46
Polkinghorne, Richard 210
Pollard, Su 31
Pompidou, Georges 421
Poole, Lord 69
poor 77–8
Pop Idol 348
Popbitch.com 5, 10, 46, 142, 238, 271, 304, 308, 470
Popcorn (Elton) 286
Popcorn, Faith 300
Pope, Alexander 76
pornography 47
Porridge 458
Porter, George 124
Porter, Peter 165
Portillo, Michael 345
Potter, Colonel Sherman T. (*M*A*S*H*) 209, 340
Pound, Ezra 526
Poundstone, Paula 417, 478
Powell, Enoch 322
Powell, Jonathan 345
Powell, Lee 303
Powell, Thomas Reed 455
power 316–17
Pratchett, Terry 159, 287, 296, 373, 386, 409, 437, 536

Prentiss, Charles
(*Absolute Power*)
465
Prescott, John 223,
335, 367
Presley, Elvis 141, 354
Press, Bill 341
Prévot, André 51
Price, Katie 386
Price, Leontyne 360
Price, Matt 261
Priestley, J.B. 189
Primal Fear 461
Princess Bride, The 389
prison 462–3
Pritchett, Matthew
'Matt' 68
Pritchett, Oliver 216
Private Eye 464
problems 281–2
Prochnow, Herbert V.
151, 289
Prokofiev, Sergei 350
prostitute 48
Proust, Marcel 97, 309
proverbs 78, 134, 137,
206, 239, 312, 323,
357
Pryor, Richard 18, 488
psychiatry & therapy
492–7
*Pub Landlord's Book
of Common Sense,
The* (Murray) 135,
414
public speaking 211–12
publicity 388
publishing 163–4
Pullen, Barry 114
Punch 340, 392
punctuality 247
Purves, Libby 321
Purvis, Andrew 7
Putin, Vladimir 338
Puzo, Mario 52, 157
Pyle, Robert M. 122

QI 6, 186, 428, 439,
463
Quatro, Suzi 141
Quillen, Robert 476
Quinn, Colin 417
Quinn, Jane Bryant 439
Quirini, Linda 205
Quittner, Joshua 433

Rabelais, François 525
race & ethnicity 140–1
racism & prejudice
141–2
*Radcliffe and Maconie
Show, The* 23
radio 390
Raiders of the Lost Ark
519
Raines, Howell 297
Ramey, Dr Estelle 137
Ramsay, Gordon 10
Randolph, John 323,
342
Rankin, Jeannette 466
Ransome, Arthur 298
Rantzen, Esther 42
Rascoe, Burton 156
Rathbone, Twiggy (*Hot
Metal*) 459
Rather, Dan 319
Rauhihi, Paul 197
Ravenwood, Marion
(*Raiders of the Lost
Ark*) 519
Ray, Ted 193
Raye, Martha 279
Raymond, F.J. 55
Rayner, Jay 25
Reade, Charles 222
Reader's Digest 197
Readman, Robert 421
Reagan, Ronald 53,
295, 316, 317, 343,
346, 416, 450
A Really Cute Corpse
(Hess) 189
Reard, Louis 306
recession 64–5
Red Dwarf 82, 108
Red Orc's Rage
(Farmer) 27
Reed, John Shelton 243
Reed, Rex 232
Reed, Stuart 484
Rees–Mogg, William
333
Reeve, Christopher 488
Reeves, Richard 132
Reeves, Vic 140, 193
Reg (*Table Manners*)
13
Regan, Donald 316
Régnier, Henri de 208
Rehnquist, William
454

Reid, Beryl 101, 233
Reid, Jimmy 332
Reiger, Alex (*Taxi*) 220,
278
Reilly, Rick 267
Reinhard, Bob 113
Reiser, Paul 185
religion 529–41
remarriage 199–200
Renan, Ernest 38, 435
Renard, Jules 52, 57,
280, 526
Renner, Jack 266
Renoir, Pierre–Auguste
364
restaurants & cafés
22–7
Restivo, Joe 244
retirement 521–3
Reuben, Reuben
(McGland) 87
Revenge of the Lawn
(Brautigan) 236
Rexroth, Kenneth 164
Rhea, Caroline 38, 42,
418
Rhea, Nicholas 537
Rice, Grantland 221
rich 74–7
Rich, Buddy 484
*Richard Bacon Show,
The* 122
Richards, Keith 357,
358
Richards, Ron 281
Richardson, Charlie
68
Richardson, Dorothy
M. 211
Richardson, John 92
Richman, Alan 25
Rickman, Dennis
(*EastEnders*) 224
Ridge, William Pett 19
Ridgway, Phil 90
Rigaux, Jean 12
right & wrong 225–6
Right Ho, Jeeves
(Wodehouse) 83, 337
Rigsby, Rupert (*Rising
Damp*) 505
Rimmell, Mark 258
Rimmer, Arnold (*Red
Dwarf*) 108
Rising Damp 505
Rivers, Caryl 299

Rivers, Joan 37, 43, 76,
90, 98, 99, 180, 184,
187, 189, 235, 283,
391, 392
*Roast Chicken and
Other Stories*
(Hopkinson) 5
Robbins, Lisa (*The
Drew Carey Show*) 86
Robbins, Tom 90, 119,
156
Roberts, Larenda Lyles
312
Robeson, Paul 374
Robinson, Anne 175,
496
Robson, Bobby 262
Rockefeller, Nelson 336
Rodin, Auguste 367
Rodriguez, Chi Chi 265
Roebuck, Peter 260
Rogers, Will 53, 55, 63,
64, 71, 112, 204,
289, 329, 341, 344,
466, 467, 506
Romanoff and Juliet
463
Romeo and Juliet 380
Ronson, Mark 352
Rook, Jean 450
Rookwood, Dan 92
Room 101 6
Rooney, Andy 431, 521
Rooney, Kevin 418
Roosevelt, Theodore
330, 383
Roren, Ned 363
Rose Marie 302
Rose, Billy 4
Rose, Stuart 288
Roseanne 8, 136, 176,
316, 482
Rosen, Marc 303
Rosenberg, Harold 366
Rosenberg, Jim 474
Rosenblatt, Roger 213
Rosenstock-Huessy,
Eugen 228, 532
Ross, Harold 165
Ross, Jeffrey 33, 37,
98, 369, 519
Ross, Jonathan 33, 83,
370
Ross, Verda 281
Rosseau, Jean–Jacques
525

Rosten, Leo 225, 229
Roszak, Theodore 510
Rotarian, The 66
Roth, David Lee 488
Rothfels, Gina 59
Rothman, Max 249
Rothschild, Baron 50
Rouse, G.M. 198
Rovin, Jeff 518
Rowen, Henry S. 340
Rowland, Helen 33,
 182, 248, 518
Rowson, Martin 331
royalty 449–51
Royle Family, The 177
Royle, Barbara (*The
 Royle Family*) 177
Royle, Jim (*The Royle
 Family*) 177
Rubenstein, Arthur 348
Ruby, Harry 418
Rudge, Helen 2
Ruffo, Titta 360
Rumpole of the Bailey
 455, 461
Rumpole, Horace
 (*Rumpole of the
 Bailey*) 455, 461
Rumsfeld, Donald 463
Runes, Dagobert D. 408
Runyon, Damon 85
Rushton, Willie 396
Ruskin, John 51
Russell, Bertrand 153,
 327, 440
Russell, Mark 55
Ryan, Jack 202, 205
Ryan, Tom 57

Saatchi, Charles 10,
 199, 220, 388, 450,
 477, 500
Sabatini, Rafael 85
Safire, William 149,
 151
Sagan, Carl 538
Sagan, Françoise 91
Saint-Laurent, Yves 86,
 93
Saki 428, 525
Sales, Raul R. de 60
Sales, Soupy 519
Salvation 460
Samuelson, Paul 64
Sanders, George 96,
 508

Sanders, Steve (*Beverly
 Hills 90210*) 417
Sandilands, John 540
Saroyan, Carol, 200
Saroyan, William 168,
 200, 514
Sartre, Jean–Paul 367
Saul, John Ralston 272,
 511
Saunders, Diane 55
Saunders, Margaret
 Baillie 59, 137
Saunders, Steve
 (*Beverly Hills 90210*)
 417
Saurès, André 68
Savage, Brian 532
Savage, Lily 88, 187,
 300
Savage, Robbie 263
saving & thrift 72–3
Sawalha, Julia 531
Sawyer, Frederick 339
Sawyer, Veronica
 (*Heathers*) 238
Scalzi, John 186
Scarlet, Earle P. 485
Scarpaggi, Antonio
 (*Wings*) 32
Schalk, Franz 359
Schimmel, Robert 149
Schnabel, Artur 357
Schneider, Bill 342
Schneier, Bruce 213
Schoenberg, Harold
 360
schools 500–3
Schopenhauer, Arthur
 207, 301
Schrute, Dwight (*The
 Office* (USA)) 192
Schumacher, Joel 382
Schwarzenegger, Arnold
 82, 325
Schwarzkopf, General
 Norman 471
science & technology
 429–46
scientists 434–6
Scoppettone, Sandra
 491
Scotland 426–8
Scott, Anne 248
Scott, Ralph 247
Scott, Ray 278
Scott, Sir Walter 427

Scully, Vin 221
sculpture 367–8
sea travel 404–5
Secombe, Harry 24, 360
*Secret Policeman's Ball,
 The* 378
*Secret World of the
 Irish Male, The*
 (O'Connor) 57
secrets 206–7
Sedaris, David 239, 509
Seers, Dudley 296
Segal, George 419
Seinfeld 30, 483
Seinfeld, Jerry (*Seinfeld*)
 30, 188
Self, Will 10, 25, 300
Sellar, W.C. 121
Sendak, Maurice 300
Sense and Sensibility
 (Austen) 215
separation & divorce
 198–9
Serafinowicz, Peter 486
Sergeant, John 141
Serling, Robert J.
 (*Wings*) 91
Seville, Bishop of 520
Sewell, Brain 365
sex & dating 29–34
Sex and the City 181,
 197
sex education 191
Seymour, Jane 133
Shaefer, Arno 431
Shakespeare, William
 320, 377, 378–81
Shales, Tom 362
Shandling, Garry 39,
 40, 192
Shankly, Bill 262, 263,
 264
Shapiro, Eugene 484
Sharf, Craig 112
Shaw, George Bernard
 14, 60, 62, 175, 207,
 272, 298, 356, 368,
 425, 427, 465, 540
Shaw, Jeff 394
Shaw, Raymond (*The
 Manchurian
 Candidate*) 388
Shay, R.E. 237
Sheirr, Harvey 302
Shepard, Sam 372
Shepherd, Cybill 88

Sherman, Joanne 438
Sherman, Mark 303
Shetterly, Will 421
Shoales, Ian 374
Shoñagon, Sei 46
Shooting Stars 140, 193
shopping 301–2
Short, Martin 287
Shreve, L.G. 16
Shriner, Herb 297, 387
Shrödinger, Erwin 435
Shulman, Milton 26
Shumacher, Jules 205
Sibelius, Jean 350
Sibley, Alex 515
Sideshow Mel (*The
 Simpsons*) 489
Sig 422
Silver, Joel 136
Silver, Leo 19
Silverman, Sarah 40,
 87, 188, 231
Simborg, Phil 46
Simon & Simon 483
Simon, Cecilia (*Simon
 & Simon*) 483
Simon, John 111
Simon, Neil 284, 417
Simonson, Lee 465
*Simple Art of Murder,
 The* (Chandler) 15
Simpson, Bart (*The
 Simpsons*) 474, 502,
 503
Simpson, Homer (*The
 Simpsons*) 2, 45, 52,
 58, 70, 74, 78, 91,
 109, 134, 153, 172,
 190, 203, 274, 309,
 344, 389, 441, 442,
 445, 463, 472, 496,
 515, 530, 537
Simpson, Lisa (*The
 Simpsons*) 78, 496
Simpson, Marge (*The
 Simpsons*) 45, 52, 58,
 109, 134, 172, 203,
 474, 515
Simpson, O.J. 461
Simpsons, The 2, 17,
 45, 52, 58, 70, 74,
 78, 106, 109, 134,
 153, 172, 190, 203,
 309, 344, 389, 426,
 441, 442, 445, 463,
 472, 474, 488, 496,

502, 503, 515, 530, 537
Sinatra, Frank 353, 388
Singer, Alvy (*Annie Hall*) 469, 494
Singer, Steven Max 41
single life 177
Siskind, Carol 34, 462
Sitwell, Osbert 166, 223, 248
Skelton, Red 282, 456
Skelton, Robin 202
Skinner, Frank 175, 263, 323, 386, 394, 487, 518, 524
Skinny Legs and All (Robbins) 90
Slater, Nigel 12, 23
Slayton, Bobby 172, 176
Sleep When I'm Dead (Barnes) 486
Slonimski, Antoni 375
Slowing Down (Melly) 142
Small Bachelor, The (Wodehouse) 284
smells 231–2
Smith Lectures, The (Smith) 109, 398
Smith, Adam 53
Smith, Alexander 121
Smith, Alfred E. 415
Smith, Arthur 109, 398
Smith, Bob 139
Smith, Chuck 246
Smith, Cyril 2
Smith, Elaine 427
Smith, Elinor Goulding 185
Smith, Gary 111
Smith, Giles 314
Smith, H. Allen 279
Smith, H.R. 465
Smith, Iain Duncan 297, 334
Smith, J. Calvin 436
Smith, Linda 94, 449
Smith, Liz 205
Smith, Logan Pearsall 220
Smith, Maggie 383
Smith, Marion 177
Smith, Reverend Sydney 110, 247, 345, 426, 476, 478, 492, 507

Smith, Stevie 536
smoking 490–1
Snead, Sam 268
Snoopy (*Peanuts*) 131
Snow, Carrie P. 177
Snowdon, Lord 368
So I Married an Axe Murderer 426
Soap 139, 203
Sobel, Robert 341
society & law 447–72
Sohl, Mort 536
Solon, Mark 402
Sombrero Fallout (Brautigan) 85
Some Like it Hot 71
Somerville, Michael 172
Sondheim, Stephen 352
Sontag, Susan 491
Soprano, Corrado 'Junior' (*The Sopranos*) 286
Soprano, Tony (*The Sopranos*) 286
Sopranos, The 286
Sorenson, Jean 31, 247
Sothern, Edward H. 168
Sowell, Thomas 511
Spadaro, Annie (*Caroline in the City*) 32
Spark, Muriel 25
Sparrow, John 102
Speaking For Myself (Day) 305
Speck, Ross 494
Spectator 376
Spencer, Dan 118
Spender, Stephen 157
Sperber, Ann M. 238
Spillane, Mickey 160
sports 255–75
Spring, Howard 338
Springsteen, Bruce 285, 343
St. Johns, Adela Rogers 42, 342
Stadler and Waldorf (*The Muppet Show*) 376
Stadtmiller, Mandy 387
Stallone, Sylvester 4, 184, 370, 387

Stanhope, Doug 38
Stanshall, Viv 179
Star Trek Nemesis 211
Stargell, Willie 274
statistics 441–2
Stead, Christina 51
Steed, Wilfred 425
Steel, Danielle 151
Steel, Dawn 284
Steele, Bob 177
Steenbergh, Thomas Van 205
Steiber, Ellen 435
Stein, Gertrude 416, 520
Stein, Joel 112
Steinbeck, John 155, 169, 237, 519
Steinem, Gloria 136, 137
Steingarten, Jeffrey 4
Stemp, Robin 314
Stendhal 236
Stengel, Casey 274
Stephen Nolan Show 364
Stephens, James 359
Stephenson, Mike 197
Sterling, John 455
Stevens, Lester 380
Stevenson, Adlai 68
Stevenson, James 217, 460
Stevenson, Robert Louis 521
Stewart, Alistair 245
Stewart, Jon 85, 187, 213, 312, 343, 416, 431, 432, 522, 530
Stiff Upper Lip, Jeeves (Wodehouse) 3
Stone, Dan G. 284
Stone, Norman 309, 414
Stone, Pam 484
Stone, Stewie 84, 531
Stoppard, Tom 273, 465
Store, the 179
Storey, Moorfield 253
Stracey, John H. 271
Straight Talk 140
Strange, Baroness 336
Strauss Jr., Johann 350

Stravinsky, Igor 350, 351, 356, 357, 510
Streisand, Barbara 391
Strickland, Bill 401
Strictly Come Dancing 362
stupidity 508–9
Styron, William 491
success & failure 283–6
Suerat, Georges 365
Sugar Kane Kowalczyk (*Some Like it Hot*) 71
Sugar, Sir Alan 288
Sugarbaker, Suzanne 82
suicide 526
Sullavan, Margaret 233
Sullivan, Frank 519
Summer Lightning (Wodehouse) 235
Sun Also Rises, The (Hemingway) 59
Sunday, Billy 248
Super Hans (*Peep Show*) 131, 399
Swanson, Gloria 520, 528
Swarbrick, Brian 266
swearing 249–51
Sweeney, Kevin 213
Sweeney, Kieran 438
Swetchine, Anne–Sophie 327
Swift, Jonathan 204, 388, 392
Swinburn, Walter 259
Sykes, Tom 14
Sykes, Wanda 41
Sylvester, Rachel 320
Synnott, Pierce 3

Table Manners 13
Tadema, Alma 365
Taibbi, Matt 67, 68
Taine, Hippolyte 512
Take it From Here 152
Talleyrand, Charles-Maurice 2, 34
Talmud, the 238
Tanglewood Murder, the (Kallen) 83
Tanner, M.J.J. 6
Tarantino, Quentin 372
Tarkington, Booth 227
Tarrant, Chris 390
Taupin, Bernie 374

Tavare, Jim 394
taxation 53–7
Taxi 30, 217, 220, 278, 504
Taylor, A.J.P. 326
Taylor, Elizabeth 200
Taylor, Rip 42
teacher 502–3
Teachers 516
Tebbit, Norman 295, 322, 458
Telemacher, Harris T. (*L.A. Story*) 140, 197, 418
telephone 209–11
television 389–90
television news 216–17
Temple, Shirley 381
tennis 271–2
Tenuta, Judy 35, 283
terrorism 470–1
Thackeray, William Makepeace 252, 497
That 70s Show 30, 353
That's My Boy 83
Thatcher, Margaret 197
theatre 375–7
there are two kinds of people in the world… 131–2
Thick of It, the 206, 207, 223, 242, 253
Thin Man, The 20
Thinking 510–11
Thirkell, Angela 73
30 Rock 136, 173, 198, 231, 253, 283, 286, 290, 413, 455, 475
Thompson, Emma 93
Thompson, Ramada (*Hot Shots!*) 39
Thoreau, Henry David 213, 227, 301
Thubron, Colin 405
Thurber, James 19, 134
Thurow, Lester 413
Thurston, John 438
Thurston, Vince 93
Tikoo, Ravi 256
time 438–9
Times, The 232, 246, 330, 507
Tindale, Paul 512
Tinniswood, Peter 121
Titus 178, 226

Titus, Christopher (*Titus*) 178, 226
Tobias, Steve (*The In-Laws*) 26
Toksvig, Sandi 11, 78, 147, 269, 353, 411
Tomlin, Lily 234, 437, 533
Toody, Officer Gunther (*Car 54, Where Are You?*) 460
Took, Barry 485
Tortelli, Carla (*Cheers*) 97, 187, 247, 285
Toscanini, Arturo 350
tourism 408–11
Townsend, Robert 289
Toxic Bachelors (Steel) 151
Tracy, Spencer 18, 77
train 401–2
transport 395–405
Trapp, Maria Augusta 476
travel & countries 407–28
A Tree Full of Angels (Wiederkehr) 208
Treneman, Ann 223
Trevino, Lee 265, 267
Trillin, Calvin 412
Trivax, Stu 468
Trollope, Anthony 2, 92, 321
Trollope, Joanna 31
Trotsky, Leon 323
Trotter, Rodney (*Only Fools and Horses*) 9
Troubridge, Sir Thomas 468
Trudeau, Margaret 135
Trudeau, Pierre 318
Truman, Harry S. 63, 341
Truman, Will (*Will and Grace*) 24
truth & lies 229–30
Tucker, Malcolm (*The Thick of It/In the Loop*) 206, 242, 249, 253, 339, 471
Tufte, Edward 430
Tully, Lee 436
Turner, Beverly 257
Turner, Lana 200

Turner, Steve 432
Turner, Toni 67
Twain, Mark 7, 14, 51, 53, 58, 92, 107, 130, 143, 146, 147, 153, 194, 226, 227, 229, 245, 250, 280, 287, 297, 307, 386, 400, 405, 434, 458, 500, 535
Two and a Half Men 114
Tyler, Steve 488
Tynan, Kenneth 233, 248, 374, 375, 390
Tyson, Mike 270, 271

Udkoff, Bob 46
ugly 97–8
Ullmann, Liv 45
Unbelievable Truth, The 412, 424
Uncle Mort's North Country 121
Unger, Felix (*The Odd Couple*) 286
Unreliable Memoirs (James) 25
unseemly greetings cards for unlikely occasions 302–3
Untermeye, Louis 158
Updike, John 416
Urquhart, Francis (*House of Cards*) 511
U.S. politics 341–2
Ustinov, Peter 76, 141, 168, 223, 230, 247, 291, 377, 384, 393, 501, 523
Utley, Michael 356

Vail, Amanda 139
Vail, Martin (*Primal Fear*) 461
Valéry, Paul 351
Van Pelt, Linus (*Peanuts*) 8
Vance, Patricia H. 179
Varano, Frank 476
Vardon, Harry 267
Vaughan, Bill 275
Vaughn, Bill 203
Veeck, Bill 273
vegetarian 13
Venturi, Ken 266

Verne, Jules 410
Very Good, Jeeves! (Wodehouse) 253
Vibes 453
Vicar of Dibley, The 486
Vicky (*American Pie*) 36
Vidal, Gore 35, 115, 317, 326, 343, 366, 464, 503, 515
Vilanch, Bruce 47
Viner, Jacob 61
violence & weapons 471–2
Vishnepolsky, Oleg 512
Viz 65, 78, 109, 135, 308, 409, 503
voice 232–3
Voice for Health 339
Voltaire 213, 317, 359, 448, 469, 533
Vonnegut, Kurt 508
Vos, Rich 188

Waits, Tom 349
Walden, George 335
Wales 428
Walker, Alice 514
Walker, Karen (*Will and Grace*) 11, 14, 52, 56, 82, 224, 298, 453
Walker, Stanley 77
Wall Street Journal 95
Wallace, David Foster 404, 405
Wallace, George 403
Walsh, Rosemary 252
Wannan, Bill 73
war & peace 465–9
War at Home, The 488
Ward, Bob 297
Warhol, Andy 32, 50, 366, 389, 415
Waring, Bird 251
Warner, Charles Dudley 295
Warner, Craig 67
Warrender, Penny (*Just Good Friends*) 278
Washington Post 487
Waterhouse, Keith 114, 189, 297, 334, 376, 424

Waters, John 153
Waugh, Evelyn 109, 416, 462, 506
Wax, Ruby 479
Weakest Link, the 496
Weale, Sally 232
Wealthy Texan (The Simpsons) 17
weather 118–20
Webber, Julian Lloyd 358
Weber, David 224
Webster, Daniel 317
Webster, Jean 132
Weed, Brian J. 208
Weed, Mr (Family Guy) 279
weight 474–5
Weinstock, Lotus 283
Weir, Bob 401
Weiss, Hazel 522
Weldon, Fay 182, 535
Weller, Paul 353
Welles, Orson 88, 383
Wells, H.G. 425
Wesker, Arnold 378
West, Mae 17, 177, 367, 385, 394, 439, 476, 509
West, Rebecca 162
Wharton, Edith 158
Whicker, Alan 523
Whistler, James McNeil 504
White, Diane 131
White, E.B. 21, 60, 157, 353
White, Edmund 41
White, Slappy 196
White, Theodore H. 316
Whitehead, Alexander 260
Whitehead, Alfred North 512
Whitehorn, Katharine 185, 208, 502, 536
Whitehouse, Mary 40
Whittle, Paul 365
Who's Afraid of Virginia Woolf 308
'Who's Who' recreations 296–7
Widdecombe, Ann 249, 402

Wiederkehr, Macrina 208
Wilde, Larry 505
Wilde, Oscar 77, 118, 143, 146, 163, 179, 230, 248, 301, 304, 348, 387, 409, 426, 436, 452, 507, 511, 528
Wilder, Billy 372, 386
Wilder, Joan (The Jewel of the Nile) 523
Wilford, G. 397
Wilkerson, Hal (Malcolm in the Middle) 95
Will and Grace 11, 14, 24, 52, 56, 82, 224, 298, 453
Williams, Bern 280
Williams, Harland 180
Williams, Jonathan 140
Williams, Kenneth 369
Williams, Pat 457
Williams, Robin 43, 184, 343, 370, 373, 420, 488, 489
Williams, Ted 273
Williams, Tennessee 230, 232, 533, 464
Williamson, Sean 134
Willis, Bruce 136
Willis, Julia 94
Willows, Catherine (CSI) 290
Wilson, A.N. 452
Wilson, Charlie 290
Wilson, Edward O. 123
Wilson, Harold 323, 330
Wilson, Scott 380
Wilson, Sloan 176
Wilson, Tom 474
Wilson, Woodrow 322
Winchester, Major Charles (M*A*S*H) 17
Windsor, Barbara 449
Winehouse, Amy 353
Wing, John 535
Wings 32, 34, 38, 91, 312
Winstone, Ray 467
Winters, Shelley 173, 197

Winthrop, Charles (Serenade) 360
Winthrop, Monica (The Carpetbaggers) 174
Wisdom, Norman 503
Wise, Anita 41, 89
Wise, Ernie 178, 196
Wismayer, Clive 62
Withers, Audrey 91
Witte, Tom 32, 251, 252
Wittgenstein, Ludwig 148
Wobbly 422
Wodehouse, P.G. 3, 14, 20, 24, 83, 128, 163, 235, 253, 284, 290, 337, 358, 366, 488, 511
Wolf, Jr., Charles 465
Wolfberg, Dennis 496
Wolfe, Alan 416
Wolff, Geoffrey 365
Wolseley, Sir Garnet 468
Woman of No Importance, A 451
women 133–4
Wonder Years, The 54
Wood, John 379
Wood, Victoria 84, 182, 304, 440
Woodburn, Kim 26
Woods, James 356
Woof73 85
Woolard, Marcy 36
Woolf, Virginia 166, 167
Woollcott, Alexander 456
Woolley, Bernard (Yes, Prime Minister) 63
words 149–50
work & business 277–92
Worm and the Ring, The (Burgess) 83
Worrell, Sir Frank 134
Wouk, Herman 154
Wozniak, Stephen 432
Wright, Frank Lloyd 116, 230
Wright, Ian 263
Wright, Jr, James C. 64

Wright, Steven 107, 115, 150, 209, 302, 400, 440, 493, 525
writer 155–60
Wrongfully Accused 408
Wurman, Richard Saul 506
Wyndham-Lewis, D.B. 391
Wynn, Early 516
Wynne-Tyson, Jon 316

Yacowar, Maurice 530
Yarborough, Cale 257
Yeatman, R.J. 121
Yeats, W.B. 165, 287
Yellow Dog (Amis) 278
Yes, Minister 107, 215, 283, 323, 325, 336, 337, 340
Yes, Prime Minister 63
Yevtushenko, Yevgeny 222
Yglesias, José 468
Young, Alan 314
Young, Judith 163
Young, Lester 84
Young, Toby 176
Youngman, Henny 7, 24, 33, 43, 75, 79, 101, 106, 248, 271, 301, 304, 308, 398, 403, 456, 481, 527
Yu, H. Thomas (Collins) 111
Yufur, Dot 252
Yutang, Lin 423

Zacharek, Stephanie 369
Zangwill, Israel 44, 508
Zappa, Frank 508
Zbornak, Dorothy (The Golden Girls) 320, 523
Zeckendorf, William 59
Zephaniah, Benjamin 7
Zewail, Professor Ahmed 438
Zola, Emile 491
Zuckerman, Mortimer 456
Zuleika Dobson 152
Zwart, Elizabeth 151